Religious Foundations
for
Global Ethics

Religious Foundations
for
Global Ethics

Robert Bruce McLaren

PEARSON

Prentice
Hall

Upper Saddle River, NJ 07458

Library of Congress Cataloging-in-Publication Data

McLaren, Robert Bruce.
    Religious foundations for global ethics / Robert Bruce McLaren.
        p. cm.
    ISBN-13: 978-0-13-148472-6
    ISBN-10: 0-13-148472-9
    1. Religious ethics. I. Title.

BJ1188.M35 2008
205—dc22

2007020659

Editor-in-Chief (Editorial): Sarah Touborg
Editorial Assistant: Carla Worner
Assistant Editor: Sarah Holle
Senior Managing Editor: Joanne Riker
Production Liaison: Fran Russello
Executive Marketing Manager: Brandy Dawson
Associate Marketing Manager: Sasha
    Anderson-Smith
Manufacturing Buyer: Cathleen Petersen
Cover Designer: Bruce Kenselaar
Manager, Cover Visual Research and
    Permissions: Karen Sanatar

Director, Image Resource Center: Melinda
    Patelli
Manager, Rights and Permissions: Zina
    Arabia
Manager, Visual Research: Beth Brenzel
Image Permission Coordinator: Craig Jones
Photo Researcher: Francelle Carapetyan
Composition/Full-Service Project
    Management: Pine Tree Composition, Inc.
Printer/Binder: RR Donnelley & Sons
    Company

Credits and acknowledgments borrowed from other sources and reproduced, with permission, in this
textbook appear on page 281.

This book is dedicated to

ALTHEA
Ab Origine Fidus

and to our children
Craig, Kirk and Christina

Contents

Preface

WHY "RELIGIOUS" FOUNDATIONS?

If we are to discuss foundations on which to base ethics on a global scale, are there grounds on which to build?

Almost every political party, social organization, mass media enterprise, and even clubs such as the Boy and Girl Scouts and the YMCA boast of some kind of "code of ethics." Even your next-door neighbor may be full of opinions on the subject. So whose ethics should we use?

In looking for a base, it is helpful to note archeological and anthropological evidence that religion in some form has been at the bedrock of every known human society. The moral development of people has been rooted in adherence to some "ultimate" set of values, and even religions which are not wedded to a concept of a personal deity, like Buddhism and Confucianism, hold firmly to norms of right behavior. *Ethics* is the studied application of such concepts to everyday practice in family life, education, social interaction, business and to ways of treating strangers, foreigners, and enemies. These are all at least potentially "global" in their implications.

It is also the case that communities of faith need to contribute if we are to resolve crises that confront us on the global scale. For instance, Larry Rasmussen notes that "a beloved world is steadily being destroyed by cumulative human activities. This is a compelling matter for religious ethics if there ever was one."[1]

It is often said that the twentieth century was born in a tidal wave of optimism resulting from a flood of nineteenth century inventions, from the steam locomotive to electric lights. It is also often noted that the twentieth century devolved into a series of wars with as many as 187 million deaths and other immeasurable destructiveness.[2] With depressions, environmental disasters, terrorism, and genocide, Winston Churchill called the century "this hideous epoch in which we dwell," and dour warnings abounded regarding the twenty-first century's end.

Perhaps it is as a consequence of such reflection that there has been a growing preoccupation with moral development and the tasks of education among academicians as well as politicians and, indeed, the public in general. Such an engagement with ethics has not always been a given. Beginning in the 1920s with the Vienna Circle, many philosophers regarded morality as a nonissue. One of their leading spokesmen declared it to be "meaningless."[3] Similarly, behavioral psychologists asserted that humans possess no innate morality; rather, they argued, people are molded through conditioning to conform to the requirements of their surroundings.[4]

The current growing absorption with moral concerns can be traced to reactions to the Vietnam War and the Civil Rights protests in the 1950s to 1970s. Today, across the United States, school districts and boards of education have begun mandating the teaching of morality with words similar to those in the California Education Code: "Each teacher shall endeavor to impress upon the minds of the pupils the principles of morality, truth [and] justice."[5] The necessity for moral education is often tied to the demands of our rapidly changing, increasingly pluralistic world.

When we talk about pluralism, what do we mean? As Harvard's Diana Eck has pointed out, mere diversity is not pluralism. Rather, "pluralism is an attempt to come to terms with plurality in a positive way. It is an interpretation of diversity, not simply its manifestation."[6] The fact is that the increasing migration of racial, ethnic, religious, and political groups invites—indeed, demands—creative dialogue. In our nation of immigrants, we must have dialogue or risk becoming a nation of ghettos.

Nearly twenty-four centuries ago, Aristotle wrote that the tendency to make judgments based on "tribal thinking" or local custom risked falling into logical fallacies. Huston Smith observed in our own time that the news media has conditioned us to think of religion as a battleground for bigots and extremists: "When bombs explode, hostages are seized, and ethnic conflicts cause the world to bleed, reporters are only too ready to reach for religion as the cause."[7] The facts are strikingly different when one considers how the religious pluralism movement began more than a century ago in the Parliament of World Religions. That event brought together in Chicago delegates from Hindu, Buddhist, Islamic, Shinto, Jewish, Christian, and a host of other traditions whose voices had never before been heard together in one setting. The event gave impetus to the academic field of comparative religions and the modern interfaith movement. Although the United States had an official Chinese Exclusion Act (1882) and other immigration restrictions, the Parliament of World Religions was able to invite Chinese representatives. The parliament helped change the religious and ethnic landscape of the United States and of other participating countries.[8] At its centennial celebration in 1993 more than 6,500 delegates came from all parts of the world. Together, they created a document, *"Toward a Global Ethic,"* that, for the first time in human history, reflects the zeal of ordinary human beings to achieve peace through the moral development of coming generations in a pluralistic world.

If religiously diverse traditions can accomplish this, one can hope that business, economic, political and scientific communities can undertake something similar that can be for the benefit of all humankind (and even of environmental ecology). Daily headlines about shattered homes, children killing children, gang violence, corporate corruption, and environmental destruction remind us of the urgency of the task. Ours is a complex nature, however, and the sheer fact of such anxious soul-searching suggests that our very quest for remedies provides a ground for optimism.

It is imperative that any book that undertakes such an exploration proceed in an interdisciplinary fashion, utilizing the resources of many lines of investigation. This book is for students, educators, legislators, and all who seek to understand the nature and sources of moral insight and how our homes, schools, and religious, political, business, and scientific institutions can share in fostering conditions for the moral development of the coming generation. Perhaps, to borrow Eric Sevareid's splendid title, it is "not so wild a dream."[9]

NOTES

1. Larry L. Rasmussen, *Earth Community, Earth Ethics* (New York: Orbis Books, 1997), p. xiii

2. Rasmussen, *ibid*, page 2

3. A.J. Ayer put it quite succinctly: "It is impossible to find a criterion for determining the validity of ethical judgments, because they have no objective validity whatever." *Language, Truth and Logic,* 2nd ed. (New York: Dover Press, 1946), 108–9.

4. One recalls the boast of J.B. Watson, founder of behaviorism, that he could program any child: "Give me a dozen healthy infants, and I'll guarantee to take any one of them at random and train him to become any type of specialist—doctor, lawyer, artist, merchant chief and yes, even beggar-man and thief." *Behaviorism,* (New York: W.W. Norton, 1925), 82.

   Francois Duchene's 1970 *The Endless Crisis*, while clearly sounding alarms, was not merely alarmist but also a thoughtful set of essays on seemingly intractable problems. There have followed almost numberless books of great penetration by writers including Kenneth Galbraith, Jean Jacques Servan-Schreiber, and Arthur Schlesinger.

   There are also numerous professional organizations including The Association for Integrative Studies; Association for Moral Education; The Society of Christian Ethics, and corresponding societies for Buddhist, Jewish, Islamic, and other traditions affiliated with the Council of Societies for the Study of Religion; the Societas Ethica based in the Netherlands; The Norham Foundation, an interdisciplinary forum for moral education and development in the United Kingdom, and the Institut fur Social Etik in Switzerland.

5. *Moral and Civic Education,* published by the California Department of Education, Sacramento, California, 1991. Section 44806 of the education code is quoted on page 1.

6. Diana, Eck, *The Dawn of Religious Pluralism* (La Salle, IL: Open Court, 1993), foreword, 1.

7. Huston Smith, "Tuning into Religion," *Christian Century,* September 11–18, 1996, 836.

8. It is known that while there were few Muslims in Chicago in 1893, today the city has more than half a million Muslims and some 70 mosques. There are two major and half a dozen smaller Hindu temples in Chicago's suburbs. Chinese, Japanese, Laotian, Tibetan, Thai, and Vietnamese Buddhist temples can be found in the area. One of the world's largest Baha'i temples and places of worship for Jains, Sikhs and Zoroastrians can be found in Chicago and its environs.

9. Eric Sevareid, *Not So Wild A Dream,* (New York: Athenium, 1979). Sevareid's dream was for him and many of his readers, one of those life-altering reflections on the human condition coming out of his experience as a war correspondent during World War II.

Acknowledgments

It is considerably more than a pleasure, it is an honor to acknowledge colleagues in the university sphere as well as in churches, synagogues, mosques, and temples who generously shared their criticisms and encouragements. They helped bring this project to fruition. Some are situated in such scattered places as Chicago, Moscow, Oxford, and South Africa and who, having heard my ideas expressed through papers presented at conferences, have generously given time and insight to strengthening the project.

I also wish to thank the following reviewers: Dr. Rhada Battacharya, Hindu scholar and professor of economics, California State University, Fullerton; Dr. Mark Biedebach, chair, board of directors, International Institute for Christian Psychotherapy, Long Beach; Dr. Ananda Guruge, dean of Academic Affairs, Shi Lai Buddhist University of the West, Rosemead, California; Dr. Benjamin Hubbard, cofounder and professor emeritus of the Department of Comparative Religions, California State University, Fullerton; Dr. John Polkinghorne, past president and fellow, Queens' College, Cambridge University, particle physicist, and canon theologian, Liverpool, United Kingdom whose many books won for him the coveted Templeton Award in science and religion and have been a great source of both inspiration and hardheaded wisdom; Dr. James Santucci, chair of the Department Comparative Religions at the California State University, Fullerton, and adjunct professor, Buddhist University of the West; Dr. Alan Suggate, professor of Christian theology, University of Durham, Durham, United Kingdom; Dr. Janice Strength, founder of the Moscow School of Christian Psychology, Pasadena, California, and Moscow, Russia; and the Rev. Jon West, Morningside Presbyterian Church. My heartfelt gratitude goes to each of these as well as to my family, friends, and neighbors who put up with my reclusive ways during research and the manuscript's preparation.

Religious Foundations
for
Global Ethics

CHAPTER 1

The Moral Proclivity

*Two things fill the mind with ever new and increasing
wonder and awe: the starry heavens above me and the
moral law within.*

—Immanuel Kant

From the period that Karl Jaspers called the "Axial Age" (c. 800–200 B.C. when nearly a dozen of the major religious and philosophical traditions still practiced today came into being) to the Nurnberg trials after World War II, it has been widely affirmed that all people know "in our hearts" what is right. Furthermore, because we know, we must be held accountable for our actions. The Nazi defendants' pleas during the trial that their actions in the death camps were simply a matter of "following orders" were rejected because, the judges said, despite training or conditioning, the officers should have known inherently that the orders were morally indefensible, and refused to obey.

This popular tradition has not been without its challengers, and not only among military personnel for whom obedience has always been a *sine qua non* but also among philosophers and religious visionaries. Compliance with the law as well as with socially engrained ethical standards. It was debated during the late seventeenth and eighteenth century Enlightenment. Such a priori "oughts" were thought to have been laid to rest by the early part of the twentieth century by recent schools of philosophy and psychology, including pragmatism, existentialism, psychoanalysis, and behaviorism. Entering the arena with newer challenges today are the sociobiologists and certain developmentalists who argue that any moral tendencies arise solely from our capacity as an evolving species to accommodate to changing environmental and social demands.

AN INTRODUCTORY OVERVIEW

Acknowledging the risk of oversimplification, our exploration in this chapter will include insights from literature in philosophy, religious studies, and psychology with some consideration of related research. It may rightly be argued that the selection is both too broad and too narrow. One cannot hope to do justice to these large and complex fields of study in the scope of a single book, much less a chapter. It is pretentious even to try. On the other hand, why limit the exploration to these three disciplines and select psychology to represent the social sciences? Many anthropologists and sociologists have contemplated moral development, and some have written eloquently on the subject.

It is also the case that the preponderance of materials published on the subject have come from the three disciplines here chosen. In fact, however, we will have many occasions in the course of this book to utilize insights from other fields, including some perhaps unexpected ones such as neurophysiology, economics, and even physics. Our overall pattern of study for this opening chapter will be as follows: origins of philosophy and religion, contributions from leading religions, and interfaces with psychology.

1.   Origins of Philosophy and Religion

It is perhaps not surprising that philosophy and religion have almost indistinguishable roots; both emerged from a deep concern to understand what is truly "real" (ontology); what goodness is, how evil emerged, and what values we should cherish (axiology); how humans come to know such things in the first place (epistemology); and finally whether there is a purposing Agent or Deity guiding the whole natural process, determining how we humans fit into the natural scheme of things (theology). Clearly, not all philosophers have been religious, yet it is interesting that the Indian philosopher Barghava declared that the whole social fabric of India has been governed since the beginning by a philosophy that was indistinguishable from religious thought and practice.

We will have occasion to inquire into different "schools" of philosophy and then consider diverse religious traditions East and West. First we will consider the schools of idealism and realism, which from Plato and Aristotle to Immanuel Kant and Alfred N. Whitehead have proposed the concept that morality is part of the fabric of reality, comprehended through reason and intuition. Then we'll note how pragmatists and existentialists argue that morality is culture based and/or individually selected.

2.   Contributions from Leading Religions, East and West

Except for Buddhism and possibly Confucianism, a personal, spiritual commitment to some Ultimate, even if only mystically perceived, is often the strongest motivation for seeking and fulfilling the perceived good or virtue. Religions East and West differ largely in their emphasis on whether a personal Creator-Deity instilled a knowledge of morals in the human psyche. The Western religions (Judaism, Christianity and Islam) maintain that God has written the moral laws on the human heart. The Eastern religions generally hold to a more naturalistic (Confucian) or quasi mystical or intuitive (Hindu and Buddhist) position.

3.   Interfaces with Psychology

From Gustrav Fechner's 19th century psychophysics, Herman von Helmholtz's physiological emphasis, and Sigmund Freud's exploration of the unconscious to the behaviorism of J.B. Watson and B.F. Skinner and the cognitive theories of Jean Piaget,

Lawrence Kohlberg, and Erik Erikson, psychology has illuminated the moral landscape. It has done so often with controversial, sometimes conflicting insights. These insights include that whatever moral proclivity exists has arisen because of its survival value to our unique species.[1] Our challenge will be to discern where the most helpful resources lie in achieving an understanding of moral development in our increasingly complex world.

A. FOUR PHILOSOPHICAL TRADITIONS

The question "Are children born with a sense of right and wrong?" would have seemed an idle inquiry among the pre-Socratic Greeks. Thales (636–546 B.C.), statesman and mathematician, was perhaps the first formally to introduce the idea of *unity* into our multivaried experiences, and while he was proposing this primarily for the sensate world, his views by implication came to mean that what *ought* to be was included with what *is*.[2] What ought to be was decided by the gods; human behavior was moral to the degree to which it conformed to the will of the deities. Inasmuch as Thales is often called the "first Western philosopher,"[3] his ideas underscore the contention that religion and philosophy were born together.[4]

Aristotle, writing two centuries later, commented on the widely held assumption that the soul is intermingled with the universe, "for which reason Thales suggested that all things are full of gods."[5] That these gods influence human moral judgment was affirmed, he wrote, by both Thales and his fellow mathematician Pythagoras (c. 582–502 B.C.). He also noted, however, that Xenophanes, their contemporary (c. 580–485 B.C.), argued in favor of "one God among gods and men . . . not at all like mortals in body or mind."[6] Heraclitus, meanwhile (535–475 B.C.), proposed that a *Logos*—a divine "word" or rational, moral principle that requires the cosmos to comply with it "as though it were the very law of life"—is our greatest virtue. "The people," Heraclitus declared, "must fight on behalf of (this) law as though for the city wall."[7]

The tradition that morality was given to mortals by a God or gods (or by a king in possession of divine sanction or the *Logos*) came to be known as "moral objectivism."[8] This tradition was first challenged as being thoroughly subjective, not objective, by a group of Greeks called *Sophists* (c. 500 B.C.). It may be, as George Stein argues, that their skepticism was more the result of "an accident of geography," which brought them into contact with other cultures and religions, than of a reasoned position.[9] Their most oft-quoted spokesman, Protagoras (c. 480–410 B.C.), set his seal on Sophist moral relativism by stating: "Man is the measure of all things."[10] Following upon the thorough-going materialism of Democritus, who proposed (c. 500 B.C.) the first atomic theory (that all things are made up of lifeless, infinitely small particles), Epicurus (341–270 B.C.) and his latter day disciple Lucretius (99–55 B.C.) denounced all religious theories of morality. All of observable nature is simply matter in motion, and pleasure is the ultimate good: "If the things that produce the pleasure (even) of the profligate, could dispel the fears of the mind . . . we should never have cause to blame them. No pleasure is a bad thing in itself."[11]

Plato (c. 427–347 B.C.), clearly irritated by what he considered the pompous skepticism of the Sophists, made Protagoras the particular target of attention in one of his dialogues named simply *Protagoras* and later in *Theatetus.* We need not dwell here on the skillful contrast that Plato draws between the modesty of Socrates and the pretentious verbosity of Protagoras. It is enough at this point simply note that for Plato, a reexamination of the role of the divine in human affairs was absolutely critical to understanding moral virtue and ethics. Philosophy and religion were inextricably wedded, and their interaction gave rise to the "school" of thought that came to be called *idealism* (or more accurately, idea-ism).

Among the more than twenty major treatises that Plato wrote in dialogue form is *Timaeus* in which a discussion between a young astronomer and Socrates centers on the nature of two worlds. The first world is a realm of perfect order and design, containing models or *ideas* that are in turn reflected in the second, material world. The first is the true reality. The second, our sensate environment, seems substantial only because it is experienced through our fallible senses. God, the ruler of the transcendent world of ideas, framed our sensate world so that through it we might "remember" the ultimate realities: the good, the true, and the beautiful. Being himself the very essense of goodness, God "desired that all things should come as near as possible to being like himself." Plato presented here an archetype of humankind, a "living creature" who is the ultimate idea of humanity, perfect in all aspects, and whom we "remember" in our inmost being as the true self.[12] As Shakespeare was later to express through the character of Polonius, if we are true to this inner self, we cannot then be false to any one.[13]

The concept of "remembrance" as a form of epistemology by which mortals know morality is more fully explicated in *The Republic* and in *Phaedo,* where Plato insisted that all "learning" is a case of recalling the heavenly life from which we came, and to which we belong.[14] Our moral quests and struggles were thought to be an exercise in repudiating the corrupting lure of the material world as we remind ourselves that we are citizens of another realm whose moral standards we already know. To develop a society of sensible, good people, nurture and education must reflect and make concrete these remembered values: "For good nurture and education implant good constitutions, and these good constitutions taking root in a good education improve more and more."

Then, almost as an aside, Plato warned of "entertainments" that seduce youth into lawless behavior: "Our youth should be trained from the first in a stricter system, for if amusements become lawless and the youths themselves become lawless, they can never grow up into virtuous citizens."[15] This was the basis for his endorsement of censorship of contemporary forms of art, literature, and entertainment in an era long before "freedom of speech" was to become a watchword.

Plato affirmed that virtue is not a matter of opinion, custom, or law but is grounded in the very nature of the soul, and it is the essential task of the soul to know, by the power of reason, how to direct the spirit and the appetites.[16]

In his book *On The Soul,* Aristotle (384–322 B.C.) surveyed the many theories of the nature of the soul, including Plato's position,[17] but gave his own opinion that it is "the cause or source of the living body. . . . It is (a) the source or origin of movement; it is (b) the end or goal of life (telos); and it is (c) the essence of the whole living body."[18]

Aristotle's departure from the position of his mentor, Plato, on the role of transcendent ideas or forms involved a difficult decision, as he later confessed: "an uphill one, by the fact that the Forms have been introduced by a friend of our own."[19] Setting up a rival theory (and eventually a rival school), which has been labeled *realism*, doubtless occasioned regret for Aristotle but, as he tells us in his *Nicomachean Ethics*, "It would be perhaps thought better, indeed to be our duty, for the sake of maintaining the truth, even to destroy what touches us closely . . . piety requires us to honor truth above our friends."[20]

In place of transcendent forms or ideas, Aristotle proposed that nature is the source and context of all good in accord with God's plan. The soul's quest for the good finds its satisfaction in the discovery of harmony in nature: "With a true view all the data harmonize, but with a false one the facts soon clash."[21] Discovery of the harmony yields a sense of pleasure that goes beyond the hedonic and is the root of real happiness. "Happiness then is the best, noblest, and most pleasant thing in the world."[22] He adds that if there are any gifts of the gods to humankind, "it is reasonable that happiness should be God-given," yet it ultimately comes to us and is appreciated "as a result of virtue and some process of learning or training."[23]

Happiness for Aristotle, however, must be the product of virtue and is clearly not the same as "pleasure" as advocated by Epicurus and Lucretius for whom pleasure was an end in itself regardless whether it involved moral turpitude and was worth pursuing unless it occasioned unpleasant social friction. The contrast between the Aristotelian and Epicurean (or hedonistic) positions could hardly have been more sharply drawn.

It is important to recall meanwhile that Aristotle, in making nature the context and source of moral virtue, did not subscribe to Plato's idea that we are born with an inner knowledge of the good: "None of the moral virtues arise in us by Nature."[24] Rather, through intellectual training and habit, we perceive the essential rightness of things in the harmonies of nature. Failure to do so reveals lack of training, poor habits, and ignorance. Knowledge of the good is thus not inborn but "dawns" on us as we gain an increasingly mature capacity for sensing the good which inheres in nature. This dawning awareness brings about its own unique apprehension of pleasure and harmony, "for moral excellence is concerned with pleasures and pains. Hence we ought to have been brought up in a particular way since youth," taught that worthy pleasure is not that of sensual indulgence but the delight of moral and intellectual discovery.[25]

The premise that moral order and purpose are imbedded in the natural order and are discoverable by reason aided by intuition evolved into the theory of natural law. The Stoic philosophers (so named because they began as a study/debating society that met on a broad colonnade, a popular gathering place called the *Stoa Poikile*, or "painted porch") led a kind of "back to nature" movement by which to discover the moral order. The Stoics particularly impressed the intelligentsia of the newly emerging Roman Republic. Among these was Cicero (106–43 B.C.), who did much to popularize Greek philosophy while advancing his own ideas and those of others. Aristotle had earlier been concerned that even among the more enlightened jurists, differences emerged between what was perceived as "naturally just" (*fusai dikaion*) and judgments handed down by human courts (*nomikon*). It would be the Stoics and later Roman jurists who resolved the conflict by balancing *jus naturale* with *jus gentium* and achieving the principle of *equity,* which is often mistakenly attributed to eighteenth century British jurists.[26]

The early Christians, like many of the Roman jurists, found the natural law concept too imprecise for resolving legal disputes. Not until the thirteenth century did Thomas Aquinas meld natural law with scholastic theology. With his declaration that God established all law as *lex naturae* in which all things participate, natural law gained its real force. Political and natural law were seen as having a common denominator in the will of God and because the church proposed itself as the sole rightful interpreter of this divine source, "it is perhaps not surprising that the Church assumed the privilege of ultimate moral judgment. It was the abuse of this prerogative (e.g., in sanctioning inquisitions and the "divine right" of kings) that led, in large part, to the Reformation."[27]

It will have been noted that many who followed Plato and Aristotle held either that we are in fact endowed with a moral knowledge from birth or that the knowledge is available through reason and intuition because the essential "good" is embedded in the very fabric of reality. This tradition has sometimes simply been called *essentialism,* which embraces both *idealism* and *realism* despite their differences on certain important points. In sum, its affirmation was that "essence precedes and determines existence."[28] The essential nature of a thing, including its inherent value (or dignity, moral virtue, etc.) is embodied in and expressed through its outward or existing form but (at the risk of redundancy), the form was determined by the pre-existing nature. This idea prevailed from classical Greece, through the Medieval era, the Reformation, and the Renaissance when, awed by the sheer brilliance of mankind who could envision such things, Shakespeare would write, "What a piece of work is a man! How noble in reason! . . . In action how like an angel! In apprehension how like a god!"[29] We will note how this concept also dominated the thoughts of the "founding fathers" of the United States (most of them of British origin and influenced by John Locke), who tied the "natural rights of man" to these inherent virtues, declaring that certain human rights are "unalienable" because they were "endowed by their Creator."[30]

The eighteenth century Age of Enlightenment witnessed a major assault on much that had gone before. David Hume of Scotland (1711–1776) was denied a professorship at the University of Edinburgh because he refused to subscribe to either essentialist philosophy or Christian theology. Moral distinctions, he insisted, are neither born within us nor reached by reason but are merely a matter of personal preference based on our subjective, emotional state—our feelings. "Reason itself is utterly impotent in this particular."[31] He further castigated religion as

Nothing but a species of philosophy (which) will never be able to carry us beyond the usual course of experience, or give us measures of conduct and behavior different from those which are furnished by reflections on common life.[32]

Despite official rejection in academia, Hume's writings were widely read, and his influence was to reach far beyond his century to the pragmatists of our own.

In Germany, Immanuel Kant (1724–1804) took a position directly at odds with Hume's and thoroughly embraced idealism, in which right and good are part of the very fabric of the universe. The Ten Commandments, Kant insisted, were perceived by Moses as the logical expression of what is eternally right. They came *through* human reason but not *from* our reason and, what is more, "No moral principle is based on any feeling,"[33] because feelings are physical in nature rather than rational.

George Friedrich Hegel (1770–1831) wrote of "the God within," in his celebrated *Philosophy of Right* (1821) and described conscience in terms of each person's becoming morally aware when participating in the universal "World Spirit."[34] Each of us participates in this universal spirit, and our knowledge of morals derives from a dialectical process of thought by which every proposition (thesis) is countered by its opposite (antithesis); the interaction produces a synthesis, so discovering moral truth is never a static thing but always a process.

In effect, Hume had thrown down the gauntlet to such essentialist thought, and despite the impressive impact of Kant and Hegel, some nineteenth century thinkers (e.g., Karl Marx, Charles Darwin, and Herbert Spencer) continued the challenge. By the late nineteenth century, the defenders of essentialism, theistic or not, had significantly declined. Friedrich Nietzsche (1844–1900) denounced essentialist thinking in general and proclaimed in his essay *Joyful Wisdom* that "God is dead . . . we have murdered God"[35]

John Dewey (1859–1952), one of the founders of *pragmatism,* declared that terms such as *God, truth,* and *morality* have value only to a community in which such words are acceptable. "The habit of identifying moral characteristics with conformity to external authoritative prescriptions . . . tends to reduce morals to dead, machine-like routine; the results are morally undesirable."[36] It might be argued that Dewey's insistence that morals are thus reduced to dead routine and that this is "morally" undesirable presupposes that morals have objective validity, which he had already denied, but that would require more space than we have in this brief survey. Meanwhile moral values, according to the pragmatists, "are only tentative and temporary statements of what ought to be done. They are never to be considered universal."[37] Charles Sanders Peirce (1839–1914) from whom Dewey derived much of his inspiration had affirmed that truth and goodness are best understood as workable hypotheses. William James (1842–1910) concurred (though tempered with humanitarianism); values such as truth and goodness are "whatever works," what has social utility, as John Stuart Mill had earlier insisted.

Exponents of *existentialism,* whose position was first formally enunciated in the nineteenth century but was not clearly established until the middle of the twentieth century, were also decrying as meaninglessness such concepts as a priori knowledge of moral values. "Existence precedes essence" was the insistent theme of

Jean-Paul Sartre (1905–1980). There is no God, he maintained, but even if there were, it would make no difference; each person must be free to make his or her own choices and must take full responsibility for them. Clearly, if there is no God, then there is no preset "human nature." Sartre wrote, "First of all man exists, turns up, appears on the scene, and only afterwards defines himself."[38] Our moral imperative is to make of ourselves what we will, without divine aid or blame. "Such is the first principle of existentialism. . . . Man is at the start of a plan which is aware of itself . . . nothing exists prior to this plan; man will be what he will have planned to be."[39]

Not all existentialists have been atheists. Soren Kirkegaard (1813–1855), who really instituted existentialism in early nineteenth century, was a resolute Christian. Martin Buber (1878–1965) was a committed Jew, but like Sartre, Heidegger, and Camus, Kirkegaard and Buber insisted on each person's taking complete responsibility for all of her or his thoughts and actions. Kirkegaard and Buber also urged making a "leap of faith," which opens the possibility of fellowship with God entirely on one's own. Morality is not inborn, found in nature, or, for that matter, in society (as pragmatists hold) but within the court of personal conscience. A number of other philosophers, Nicolas Berdyaev, Etienne Gilson, Karl Jaspers, and Paul Tillich would join Kiekegaard in advocating an existential leap of faith to gain a knowledge of moral principles, which can come only to those who persevere.

Meanwhile, the essentialist traditions are by no means dead in our century. The writings of Gabriel Marcel, William Hocking, Ortega y Gasset, and Jacques Maritain (whom T.S. Eliot called "the most powerful force in contemporary philosophy") attest to the durability of these traditions. It is probable that a fair majority of ordinary citizens would concur, even if they are acquainted with only the more popular expressions of them. It may be observed that the different schools of philosophy diverge, sometimes sharply on the matter of morality. Many lament this, as did an Illinois legislator who said, "I took a course in philosophy once, but all I can recall is that it was a damn dim candle over a damn dark abyss."

Frances Bacon suggested back in the seventeenth century, "A little philosophy inclineth man's mind to atheism, but depth in philosophy bringeth men's minds about to religion." For this reason, realizing that we have not yet "settled" the matter of innate moral wisdom, we will turn our attention at this point to the positions of some major religious traditions East and West.

B. CONTRIBUTIONS FROM LEADING RELIGIONS EAST AND WEST

Except for the valiant efforts of a limited number of travelers and missionaries, a formal study of the world's leading religious traditions was not undertaken until about the middle of the nineteenth century. By then, numerous missionary groups had begun sharing information both within and across denominational lines as a more organized and carefully documented effort. The most salutary culmination of this was the creation of a Parliament of the World's Religions held in Chicago, Illinois, in 1893.[40] The parliament brought together the widest spectrum of representatives of the major religious traditions ever assembled. For a variety of reasons—including the interruptions of World War I, vast realignments of international commerce, the Great Depression, and World War II—the Parliament did not convene again for a century. Its centenary meeting in 1993 drew more than 6,500 delegates and a crowd of 30,000 to hear the Dalai Lama speak on the need for the moral leaders of the world to create a document providing a global ethic.

1. Religions of the East

Hinduism. In an effort to explore some of the major religious traditions for their contribution to understanding the human sense of moral urgency, it will useful to begin with the oldest of the "living" religions, *Hinduism.* This is done not only because of its antiquity and its place in the Eastern traditions but also because it has much to tell us about the origins of moral perception and inclination.

Interestingly, not until 1924 could an acceptable date for the founding of Hinduism be established by the academic communities of India. It was decided then that the earliest informal character of Hinduism emerged in the Indus Valley about 2,500 B.C. A thousand years later, around 1,500 B.C., a migrating population of Aryans (the "noble people") came to the Indus area from southern Russia, conquered the region, and established their priests, the Brahmins, as spiritual and temporal rulers.[41] Hinduism has thus been identified with India since 1,500 B.C., with the conviction that its ritual celebrations of the cosmic "oversoul," called *Brahman,* was derived even earlier in the age of seers who heard "the sacred sounds" and from them composed the hymns known as the *Vedas.* Some gods and deities from the Indus Valley civilization were apparently incorporated and became prototypes for later representations of manifestations of deity, such as Shiva.

The Western world popularly understands the Hindu religion to be polytheistic. In fact, the many deities named in this tradition and the many portrayals of gods are said to be evidence that the lay mind simply could not envision a wholly transcendent, infinite, impersonal Brahman and the names and images of the many different manifestations were developed: *Vishnu,* the creator; *Shiva,* the destroyer; and *Kali,* the black goddess of death. There were gods for mountains and volcanoes, storms, and fertility ad infinitum. Nevertheless, for the truly enlightened Hindu, there is but one deity, *Brahman* also called *Atman,* an all-pervading spirit. "All the Vedic deities, indeed all things and events are to be regarded as manifestations of one Power at the heart of the world."[42]

Inasmuch as the Brahman Atman is to be found throughout all nature, we humans are said also to participate in the "Divine Spirit" so in that sense we are "born" with the capacity for divine insight into right and wrong. This is reminiscent of Plato's position discussed in the preceding section. But why, then, do we not always do the good? The Upanishads, sacred scriptures composed about 800–600 B.C., proclaim that Brahman, the supreme being, transcends all moral distinctions. Knowing this and being immersed in its light, the yogin or wise man, the true Brahmin, remains tranquil in the face of such perplexity. "Such a one the thought does not torment: 'Why have I not done the good? Why have I done the evil?' He saves himself from both these thoughts."[43]

This apparent moral relativism is not to suggest that Hindus are indifferent to moral distinctions. In the Aruneya Upandishad, the *yogin* is required to renounce deceit, envy, greed, pride and wrathfulness; to practice chastity, noninjury, and truthfulness; and to do without worldly possessions. These constitute the way to self-realization. If Shakespeare's Shylock in the *Merchant of Venice* were to ask "By what compulsion must I?" concerning such ethical requirement,[44] the Hindu would not reply, "God commands it" or "It is by nature the right thing to do." Instead, The Law Book of Manu (c. 250 B.C.) sets forth moral precepts of high order, and its twelve chapters contain maxims that became institutionalized and then made compulsory. In other sacred texts such as the Bhagavad Gita, the Mahabharata, and Puranas, moral behavior is exalted as making possible a reincarnation after death into a higher order of life: "Whoever worships Krishna with utter devotion (bhakti) dwells in me. Be well assured that he who worships Me, does not perish." Morality, then, is grounded in the decision for devotion to the all-encompassing Deity and in contemplative study of that which is our birthright: oneness with God.

Buddhism. The Eastern religion of *Buddhism* was born of a despair that devotion, study, and the anxious anticipation of reincarnation to a better status did not in fact lead to a better moral life. Nor did the practices ease one's spirit amid the frustrations and longings of life.

Gautama (later named Siddhartha) was born about 560 B.C., the son of an Indian raja. He left his family's palace at the age of twenty-nine to find some meaning for the many forms of suffering he had witnessed in the world. His enlightenment came, as Coomaraswamy tells us, only after years of wandering and privation when, quite suddenly while meditating under a bodhi tree, "a great peace came over him as the significance of all things made itself apparent."[45]

The moral expression of Buddhist enlightenment first entails abandoning the "heresy of individuality" which is "the first great delusion, because there is in fact, no being, only an everlasting becoming."[46] In striving for individuality, we always want things, or status, or some tangible evidence that we *are* and have some permanent or perhaps even eternal selfhood to be prized. Such desires always disappoint and often cause pain and anguish not only for ourselves but also for others against whom we compete. Ridding oneself of all desire is thus a concomitant to overcoming the heresy of individualism to which most humans subscribe (especially in the Western world where it is perhaps prized above everything else).[47] This is not to say that Buddhism is simply a shrugging off of personal responsibility or social involvement; it also requires a moral discipline. The path to full enlightenment, which the Buddha taught in his famous *Sermon at Benares,* entails the "eightfold way" of right views, right aspirations, right speech, right conduct, right livelihood, right effort, right mindfulness, and right contemplation.[48] To become a monk, one has to bind oneself to the Ten Precepts, which prohibit destroying life, taking what is not given, being unchaste, lying, accepting money, and so on.[49]

What is of special concern here is how these moral insights were derived. The Buddha made no suggestion that a deity planted them in our hearts, so we could say we were "born" with them, not that they were given in response to prayerful or intellectual quest. The tradition that the insights were "revealed" to the Buddha at the time of his enlightenment implies that there is an objective moral frame of reference—but "revealed" by whom? The Buddha was not an atheist in the usual meaning of the term but was non theistic in the sense that he declared "existence" to be an inappropriate category for that which we encounter in meditation.[50] Morality is not embedded in nature, which is full of mortal striving, but it comes by way of intuition through meditation—and morality is perhaps best understood in the context of *karma,* "moral energy," available to the questing spirit. The Buddhist concept of karma briefly stated is this:

> Any act, good or evil, once committed and conceived never vanishes but lives potentially or actively as the case may be, in the world of minds and deeds. This mysterious moral energy is embodied in and emanates from every act and thought.[51]

The Buddha did not deny the Hindu tradition of reincarnation but declared that the ultimate hope of humankind must be to go beyond, to Nirvana. This is not the nihilistic extinction of popular misrepresentation but a positive sense of release from the anguish and tragedies of this world with its ignorance and egoism. In a Buddhist hymn of victory are these words:

> In thoughtfulness let one remove belief in self,
> And pass beyond the realm of death.
> The king of death will never find
> The man whom thus the world beholds.[52]

Confucianism.   Named for its founder K'ung Fu-tsu (born c. 550 B.C. in the Province of Shantung) *Confusianism* is a title used mostly by Westerners. The Chinese are more accustomed to speak of *Ju Chaio,* "teaching of the sage." More an ethical philosophy than a religious system in its earliest form, Confucianism in its earliest teachings avoided theological argument and the trappings of a organized religion. The chief virtue espoused is *Jen* (sometimes transliterated *Ren*), which includes compassion and "human heartedness." The fully actualized "noble person" is *Chun Tsu,* who has been able to cultivate character by having had good role models (parents, family, sage companions) and disciplining the mind to do what is socially "fitting." One considers the mandates of heaven (*Tian*) and observes the proper rites and ceremonies (*Li*). The latter, "based on heaven, patterned on earth" as Confucius said, extend from propriety in serving tea and good form in archery and chariot driving to proper conduct at funerals and sacrifices to ancestors. In short, every appropriate behavior reveals one's true humanity.

As noted, Confucius generally avoided discussions of deity or traditional religious themes. Nevertheless, Confucianism, as Hume reminds us, "has always taught not only the existence of a Supreme Being, but also divine supervision over the world."[53] In the *Analects,* written either by K'ung Fu-tsu or one of his pupils, one may read, "At fifteen my mind was fixed on learning. By thirty my character had been formed. At fifty I understood the Mandate of Heaven."[54] The moral proclivity arises then from within, as an earnest desire to be fully human, following the mandate to make a more humane society.

How K'ung-Fu-Tsu came to understand Heaven's mandate is the key to the Confucian concept of morality in general. We know from the *Analects* that he was a diligent student of literature, government, natural science, and history and that he avoided the gymnastic arts and studies of the supernatural.[55] The Confucian *Book of History,* a record of China's history that dates as far back as 2300 B.C., makes a clear link between social justice, communal welfare, governmental responsibility, and the observance of religious belief and worship.[56] Yet the connection between religious belief and morality appears to have been more intuitive than by divine decree or "inspiration" in the pious sense.

The centerpiece of K'ung Fu-tsu's teaching, it is worth reiterating, is Jen, which may be translated "the virtue of perfect humanity." He appears to have affirmed a belief in the essential goodness of people, so that the discipline of *I,* or "righteousness" would prompt appropriate behavior in all situations requiring a moral choice. The virtue of *Shu* is the obverse of the Golden Rule: "Do not do to others what you do not want done to yourself."[57] This is not merely a negative phrasing; the positive side is stated in *Chung Yung,* in which Confucius is noted to have said, "Set an example in behavior toward a friend, as I would require him to behave toward me."[58]

For K'ung Fu-tsu, virtue meant being as fully human as one could be, which required social interaction. Presumably he would have agreed with Socrates, who said that a man would have to be either a beast or an angel to live alone. Maintaining proper interaction required acknowledging the essential relationships of ruler and subject, father and son, husband and wife, elder and younger brother, teacher and pupil, and friend and friend. In the last case, the rule of reciprocity must prevail because members neither should presume to be "above" the other. The Chun Tsu, as noted, is a specific designation in Confucian ethics that denotes the ideal, or superior individual. The formulation appears over a hundred times in the Analects.

Interestingly, the concept of a superior individual does not include "superior women." Confucianism is the only thoroughly masculine-dominated religious tradition of the world's "great" religions. The downplaying of the consideration of women, half of the world's population, must be of concern as we search for the origins of the moral proclivity. In other aspects, Confucianism seems to have much in common with the humanism of eighteenth century Western philosophy, and, in all honesty, we must confess that in the West, too, the role of women has only recently been accorded long overdue attention.

2. Religions of the West

Judaism, Christianity, and Islam are the leading Western religious traditions, all three of which are distinctly and almost aggressively monotheistic in contrast to those of the East considered in this brief survey. These Western traditions hold that there is but one omnipotent, transcendent God who is the author of all things including the moral standards that are to guide and judge human behavior.

Judaism. In *Judaism,* the premise that God not only created human beings along with all other natural creatures but also created humans in God's own image is unequivocal.[59] It is significant that God's image transcends gender distinctions; the word *Shekhinah (Presence)* is a feminine name for God in both the Talmud and in Kabbalistic literature. Furthermore, it is asserted that as our creator, God knows us even before we are conceived[60] and establishes his law in our hearts.[61]

Faith is a way of knowing just as the senses and reason are ways of knowing. The epistemology of faith is such that we can search out God's moral imperatives,[62] but even when the task falters, God may break through to our conscious minds and reveal his word or law directly.[63] It is also the case, however, that when God's word is ignored or law violated or when people use religion to camouflage their injustices, God's moral law will be reiterated through chosen spokespersons, or prophets. A Deborah, an Isaiah, or an Amos will rise to rebuke the people and call for repentance and a return to the paths of justice and ethical behavior.[64] Perhaps the most insightful passage in Hebrew scripture relates what God requires us "to do justice, and to love kindness, and to walk humbly with your God."[65]

An interesting contrast between the Eastern and Western religious traditions lies not only in the direct relationship between God and "his" people (in Jewish tradition, God is invariably spoken or written about as male except for certain important inferences[66]) but in the many specific moral laws that have direct application to daily life. These range from birthing rituals to personal cleanliness, food restrictions, business practices, and burials.[67] "We cannot be Jewish just by *being*—to remain Jewish is a process" wrote Abraham Heschel.[68] It requires an understanding that Judaism does not separate belief from behavior, sacred from the secular in human conduct. "God," says Heschel, "is concerned with everydayness." Thus, although the Eastern traditions do in fact impose requirements of right conduct, these tend to be in terms of general principles (e.g., Buddhism's "right views, right aims, right speech," etc.) and are often characterized as ultimately impersonal inasmuch as self-hood itself is a questionable concept. Jewish tradition is seldom general and never impersonal but gives explicit moral and ethical instructions. Hebrew scriptures (pronounced complete by about the year 90 C.E.) the *Mishnah,* or "traditions" (codified about 220 C.E.), the *Talmud* (c. 390 C.E.), and the *Midrash* (expositions on the scriptures) gave the Jewish people specific moral guidelines.

Rabbi Abraham Sachar's *History of the Jews* reminds us, however, that the traditions and commentaries were

> never intended to be authoritative legal codes, but in effect became just that. Even obsolete laws . . . became sacred and were discussed and expounded as if they still had vitality, and what some of the rabbis had feared came true. The great compilation tended to overshadow the Scriptures which it was created to expound.[69]

Christianity. This very concern that traditions and adherence to written moral codes threatened to overshadow the word of God in part gave *Christianity* its initial controversial aspect.

This concern existed before Jesus came on the scene, and his many conflicts with the Pharisees and other religious leaders arose from Jesus' anxiety that Hebrew tradition had, especially among the Pharisees and their followers, retreated to rigid legal demands, for example, the Ten Commandments' prohibition of any form of work on the Sabbath. There were literally hundreds of regulations such as defining how many yards a person might walk on the Sabbath, or in the episode of the denouncement of Jesus for plucking a handful of grain to feed his disciples. Countless other traditions had allowed the faith to become "Hellenized," or so compromised by Greek influences as almost to cease being authentic Judaism.[70] The apostle Paul, who never thought of himself as other that a faithful Jew, noted that God's law was "written upon the human heart"[71] to give the human spirit wings, not a heavy burden to bear. Love for God and for one's neighbor was to be a liberating force. Jesus' charge was that the scribes and Pharisees "bind heavy burdens, hard to bear . . . [but] have neglected the weightier matters of the law, justice and mercy and faith."[72]

It must never be overlooked that Jesus' faith was deeply embedded in the religion of the Hebrew people. The ethics in which he was raised can be summed up in the Hebrew word *halakhah*, "walking in obedience," which encompassed both faith and ethics. He doubtless began each day, as did every faithful Jew, with the prayerful reminder: "Shema Israel, Adonoi Eluhenu, Adonoi Echad." ("Hear, O Israel, the Lord our God, the Lord in One") and took up "the yoke of the Kingdom" to begin his *halakhah* on the highway of the Kingdom. Furthermore, while he chafed at the Pharisees' oppressive use of the laws of Israel, for him the Torah was authoritative, and he strove to fulfill "every jot and tittle."[73] He insisted among his disciples, "I tell you, unless your righteousness exceeds that of the scribes and Pharisees, you will never enter the Kingdom of Heaven."[74]

The key to Jesus' moral teaching was in his insistence that the very essence of God is love[75] and that if we know God (one definition of the Hebrew verb "to know" is "to become one with. . . ."), we will also be people of love. Those who are not loving, which includes not forgiving, not becoming reconciled in their relations with fellow humans, simply do not know God, no matter how pious they may be.[76] Furthermore, love embraces not only friends and relatives[77] but also strangers[78] and even one's enemies.[79]

This last emphasis, loving one's enemies, is perhaps most characteristic of Christian ethics but is deeply rooted in the Hebrew consciousness (cf. Exodus 23: 5 and Proverbs 25:21) and remains what makes it so difficult to be understood or accepted even among many who call themselves Christians. Nothing was so impressive to the ancient Romans. "See how these Christians love each other," wrote a Roman statesman, Tertullian, who later converted to Christianity. Tragically, nothing is so conspicuously absent among many modern churchgoers who seem to pride themselves on excoriating not only their nations' enemies but even fellow Christians whose interpretation of the faith differs from their own.[80]

The focus on love is by no means a mere sentimentality because loving the enemy, especially in time of war, can bring down condemnation on one's head. It is useful to reflect that an official definition of a traitor is "one who gives aid and comfort to the enemy." As the Scribes and Pharisees were intolerant of non-Jews and resented Jesus' fraternizing with Gentiles and "sinners,"[81] so even today many who label themselves as Christians reject those who seek ways to work with refugees, the jobless, and the racially diverse.

As to the origin of love as a basis for ethical behavior, the New Testament is clear: "We love, because God first loved us."[82] God not only instilled the capacity for love in our human natures but also established his law, "Thou *shalt* love"[83] in our hearts. "Love is the fulfilling of the law."[84] All laws designed to secure domestic tranquility and international peace are fulfilled in the exercise of love, as was demonstrated in the first century Christianity communities with efforts to care for the sick, eliminate hunger, and shelter the homeless.[85] Eventually in Rome, the practical exercise of love resulted in abolishing infanticide and gladiatorial combat and setting up hospitals, food distribution centers, and schools. Perhaps Will Durant expressed best the consequences of all this in describing how Christianity supplanted the vast power of the Roman Empire: "They turned from Caesar preaching war, to Christ preaching peace; from incredible brutality to unprecedented charity; from a life without hope or dignity to a faith that honored their humanity."[86]

The essence of Christianity is not in the trappings or traditions of the church but in becoming so identified with Christ that we truly become one with him who fully identified with God. "For me to live," wrote Paul, "is Christ."[87] Again, "It is no longer I who live, but Christ lives within me."[88] This ontological identification is, according to Christian teachings, made possible because, in the fullest sense, we are born with the capacity for knowing it; we are born in the image of God. If Christians become at one with Jesus, as he became one with God, even if, like many of his followers, Christians are executed or assassinated for the faith, they believe they will share in his resurrection from death and be reunited with all whom they loved (including enemies!) in God's Kingdom.[89] Indeed, the belief among many Christians is that God's love for all creation holds the promise that even if others have not known Jesus as Christ in this life, they still have hope for the resurrection by having shared in the spirit of love (and the morality it implies) during their pilgrimage through this world.

Islam. The third in the trilogy with Judaism and Christianity is *Islam,* which traces its historic lineage to Abraham. The founding date of Islam on Western calendars is usually given as 622 A.D. although the date among Muslims, the followers of Islam, is denoted *Anno Hegirae* (abbreviated A.H., for the year of Muhammad's migration from Mecca to Medina), marking the beginning year. Like Judaism and Christianity (to both of which the Qur'an refers as "the people of the Book"), Islam provides guidelines for all areas of life, political and domestic, as well as spiritual, and maintains that these directives are directly from God whom its calls Allah. Unlike the other two religions, Islam (which means "submission") has never had a priesthood or a mediator between God and humankind. Each believer has a direct relationship with God providing the believer is truly Muslim, "one who submits" heart and mind to God's holy will.

If the foundation of Christian ethics is love, with its numerous ramifications, the foundation of Islamic ethics is found in the "Five Pillars," which include certain obligations: (1) repetition of the creed (or *Kalimah,* watchword), (2) prayer, (3) alms giving, (4) fasting during Ramadan, and (5) the pilgrimage to Mecca. In brief, these may be understood as "acts of service" (*ibadat*) including the following:

1. Daily affirmation of the creed in the original Arabic: *La ilaha illa Allah; wa-Muhammadan rasulu Allah:* "There is no God but Allah; and Muhammad is his messenger."
2. The call to prayer is heard from the minaret of every mosque five times daily and is directed toward the sacred mosque in Mecca.
3. Generosity is a key characteristic of the Islamic life and derives from the directive that a fifth of all the faithful acquires (including "booty" from war) belongs to Allah, to the Apostle, near relatives, the needy and the wayfarer.
4. To prevent distraction from worship and the practical needs of others, fasting, during the month of Ramadan (the ninth month of the Islamic lunar calendar) is required as is abstention from drinking, smoking, and sexual intercourse during daylight hours (the distinction between daylight and nighttime hours being determined by the ability to distinguish between a white and a black thread in ordinary light).
5. At least once during the lifetime of each man and woman, a *hajj,* or pilgrimage to the holy city of Mecca in the twelfth month of the lunar calendar is required. This is to emulate Muhammad's pilgrimage shortly before his death in 632. To reinforce the theme that all faithful are brothers without regard to nation, race, or other worldly involvements, all pilgrims dress in a simple white garment and begin a sevenfold procession around the Kaaba, a square stone building presumably built by Abraham and containing a black rock given to Abraham by Gabriel. The procession is followed by travel to Arafat, where prayers of confession and the sacrifice of an animal are offered. Finally, the shearing of the men's hair and the trimming of the women's opens three days of celebration and a farewell before the Kaaba and the homeward journey.

This five-part discipline, often called the "Five Pillars of Islam" or *ibadat* (acts of service) might well be seen as at least a minimal "ethical foundation" for Islam, but this is not to suggest that it is the literal equivalent to the foundations of the other traditions we have considered.

It is important to remember that Islam is not correctly called "Muhammadanism" because the prophet Muhammad (570–632 B.C.E.) did not actually create the religion. Islam is the message of Allah revealed to all of his prophets, who were human beings chosen by him to deliver his message to mankind. Thus, Abraham, Ishmael, Isaac, Jacob, Moses, John, Jesus, and finally Muhammad (the peace and blessings of Allah be upon them all) were all prophets of Islam. Muslims are told not to differentiate between the prophets of Allah as being inferior or superior to one another. Every Muslim must believe the truthfulness of Moses, Jesus, and all other prophets of Allah.[90]

One of the most prevalent misconceptions about Islamic ethics is that it is enjoined to "spread the religion by the sword." The sacred scripture of Islam, The Holy Qur'an, is quite explicit: "Let there be no compulsion in religion."[91] To be sure, when Muhammed began preaching, he encountered hostility from among his countrymen and had to defend himself to avoid capture and death. With increasing opposition, he found it necessary to create a small army and finally established himself at Medina. There he built a mosque and eventually returned to his home city of Mecca, where he set up a theocracy from which to rule all Arabia. Although said to have been unlettered, he admired the centers of learning he found among Jews and Christians during his travels and was determined to advance education among his followers. As Islam spread across Europe, the pattern of hostility and retaliation, familiar to all who traveled in those days, necessitated a strong military backup. With mounting successes, the armies of Islam came to be respected and feared, hence the reputation of spreading the religion by the sword. Central to the Qur'an's message (and remarkably similar to Acts 10:34–35 in the Christian Bible), however, are these words: "Whoever submits his whole self to God, and is a doer of good, he will get his reward with his Lord."[92] The key word here is "whoever." Islam is an inclusive faith, not the exclusive religion of any one group such as the Taliban or others who have perverted the tradition for political gain (in much the way some Christians did during the Crusades and the Inquisition).

Islam proposes a revolutionary concept of the unity of humankind, totally rejecting barriers of color, race, and language, by regarding all men as created equal. This concept appeared centuries before the Magna Charta or Bill of Rights. Indeed, in Islam, the only distinction to be made among people is precisely on moral and ethical grounds. Allah (who addresses humankind from the vantage point of the royal "We"), declares: "O Mankind, We created you from a single (pair), of male and female, and made you into nations and tribes, that you may know each other. Verily the most honored of you in the sight of God, is he who is most righteous."[93]

Among the ethical concerns of Westerners about Islam (and the source of a great deal of misunderstanding), the role of women is perhaps the most troubling. Can a religion that imposes a second-class status on half of its population be morally trustworthy?

It should be noted from the outset that Muhammad was keenly aware of his debt to his wife, Khadijah, for providing him the necessary time and resources for spiritual reflection and for receptivity to the inspiration that led to the founding of Islam. Second, having renounced the polytheism and idol worship of his Meccan background, he set about to abolish its harsh practices, such as the burial alive of unwanted babies, unregulated polygamy, and denial of property ownership to women. Third, he pointed to God's direct inspiration in the Qur'an that women are to be reverenced.[94] A man might have as many as four wives at one time but must treat them with respect and absolute equality in terms of worldly support.[95]

Other areas of the Islamic moral and ethical stance that sometimes perplex non-Muslims include marriage, divorce, ownership of property, and public comportment (often with specific reference to requiring women to wear veils). Obviously, these are not inborn convictions; they are not a priori but are to be found either as injunctions from God via the Qur'an, or are in the Hadith, a body of literature of the "sayings" of Muhammad outside the Qur'an. Finally, it should be noted that Islamic legal traditions may vary from country to country. For example, while the Qur'an and the Hadith permit marriage to four wives, polygamy is now illegal in Turkish law, which nevertheless remains informed by the Qur'an. An even more striking example might be the practice of requiring girls to be circumcized in some African Islamic communities. Many non-Muslims consider this brutality, but the fact is that such a practice has no place in Islam; it is purely a matter of cultural, tribal tradition.

In Islam, the primary moral obligation is to seek God's will as revealed in the Qur'an, in the Hadith, or in the courts of the community of faith. Keeping that in mind, we consider these issues in order.

As to marriage, the Qur'an instructs: "Keep the tie of marriage sacred," and if a man cannot afford to be married, he must remain strictly celebate until God provides a means for him to marry.[96]

Divorce is legally possible according to the Qur'an, but Muslims are warned, "Of all things permitted by law, divorce is the most hateful in the sight of God." As to the wives, the Qur'an sternly admonishes husbands: "Fear God, and turn them not out of their houses."[97] The divorced wife is not required to give up her dowery.[98]

The right of wives to inherit and own property independently of the husband is an area in which in the Qur'an was centuries ahead of many Western traditions. As recently as the nineteenth century, for example, most European and American women could niether own property nor vote. The Bible is simply silent on such matters, which are left to be decided in secular courts. It is true that in Islam, a girl can inherit only half as much as her brother.[99] Inasmuch as she has no obligation to share the inheritance with her original family (as he does) but takes her inheritance into her marriage, the division is more equitable than may be apparent.

Westerners are usually more "put off" by the Islamic custom of women going veiled in public than by any other evidence of inequality. But the veil, as one Muslim woman has written, "so seemingly oppressive to Western eyes, at least has allowed women to observe without being observed, affording their wearers a degree of anonymity that on some occasions has proven useful."[100] Stories and movies depicting harems have also titillated Western imaginations, but the word *harem,* which is often translated as "forbidden place," actually has its root in the word *beloved.* Because their women were to be cherished in a predatory world, the early Muslim households kept their women safe in secluded areas, often in carefully guarded gardens.

Today, in much of the Muslim world (except for Saudi Arabia and some gulf states), women have the right to vote and have gained access to education, the work force, and travel abroad. Some are beginning to enter into politics. It is also of interest that many Muslim women have compared their lot quite favorably to that of non-Muslims whose women are exploited for commercial profit in television, advertising, and the movies. The rise in divorce with its accompaniment of lower economic security, abandoned "latch key" children, delinquency, and social unrest appear to many Muslims evidence that the price of "freedom" in Western societies is too high.

To trace and illuminate the ethical foundations of Islam, one may look to the Qur'an as the ultimate authority and arbiter on human rights. The conference of Riyad, March 23, 1972 (Safar 1392 of the Hagira), the initial meeting with Saudi canonists, it was asserted that the constitution of Saudi Arabia and its laws, whether in civil matters or questions of personal status, were founded exclusively on the Qur'an, according to the revelation received fourteen centuries before.[101]

While this may seem arbitrary and rigid to non-Muslims, openness to dialogue is also sacred to the Muslim mind. The Qur'an explicitly says, "Speak fair to the people,"[102] "call unto the way of thy Lord with wisdom and fair exortation,"[103] and "argue not with the People of then Scripture (Christians and Jews) unless it be in a way that is better."[104] Furthermore, "Where there is common good, there is the law of God."[105] A member of the Saudi delegation to the Conference of Riyad (not named) spoke to the question of the relation of ethics to religion: "By religion is understood the way in which man actualizes his relations with the suprahuman and mysterious forces on which he believes to be dependent."[106] This superhuman agent that guides him or her is choice the between ethical alternatives. The Saudi delegate continues on a more urgent note:

> It is a command of the Qur'an that justice in the exercise of authority should be absolute. The Qur'an asserts that all mankind, born of the same father and mother forms one single family, that the Creator has ordered men according to nations and tribes to know and assist one another for the good of all; Islam bans any kind of enmity among men, any kind of hatred, contempt or oppression.[107]

If a common theme can be discerned in these three Western traditions—Judaism, Christianity, and Islam—it would seem to be that humans are indeed born by the grace of God and are endowed with the capacity to seek God's will. It is in our nature to acknowledge that as God loves us, we must also love God and all that God has created. Love is at the root of our moral standards and our moral proclivities. To depart from these is to abandon our birthright, our essential nature, and our intended destiny.

C. INTERFACES WITH PSYCHOLOGY AND RELATED DISCIPLINES

In their 1984 landmark book *Morality, Moral Behavior, and Moral Development,* Drs. Kurtines and Gewirtz set forth three major themes around which their collection of essays would revolve: the need for theoretic models, the need for increased methodological rigor, and the need to clarify and refine the boundaries between philosophical and psychological issues.[108] What is attempted in this brief discussion is to focus on the third concern, to expand the field of study and suggest that clarity of boundaries need not be sacrificed while inviting interdisciplinary dialogue.

It is useful to recall that among psychologists, one of the first to make explicit his concern for the spiritual foundations of moral development was Gustav Fechner (1801–1887). He was the originator of the science of psychophysics, which in turn gave rise to physiological psychology. While he identified himself as a Christian,[109]

Fechner often quoted other religious traditions and was especially attracted to the Zend Avesta (Book of Law) of the Zoroastrian tradition.[110] His conviction was that psychology, as its name originally implied, was to be a study of the soul (*psyche*), the organizing self that is capable of reflecting on and evaluating its own nature and, by implication, authenticate the reality of the souls of others. "All our psychology, insofar as it is not merely the observation of oneself, assumes a belief in the souls of others."[111] His effort to reduce all perceptions, whether of self or other selves or any other kind of sensation to specific numbers, and thus make them quantifiable, became known as "Fechner's law."[112]

Fechner believed that God has so designed us that we can perceive the Divine Will, including moral and ethical precepts, directly and that the experience of them is as subject to verification as any other subjective perception such as goodness and beauty.[113] If an increase in a stimulus can be precisely correlated with an increase in sensation, then a quantitative relationship can be established between the physical and the mental/spiritual. Fechner demonstrated how seemingly irreconcilable data can be bound together in rational unity.

1. Experimental Psychology

The whole field of *experimental psychology* began with Fechner, and he so impressed his contemporaries Wilhelm Wundt, Will James, and G. Stanley Hall that they wrote special tributes to his work.[114] Edwin Boring notes, "It is hard to see how the new psychology could have advanced as it did without (Fechner's) *Elemente der Psychophysik*, in 1860."[115]

Toward the end of the nineteenth century, the formal establishment of a psychological laboratory by Wilhelm Wundt in Leipzig in 1879 provided clear evidence that the field had become quite consciously experimental. Some historians argue that William James' laboratory at Harvard, begun four years earlier in 1875, should be listed first. But in James' case, the work done seems almost casual by comparison with Wundt's rigorous and systematic studies on the physiological basis of human experiences and behavior. It is beyond the scope of this presentation to trace the diverse paths of psychology from the physiological emphases of Helmholtz, Donders, Lotz, and Brentano to the medical orientation of Sigmund Freud in Vienna, the structuralism of Titchener at Cornell, and the behavioral conditioning theories of J. B. Watson at Chicago or B.F. Skinner at Harvard. Perhaps the major trend to note during the generations that included and followed them was the almost frenetic anxiety to be considered "scientific." For many of them, this meant abandoning concerns for moral or "spiritual" matters except as they aided individuals in coping with their social environment.

In his book *The Death and Rebirth of Psychology*, Ira Progoff describes what he regards as a historic change in the direction of the field. Sigmund Freud, he stated, was on the right track in his exploration of the unconscious, "but [his] conception of the unconscious has led beyond itself, first . . . in the works of Freud himself and Jung; then in the later writings of Adler, Jung and especially Rank."[116] In the wake of two world wars, rising crime rates, domestic disintegration, and the apparent evaporation of cultural values, psychology, according to Progoff, must "fulfill itself by leading what Jung called 'modern man in search of a soul,' to a soul beyond psychology."

Whether or not psychologists have the capability or even inclination to seek the human soul, the traditional concern for moral rectitude has recently become of considerable importance to many in the field. The moral proclivity among human beings is now widely considered a verifiable reality. To be sure, William James nearly a century ago suggested that many preconditions for morality, such as free will and reason, are not fully subject to psychological investigation because our instruments "will surely never grow refined enough to discover [them]."[117] In 1932, Sigmund Freud, author of *Psychoanalysis*, conceded that "scientific thought is still in its infancy"[118] and psychology must proceed the best way it can, testing hypotheses by making careful observations. Accordingly, he hypothesized that humans are born with at least three innate mental components: the *id* (containing genetically determined characteristics, including instincts and survival needs), the *ego* ("that part of the *id* which has been modified by the direct influence of the external world," comprising the "self" and "representing what we call reason and sanity"[119]), and the *superego*, into which one incorporates the certain attributes, characteristics, and affective behaviors of one's parents and the standards of one's society and culture.

For Freud, however, the notion that we are actually born knowing right and wrong would have been absurd. Nevertheless, he affirmed that we are provided, as an evolutionary mechanism of survival, the superego so that the proclivity for the moral quest is indeed "built-in." He eschewed any notion that a deity provided this; God was simply one's earthly father "clothed in the grandeur in which he once appeared to the small child" and projected outward onto the cosmos.[120] Freud expressed his hostility to a religious interpretation of the superego as something "provided" in his vehement statement: "Of the forces which dispute the position of science, religion alone is a really serious enemy."[121]

Many psychoanalysts have departed from Freud on this point, including his early disciples, Carl Jung and Erik Erikson, as well as the British D.W. Winnicott, the American Ana-Maria Rizzuto, and others. Robert Coles of Harvard declares that Freud's use of such undemonstrable entities as id and superego is no less a metaphysical exercise than concepts of God and the human soul. He describes it as

> ironic and dismaying to find both Freudian and Marxist thought so arrogantly abusive when the subject of religion comes up. True, religious thought, like everything else, has lent itself to tyranny and exploitation of people. But so has Marxist thought, and Freudian thought . . . The writings turn into the "movement" with a few anointed ones, with "schools" and splits and expulsions; "punitive orthodoxy."[122]

Meanwhile, the work of *developmental* cognitive theorist Jean Piaget offers four distinct stages of development in which the child uses the senses and motor skills to understand the world: the *sensorimotor* (birth to 2 years, when the infant organized its activities to gain control over the environment); the *pre-operational* (ages 2 to 6 years, which involves symbolic thinking, including language); the *concrete operational* (ages 7 to 11 years, requiring increasingly complex logical processes); and the *formal operational* (age 12 and up, hypothetical and abstract reasoning capable of moving from the actual to the possible). It is noted that for Piaget, ethics and moral judgment must wait for this fourth step when the cognitive capacities are more mature. Piaget held that no consideration of moral thinking or ethical judgment was inherent in the newborn but, significantly, that these stages reveal a natural unfolding of the child's nature and that children are by nature proactive, seeking new experiences and knowledge and striving for mental equilibrium when earlier conceptions prove inadequate. Such equilibrium may be considered a kind of moral balance.[123]

Within that framework, however, are other stages related directly to the child's perception of moral and ethical principles. Between the ages of 3 and 11, Piaget noted, children adhere to a morality of restraint in which "playing by the rules" is mandatory to be rewarded and to avoid punishment. By the beginning of adolescence, in conjunction with the stage of abstract reasoning, the child begins to extract socially acceptable principles underlying the rule and to monitor her or his own value judgments.[124]

Lawrence Kohlberg also described moral development as a stage-by-stage process; he proposed not four but six distinct *age-periods* (each with sub stages) during which the child moves from being an egocentric to becoming mature and seeking principles. The stages or age-periods are further grouped into three levels seen in such descriptive terms as "do what satisfies me" (ages 0–2), "avoid punishment" (ages 2–3), and a hedonic "do what pleases me" (4–7), all of which Kohlberg labels the *preconventional,* or premoral, level. From 7 to 10 years of age, the idea is to gain approval, be a good boy/girl, while from 10 to 12, a law-and-order orientation sets in. This is the *conventional* level. Finally, the *postconventional* level includes gaining the respect of others (13 to 15), developing internal principles (15 to 18), and perhaps even discovering "eternal principles" based on a kind of cosmic commitment to eternal values.[125] Of special interest to the present writer was a comment that Kohlberg made during a personal conversation in San Francisco a year or so before he died. He was tempted, he told me, to drop the final, sixth stage from his list. Apart from Albert Schweitzer and Mother Teresa, he said, he could find almost no one to exemplify it. Just before his death in 1987, however, he had moved ahead, setting himself the additional task of formalizing a seventh stage, incorporating religious insight that prompts conscious moral effort.

Critics have found some serious problems with Kohlberg's position. Among these is Carol Gilligan of Harvard, who objects that his theory that focuses on issues of justice, is of male orientation, and fails to acknowledge gender differences.[126] Women, Gilligan insists, are more likely to solve problems of human relations in terms of caring, nurturing, and altruism, in comparison to men who are more rule oriented and legalistic.

Others find a problem with Kohlberg's insistence that the sequence of stages is unchanging and the process of maturing from one to the other is irreversible. In point of fact, the "backsliding" of people from higher to lower ethical stages (e.g., the once honest accountant who starts cheating on taxes) is a familiar phenomenon. Then, too, Piaget and Kohlberg used similar techniques in assessing children's moral development, eliciting verbal rationale for the judgment of specific acts in hypothetical situations. Carol Schuster points out, however, that "there is often a discrepancy between what a child can verbalize as being right, and what he would actually do in a similar value-choice situation."[127] Doubtless many adults, too, would be offended when asked if it is ever right to lie to the government or stand by idly while another person is being physically attacked, yet those same adults might fabricate numbers on their income tax or hasten from the scene of a street mugging to avoid getting involved. Again, critics fault Kohlberg for attending only to the verbalization of clients about rules and obedience to the neglect of issues of personal sacrifice and weighing one's own needs against those of others.[128]

It may be that, had he lived longer, Kohlberg would have addressed these issues. It is reported that he was concerned about the nature of moral discernment as quite possibly a distinct, inborn human trait. As mentioned, shortly before his death he had begun exploring the field of meta-ethics, normative moral behavior, and the spiritual domain.[129] What he might have concluded in the process of such exploration we may never know, but the epistemological question central to the whole enterprise still needs attention. If there are universally valid moral truths, do we know them because of an inborn capacity? Is this capacity operational at birth, or does the knowledge "dawn" on us as we move through successive stages of development? In any case, it would seem that Kohlberg's assumption has the prospect that moral values have objective, extramundane reality.

2. Sociobiology

Perhaps the most rigorous insistence on defining the origins of moral perception in terms of biology and evolution comes from the relatively new field of *sociobiology*. Originally the title of a book by Edward Wilson of Harvard, sociobiology proposes that neither courage, altruism, nor spiritual inspiration prompts our actions, even our most generous impulses. All represent biologically evolved traits to ensure the survival of the species. "Innate censors and motivators exist in the brain that deeply and unconsciously affect our ethical premises; from these roots morality evolved as instinct."[130] To put his position in starkest form, Wilson insists, "Human beings are guided by an instinct based on genes."[131] When asked if he completely discounts intuition as a source of moral insight, he replies in the negative. But he qualifies his response: "Ethical philosophers intuit the deontological canons of morality by consulting the emotive centers of their own hypothalmic-limbic system."[132]

An Aristotelian might find in Wilson's premise a suggestion of teleological importance. If the moral sense is part of the given structure of the organism, humankind appears to have been preprogrammed for moral behavior, and this has enabled us to survive and to thrive. If that is not the case, natural selection does not satisfy the question as to why humans require the moral sense to prevail when countless other species have survived eons of history without it. Furthermore, if Piaget and Kohlberg are correct that morality and intelligence are correlated, it may be concluded that the moral sense does not reside in the hypothalmus-limbic system (as Wilson proposes) but in the neocortex. Philip Hefner seems to come close to this conclusion in relating the "good," the cognitive goal of the moral quest, with basic human needs that supply their own inherent "ought." He quotes R.M. Hare's *Language of Morals* and Philippa Foot's *Essay in Moral Concepts* to epitomize this argument that "the practical implication of the use of moral terms is that the virtue of oughts turn out to be needs."[133]

Yet Hefner sees an inherent flaw in confusing such terms as *needs* and *wants* and in uncritically linking them with *oughts*. This is especially important in the science of psychology, which incorporates the insights of many disciplines. He urges a carefully articulated religious hypothesis in which to frame the understandings from other disciplines in ascertaining the whole truth about what is and what ought to be.[134] In this, he appears to agree with Albert Einstein's declaration that "science can only ascertain what is, but not what should be, and outside of its domain judgments of all kinds remain necessary."[135] He notes that religion, the age-old endeavor of mankind to become clearly and completely conscious of values and goals, does not conflict with science, which must also deal daily with humane concerns. Science, as C.P. Snow acknowledged a generation ago, cannot be indifferent to these concerns, "letting the conscience rust."[136] If we can redefine the roles of science and religion in terms less weighted with dogmatism, then Nobel Laureate Charles Townes' call for a convergence of the disciplines can be sustained: Science and religion are so intimately related to our decision making that "converge they must, and through this should come new strength for both."[137]

Such "new strength for both" may be emerging, as John and Janice Baldwin express in their book *Beyond Sociobiology*. They write of "the ultimate goal of balanced social theories [being] to integrate data on natural selection and natural learning with data on physiological mechanisms."[138] Our failure thus far to be able to predict with scientific accuracy the moral choices of individuals, much less those of societies, they claim, is due to our having depended on outmoded nineteenth century interpretations of data (e.g., Malthusian rationalism and laissez faire competition, which work predictably only at the subhuman levels of nature).

Nobel Laureate Roger Sperry, a *neurophysiologist,* would go even further to state that we do not even know how the mind works because we have falsely concluded that the mind is nothing more than brain circuitries in action. "Human consciousness," he declared, "plays a causal role and is neither identical to, nor reducible to, neural events."[139] The field of psychology is greatly strengthened (and challenged) by such input by those who work directly with the brain, which is the seat (if not the origin) of conscious and purposing behaviors, including moral decision making.

Another Nobel Prize–winning neurophysiologist, John Eccles, in his Gifford Lectures on *The Human Psyche,* affirms with Sperry that personality emerges from, but is not reducible to, the brain.[140] He is joined by philosopher Karl Popper,[141] psychologist Daniel N. Robinson,[142] and mathematical physicist Roger Penrose of Oxford. They state, quite independently, that the mature human being emerges from the neurophysical system to "stand apart" from the brain in order to use it, train it, and even interact with it.[143] This is not to say (and Penrose stopped short of saying) that the self becomes wholly independent of the physical laws that control neural functions,[144] but that it is capable of perceiving transcendent "realities" in much the way Plato believed we perceive ultimate beauty, moral goodness, and truth. Penrose points out that truths, such as abstract mathematical concepts like Einstein's $E = MC^2$, operate everywhere and for all time. These ultimates are *discovered* by the self, not just made up. He stated:

> Moreover, such mathematical properties, though often not at all anticipated by human beings before appropriate insights came to light, have lain timelessly within the platonic world, as unchangeable truths waiting to be discovered—in accordance with the skills and insights of those who strive to discover them.[145]

D. IMPLICATIONS FOR GLOBAL ETHICS

If this chapter's premise that humankind has a proclivity, or at least a strong disposition, for affirming a moral imperative at the very heart of "the world" holds, a burning question remains: Why then is there so much evil, violence, and destructiveness in the world? Why, as individuals, do we lie to and betray each other, especially those whom we have pledged to love? Why, as societies, do we contract to follow specific rules for the well-being of all and then violate those agreements in cleverly disguised manipulations in the name of corporate responsibility? Why, as nations, do we so readily go to war against other nations, even when we have not been damaged or even threatened with violence by them? This enthusiasm goes back at least as far as the self-aggrandizing Roman Empire, ancient Egypt, and fourth century B.C. Mesopotamia, "the cradle of civilization."

One answer to this dilemma is that if there were no such moral inclination, we probably would not even be asking such questions. Clearly, something within our nature stands apart from our self-destructive behaviors, judges them, and sets up regulations and laws that would keep them in check. But what is the source of this capacity for moral discernment? One response, at the heart of most Western religions, is in the *Imago Dei:* We are created in the image of God and inherent in our very nature is God's spirit of righteousness. Not all religious traditions, to be sure—Hinduism, Taoism, Buddhism, and Confucianism being among them—incorporate such a conceptual model. Yet there are elements, even in these traditions, that reveal an openness to consider the ramifications of such a concept, and Zoroastrianism with its issues of conflict between light and darkness is another.

The problem of evil is evidentially a theological concern. The ancient story of Adam (which some view as a term for humankind in general) is helpful primarily because it suggests that there was never a time when our species did not know and acknowledge God's sovereignty and righteousness. At some point in our species' history, we became conscious of our capacity to choose to live in accord with God's will for us or to satisfy our craving for independent authority. The choice to go the latter way led us into conflict with God (a condition called *sin*) apart from whom there is only a brief biological life wherein "the wages of sin is death,"[146] a condition also dealt with in the Hindu and Buddhist conceptions of *karma.* This results inevitably in eternal estrangement. God's forgiveness and restoration to life is our only hope.[147]

Delegates to the Parliament of the World's Religions meeting in Chicago in 1993 sought to reify these concerns and for the first time in human history provided a document, *Towards a Global Ethic*,[148] supported by all major religious traditions. One hundred sixty representatives of 6,500 attendees from every religious group that could send them signed this document which began unabashedly:

> Our world is experiencing a fundamental crisis: a crisis in global economy, global ecology, and global politics. Hundreds of millions of human beings on our planet increasingly suffer from unemployment, poverty, hunger, and the destruction of their families. Children die, kill and are killed. It is increasingly difficult to live together peacefully in our cities because of social, racial and ethnic conflicts, the abuse of drugs, organized crime. Even neighbors often live in fear of one another. Our planet continues to be ruthlessly plundered. Religion often is misused for purely power-political goals, including war.
>
> These blights need not be. An ethic already exists within the Religious teachings of the world which can counter the global distress. As religious persons we base our lives on an Ultimate Reality. We have a special responsibility for the welfare of all humanity and care for the planet earth. We do not consider ourselves better than other women and men, but we trust that the ancient wisdom of our religions can point the way for the future. [There will be] no new global order without a new global ethic."[149]

It is with this kind of vision and hope that this present book is proffered. Gustav Fechner, with whom the section on psychology in this chapter began, may have been right after all. According to him as well as to Plato, the Hebrew prophets, and countless others including Nobel Laureates such as physicist Charles Townes and neurobiologist John Eccles, humans have come into the world with a predisposition for seeking and finding eternal verities including the morally good. We have a natural proclivity to do so.

NOTES

1. E. O. Wilson, *On Human Nature,* (Cambridge, Massachusetts: Harvard University Press, 1978.), 5.
2. W. K. C. Guthrie, *A History of Philosophy,* 4th ed., Vol. 1 (Cambridge: 1962), 45–72.
3. Walter Kaufmann, *Philosophic Classics,* 2nd ed. (Englewood Cliffs, NJ: Prentice-Hall, 1968), 6.
4. Robert B. McLaren, *The World of Philosophy* (Nelson-Hall, 1983), 1–2.
5. Aristotle, *De Anima,* A5 411a; K 93 in *The Oxford Translation of Aristotle,* vol. 8, ed. and trans W.D. Ross (New York: Oxford University Press, 1908).
6. Cf. Kathleen Freeman, *An Ancilla to the Pre-Socratic Philosophers,* quoted in Kaufmann, *op. cit., Philosophic Classics,* 13.
7. Ibid., 17.
8. George P. Stein, *The Forum of Philosophy* (New York: McGraw-Hill, 1973), 203.

9. Ibid.

10. Kaufmann, *Philosophic Classics,* citing the phrase from Protagoras' "Truth or Refutory Arguments" with more accuracy: "Of all things the measure is Man, of things that are, that they are, and of things that are not, that they are not," 53.

11. Epicurus, "The Nature of Pleasure," trans. Cyril Bailey, Gordon Clark, and T.V. Smith, *Readings in Ethics* (New York: Appleton-Century-Crofts, 1950), 93. *Cf.* Lucretius, *De Rerum Natura,* trans. W. E. Leonard (New York: E. P. Dutton, 1921) 174–179.

12. Plato. Timaeus, *The Dialogues of Plato,* Benjamin Jowett, translator. (Chicago: Encyclopedaedia Britanica, Inc. 1952), 448. 29E–30 A–D.

13. William Shakespeare, *Hamlet,* act 1, scene 3.

14. Plato, *Phaedo,* trans. Benjamin Jowett, in *Great Books of the Western World,* vol. 7 (1952), 228–229.

15. Plato, *The Republic,* trans. Jowett, in *Great Books of the Western World,* 344.

16. In the *Phaedrus,* Plato presents the analogy of a charioteer who must tame the impulses of two horses, each plunging off in different directions. The horses represent the spirit and the appetites. The charioteer, the soul, needs both steeds to achieve his destiny but must keep constant control to avoid chaos and disaster.

17. Aristotle, *On the Soul,* Book I Chapter 2, trans. J.A. Smith, *ibid.,* vol. 8, 633.

18. Ibid., 645.

19. Aristotle, *Nicomachean Ethics,* trans. W.D. Ross, in *Great Books of the Western World,* Volume 9, ibid., 341.

20. Ibid.

21. Ibid., 344.

22. Ibid. Book II. 348.

23. Ibid., 350.

24. Ibid., 348.

25. Ibid., 350.

26. Arthur Nussbaum, *A Concise History of the Laws of Nations* (New York: Macmillan, 1962), 16.

27. Robert B. McLaren, *Christian Ethics: Foundations and Practice* (Englewood Cliffs, NJ: Prentice-Hall/Simon and Schuster, l994), 180.

28. Ibid.

29. Shakespeare, *Hamlet,* act 2, scene 2.

30. From "The unanimous Declaration of the thirteen United States of America", 1776

31. David Hume, "A Treatise of Human Nature," quoted in *Ethics,* ed. Oliver A. Johnson (New York: Holt, Reinhart and Winston, 1965), 165.

32. David Hume, *Concerning Human Understanding,* in *Great Books of the Western World,* Volume 35, ibid., 502.

33. Immanuel Kant, "Preface to the Metaphysical Elements in Ethics," trans. Thomas Abbott, in *Great Books of the Western World,* 365.

34. Georg F. Hegel, *The Philosophy of Right,* trans. T.M. Knox, *Great Books of the Western World,* 12.

35. Harold Titus, Living issues in philosophy. (Newyork: Van Nostrand Reinhold 1970), 306.

36. John Dewey, *Democracy and Education* (New York: Free Press, 1966), 357–358.

37. Van Cleve Morris, and Young Pai, *Philosophy and the American School* (Boston: Houghton-Mifflin, 1976), 250.

38. Jean-Paul Sartre, *Existentialism and Humanism,* trans. Philip Mairet (London: Methuisn, 1948), 18.

39. Ibid.

40. Joel D. Beversluis, ed., *A SourceBook for the Community of Religions* (Chicago: Council for a Parliament of the World's Religions, 1993).

41. Ninian Smart, *The World's Religions* (Englewood Cliffs, NJ: l989), 50–51.

42. Robert E. Hume, *The World's Living Religions* (New York: Charles Scribner's Sons, l959), 26.

43. *Thirteen Principle Upanishads,* trans. Robert E. Hume (New York: Oxford University Pres, l931), 289. Cf. *Sacred Books of the East,* ed. F. Max Muller (New York: Oxford University Press, 1910).

44. *Bhagavad Gita,* 9:29,3l, Hume, *World's Living Religions,* 30. Cf. Sarvepalli Radhakrishna, *Indian Philosophy* (Princeton, NJ: Princeton University Press, l957), 134.

45. Anana K. Coomaraswami, and Sister Nivedita, *Myths of the Hindus and Buddhists* (New York: Dover, 1967), 247.

46. Ibid., 249–250.

47. Quinter Lyon, *The Great Religions* (New York: The Odysee Press, 1957), 178. "Unenlightened humanity is full of desire."

48. Sarvepalli Radhakrishnan, *Indian Philosophy,* 2nd ed., vol. 1 (New York: Macmillan, Company, l948), 350.

49. Brahmana Shatapatha, *Sacred Books of the East,* ed. Max Muller (New York: Charles Scribner's Sons, 1901), 146–149.

50. Lyon, *Great Religions,* 185. Cf. D.T. Suzuki, *Outlines of Mahayana Buddhism* (New York: Schocken Books, 1970), 31–32.

51. Suzuki, *Outlines,* 183.

52. Ibid., 339.

53. Robert Hume *The World's Living Religions* (Newyork: Charles Scribner's Sons, 1959), 111.

54. Ninian Smart, *The World's Religions* (Englewood Cliffs, NJ: Prentice Hall 1989), 105.

55. Hume, 113.

56. H.G. Creel, *The Birth of China* (New York: Reynold and Hitchcock, 1937). Cf. F.C.M. Wei, *The Spirit of Chinese Culture* (New York: Chalres Scribner's Sons, l947), chap. 2.

57. *Analects,* op. cit., Book XV, Chapter 23.

58. *Chung Yung, or Doctrine of the Mean,* trans. James Legge (Shanghai, n.d.), chap. 13, sec. 4.

59. Genesis 1:27.

60. Psalm 139: 13–16; Jeremiah 1:5.

61. Jeremiah 31:33.

62. Deuteronomy 4:29; Jeremiah 29:13.

63. I Samuel 15:10; Jeremiah 1:4; Ezekiel 1:3.

64. Judges 4:4; Isaiah 1:10; Amos 7:14,15.

65. Micah 6:8.

66. Anne Bennett points out that designations for God appear at times to be distinctly feminine: The *Spirit of God,* in Hebrew, *Ruach,* is feminine gender; the Voice of God, *Bat Kohl,* is a double feminine, "understanding" is *Binah,* again feminine; mercy (of God) is *Rehem,* feminine. Cf. Anne McGrew Bennett, *Woman-Pain to Woman-Vision* (Minneapolis, Fortress Press, 1989), 93.

67. The entire book of Leviticus is a set of prescriptions for details of the daily behaviors required for the life of the faithful.

68. Joseph Lowin, *Jewish Ethics* (New York: Shocken Books, Hadassah, l986), 7.

69. Rabbi Abraham Leon Sachar, *History of the Jews,* 2nd ed. (New York: Alfred Knopf, 1943), 148.

70. "I will put my laws into their minds, and write them on their hearts, and I will be their God, and they shall be my people," Hebrews 8:10.

71. Hebrews 10:16, doubtless quoting Jeremiah 321:33. The "profound Hellenization" of Judaism is a point concurred in by Jacob Neusner, *From Politics to Piety: The Emergenge of Pharisaic Judaism* (Englewood Cliffs, NJ: Prentice-Hall, l973), 4.

72. Matthew 23:4; 23–24.

73. Matthew 5:17.

74. Matthew 5:20.

75. I John 4:8.

76. I John 4:19, 20.

77. Luke 6:32.

78. Luke 10:25–37.

79. Matthew 5:44. Cf. William Klassen's insightful book, *Love of Enemies* (Philadelphia: Fortress Press, 1984).

80. Jacques Ellul, *The Subversion of Christianity* (Grand Rapids, MI: Fortress Press, 1986), chapter 8; Daniel MaGuire, *The Moral Revolution* (San Francisco: Harper and Row, 1986), 54; McLaren, *Christian Ethics,* 224–226.

81. Matthew 9:10.

82. I John 4:19.

83. Hebrews 8:10.

84. Romans 13: 10.

85. Acts 4:34.

86. Will Durant, *Caesar and Christ* (New York: Simon and Schuster, 1944), 667.

87. Philippians 1:21.

88. Galatians 2:20.

89. John 17: 18–26.

90. *Islam at a Glance* (Garden Grove, CA: Islamic Society of Orange County, 1994), 3.

91. *The Holy Qur'an,* trans. Abdullah Yusuf Ali (McGregor & Werner, 1946), S.II. 256.

92. Ibid, S II, 112.

93. Ibid. S. XL1X. 13.

94. Ibid. S. IV, 1.

95. Ibid., S IV. 3.

96. Ibid. S XXIV. 33.

97. Ibid. S LXV. 1.

98. Ibid. S IV 20–21.

99. Ibid, S IV. 11.

100. Arvind Sharma, ed. *Women in World Religions* (New York: SUNY Press, 1987), 241.

101. Conference of Riyad on Moslem Doctrine and Human Rights in Islam. Beirut, Lebanon:

102. *Holy Qur'an*, II, 83.

103. Ibid., XVI, 125.

104. Ibid., XXIX, 46.

105. Notes, kept anonymous as submitted by delegates to *The Conference of Riyad*, Saudi Arabia, March 23, 1972 (Safar 1392 of the Hagira).

106. Ibid.

107. Ibid.

108. William M. Kurtines and Jacob L. Gewirtz, *Morality, Moral Behavior, and Moral Development* (New York: John Wiley, 1984), preface.

109. Gustav Theodor Fechner, "About Christ," trans. Walter Lowrie, *Religion of a Scientist* (New York: Pantheon Books, 1946), 265–266.

110. Ibid., *Zend Avesta, Ueber die Dinge des Himmels und des Jenseits, vom Standpunct der Naturbetrachtung,* 1851.

111. Ibid., "The Three Motives and Grounds of Faith," *Religion of a Scientist,* 87.

112. S = C log R, where S = sensation; R = the stimulus numerically estimated; and C = a constant to be separately determined by experiment. Will James reported that Fechner tabulated and computed no fewer than 24,576 separate judgements. Cf. William James, *Psychology* (1890, as *Principles of Psychology;* Cleveland: World Publishing Company, 1948), 21.

113. Cf. Fechner's his book on exprimental aesthetics, *Vorschule Aesthetik* (1876).

114. Wilhelm Wundt, *Gustav Theodor Fechner,* an address delivered in 1901 on the centenary of Fechners birth; William James, "Concerning Fechner," *A Pluralistic Universe,* 1909, Lecture IV, G. Stanley Hall, *Foundations of Modern Psychology* (1912), chap. 3.

115. Edwin G. Boring, *A History of Experimental Psychology* (New York: Appleton-Century-Crofts, 1957), 283.

116. Ira Progoff, *The Death and Rebirth of Psychology* (New York: Julian Press, 1956), 15.

117. James, *Psychology,* 457.

118. Sigmund Freud, "New Introductory Lectures on Psychoanalysis," *The Major Works of Sigmund Freud* (Chicago: Great Books of the Western World, 1952), 884.

119. Ibid., "The Ego and the Id," 697–698.

120. Ibid., 876.

121. Ibid., "New Introductory Lectures," 875.

122. Robert Coles, *The Spiritual Life of Children* (Boston: Houghton-Mifflin, 1990), 7–8.

123. Jean Piaget, *The Child's Concept of Time,* trans. A.J. Pomerans (New York: Basic Books). Cf. Jean Piaget and Barbel Inhelder, *The Child's Construction of Quantities: Conservation and Atomism* (London: Rutledge and Kagen Paul, l974).

124. Jean Piaget, *The Moral Judgement of the Child* (New York: Free Press, l965).

125. Lawrence Kohlberg, *The Philosophy of Moral Development* (San Francisco: Harper & Row, l981). Author's Personal Conversation with Dr. Kohlberg.

126. Carol Gilligan, Janie Ward, and Jill Taylor, *Mapping the Moral Domain* (Cambridge: Harvard University Press, 1988), chap. 3.

127. Clara Schuster and Jarrell W. Garsee, "Theories of Moral Development," *The Process of Human Development,* 3rd ed., ed. Clara Schuster and Shirley Ashburn (Philadelphia: J.B. Lippincott, l992), 335.

128. Nancy Eisenberg and Paul H. Mussen, *The Roots of Prosocial Behavior in Children* (Cambridge, England: Cambridge University Press, 1989), 124.

129. Schuster and Garsee, Jarrell, "Theories of Moral Development," 335.

130. Edward O. Wilson, *On Human Nature* (Cambridge: Harvard University Press, 1978), 5.

131. Ibid., 38.

132. Ibid., 5.

133. Philip Hefner, "Is/Ought," *The Sciences and Theology in the Twentieth Century* (Northumberland, England: Oriel Press, l981), 68.

134. Ibid., 76.

135. Albert Einstein, *Out of My Later Years* (New York: Philosophical Library, 1950), 25.

136. Charles P. Snow, "The Moral Un-neutrality of Science," *Science* 133, no. 3448 (1961): 256.

137. Charles Townes, "The Convergence of Science and Religion," *Think,* March 1966: 7.

138. John D. Baldwin and Janice I. Baldwin, *Beyond Sociobiology* (New York: Oxford/Elsevier, 1981), 260.

139. Colwyn Trevarthen, *Brain Circuits and Functions of the Mind, Essays in Honor of Roger Sperry* (Cambridge, England: Cambridge University Press, 1990), 384.

140. Sir John Eccles, *The Human Psyche: The Gifford Lectures* (Heidelberg: Springer-Verlag, 1992), 13–15, 236, 241.

141. Karl Popper, and John Eccles, *The Self and Its Brain* (Heidelberg: Springer International, 1977), 144; and in the Dialogues: II, IV, V, VI and VIII.

142. Sir John Eccles and Daniel N. Robinson, *The Wonder of Being Human* (Boston: New Science Library, 1985), chap. 3.

143. Ibid.

144. Roger Penrose, *Shadows of the Mind* (New York: Oxford University Press, l994) 350.

145. Ibid., 416.

146. Romans 6:23.

147. Cf. Hinduism's *Rig Veda,* 5.85. 7–8; Judaism's Psalm 103: 1–4, 10–12; 130:3–4; Christianity's Matthew 6: 1–4; 14–15; Mark: 11:25; James 2:13; Islam's Qur'an S: 2. 195; 3:141; 149 4:106; 5:12, 16; 16:120.

148. *Towards a Global Ethic: An Initial Declaration* (Chicago: Council for a Parliament of the World's Religions, 1993).

149. Ibid., 3.

CHAPTER 2

The Moral Person

*Important as the struggle for existence has been, . . . yet
as far as the highest part of our nature is concerned
there are other agencies more important. For the moral
qualities are advanced . . . much more through the
effects of habit, the reasoning powers, instruction,
religion . . . than through Natural Selection.*
—Charles Darwin

If there is a proclivity in human nature to seek the true, the just, and the good in personal and social affairs as Chapter One avers, why, then, do we witness so many manifestations of violence and corruption in our world? We considered this question briefly in the concluding pages of that chapter, but a deeper probe demands our attention. Why, for example did our species bring about the violent deaths of more than 170 million persons in the wars of the century just passed? Why the horror of abductions, enslavement, and torture in so many countries and the "globalization of hate" reported by Amnesty International?[1] Why the inequities of extreme wealth and grinding poverty in some developing countries, such as India and much of Asia and South America? And why the exploitation and/or neglect by wealthier nations whose leaders are fully aware of the suffering, in sub-Saharan Africa, for example, where as many as 60 percent of the population experience severe malnutrition and disease? If we truly have a moral proclivity, why the apparent necessity for a "war on terror" at staggering costs of human life and resources? Why the bombing raids that reduced to rubble not just a few houses but whole villages, historic cultural treasures, and the environment itself? Nor can we omit the issues of private and corporate corruption amounting to billions of dollars annually, crime at all age and social levels, environmental pollution and destruction, the abuses of family members and self-destruction via drugs, and the AIDS crisis. The latter threatens millions of deaths annually. The list of evils mounts with mind-numbing intensity, and it is worse than naiveté if we shrug it aside.

Six decades ago, Reinhold Niebuhr addressed similar questions in his prescient book, *Moral Man and Immoral Society*. Emerging from the bubbling optimism of the postwar 1920s, the despair of the Great Depression of the 1930s, and the dread of another world war, he wrote forcefully of human egoism and "our entrenched, predatory self-interest."[2] As individuals, we may resist such involvements by conforming to ethical standards elaborated by the culture in which we live. As members of groups, however, we often find it expedient to justify limiting the freedoms of others "for the good of the whole." This provides a means for group egoism to create political power structures that perpetuate inequalities within the group. Niebur says, "The literature of all ages is filled with rational and moral justification of these inequalities."[3]

A romantic overestimation of human virtue has persisted, especially in contemporary middle class cultures despite the conflicts breakingout across racial and ethnic lines and in times of war when someone or some nation is officially identified as "the enemy." The fantasy prevents our recognizing the stubborn, sometimes brutal, character of collective egoism, which could not exist if individual egoism were not already at work. Folk wisdom reflects this: "Each of us is capable of becoming a killer." By way of justification, a U.S. Court of Appeals judge stated: "If stakes are high enough torture is permissible," and *The Washington Post* recently published an echo of this attitude in a government official's declaration: "If you don't violate someone's human rights some of the time, you probably aren't doing your job."[4] Such rationalization may be behind the ancient argument for a doctrine of "original sin," which appears to originate in ourselves or may be, as John Calvin proposed as much an inborn trait as poison in a rattlesnake.

During Niebuhr's lifetime, and despite the turmoil that occurred anticipations of global brotherliness lingered through the League of Nations, the Kellogg Peace Pact, and industrial unions, all of which ultimately failed to meet expectations. This has underscored the urgency to find new methods for achieving a realistic and viable ethical social framework for what many in the l940s and 1950s predicted would be "one world," a global society. The danger remains, however, that one or more political powers will seek domination over the others in order to impose their own vision of that unified world.

More recently, Samuel Huntington wrote in his book *The Clash of Civilizations* of the self-deluding hegemonic dreams of Western cultures, which blind both individuals and whole segments of society to the causes of conflict. We are only beginning to realize that "the most important distinctions among peoples are not ideological, political or economic. They are cultural. People define themselves in terms of ancestry, religion, language, history, values, customs. . . . They used politics to define their identity."[5] These elements of identity become their civilization. The time has passed when Western nation states (Britain, France, Spain, etc.) would fight their major battles among themselves, ignoring the fact that non-Western societies were developing their own identities, economic wealth, and cultural traditions. The latter would create the basis for their military power and political influence. "Non-Western societies increasingly assert their own cultural values and reject those 'imposed' on them by the West."[6] We can anticipate clashes among these ethnic/cultural societies (civilizations) to be of increasing frequency and intensity unless we can move beyond our several universal pretensions and find common ground in our religious and cultural commitments on which to build a global ethic.

What can be the role and strategy of an individual person, a prophet such as Abraham, Buddha, Jesus, or Mohammed, nurtured in the traditions of a familial, tribal, and cultural history, trying to marshal the moral resources on which to build both within and beyond his or her culture a viable ethic? This is no small undertaking that can be cobbled together from bits and pieces of customs and laws. Such persons must consider the complexity of human nature (including his or her own) of the people with whom they work and who paradoxically manifest the very collective behaviors that run counter to the vision of what "should" be. Such persons must also be keenly aware of and responsive to whatever transcendent source of inspiration may come to him or her and that radically alters his or her perspective.

Human nature, to paraphrase an old saw about the weather, is something everybody talks about but nobody knows much about. Questions abound. Are we essentially amoral animals destined to claw our way to whatever eminence we can achieve, machinelike creatures to be programmed, or sentient beings at some balancing point between the physical and spiritual? If we are to understand the nature and role of the moral person, it is not merely gratuitous that we first clarify the meaning of personhood.

From the standpoint of evolution, it may be that the emergence of morally aware, loving, justice-seeking beings is the most significant event in cosmic history. Indeed, Charles Darwin's quotation at the opening of this chapter suggests this. Humans apparently represent a unique creature in their solar system; there is no solid evidence for anything comparable or even for the bare building blocks such as living cells. As introduced in the first chapter, the effort here is to draw on the disciplines of philosophy, the major religious traditions, and the social sciences and to integrate the insights from each.

A. THE IDEA OF PERSONHOOD

It has not been determined just when prehistoric tribespeople began to speculate on seeing a cherished mate or child die or perhaps on killing a wild beast, that some essence of the deceased might have survived apart from the body. Some anthropologists and art historians surmise that cave paintings made during the Upper Paleolithic Period (c. 15,000 B.C.) were efforts to retain some essence of the deceased and keep them close. Some painters depicted hunters and their intended prey to capture or "fix" whatever might be called that essence (personhood?) of the animal so the hunters would prevail.[7] That they did conceive of something akin to personhood is evidenced in the practice of paying homage to and in some instances worshipping the images of such creatures. It is also known that Neanderthal tribespeople placed flowers and other treasured items in the graves of those whom they buried in the apparent conviction that as persons, they lived beyond their mortal forms.[8]

The more sophisticated descendents of the early Greeks, notably Heraclitus, Xeno, and Democritus, wrote of the inner person as *psyche* or "soul" (the study of whose nature gave rise to *psych*ology), which had at least the potential for immortality. Plato proposed that the soul is the offspring of the eternal "World-Mind." In his concept of "remembrance," he established the origin of our selfhood to have been in the transcendent realm of "ideas" from whence we were born into this material world.[9]

Aristotle described "active reason" as the apex of the soul that is divine and creative. He also insisted that humans, like all living things, are directed toward a *telos* or "end" toward which we must move. The telos of the acorn, for example, is to become an oak tree able to bear acorns of its own. Each created being, accordingly, has a destiny to fulfill but unlike the acorn, nothing is set or biologically inevitable about the survival of the self. We must consciously strive to become the persons we were intended to be, sometimes against wayward temptations. This, according to Plato, requires reason and moral character.

Many philosophers with diverse variations on the theme who followed, down to the present tended to identify the self with mind and spirit. George Berkeley (1685–1753) declared that the "Something," which knows and perceives, exercises different operations as willing, imagining, remembering, is what I call *mind, spirit, soul* or *myself*."[10] From Plato and Aristotle to Augustine, Aquinas, Descartes, Spinoza, Kant, and Hegel, there has been agreement that the human self or personhood differs from the identity of the lower animals not just in degree but also in kind. They also agree that the self is not an object but a subject. One does not "have" a soul; one *is* a soul. A modern Hindu philosopher, the late Sarvepalli Rhadakrishnan, expressed this well when he noted, "The self is not an object which we can find in knowledge, for it is the very condition of knowledge. It is different from all objects, the body, the senses, the empirical self itself."[11]

The importance of this last observation is the fact that contemporary psychology, asserted to be a science, has tended to follow Charles Darwin's insistence that the identity we call "mind" is *not* significantly different between humans and "lower" animals; the distinction is one of degree, not of kind.[12] Many are suspicious of subjective interpretations of mind or personhood and tend to regard writings on the subject prior to William James and Sigmund Freud as mere speculation. This fact is particularly interesting because in physics, perhaps the most demanding of the physical sciences, it is clearly understood that, as Werner Heisenberg expressed it, any kind of *objective* knowledge (e.g., the action of atomic particles, their position and momentum) is actually quite elusive because the *object* of study is discernable only by the *subjective* choice (i.e., by the way one approaches the study). Subjective choices are possible only because of the phenomenon called *consciousness*, the capacity for free-ranging imaginative consideration of possibilities.[13]

There are those, particularly among psychologists and sociobiologists, who conclude that a scientific understanding of the human condition must discount consciousness as anything more than an illusion. Personhood is regarded as mere accumulation of responses to stimuli, or habit systems. A significant number of neuroscientists concur that if the conscious self cannot be found among the neurons and synaptic connections of the brain, its objective reality cannot be scientifically defended.[14] This is perhaps the most serious challenge to our undertaking, although it is not entirely new or confined to Western thought. It finds its resonance in the writings of the Hindu and Buddhist traditions as we note presently.[15]

Nobel Laureate John Eccles, disagreeing with many of his contemporaries, charges that, according to them, "the existence of mind or consciousness . . . is relegated to the passive role of mental experiences accompanying some types of brain action, as in psychoneural identity, but with absolutely no *effective* action on the brain" (italics in original).[16] In point of fact, he notes, (P.E.T.) scans reveal very real effective action of conscious thought on the physical structure of the brain. Indeed, the progress of human civilization has depended on the conscious commitment of people to create technical inventions, artistic productions, and conditions for justice, truthfulness, loyalty, and love, which can be sustained and secured by laws enacted by morally concerned people.

Physicist Roger Penrose agrees with Eccles, noting that a person can only speculate why those who deny that humans are conscious beings have felt such a need to refute their own consciousness by which they make such claims:

> Consciousness seems to me to be such an important phenomenon that I simply cannot believe it is something just accidentally conjured up by a complicated computation. It is the phenomenon by which the universe's very existence is made known. I would even say that all the mathematical descriptions of a universe that have been given so far must fail this criterion. It is only the phenomenon of consciousness that can conjure a putative "theoretical" universe into actual existence.[17]

If one can accept that consciousness is a reality, that most people have the capacity to perceive such distinctions as truthfulness and lying, loyalty and betrayal, good and evil, we can begin the quest for developing the moral person.

Attempting to bridge the growing gap between philosophy and psychology, W.H. Werkmeister reflected on the phenomenon of the "Self" transcending and judging itself and wrote that perhaps the most remarkable feature of the human person is that he or she lives

> not simply in conformity with the laws that govern the realm of nature, but in conformity with the *concept* of laws as well. It is insight into, and understanding of those laws that make possible our self-directed responsible action. We become self-legislative, capable of imposing laws on ourselves.[18]

From a moral point of view, such imposition of laws by humans on ourselves is the fullest expression of responsibility. In this vein, Karl Popper and John Eccles reflected in *The Self and Its Brain* on the moral importance of personal responsibility, defining personhood in terms of Immanuel Kant's dictum that "a person is a subject who is responsible for his actions." Popper referred to "that greatest of miracles: the human consciousness of self"—a self, that is, which takes responsibility for itself[19]

B. FOSTERING PERSONAL MORALITY

In simplest terms, the moral person is one who, when making choices that will affect the safety and well-being of others, takes responsibility for the decisions made and consciously strives to do what is needed to ensure the happiest, healthiest, and most fulfilling outcome for those others. It is refreshing to remind ourselves that the framers of the Bill of Rights emphasized "Life, Liberty and the Pursuit of Happiness" as God given and unalienable. Can such an attitude and commitment to the well-being of others be taught?

When someone suggests that morality can or should be taught in the schools, the immediate rejoinder is fairly predictable: "But whose morals?!" This is an effective if unfortunate conversation stopper, implying that morality is a private matter and that every person is her or his own authority. The boast is a common one: "I am a self-made man." John Dunn's "No Man Is an Island" reminds us that even the most rugged individualist is born into family, community, and historical cultural traditions we can too easily discount.

Morality is often equated with virtue, but when asked whether virtue could be taught, Socrates replied in words that still haunt the educational community: "I confess with shame that I know literally nothing about virtue." He was not trying to be evasive; he strove for an adequate definition to help students avoid both the relativism of the Sophists and the rigidity of traditionalists.[20] His execution by Athenian social conservatives (c. 399 B.C.) who resented and feared his "radical" ideas interrupted the definition effort.

Perhaps Socrates would have been even more dismayed today when efforts at definition have yielded only vagueness and confusion. Marvin Berkowitz of Scotland relates that his country's efforts to identify and educate moral persons have produced "a cornucopia of moral characteristics" but

> a fragmented curriculum with such varied topics as values education, character education, moral education, personal and social education, citizenship education, religious education, morality, and democratic education among other rubrics.[21]

These terms are neither synonymous nor interchangeable. One can speak of moral values, but not all values (e.g., in the realm of the arts) are decided on moral grounds. Furthermore, in a pluralistic society, some means of mediating among conflicting social values imported from widely diverse cultural backgrounds may be required to keep peace and promote creative interaction.

Some of the fuzziness in meaning may be alleviated if the field of study can be reduced to the distinction between morals and ethics, law and custom, and "good" behavior, manners, and etiquette. We address these presently, but meanwhile we should acknowledge the frustrations of guilt and self-doubt experienced even among those striving most valiantly to overcome their moral deficiencies. If we know what is right by both intellectual assent and moral commitment, why do we violate "our better natures" in matters of behavior? This was an issue that Sophocles tried to probe as a tragic theme in his dramas two and a half millennia ago (*Ajax, Antigone, Oedipus, Electra,* etc.). Omar Khayyam lamented, "I myself am heaven and hell," and Goethe echoed, "Two souls, alas, dwell in my breast." Yale law professor William Stuntz, observed, "We are endlessly self-justifying, eager to find ways to do what we want even when the law written on our hearts tells us we are doing wrong."[22]

The phrase "written on our hearts" echoes the theme undergirding the Nürnberg trials when, as noted in Chapter 1, Nazi war criminals were told that their plea that they were "only complying with orders" was indefensible. They "knew in their hearts" what was right and should have disobeyed their commanders. Perhaps the human race has never been free of such inner conflicts. While we may think ourselves to be recipients of divinely revealed commandments, we also experience a kind of moral schizophrenia. This is what the apostle Paul called inner warfare: "I can will what is right but cannot do it. The evil that I do not want is what I do." Those under the added pressure to do evil in the service of the tribe or state, which requires unquestioning devotion, are truly conflicted. All effort to become "moral persons" may seem hopeless. This is but one of several related issues that Reinhold Niebuhr addressed in *Moral Man and Immoral Society*, warning, prophetically, of an imminent protracted era of international violence. "The unqualified character of this devotion is the very basis of the nation's power and of the freedom to use the power without moral restraint."[23]

To avoid becoming distracted by the many terms introduced by Dr. Berkowitz (and to which he referred as "The Tower of Babel"), we limit ourselves here to the distinctions between a few key terms.

Morals are often proffered as a set of principles rooted in the natural order although we will note a philosophical division. There are those advocating that nature is simply amoral, an interaction of things, events, and pressures. If this were the case, these nagging questions remain: What is the source of the moral authority, the "ought" against which a moral act can be tested? Does this not presuppose an "Authority," a "Deity"? Or is it that the natural order is inherently a process that provides for some form of natural law, which a nontheist can promote for developing rules of conduct discoverable by the humanly unique power of reason? The Ionian philosophers of sixth century B.C. (e.g., Thales, Anaximander, Heraclitus) laid the groundwork for early naturalism as they sought to explain all phenomena in terms of matter and physical forces. They had little to say about morals, but later philosophers such as Epicurus and Lucretius followed their lead and reduced all such considerations to immutable physical laws. This was clearly in rejection of metaphysical or transcendental influences. Lucretius (c. 99–55 B.C.) was an outspoken atheist who advocated that moral behavior was that which conformed to the natural order of things. It is when people go against the natural order, for example by violating nature's requirement for protecting one's offspring, that sin or evil arises. In his *De Rerum Natura*, Lucretius refers scornfully to the religiously motivated murder of Agamemnon's daughter:

> . . . sinless woman, sinfully foredone;
> A parent felled her on her bridal day,
> Making his child a sacrificial beast to give the ships auspicious winds for
> Troy.[24]

One consequence of Lucretius' point of view, which he accredited to his philosophical mentor Epicurus (c. 342–270 B.C.), although in fact it can be traced back to Aristippus (c. 435–356 B.C.), is hedonism, "the pleasure principle." Aristippus had declared pleasure to be the one and only good and the most intense pleasure, the highest aim of life. Epicurus modified this when he noted that hedonism can lead to such virulent egocentrism as to make a person antisocial and lead to isolation, grief, and pain. It was better, he said, to seek not the most intense pleasure but that which produces long-run satisfaction, which requires a degree of self-restraint, friendship, and wisdom.

This kind of "Naturalism" was for the next two and one-half millennia largely overridden in the emergence of Judaism, Zoroastrianism, Christianity, and Islam (and less clearly in the Confucian concept of Li, or propriety, vaguely related to the Tao or cosmological principle).[25] The suggestion that people "ought" to behave in a certain way toward others kept begging the question of Shakespeare's Shylock: "On what compulsion must I? Tell me that." For the monotheist, it is proposed that the moral imperative emerges when one's selfhood is realized as personhood in the presence of other persons and that one owes to each other person "to do justly, love mercy and walk humbly with God." In those moments during which some moral obligation becomes evident, there is a shift from the impersonal "one ought to do . . ." to the intensely personal "I ought to. . . ." Then one can understand Johann Fichte's insistence (in Ethik, 1798): "If I ought, then I can, and I must."

During the period variously labeled the Age of Enlightenment or Age of Empiricism (roughly from the time of Frances Bacon [1561–1626] through Locke, Voltaire, and Bentham (late eighteenth to early nineteenth century), the naturalist spirit resurfaced. It was openly advocated by Thomas Hobbes (1588–1679), Jeremy Bentham (1748–1832) and to a modified degree (and without the hedonism) by John Stuart Mill (1806–1873). Bentham was quite emphatic in his support of this consequence of "un-romanticized" naturalism: "Man is a pleasure-seeking, pain-avoiding animal." Bentham's Principle of Utility defines any act or object that yields an advantage or a benefit as good. The word *ought* is irrelevant in making choices; what matters is the consequences. All one needs to do is make one's choices intelligently with those consequences in mind.[26]

A provocative modern expression of materialistic naturalism as a ground for morality made by biologist Richard Dawkins, who contends that all human behaviors can be traced to "the selfish gene" that knows no law but survival and governs our actions, which we only imagine to be freely initiated.[27] Some people declare that many behaviors widely regarded as "deviant" or even criminal should not be moral or legal issues because they can be observed elsewhere in nature among certain birds and mammals (such as stealing food or driving a weaker animal from its lair).

Chandler Burr has suggested, however, that seeking moral guidance for any human behavior, such as homosexuality, from analogies with nature is an act of hubris, or more likely of sheer hype.[28] Nature does not provide a standard set of behaviors that apply to all species; some behaviors are species specific, as with the black widow spider who devours her mate after copulation. Even with such "basic" instincts as maternal protection of offspring, "nature" is not consistent as exemplified in the frequent abandonment of eggs and hatchlings by reptiles and by many migratory birds when an early winter sets in.

Whether the term *nature* is even appropriate to imply a coherent whole may be questioned. The fact seems to be that what we have is a planet on which live countless species, each with its own patterns for self-preservation. Deadly competition is endemic. The emergence of moral concern may be one of the most distinctive hallmarks of being human.

An alternative approach to the "nature" controversy became a hallmark of Aristotle's departure from Plato's Idealism (or more accurately, Idea-ism), so it will be useful briefly to reprise their concerns, which still echo in much modern debate. Recall that Plato proposed that nature does not compose the real world but provides only material objects that are copies of a transcendent realm of perfect "Forms" or "Ideas." Our minds recall dimly a preexistence in that realm of "Eternal Ideas," so that what we find in the natural order gives us clues and reflections. The "Good," the foundation of morality, is unobtainable in this imperfect world, but we find reflections of goodness in daily encounters with people, customs, and laws because the idea of goodness is part of our *ontos*, or inner being. The essential self draws its understanding of morality from the transcendent realm dimly remembered and refines its understanding through discipline of the mind.

Aristotle did not reject outright the concept of the "Forms" or "Ideas" but insisted that we can know the good, true, and beautiful only as we encounter them in nature. In seeking the good, or moral, life, we search in daily encounters in the natural, hands-on world. Elements of "good" may be discovered in health, wealth, proficiency in required skills (for example, carpentry, musical composition, swordsmanship, and statesmanship). What we experience in the finding Aristotle called *eudaemonia*, a term difficult to translate but that roughly implies happiness, well-being, and enlightenment.

One must consider, however, that while happiness may include pleasure as the reward of the quest, the search for pleasure in and for itself apart from humane consideration can easily lead to excesses and the destruction of both goodness and happiness. One must use reasonable caution in seeking specific goals as, for example, health and athletic skill, to proceed with moderated enthusiasm that avoids the kind of cutthroat competition often destructive to decent human relationships. For Aristotle, moderation became a "golden mean" by which to avoid extremes. The virtues we cherish are to be achieved through diligent, intelligent, moderate practice. In his Nicomachean Ethics he wrote:

> Men become builders by building and lyre players by playing the lyre; so too we become just by doing just acts, temperate by doing temperate acts, brave by doing brave acts.[29]

Indeed, is the very act of such "learning by doing" has a certain ethic as might be exemplified in the sportsmanship present or absent in given a sport. Aristotle would doubtless applaud the generosity accorded cyclist Lance Armstrong when, during the 2003 Tour de France, his competitors halted the race to give him the time required to recover from an accidental fall. "Of course," said Jan Ullrich, of Germany, "if I would have won this race by taking advantage of someone's bad luck, then the race was not worth winning." Courtesy and generosity are often learned in performing in accord with unwritten but acknowledged standards.

The influence of Plato and Aristotle on life and thought during the Middle Ages was profound; Aristotle in particular was recognized as an authority on such wide-ranging topics as logic, poetics, the classification of plants and animals, and the nature of the soul, which he termed "the principle of all animal life. " This term even included God, whom he called not only "the Prime Mover" but also "the universal animal."[30]

In Aristotle's "form-matter hypothesis," he affirmed that as the earth beneath our feet is primal matter, inchoate, and virtually formless, our quest takes us upward on the scale of matter to more complex entities such as moss, plants, trees, animals, and finally man. The highest feature of a human is the mind, the locus of reason. Furthermore, as we move upward on the scale of things, matter becomes less and less important but form more so. Above humans are the heavens, and above heaven is God, pure form and no matter. Matter is thus the principle of *potentiality,* form the principle of *actuality* endowing matter with that which could not exist before. As pure form, God is the ultimate actuality, ultimate being, the unmoved mover.[31]

As noted, Aristotle's contention was that there is a moral order and purpose in nature that can be discerned by reason. He proposed that we all have a duty to seek what is true (as in precise scientific observation) and what is good. We are to establish rules based on nature's laws to ensure that right will be done. Aristotle elaborated a distinction between "natural law," which points us to the naturally just, and "the laws of nature," which are often "red in fang and claw," profligate in destruction of life. He did not hold to the later Spencerian style "survival-of-the-fittest" point of view, however.[32] This was part of Aristotle's appeal for some later Roman jurists (Cicero and Gaius) and for Thomas Aquinas, who found much in Aristotle that he could accommodate to Christian thought.

Philosophy became wedded with theology when Thomas Aquinas (1224–1274) recast Aristotle's view of "The Good" in terms of Christian theology. The restatement became not only official dogma of the Roman Catholic Church but continues its influence today in neo-Thomism, a philosophy shared in large measure by Roman Catholics and protestants alike. The emphasis on the discipline of reason is of special interest because Aquinas taught that reason is one of the most distinctive of human potentialities. Reason was second only to faith, which brings us into closest proximity with God, although love and contemplation of truth are the most ennobling characteristics of truly human life. Indeed, this emphasis of Aquinas set Christianity in a unique position among the world's religions, as we will note presently. Neither in Hinduism, Buddhism, Taoism, Sikhism, nor the other major Eastern traditions is there a suggestion that we reveal God's image in our human nature; some, like Buddhism, question even the reality of a personal deity.

During the Western Renaissance and the following Age of Enlightenment (from Locke, Diderot, and Kant through Hegel), were both elaborated and challenged by the claim that humankind behaves morally only because of the need to conform to established customs, rules of law, and social contracts (as proposed by Hobbes, Locke, and Rousseau). Struggling to understand the role of instinctive behavior, Charles Darwin (1809–1882) wrote of "an ennobling belief in God," affirming in his history-making treatise *The Descent of Man* that

> of all the differences between man and the lower animals, the moral sense or conscience is by far the most important. [It has] "a rightful supremacy over every other principle of human action . . . summed up in that short but imperious word *ought*. It is the most noble of all attributes of man, leading him without a moment's hesitation to risk his life for that of a fellow creature.[33]

While remaining an agnostic, Darwin was aware that concern for the well-being of others is at the heart of most of the world's better known religions, which were often begun by a single visionary—Abraham, Confucius, Isaiah, Jesus, Mohammed—who, seeking to correct certain social deficiencies or corrupting forces, drew upon some transcendent reality to establish a moral foundation.

Having devoted the first chapter to the search for a moral imperative, we may visualize the way moral principles evolve into customs or cultural mores, ethical rules, the establishment of laws to safeguard the pragmatic demands of society, good manners, and etiquette. The following might be termed a "bottoms-up" diagram, using the "Transcendent Source: Nature or Deity" as our foundation:

Etiquette
∧
Manners
∧
Laws
∧
Ethics
∧
Customs
∧
Morality
∧
Religion
∧
Transcendent Source (Nature? Deity?)

People do not ordinarily start out seeking the moral foundations that undergird morality, social customs, ethics, laws, and so on. We are born into families that have already accommodated more or less to the customs of the society around them, are instructed both formally and informally to obey prevailing laws, and teach our children manners and rules of etiquette. Given the alterations in family arrangements, some children may have simply learned to conform to the customs, laws, and so on, of their community and, in the absence of a well-knit family, join gangs or perhaps the military that enforces rules of behavior rigidly without much philosophical reflection. This will be more fully explored in the last section of this chapter when we engage the contributions of the social sciences.

The usefulness of the preceding diagram of categories may become clearer as we try to examine, albeit briefly, the processes of moral development within a given society.

Customs are the patterns of behavior relating to a people's efforts to act out perceived moral demands. Customs reflect habits, social conventions, and "the way things are done" (or *not* done) in society and comprise the loosely articulated requirements that furnish the community's general character. These often give rise to the folktales, myths, sagas, and legends that eventually become the trademark of that people and its era.

Ethics represent a studied application of moral principles and the customs that have arisen because of them. The root Greek word *eiotha* (literally, "place of dwelling") referred to formal customs and could be expressed by answering the question "How are things done where you come from?" Julius Caesar's advice to his troops, "When in Rome, do as the Romans do," was an ethical directive to emulate the customs of the Romans, not a moral one. The charge was to conform to the standards of the immediate situation, even if it required acting wrongly according to their own "higher" Roman moral standards.

Many ethicists would argue that ethics seldom actually conflict with moral principles because in a sense, these principles have grown out of the underlying moral imperatives that molded the subsequent social customs. It is not uncommon, however, in professional life, for example, to have to make ethical decisions when no clear moral or customary guidelines are at hand. Medical ethics often has to depend on the cultural or social *ethos*, the consensus of community values, to determine whether an experiment or operation will be justified (or even permitted), for example, cloning, or using stem cells from human embryos to grow new tissues. Another contemporary example would be the practice of employing people from a different culture (e.g., Australian or African tribes) in which no restrictions apply to test new drugs, a practice that is prohibited in the first society. "Protecting Communities in Biomedical Research" is a highly perceptive article in *Science* that employs terms such as "respect for culture" and "informed consent" to illustrate concern within the profession for adequate ethical guidelines. It is no mere exercise in casuistry.

Laws are established to guarantee the enforcement of ethical principles in a more sophisticated culture. The moral person is inevitably drawn into consideration of formal expressions of both custom and ethics. Justice Oliver Wendell Holmes expressed it eloquently more than a century ago:

> The life of law has not been logic; it has been experience. The felt necessities of the time, the prevalent moral and political theories, institutions of public policy, avowed or unconscious, even the prejudices which judges share with their fellow-men, have had a good deal more to do than the syllogism in determining the rules by which men should be governed. The law embodies the story of a nation's development through many centuries, and it cannot be dealt with as if it contained only the axioms and corollaries of a book of mathematics.[34]

It would appear that the laws of a society, no matter how tightly reasoned, are doomed to obsolescence if they are not grounded in morals, customs and ethics. In 1966, the late Earl Warren, then Chief Justice of the United States Supreme Court, called for the establishment of an institute on law and ethics to explore their interrelationships. "The law," he wrote, "floats on a sea of ethics, and the sea seems to be draining away."[35]

Good manners might seem to be virtually synonymous with etiquette, but in fact each has its distinct place in social discourse. Also, at some points, good manners appear so closely related to the moral demand (e.g., to respect other's property) to be almost indistinguishable from morals except to the most sophisticated sensibility. Respect for other's of view appears grounded in a commitment to the values of pluralism and rooted in moral values. Manners tend to be prescribed behaviors that parents and teachers invoke to help their children through the stages of socialization. They include such common and well-nigh universal graces as respect for their political views or religious preferences of others, patience where those virtues are not reciprocated, and tolerance when it is found that other people have different modes of social interaction from one's own. It is not uncommon to encounter adults who are deficient in self-control, as in the common experiences of "road rage" or playing a radio so loud as to make conversation difficult even in the next room or apartment; not "taking one's turn" when standing in line at the theater or checkout counter at the grocery store. The list of other people's lack of respect for what constitutes good manners seems at times almost endless. Most of the major religions have developed lengthy lists of social regulations, as we will discover.

Rules of *etiquette*, by way of differentiation, evolve as models for conduct among members of a profession including the proper salutation for nobility and judges; nurses standing when a physician enters the room; knowing which fork to use at a formal banquet; a gentleman holding the door open for a lady or for someone burdened with a load of packages. These practices are clearly artifices and tend to become remote from real manners so that one might know precisely how to speak courteously to a lady in public yet treat her with disrespect in private (as famously cited by Oscar Wilde). During the decadent, courtly days before the French Revolution, one scholar lamented that the most prized of teachers was not a philosopher or mathematician but a dancing master. The cloying deference toward one's "superiors" in royal society has long been a staple of playwrights and novelists.

The rules for developing a moral person appear to call upon all of these, from morals to etiquette, in some measure. It is when coherence among them breaks down that society fragments and sets individuals adrift. Real danger emerges when a crisis in society erupts as in time of racial conflict, severe food shortages that lead to famine, regional or civil war sets brother against brother, and mob rule or thirst for revenge launches atrocities that grow to terrorism. Then the ancient question of "original sin" is raised. It may be that sin "originates" in each of us, but the question persists: If we are children of God, or even if just the spawn of nature, why do we violate ourselves and each other in such monstrous fashion?

C.   CONTRIBUTIONS OF MAJOR RELIGIONS

The first chapter of this text opened with a quotation from Immanuel Kant expressing "wonder and awe" at the moral law he felt had somehow been planted within human nature. Such a statement reflects a conviction central to both Hebrew and Christian traditions, as well as that found in the Islamic Qur 'an,[36] and was a major theme among the early Greek writers.[37] One of our contemporaries at Oxford University, physicist Roger Penrose, affirms a "genuine relationship—still mysterious— between the Platonic mathematical world and the world of physical objects," and proposes that "the ideal concept of the good" as well as of the true and beautiful must also be attributed to a transcendent reality awaiting discovery just as mathematical truths await discovery.[38]

It is common knowledge that there are different and sometimes competing "schools" in philosophy and psychology, and, of course, the same is historical fact for religious denominations. Nevertheless, because of the creation of ecumenical councils and the emergence of bodies such as the Earth Charter Movement and the Parliament of the World's Religions, increased consensus is emerging among religions concerning the meaning of morality, the nature of the moral person, and how we may improve our moral and ethical relations.

1. Eastern Religions

Eastern religions vary significantly Western religions (especially Hebrew and Christian), which emphasize the intensely personal nature of humans as created in God's image. The Holy Qur'an does not assert that humankind bears God's image but that humans were created to be God's vice gerents on earth. (Surah II, Section 4:30)

The Eastern traditions have been more ambiguous on the nature of deity, and how that affects the human condition.

Hinduism.   Presents many personalized "sub" deities in the Vedic literature, but the sacred writings of the Upanishads, declare only one deity, *Brahman*, who is best understood as the impersonal *Atman*, or world soul: "That Self is indeed Brahman, consisting of knowledge, mind, life, sight . . . right or wrong and all things."[39] To become one with that universal self is to become Brahmana, one whose self is "smaller than small, greater than great, hidden in the heart of the creature; free from desires, free from grief."[40] *Hinduism* holds that the individual is at most a temporary emanation of the impersonal cosmic self and is not truly responsible before such an impersonal deity as Western traditions have it. Judgment for living an evil life is simply self-ordained. Evil things happen to those who do evil, not so much as "punishment" but simply as in the nature of things. The Vedic literature exhorts, "If we have cheated, done wrong, cast all these sins away like loosened fetters." (Rig-Veda v.85.6-8).

Buddhism.   Because of the unsatisfactory vagueness of such exhortations (to some), there were many early attempts at reform in Hinduism, the most popular of these being *Buddhism*.

Officially atheistic, Buddhist tradition has a reverence for the memory of the Gautama Buddha and other leading figures in Buddhist history but not for a personal creator or deity. When asked about this in a 1988 interview, His Holiness the Dalai Lama replied, "For the Buddhist, the universe had no first cause and hence no creator, nor can there be such a thing as a permanent, primordial pure being."[41] However, he added, this fact really does not matter because whether one chooses to believe in a personal deity is purely a matter of preference. "For certain people, the idea of God as creator . . . is beneficial. For someone else the idea that there is no creator is more appropriate. Everything depends upon oneself."[42]

Buddhism proposes that one must divest oneself from preoccupation with the self. "First, banish every ground of 'self.' This thought of self shades every lofty good aim; cut out the love of self, like an autumn lotus."[43] Human nature is deemed essentially good (no fixed point on a moral compass is identified, however, so that one could tell whether she or he is now closer or further from an absolute standard of goodness). This renders "salvation" in the traditional religious meaning of the term unnecessary beyond our achieving "enlightenment." This enlightenment reveals a moral law and truths superior to the general prescriptions for the good life in Hinduism, but it required a specific set of disciplines, subsequently identified as the *Four Noble Truths*: (1) recognition that all life is suffering, (2) the suffering is the result of cravings, (3) release from which is achieved by abandonment of all craving and complete nonattachment, which leads to (4) *The Noble Eightfold Way*.

While Chapter One touched on the eightfold way, elaborating on it more fully will be useful to see that each makes possible the maturing of the moral person. In his famous sermon to a gathering of monks in the Isipatana deer park at Benares, (c. 489 B.C.), Prince Siddhartha, the Buddha ("the Enlightened One") detailed the Eightfold Way:

1. Holding *right views* or outlook: acknowledging the reality of suffering, from birth pangs through the tribulations of life to the time of death.
2. *Right aspirations*: resolving to renounce the world with its cravings and to do no harm.
3. *Right speech*: abstaining from lies, slander, and gossip.
4. *Right conduct*: abstaining from stealing, lechery, and taking life.
5. *Right livelihood*: engaging only in honorable vocations.
6. *Right effort*: striving with all one's heart to do good and renouncing negative qualities in all willing and acting.
7. *Right mindfulness*: being aware of one's body and health conditions, alert to all happenings in one's immediate surroundings and in the world, and being free from wants and discontent.
8. *Right contemplation*: enjoying the rapture of concentration free from lust or nagging regrets and dwelling in serenity that is bred of concentration on the cessation of suffering.

The truly moral person is one who has engaged all of these steps and thus become a Buddha, an enlightened one.[44]

Confucianism. In striking contrast to both Hinduism and Buddhism, *Confusianism* seems unconcerned with the issue of personhood as such, accepting self-conscious identity as a given. However, the founder K'ung Fu Tsu, born approximately 550 B.C., proclaimed that human nature is essentially good. He did not argue the point and did not base it on an assumption that we were created good by a benevolent deity but that T'ien (Heaven; also a term for a kind of cosmic Providence) is "The Good." Our native tendency is to follow the Tao, "The Way of Heaven," which embodies supreme wisdom characterized by tranquility and simplicity.[45] The good life, the way of the Tao, provides the only true happiness—"Set your heart upon the Way"[46]—while a life that is out of harmony with this cosmic "Good" can yield only unhappiness.

Goodness is presented in the Confucian tradition in a distinctly masculine framework. The expression "superior man" describes what we would term "the moral person," and occurs 105 times in the Analects. However, the only single reference to women is decidedly negative, the personhood of women is equated with people of low birth. If you are friendly with them, they get out of hand, and if you keep your distance they resent it."[47] This is a cultural departure from that found in early Eastern thought; the earliest forms of both Hinduism and Buddhism accorded women higher status.[48] This is a matter we will deal with in a later chapter under the heading of Gender Roles in Transition.

2. Western Religions

As has been noted, *Western religions* proclaim a personal deity and affirm full personhood for all human kind. They are perhaps best represented, at least in numbers of adherents, by Judaism, Christianity, and Islam.

Judaism.   Historically preceding and undergirding both Christianity and Islam, *Judaism* was the first major religion to proclaim faith in a single, creative deity but whom, Maimonides (c. 1135–1204) cautioned, should not be called "a person" for fear of reducing God to mortal terms. Yet God can be approached in prayer much as we engage other persons in conversation. Scripture reminds us, said Maimonides, that "God is Spirit" and it was that spirit that brought the world into being. Transcending all created things, God created humankind "in the image of God," giving us the assurance that as God is personal in nature (though not "a person"), we too are personal beings "in His image."

The grandeur of this imagery is stressed in Psalm 8 where the writer, overed by the magnitude of the starry heavens, asked, "What is man that thou art mindful of him?" The answer came in the revelation that we are so endowed above all other creatures that we are "but little lower than the angels" and have been granted dominion over the earth and other creatures. Yet the prophet Jeremiah warned that "the heart is deceitful above all things," (Jeremiah 17:9), so the most earnest prayer of the psalmist was "create in me a clean heart, O God." (Psalm 51:10) Here an intense focus is placed on our personhood; we are creatures capable of envisioning a deity whom we can approach in the expectation of dialogue, who has created us to be in some astonishing way like God yet by our own deviousness are estranged from God (and from each other).

This estrangement is another distinguishing feature of Western religions; the prophet Jeremiah declared, "The heart is deceitful above all things, and desperately corrupt." The disaffection, amounting to antagonism, is the clearest evidence of mortal sinfulness. (Jeremiah 17:9). The author of Psalms 14 tells us, "There is none that is good . . . they are all alike corrupt." By acknowledging ourselves as responsible for this predicament, we are invited to seek restoration to the initial fellowship for which God created us. (Jeremiah 29:13) According to this conviction, ours is a personhood of an intense and lasting nature, no mere illusion.

The moral person, then, is the one who confesses this estrangement and who seeks not merely to make amends for violating God's commands and for any damage done to a neighbor but also prays fervently, "Create in me a clean heart, O God, and renew a right spirit within me." (Psalm 51:10)

Christianity.   As the New Testament makes clear, *Christianity* presents Jesus as standing in direct line with the prophets of Israel and regarding human sin with utmost seriousness. He began his ministry with: "Repent, for the Kingdom of Heaven is at hand." (Matthew 4:17) The verb *repent* comes from the Greek *metanoia,* requiring a radical alteration of mind and lifestyle. Jesus is not vague about what he means: "From within, out of the heart, evil thoughts proceed; fornications, thefts, murders, adulteries, coveting, wickedness, deceit, lasciviousness, railing, pride, foolishness: all these evil things proceed from within." (Mark 7:21-23). Neither nature nor the environment can be blamed for making us something other than God intended. In sinning against God or other people, we are ontologically altered at the core by our own perverse being.[49]

For twenty centuries Christian tradition has reaffirmed these convictions; the early Church Fathers and then later Augustine, Aquinas, Luther, Calvin, and theologians down to the present have echoed them. Each gives in his or her time a version of these in the intervention of God, who is not willing that anyone should perish because of his or her deviation from God's plan: but rather, "God was in Christ, reconciling the world to himself."

In Reinhold Niebuhr's book, *The Self and the Dramas of History,* this is a central theme in his chapter, "The Uniqueness of the Human Self." Referring to the Biblical affirmation that "God made man after his image and likeness,"[50] Niebuhr emphasized three implications of this. First is the human capacity for *dialogue* within oneself, with the neighbor, and with God. "We may safely say that the human animal is the only creature which talks to itself."[51] Most of us, when we reflect on it, are aware that the internal dialogue proceeds on many levels—between the self that is aware of its obligations and the self that observes decisions being made, the self that is in the grip of biological urges, and the self that is organizer of long-range purposes that may require deferring those urges.

Second are the dialogues we hold with other persons who may or may not choose to reveal their own inner selves so that, as Shakespeare's Lady Macbeth insisted, "False face must hide what the false heart doth know." This capacity consciously to conceal one's secret self from others is other evidence of the uniqueness of selfhood but is less remarkable than the proclivity to lie to one's self about one's self, a phenomenon of which modern psychology, especially since Freud, has made a great deal.

Finally—and most crucial to the Western religious' understanding of selfhood—there is dialogue with God. The affirmation that we are created in God's image is historically an astonishing claim given that in the ancient world, the gods were often portrayed as having little but distain for humans; worshippers had to curry favors by offering sacrifices. The most important implication of the Christian gospel is that we are capable of having dialogue with our creator, learning God's will for our lives, his judgment on our failures, and his redeeming love. The social implications are wide ranging. St. John writes, "Beloved, let us love one another, for love is of God. He that loves not knows not God; for God is love." (I John 4:7)

Indeed *love,* in Christian tradition, is the ultimate word in defining human selfhood. Other species exhibit affection in many and often touching ways, and the "maternal instinct" is a powerful force in the familial life of, for example, a mother bear who will fight to the death to protect her cub. However powerful a bond it appears to be, it does not last beyond a limited time in the cub's life. The day will come when the mother will drive the cub up a tree with growls and swats and then abandon it. If she and her cub should meet a month later on some forest trail, there will be slight recognition between them.[52]

Beyond the *eros* of natural attraction (what Aristotle called "concupiscent love") and the *phileo* of brotherly affection (sometimes strong enough to prompt one to lay down his life for the other, as military comrades sometimes experience), there is *agape*: a bond between persons that promises to outlast death itself. Plato and Aristotle both suggested that such a transcendent bond must exist but offered few examples. Not until the apostle Paul identified it as the love that Jesus fulfilled on the cross (the love that prompted him to be willing to die not only for friends but also for his enemies so they too might be forgiven) did *agape* became the ultimate characterization of the Christian person. Agape enables one to transcend normative definitions of humanness so that in theological parlance, in becoming "one with Christ," the individual becomes a new kind of person, a "new being."

Paul Tillich wrote, "If I were asked to sum up the Christian message for our time in two words, I would say with Paul: It is the message of 'New Creation.' "[53] If God was truly "in Christ, reconciling the world to Himself," then the apostle Paul's words to the Corinthians says it all: "If anyone is in union with Christ, he is a new being; the old state of things has passed away." (II Corinthians 5:17). The "new being," fully identified with Christ, is now capable of this perfect love that fully embraces even the enemy. The writer of I John 3:14 expressed this: "We know that we have passed out of death into life, because we love the brethren." But such assurance comes with a caveat: "He who does not love remains in death." As death is separation or apartness from God, our conflicted generation has become, in Tillich's words, "the generation of world wars, revolutions, mass migrations. Multitudes as numerous as whole nations still wander over the face of the earth or perish when artificial walls put an end to their wanderings."[54]

Islam.   While making no direct claim that our personhood bears the "image of God" as do Hebrew and Christian scripture, the *Holy Qur'an* of Islam makes two distinct assertions. First, humankind began with Adam (Man) being created as God's "Vice gerent on earth"[55] and second humans are not (as Psalm 8 has it) "little lower than the angels" but indeed are actually *higher* than the angels, who are told to "bow down to Adam."[56] Interestingly, the angels' surprised response is to ask God, "Wilt Thou place therein one who will make mischief . . . and shed blood?" to which God replies, "I know what ye know not."[57]

To appreciate fully the importance of the Holy Qur'an in revealing God's will concerning humankind, it will be helpful to note Ninian Smart's observation: If you were to look for a rough equivalent to the Christian Incarnation (the divine nature of Jesus) in Muslim piety, it would be the Qur'an. It is divine thought and divine law incarnated in words.[58] Perhaps most Christians proclaim that the Bible is "the Word of God," many would insist instead that Christ is the incarnate Word while the Bible contains rather a record of God's dealing with humankind (and underscores our often stumbling response). Islam as both a faith and a governmental force gives to the Holy Qur'an absolute centrality in presenting God's message to his creation.

This being the case, it is worth noting that there is no discussion or debate as to human personhood per se. The Quran instead affirms that God, "the Cherisher and Sustainer of the Worlds" has created us as conscious, self-aware beings[59] who realize "in our inner souls" God's love and care.[60] Our most natural response is one of worship during which we also seek God's help to live a more moral life.[61] Perhaps even more tellingly in terms of Islamic affirmation of our personhood is our awareness of God's judgment and that all humans are in the same moral predicament. We need each other's help in a mutually uplifting fellowship, the sacral community.[62]

Of crucial importance is the debate lasting more than two thousand years as to whether the Holy Qur'an asserts that humankind bears God's image. In point of fact, while the Qur'an does not present it as an arguable issue, (Surah 15:29; 32:9; 38:72), the Haddith literature (n. 4731) makes it quite clear that mankind was created in the image of God. Compare Surah: 15:29; 32;9; 38:72.

The Qur'an identifies three kinds of persons. First are those who, recognizing the vast difference between God's perfection and human imperfection, fear God and by being steadfast in prayer find that God is merciful and compassionate. Remarkably (especially considering the era in which this revelation took place), it is made clear that "Whoever submits his whole self to God, and is a doer of good . . . will get his reward with his Lord." (Surah II :1-5, 112)[63] This passage has a striking resemblance to Acts 10:34, 35 in the New Testament and with which Muhammad may have been acquainted: "God shows no partiality, but in every nation anyone who fears Him and does what is right is acceptable to him." (Surrah II: 12) This is not to suggest that Muhammad was influenced by Christian scripture but that the similarity reveals an area of common insight into God's will.

Second are the out-and-out atheists as distinct from those who merely hold "mistaken notions" of God. (Sura II 6)[64] Yusuf Ali affirms God's compassion for those who are without faith but are earnestly seeking God: "Where there is such desire, the grace and mercy of God gives guidance." But some atheists have so hardened their hearts and closed their minds that "it is the same to them whether thou warn them or do not warn them; they will not believe." Here, in a passage reminiscent of Exodus 4:21 where God hardened Pharaoh's heart, the Holy Qur'an tells us "God hath set a seal on their hearts and on their hearing, and on their eyes as a veil; great is the penalty they (incur)." (Sura II. 7)[65] In the psychology of faith, once one chooses to reject communion with God, the "hardening of hearts" seems to become as inexorable as gravity's action on a person who deliberately steps out of a tenth floor window. That law, too, is God's doing and will not be suspended for our convenience.

The third kind of person is the hypocrite. "When they meet those who believe, they say 'We believe.' But when they are alone with their evil (companions) they say: 'we are really with you. We were only jesting.' (Sura II. 14)[66] Hypocrisy takes many forms: deception (trying to deceive God as well as one's neighbors), arrogant compromise, "trying to get the best of both worlds, by compromising between good and evil"; (Cf,. A. Yusuf Ali's commentary on p, 19, *The Holy Qur'an*, published by Amana Corp., Brentwood Md. 1934) and cynicism, which says "faith is good enough for fools"[67] "cynicism may be the greatest folly in the eyes of God." (ibid. p. 19) It is the cynics who are the fools. "God will throw back their mockery on them." (ibid.)[68]

Although not discussed in specifics, personhood is clearly of great importance in Islam. One's choice to be one kind of person or another is critical and, in the end,

Jainism

One should treat all creatures in the world as one would like to be treated.
Mahavira, *Sutrakritanga*

Judaism

What is hateful to you, do not do to your neighbor. This is the whole Torah; all the rest is commentary.
Hillel, Talmud, *Shabbath* 31a
One must also include Love your neighbor as yourself.
Leviticus 19:18

Sikhism

I am a stranger to no one; and no one is a stranger to me. Indeed I am a friend to all.
Guru Gbranth *Sahib*, p. 1299

Taoism

Regard your neighbor's gain as your own gain, and your neighbor's loss as your own loss.
T'ai Shang Kan Ying *P'ien*, 213–18

Unitarianism

We affirm and promote respect for the interdependent web of all existence, of which we are a part.
Unitarian Principle

Zoroastrianism

Do not do unto others whatever is injurious to yourself.
Shayast-na-Shayast 13.29

There is no suggestion here that "all religions are basically alike." Even a casual study of the traditions will reveal major differences, but the list serves as a reminder that we as persons—citizens of the world—can find some common ground on which to build a global ethic. On such a foundation we may at least begin to construct a more harmonious worldwide fellowship. These "golden rules" provide an excellent agenda for family discussion around the dinner table and suggest that opportunities abound for selecting good stories, essays, and books that parents can read to their children and discuss later. Chapter 3 will explore some strategies for such a family venture.

E.   INSIGHTS FROM THE SOCIAL SCIENCES

Much of the literature in the social sciences seems to suggest that moral development from infancy to old age could be a fairly straightforward affair if only we apply the right motivational, educational, and/or conditioning techniques and reinforce the whole with effective social, legal, and political strategies.

A common approach found in scores of books from Hartshorne and May in the 1920s to Thomas Lickona, William Damon, and Larry Rassmussen in the present is to begin by presenting a veritable litany of social ills that include everything from broken homes, delinquency, and violent crime to racial conflicts and all-out war, all of which, authors note, are on the increase. There is ample justification for accepting this, but it is not the whole story, nor is it entirely appropriate. The human condition will not be understood by the time we have exhausted all arguments for the human species being declared basically good, morally neutral, or ontologically deviant.

In his perceptive *Raising Good Children*, Thomas Lickona describes the abrupt change in moral orientation in the post-World War II years, contrasting the "Old Morality" with the "New Morality." The old, he writes, "with its roots in religion, speaks of respect, service to others, sacrifice, resistance to temptation, and moderation in the pursuit of pleasure."[71] He might well have included philosophy with religion because from Socrates onward, many of these same virtues have been given considerable attention. But the "New Morality," Lickona tells us, "celebrates self-centeredness and self-indulgence."[72] One might argue against characterizing a whole field of study with such a sweeping criticism, but certainly much of "pop psychology" openly rejected the traditional moral consensus still to be found among the major traditions and has drawn extensively (if superficially) from Sigmund Freud, J.B. Watson, B.F. Skinner, and others.

Among the most influential "stage" theorists (and given due credit by Lickona) have been Freud, Jean Piaget, Erik Erikson, and Lawrence Kohlberg. Each has identified periods in the life span when moral insights occur and are acted on, laying the foundation for successive stages. These are sufficiently well known not to require extensive exploration here except to observe that the emergence of insight is represented as a virtually automatic and inevitable stage. Note, for example, that Freud assumed that from birth to roughly three years of age, all children go through an oral, anal, and then phallic stage during which they encounter either pleasure or conflict.

Depending on how the conflicts are resolved (e.g., termination of breast feeding, imposition of toilet training, punishment for masturbating or for showing too intense preference for the parent of the opposite sex), successive stages of development may be deflected, resulting in emotional trauma and neurotic behavior. The conflicts may be so great as to become "complexes" of several disorders buried deep in the unconscious mind inaccessible to consciousness. They may lurk there and, like pus under a scab, poison the entire person.

Two later stages, latent and genital, corresponding roughly to elementary school years and early adolescence, respectively, were of less concern to Freud, who considered that the first seven years of life represented the period most critical to adult personality formation.

Ultimately, Freud's theory of personality development may be described as fatalistic, rooted in conditions largely beyond our control, and pessimistic as revealed in his *Civilization and Its Discontents*. In that series of lectures in 1929, he announced: "Men have brought their powers of subduing the forces of nature to such a pitch that by using them they could now very easily exterminate one another . . . hence their unrest, their dejection."[73]

In contrast to Freud's psychosexual stages, which clashed with environmental demands (including family moral values), Erik Erikson, a fellow psychoanalytic theorist, introduced two quite different experiences of a more social nature during the first three years life. Children, he wrote, come to trust or mistrust themselves and others during the very first year of experience with caretakers. Ideally, self-confidence and trust in their parents and family lead to a well-balanced child. During the second stage—ages two to three years—as children gain some skills like walking and climbing and begin asserting themselves as individuals, they find themselves in conflict with their caretakers. This leads to a sense of autonomy and, at times, feelings of shame and guilt. The importance of these stages for later development is seen in the discovery that trust, mistrust, and guilty feelings are a part of life's encounters (Erikson was the first to propose a developmental model that extended over the life span). We cannot trust everyone we meet, and sometimes we do things that *should* make us feel guilty. When we are confronted with people who do cruel, exploitive, or deceitful things but who express neither guilt nor remorse, we feel alienated and come to view them as monstrous or sick.

Jean Piaget was more engaged with cognitive than moral development during those first years that preoccupied Freud and Erikson. Moral norms, Piaget wrote in *The Moral Judgement of the Child* (1976), have three characteristics: they are generalizable to all situations, they last beyond the immediate situations to which they apply, and they are associated with self-assessment or autonomy.

> From two to seven years, none of these conditions is met. To begin with, norms are not generalized but are valid only under particular conditions. For example, the child considers it wrong to lie to his parents and other adults but not to his comrades. Second, instructions remain linked to certain represented situations. . . . Good and bad are defined as that which conforms or fails to conform to the instructions one has received.[74]

Piaget's concern with moral development remained grounded in his concern for understanding the evolution of moral reasoning: how children interact with their family, peers, and environment to reach conclusions about what action is best. His approach was more descriptive than prescriptive.

Lawrence Kohlberg was also concerned primarily with moral reasoning; he identified six stages that divided into three levels. The preconventional level included the obedience-and-punishment stage (obedience to commands to avoid punishment) and the hedonistic-instrumental stage (obedience to get a reward). Children, he wrote, may remain in this level from one to nine years of age.

The conventional level spans adolescence and, for some, all of the adult years. Its stages include the "good boy–nice girl" morality in which each strives for approval for complying with a list of virtues; and the "law-and-order" or conformity to duty stage. Some have referred to this as the "John Wayne" orientation; everyone is expected to abide by it.

The postconventional level contains the "social contract" stages, which are more philosophical and open to modifying rules that serve human rights. Beyond this community-based orientation is the sixth or "universal ethical principles" stage.

The quest here is for conduct guided by moral insights that transcend personal and social regulations. During the present author's conversation with Dr. Kohlberg shortly before his death in 1987, he said he had difficulties with stage six because he could not find enough real-life exemplars. "Perhaps I've pushed too far," he said. Evidently, he resolved the concern because he shared with other colleagues later that year that he was about to propose a seventh stage, "more religious and transcendental in substance," affirming his belief that there is a universal morality.[75]

In assessing the work of these theorists, it is instructive to note that Freud has often been criticized as being unscientific because he made few predictions that could be tested (a key element in the scientific method). The realm of the "unconscious" is almost by definition impossible to demonstrate, much less explore. Furthermore, his "stages" were constructed almost entirely based on the recollections of adult male patients. Female psychologists have objected that his concepts of "penis envy" and the castration and Electra complexes are considered extremely sexist and without substantiation when female patients were involved.

Erikson, too, has come under some criticism for the fact that "all of the subjects of his psychobiographies and most of his case samples were male."[76] His tone of optimism has made his perhaps a more welcome voice than Freud's, and he has made a major contribution to the language by popularizing such terms as *identity crisis* and *the life cycle.*

Piaget's work has given the study of cognitive development a much needed boost, although he has been faulted for underestimating the mental capabilities of children, especially infants. Furthermore, his focus on developmental stages has been said to overestimate the periods of stability between the change into an advanced stage (which is less abrupt than he thought).

Among the sharpest criticisms of Kohlberg's stage theory have come from women co-workers, especially Carol Gilligan, on lines of criticism similar to those of Freud and Erikson: Kohlberg's conclusions are based almost entirely on studies of male subjects. His insistence that progress through the stages that he outlines is unvarying and irreversible has also been challenged; after all, most us of have noted periods of "backsliding" in our moral progress. The most serious complaint may be, however, that he is merely an observer of stages, mapping the presumed progress, concerned not with whether responses to his test questions were right or wrong, good or bad, but simply how the subjects arrived at such conclusions. "Kohlberg was criticized, for educating for moral reasoning, which was unrelated to behavior. It was a wasted enterprise because such capacities had nothing to do with what people actually do."[77] Coming to his defense, Berkowitz reminded the critics that a substantial literature demonstrates a significant relation between one's capacity for moral reason and one's moral behavior. The criticism remains a valid one, however, because as Hartshorne and May demonstrated in the 1920s (after investigating the behavior of 11,000 children), youngsters can be taught to give "all the right answers" to moral questions yet still engage in lying, cheating, and even stealing.[78] Those of us who have had experience counseling in detention homes and prisons can attest to this, and Berkowitz is quick to acknowledge that "there is no necessary isomorphism between reason and behavior . . . due to the complexity of the moral person."[79]

This brings us, of necessity, to the question at the very core of our study: How are we to set up the conditions for nurturing moral development?

Perhaps the best place to begin is to recognize that because we live interdependent lives in family and other groups, morality begins in responding to other people through sympathetic, cooperative, helpful, altruistic, comforting, giving and rescuing actions.[80] It is important to note that these emphasize here is on actions, not merely intentions; an old adage has it that "the road to Hell is paved with good intentions," which are never acted on. Second, a distinction should be noted between helping and altruistic actions. Helping is a valuable experience as children follow their parents or other caretakers about the house picking up and cleaning. This is usually done as reciprocal behavior in the hope for some pleasurable reward, even if just a smile or pat on the head. Altruism, on the other hand, involves carrying out actions to benefit others without any thought of reward; it is done simply because the actions are good and right to do (e.g., the ancient Good Samaritan story from Luke).

Third, comforting involves the capacity for empathy, the ability to identify with another person's pain or distress and so seek to alleviate it. William Damon writes of numerous observations of infants who exhibited strong, often tearful, reactions upon witnessing other children in pain and describes specific techniques for measuring such reactions in the laboratories at the University of California at Los Angeles (U.C.L.A.).[81] "There is also solid evidence that a child's ability to empathize is associated with her or his tendencies to engage in prosocial acts such as helping a sharing." This sensitivity may encourage the child to engage in charitable behavior and impart a humanitarian flavor to later emerging political and ideological views.[82]

Empathy is highly correlated with secure attachment to the parents, especially the mother, as Thomas Licona reports. Researchers Waters, Wippman, and Stroufe rated babies' attachment to their mothers at 15 months of age. These children were "tracked" through nursery school (age three) and were found to tend to be social leaders. "Other kids sought them out; they frequently initiated activities. When another child showed distress, a securely attached child was likely to respond with empathy."[83] However, it is equally important to note the attachment to the fathers. The relationships are different, but researchers have found that "children with highly involved fathers tend to exhibit higher cognitive competence, advanced developmental functioning, better peer relations, and increased empathy."[84]

Conversely, children who are not encouraged to be kind, generous, and attentive to the needs of siblings and peers may become "empathically dysfunctional," engaging in antisocial behavior. "Young people convicted of violent crimes often express their lack of feeling for their victim's distress."[85] Nearly two centuries ago, novelist Mary Wollstonecraft, author of *Frankenstein,* warned, "Those who are able to see pain, unmoved, will soon learn to inflict it."[86]

Fourth, rescuing requires all of the three preceding elements, plus the courage to act even at the risk of one's own safety. All who have had experience working with very young children can relate episodes in which a youngster witnessing another in a situation of danger would either ignore the child, try to help, or call for help. Responses may vary according to the situation; a child fallen in the street or in danger of drowning might evoke a more urgent reaction but also may merely attract curiosity with no effort to help. There might even be some who react with ridicule: "Don't be such a wimp!" Rather than try to generalize or suggest that some children are just naturally good and courageous while others are born bad, cruel, or apathetic, Norma and Seymore Feshmach of U.C.L.A. designed a ten-week program that involved role-playing. Using "affect-identification" exercises, they found that children showed increased prosocial activity during the course. How long the effect lasted was not determined.[87]

It may be that direct instruction in such experiences as Sunday School training regarding the Ten Commandments, the Sermon on the Mount, exhortations from the Qur'an, etc., can be reinforcement for the influence already established in the home. The prospect for a carryover of family-centered nurturance of such moral behavior as helping each other is better supported in the reports of youth who come forward to volunteer after fire or earthquake disasters in the immediate neighborhood and to gather food and clothing for homeless people in the inner cities. It took moral courage to do the risky clean-up work in the rubble that followed the Rodney King riots in Los Angeles while trouble still brewed.

Perhaps most dramatic were the stories of hundreds of Christians who risked their lives during World War II by welcoming and rescuing neighboring Jews and other victims of the Holocaust.[88] Extensive interviews with 406 such rescuers (and a matched sample of nonrescuers) revealed that the former group had strong identification with parental models of strong moral conviction; home discipline that tended toward leniency, emphasis on providing reasons for certain behaviors being appropriate or not, and explicit communication about the obligation to help others in a spirit of generosity. In contrast, the nonrescuers came from families with low commitment to altruistic behavior and, in some cases, scorn for the whole notion of morality.[89] Similar studies of participants in the Civil Rights movement in the 1960s revealed a family history of church participation and frequent altruistic actions on the part of family members, some of whom had often risked their lives out of commitment to what they deemed morally right action.[90]

Among other early values that children must learn is the virtue of truth telling. Lying is often a frightened effort to conceal a weakness (e.g., boasting of some unacquired skill or feat of strength). It can be employed to cover an embarrassing deficiency such as having made a failing grade on a spelling test. Laying the groundwork for adult truthfulness is of critical importance for the whole society. We have witnessed much cynicism in recent years about "big business" not representing products truthfully (e.g., the auto and tire industries knowingly selling defective merchandise; television advertising whose false claims necessitated the Truth in Advertising laws; the tobacco industry putting millions of customers at deadly risk for decades [with an annual death toll of 400,000] for the sake of profit). As is well known and being emulated in parts of Europe, local and national lawsuits are being launched to recover billions of dollars in government costs for health care.

It is certainly clear that there can be no progress in science unless researchers can be counted on to be rigorously truthful. In a remarkable instance of this, astrophysicist Andrew Lyne, after years of effort to locate planets beyond our solar system, was invited to announce his success at an international conference. Ten or twelve days before the conference, he discovered a slight inaccuracy in his calculations. He seriously feared this might end his career, but he admitted publicly that his efforts had failed. Instead of disparagement, he received an enthusiastic round of applause for his honesty.[91] To be sure, the skeptic might retort that if a scientist lies, other scientists will discover the deception in short order and will unmask the person as a fraud. Merely avoiding "getting caught" is not a virtue, however. Those who have been schooled in honesty and adhere to a rigorous habit of self-discipline do not need negative inducements.

The habit of adhering to the truth is apparently learned first and most lastingly in the home. In their book *Home Rules*, Denis Wood and Robert Beck emphasize "the enculturing power of the home," pointing out that children actually feel most secure when rules for behavior are clear and uniformly applied and every day is filled with regulations, many so subtle and seemingly inconsequential as not slamming or kicking the door and not opening it to just anybody. By learning to comply with countless small, specific rules, especially those related to truth telling, "children are internalizing a vast cultural system of values and meaning."[92]

Within the cultural system, perhaps the most foundational values are respect and love. When these are absent, the others may not be realized at all. If an individual respects others, he or she will not steal from them or hurt or humiliate them but will be quick to offer help both material and emotional when needed. The element of love is the most difficult because while a person can easily absorb admonitions like "Love thy neighbor," it is quite something else to love one's enemies and "pray for those that persecute you." Many—perhaps most—people find this an ideal beyond their capacity to actualize now or even in the distant future, but the fact that morally concerned persons are willing to entertain the possibility, however remote, offers some ground for optimism. Francis Fukuyama urges us to consider that "human beings are designed to create moral rules and social order. If technology makes older forms of community difficult, then we will seek out new ones."[93] And if it turns out that the moral rules are not simply humanly contrived but revealed to us from some transcendent source and that we are "designed" to receive them, we will have even more reason to consider the right of each person to all the generosity, helpfulness, compassion, and "rescuing" of which we are capable.

F. IMPLICATIONS FOR GLOBAL ETHICS

It is hoped that in our quest for exemplars of moral persons, John Donne's often quoted "no man is an island" will be received as more than a poetic cliché. His metaphor is as timely today as in the seventeenth century, prompting Douglas Sturm to affirm that "whatever else is true about us, we are all denizens of an ongoing community of life."[94] Donne's observation was and is apt: "Every man is a piece of the continent, a part of the main."

Sturm points to Karl Jaspers' description of a remarkable era between 800 and 200 B.C.E. that he dubbed the "Axial Age." It was a period when spiritually alert individuals from very different backgrounds independently established new religions, offering possibilities of a unified human community: Zarathustra and Zoroastrianism (c. 600 B.C.E.), Lao Tze and Taoism (c. 604 B.C.E.), Mahavira and Jainism (c. 600 B.C.E.), Gautama and Buddhism (c. 560 B.C.E.), and Confucius and Confucianism (c. 550 B.C.E.). Each of the founders was profoundly grasped by a vision of a united humanity.

Remarkably, the "founders" of these religious movements were not collaborators in think tanks but unique, unrelated individuals, and each of the religions that they founded remains near the top of the major traditions still in practice around the globe.

It is important for us to remember—and Sturm does not neglect the point— that "the principle of human solidarity has constituted an important axis on which the understanding of history has turned throughout subsequent centuries."[95] The crucial role of religious insight and commitment in such "understanding of history" deserves acknowledgment, not only in the publications of the national and world councils of churches; comparable organizations of Jewish, Islamic, and Buddhist origin; and the Earth Charter Movement, but also in the United Nations' primarily secular Universal Declaration of Human Rights of 1948. The "rights," as in Thomas Jefferson's Declaration of Independence are not available in all cultures, to a clear pronouncement of God, or even, as in the case of the 1948 Declaration, based on universal moral standards. "Anthropological science demonstrates that there are no universal moral standards, because morals are always dependent on particular cultural traditions."[96]

When one reads extensively in the sacred literature of the many religions' proffering something very much like the Golden Rule (as quoted in the earlier section and contributions of the major religions), one becomes aware that, as Ewert Cousins describes the need for religiously informed discussion, "the threats with which we are now confronted are not just to the survival of certain groups of people, they are threats to the survival of all human kind."[97] These threats include, among many others, the careless dumping of toxic waste polluting the soil, air, and water required for survival; the astonishing spread of HIV and AIDS across whole continents resulting in deaths of millions; political and economic exploitation of whole populations resulting in unemployment, homelessness, and death of hundreds of millions; and the ever looming threat of weapons of mass destruction from biological to nuclear agents. These issues are very much a part of religious conferences such as the Parliament of the World's Religions, the British Society for the Study of Christian Ethics, and the European Societas Ethica, and in the curriculum of departments of comparative religions on almost every major university campus in the United States and elsewhere.

Hans Kung, discussing the many wrenching problems of our time with students and colleagues, has written, "No one can still have any serious doubts that a period of the world which has been shaped more than any before it by world politics, world technology, the world economy and world civilization needs a world ethic."[98] But he is careful not to suggest a simplistic ideology that all people would automatically embrace.

> "Here a global ethic means neither a global ideology, nor a single unified global religion transcending all existing religions, nor a mixture of all religions. The religions of the world are so different in their views of faith and 'dogmas,' their symbols and rites, that a 'unification' of them would be meaningless, a distasteful syncretistic cocktail." An ethical minimalism would only do violence to the Torah,

the New Testament, the Qur'an, the Bhagavad Gita, and the Sayings of Confucius. For hundreds of millions of people these remain the foundation for faith and life. Instead, "a global ethic seeks to work out what is already common to the religions of the world. . . (it) does not reduce the religions to an ethical minimalism, but represents the minimum of what the religions of the world have (to offer). [A global ethic] invites all, believers and nonbelievers to make this their own."[99]

To some, this seems overly modest as a fledgling first effort, but Kung points out that the Council for the Parliament of the World's Religions out of which this document emerged represents the first time in the history of religions worldwide when such an effort was even tried.

NOTES

1. Amy Chua, "Power and Prejudice: Globalizing Hate," *Amnesty Now* (New York: Amnesty International USA, 2003), 5–7.

2. Reinhold Niebuhr, *Moral Man and Immoral Society* (New York: Charles Scribner's Sons, 1932). In the Introduction (p. xiii), he credits John Dewey with coining the phrase.

3. *Ibid.*, 8.

4. Eyal Press, "Tortured Logic," *Amnesty Now*, op. cit 20–21.

5. Samuel P. Huntington, *The Clash of Civilizations and the Remaking of World Order* (New York: Touchtone/Simon and Schuster, 1996), 21.

6. *Ibid.*, 28.

7. Helen Garner, *Art Through the Ages* (New York: Harcourt, Brace, Jovanovich, 1975).

8. Annemarie De Waal Malefijt, *Religion and Culture* (Prospect Heights, Il.: Waveland Press, 1968), 31–32.

9. Plato, "Menno," 71a, from *The Dialogues of Plato*, trans. Benjamin Jewett *Great Books of the Western World*, vol. 7, (Chicago: Encyclopedia Britannica, 1971), 174.

10. George Berkekey, *A Treatise Concerning the Principles of Human Knowledge* Great Books of the Western World, vol. 35 (Chicago, The Encyclopedia Britannica, 1971), 413.

11. Sarvepalli Radhakrishnan, "Human Personality," in *The Self*, ed. Moustakas Clark (New York: Harper & Row, 1956).

12. Charles Darwin, *The Descent of Man*, Great Books of the Western World, vol. 49 (Chicago: Encyclopedia Britannica, *The Great Books*, 1971). Darwin argues this extensively in chap. 2 and 3.

13. Werner Heisenberg noted that classical physics was incapable of creating anything that is essentially more than an aggregate of its parts (such as mind–brain connection), but a quantum event is "perceived" as creating it by combining diverse aspects of the prior situation into a new unified whole. Classical physics, writes Henry Stapp, "has no rational place for consciousness. If consciousness is put into the theory at all, it must simply be put in 'by hand,' rather than by virtue of the logical structure of the theory. The logical situation in quantum theory is quite different: there is an absolute logical need for something else, such as consciousness." H. P. Stapp "Quantum

Propensities and the Brain-Mind Connection," *Foundations of Physics* (quoted in), John C. Eccles, *How the Self Controls Its Brain* (Heidelberg: Springer-Verlag, 1994), 51.

14. Francis Crick quotes with admitted astonishment the definition of "consciousness" from the *International Dictionary of Psychology* "a fascinating but illusive phenomenon; it is impossible to specify what it is, what it does or why it evolved." He then adds, "Nothing worth reading has been written on it." Crick himself believes that consciousness is a reality but is an aspect of the brain's behavior, not separate from it. See Crick, *The Astonishing Hypothesis* (New York: Simon and Schuster/Touchtone Books, 1995), preface, 259. See also in Part 1 of Additional References: Pribram, Rensch, Wilson, Blakemore, Edelman, Dennet, Crick, and Searle.

15. "The person is a temporary putting together of five kinds of impermanent events: bodily; perceptions, feelings, dispositions and states of consciousness." This description of the Theravada Buddhist analysis of personhood arose from the fact that the original Buddha did not believe in anything "beyond" in the form of a personal deity or God or absolute. See Ninian Smart, *The World's Religions* (Englewood Cliffs, NJ, Prentice-Hall, 1989), 77–79.

16. John C. Eccles, *The Human Psyche* (Heidelberg-New York: Springer-Verlag, 1980) 17.

17. Roger Penrose, *The Emperor's New Mind: Concerning Computors, Minds, and the Laws of Physics* (Oxford, England: Oxford University Press, 1989), 447.

18. W.H. Werkmeister, *Man and His Values* (Lincoln, NE: University of Nebraska Press, 1967), 19. The enormous demands made on the conscious, self-reflective, and proactive human mind is perhaps nowhere better illustrated than in the observation by Thomas Pettinger Jr. in a review of Michael Crichton's book *Airframe*: "Among the artifacts of the Earth, there is none more complex than a commercial jetliner." Pettinger understands, perhaps even better than Crichton, the incredible complexity of an airliner's architecture, aerodynamics, and built-in communications and self-monitoring systems produced not by a vague, illusory "consciousness" but by the inventive human mind. *Los Angeles Times* (December 15, l996), 3, (Book Review sect.)

19. Karl Popper and John C. Eccles, *The Self and Its Brain* (Heidelberg: Springer-Verlag, l977), 144.

20. Plato's *Meno*, 71a, from *The Dialogues of Plato*, Benjamin Jowett, translator, *The Great Books*, Volume 7, Chicago: The University of Chicago Press, l971. p. 174.

21. Marvin W. Berkowitz, *The Education of the Complete Mora Person* (Aberdeen, Scotland: Gordon Cook Foundation, l999), 4.

22. William Stuntz, "Pride and Pessimism in the Courts," *First Things* (New York: Institute on Religion and Public Life, 1997), 27. Romans 7:18–19.

23. Niebuhr, *Moral Man*, 91.

24. Lucretius, *De Rerum Natura*, trans. W.E. Leonard, (New York: E.P. Dutton, 1921), 6 (I 113–117).

25. T.H.H, Dubs, *The Works of Hsuntse*, trans. from the Chinese (London: Probsthain. 1928), 223, quoted in John B. Noss, *Man's Religions*, 4th ed. (London: Macmillan, 1970). Noss is careful to point out (pp. 302–03) that Hsuntse cautioned against making too much of Confucius' "Way of Heaven," saying, "The way to do things is neither the way of Heaven nor that of earth, but of man." Yet he still acknowledges that humankind is still a part of the whole cosmological principle "whereby Heaven and earth unite."

26. Jeremy Bentham, *An Introduction to the Principles of Morals and Legislation* (London: Oxford University Press, 1879), chap. 10.

27. Richard Dawkins, *The Blind Watchmaker* (London: W.W. Norton, 1985).

28. Chandler Burr, "Homosexuality and Biology," *Atlantic Monthly,* March 1993, 448.

29. Aristotle, *The Nicomachean Ethics,* Book X, chap. 5, trans. W.D. Ross, Great Books of the Western World, vol. 9, (Chicago: The University of Chicago, Great Books of the Western Worlds vol. 9, 1952).

30. Aristotle, *Nicomachean Ethics,* book 1 vol. 8, 631.

31. Robert B. McLaren, *The World of Philosophy* (Chicago: Nelson-Hall, 1983), 31.

32. "Survival of the fittest" was a term coined not by Charles Darwin but by his cousin, Herbert Spencer, *Principles of Biology* (1865), pt. 3, chap. 12, sect. 164.

33. Charles Darwin, *The Descent of Man* (New York: Random House, n.d.), 491.

34. Oliver Wendell Holmes, *The Common Law* (Boston: Little, Brown 1881), 1.

35. Earl Warren, quoted in *All to the Good* (New York: World Publishing Company, 1969), 1.

36. In *The Holy Qur'an* (Sura xv, 29), we read of God's breathing his spirit into humankind and thus, according to translator and commentator Abdullah Yusuf Ali, imparting "the faculty of God-like knowledge and will." (McGregor & Werner, 1946), 643. The reference Sura xv, 29 signifies Surah (or chapter) 4, verse 29.

37. In *Timaeus,* Plato wrote of two worlds, the first being that of perfect order and design, reflected in the second (our mortal world). In both *Phaedo* and *The Republic,* he further argued that our "learning" is actually a "remembering" of that perfect world which we inwardly perceive.

38. Roger Penrose, *Shadows of the Mind* (New York: Oxford University Press, 1994), 416. Eccles John C. *Cf. How the Self Controls,* 179–81. Dr. Eccles proposes that we, as persons, direct our brains to seek out and disclose truths and moral goodness that are already "there" to be found; the cosmos is designed that way.

39. S.E. Frost, ed., The Brihad-Aranyaka Upanishad, 4th Adhyaya, 5, 21, *The Sacred Writings of the World's Great Religions* (New York: McGraw-Hill, 1972), 28–29.21.

40. Ibid., "The Katha Upanishad", NY: 35.

41. H. H. Dalai Lama, *The Bodhgaya Interviews*, ed. Jose Cabezon (Ithaca, NY: Snow Lion Publications, 1988), 12.

42. Ibid., 13.

43. F. Max Mueller, ed. *Sacred Books of the East,* vol. 19, (Oxford, England: Oxford University Press,) 261.

44. Sarvepali Rahakrishnan and Charles A. Moore, *Indian Philosophy* (Princeton, NJ: Princeton University Press, 1957), 274–78. See also Noel Pliney Jacobson, *Buddhism* (Carbondale: Southern Illinois University Press, 1966), 74–82; and H.H. the Dalai Lama, *Ethics for the New Millennium* (New York: Penguin Putnam, 1999), sec. II.

45. *The Analects of Confucius,* trans. Arthur Waley (New York: Random House, Vintage Books, 1938), 30.

46. Ibid., book VII. 6.

47. Ibid., book XVII. 25.

48. Surendranath, Dasgupta, *History of Indian Philosophy* (Cambridge: Cambridge University Press, 1932), 33–35. Nancy Barnes, *Women in World Religions* (Albany: State University of New York, England Press, 1987) 105.

49. Robert B. McLaren, *Christian Ethics: Foundations and Practice* (Englewood Cliffs, NJ: Prentice-Hall, 1994), 10.

50. Reinhold Niebuhr, *The Self and the Dramas of History* (New York: Charles Scribner's Sons, 1955), 3.

51. Ibid., 6.

52. The herd life of some species such as whales and elephants may suggest something more, but studies so far have been few and inconclusive.

53. Paul Tillich, *The New Being* (New York: Charles Scribner's Sons, 1955), 15.

54. Ibid., 171.

55. A. Yusuf Ali, trans. and comm., *The Holy Qur'an* (Sura II, 30) (Brentwood, MD: Amana Corporation, 1983), 24.

56. Ibid., (Sura II, 34–35), 25.

57. Ibid. At the risk of seeming irreverent, this looks to a Western eye like a revelation that God has a keen sense of humor. The angels are clearly surprised: "Wilt Thou place (in the Garden) one who will make mischief therein and shed blood, while we do celebrate Thy praises, and glorify Thy holy name?" (Sura II, 30–31, 34). But God proceeds to place humankind on a higher plain than the angels, saying in effect: "I know something you don't know," and begins to instruct Adam in all the ways of nature.

58. Smart, *The World's Religions*, 281.

59. Ali, *Holy Qur'an* (Sura, I, 2), 14.

60. Ibid. (Commentary 20), 14.

61. a. Ibid. (Sura I, 5). See also Seyyed Hossein Nasr, *Introduction to*
    b. *Islamic Cosmological Doctrines* (Albany: State University of New York Press, 1993), xv.
    c. Ibid. (Sura II, 1–5, 112).
    d. Ibid. (Sura II, 6).
    e. Ibid. (Sura II, 7).
    f. Ibid. (Sura II, 14).
    g. *Holy Qur'an* (Commentary 34), 19.
    h. Ibid., (Commentary 36) 19.
    i. Ibid. (Sura II, 15).

62. Alfred North Whitehead, *The Aims of Education* (New York: Macmillan, 1957), 1–2.

63. A.J. Ayers, *Language, Truth and Logic* (New York: Dover, 1936), 108–9.

64. Frost, The Bhagavad-Gita (Lesson the Second 11,12), *The Sacred Writings of the World's Great Religions* (New York: McGraw-Hill, 1972), 47.

65. Ibid. (Lesson the Second, 33).

66. Cf. references such as "An eye for an eye, tooth for tooth, hand for hand . . ." (Exodus 21:24) and "He who spares the rod hates his son" (Proverbs 13:24).

67. "He who conquers and keeps my works . . . I will give him power over the nations (Revelation 2:26–27). Even the name Canaan (which means black) was invoked during days of slavery in the United States to keep the black race in servitude. The Holy Qur'an does not advocate female circumcision, but pre-Islamic culture does in some parts of the Islamic world.

68. Robert Conot, "When Inhumanity Was Tried in Court," Part IV, *Los Angeles Times,* November 17, 1985, 3.

69. Nancy Eisenberg and Paul H, Mussen, *The Roots of Prosocial Behavior in Children* (New York: Cambridge University Press, 1989), 1. A full decade after Eisenberg and Mussen wrote these words, the September 6, 1999, issue of the *Los Angeles Times* gave front page coverage to the massacre of proindependence supporters in East Timor by Indonesian militias: "Thousands flee in terror, a car bomb killing scores of people" in Dagestan, signaling a reopening of the Islamic war for independence: Twin car bombs exploded in Tiberias and the port of Haifa with deadly results in protest of the peace efforts between Israel and Palestine. "History seems to be repeating itself endlessly."

70. McLaren, *Christian Ethics*, 37.

71. Thomas Lickona, *Raising Good Children* (New York: Bantam Books, 1985), 5.

72. For a brief but succinct treatment of Freud's stage theory, see James W, Vander Zanden, *Human Development*, 7th ed., (New York: McGraw-Hill, 1999), 37–42.

73. Sigmund Freud, *Civilization and Its Discontents*, ed. Robert Maynard Hutchins et al., *Great Books of the Western World*, vol. 54. (Chicago: Encyclopedia Britannica, 1952), 802.

74. Jean Piaget, *The Moral Judgement of the Child* (New York: Free Press, 1981).

75. James W. Vander Zanden, *Human Development*, 6th ed. (New York: McGraw Hill, 1997), 277–78. In the seventh edition, Vander Zanden adds, "It is Kohlberg's view that what is moral is not a matter of taste or opinion—there is a universal morality" (New York: McGraw-Hill,), 290.

76. Vander Zanden, *Human Development*, 45.

77. Berkowitz, *The Education*, 10.

78. H. Hartshorn and M.A. May, *Studies in the Nature of Character,* vol. 1 (New York: Macmillan, 1928), 411.

79. Berkowitz, *The Education*, 10.

80. Vander Zanden, *Human Development*, 7th ed., 291.

81. William Damon, *The Moral Child* (New York: Free Press, 1988), 17.

82. Ibid.

83. The report references E. Walters, J. Whippman, and L.A. Stroufe, "Attachment, Positive Affect, and Competence in the Peer Groups"; see Lickona, *Raising Good Children*, 48.

84. Clara, Schuster, and Shirley Ashburn, eds., *The Process of Human Development* (New York: J.B. Lippincott, 1992), 685.

85. Ibid., 17–18.

86. Mary, Wollstonecraft, quoted in Larry L. Rassmussen, *Earth Community, Earth Ethics* (Maryknoll, NY: Orbis Books, 1997), 344.

87. A. Blasi, "Bridging Moral Cognition and Moral Action: A Critical Review of the Literature," *Psychological Bulletin,* 1981: 593–637.

88. Eisenberg and Mussen, *The Roots of Prosocial Behavior*, 1.

89. *Ibid.*, 74–75.

90. Ibid., 75–76, quoting D.J Rosenhan, "Learning Theory and Prosocial Behavior," *The Roots*, 75–76.

91. *Science*, September 29, 2000, 260–62.

92. Dennis Wood, and Robert J. Beck, *Home Rules* (Baltimore: Johns Hopkins University Press, 1994).

93. Francis Fukuyama, "The Great Disruption," *The Atlantic Monthly,* May 1999, 78.

94. Douglas Sturm, "Identity and Otherness: Summons to a New Axial Age," *The Earth Charter Movement* (Forum on Religion and Ecology, Bucknell University, 1999), 2.

95. *Ibid.*, 5.

96. Cees Maris, "Franglais: On Liberalism, Nationalism and Multiculturalism," *Nation, State and the Coexistence of Different Communities* (Kampen, The Netherlands: Kok Pharos Publishing House, 1995), 61.

97. Quoted in Sturm, p. 5.

98. Hans Kung, *A Global Ethic"* Identity and Otherness," *Ethic*, New York: Continuum International, 1993), 7.

99. *Ibid.*, 8.

ADDITIONAL REFERENCES

It is inevitable that when writing a book or even an article, the writer is indebted to sources for which documentation is not strictly required but were still of immense value in advancing ideas and insights. Sometimes these were little more than suggestions but still worthy of recognition. The following are among the most helpful resources and deserving of sincere gratitude.

1. Studies of the Mind

Blakemore, C. *Mechanics of the Mind*. London: Cambridge University Press, 1977.

Crick, F., and C. Koch. "The Problem of Consciousness." *Scientific American*, 1992, 111–17.

Dawkins, R. *The Selfish Gene*. Oxford, England: Oxford University Press, 1976.

Dennett, D.C. *Consciousness Explained*. London: Allen Lane/Penguin, 1991.

Edelman, G.M. "Group Selection and Phasic Reentrant Signaling: A Theory of Higher Brain Function." In *The Mindful Brain*, Schmitt. Cambridge MA: M.I.T. Press, 1978.

Ornstein, Robert E. *The Psychology of Consciousness*. 2nd ed. New York: Harcourt, Brace, Jovonovich, 1972.

Pribram, K.H. *Languages of the Brain*. Englewood Cliffs, NJ: Prentice-Hall, 1971.

Rensch, B. *Biophilosophy*. New York: Columbia University Press, 1971.

Rensch, B. "Polynomistic Determination of Biological Processes." In *Studies in the Philosophy of Biology*, ed. F.J. Ayala and T. Dobzhansky. London: Macmillan, 1974.

Searle, J.R. *The Rediscovery of the Mind*. Cambridge, MA: M.I.T. Press, 1992.

Wilson, E.O. *On Human Nature*. Cambridge, MA: Harvard University Press, 1978.

2. Philosophy

Ayer, Alfred. *Language, Truth and Logic*. New York: Dover Press, 1946.

Carnap, Rudolp. *Testability and Meaning*. New Haven, CT: Whitlock's Inc., 1954.

Kaplan, Abraham. *The New World of Philosophy*. New York: Random House, 1961.

McLaren, Robert B. *The World of Philosophy*. Chicago: Nelson-Hall, 1983.

Maslow, Abraham. *New Knowledge in Human Values.* New York: Harper & Row, 1959.

Walters, James W. *What Is a Person? An Ethical Exploration.* Urbana: University of Illinois Press, 1997.

White, Morton. *The Age of Analysis.* New York: New American Library, 1955.

Wittgenstein, Ludwig. *Philosophical Investigations.* Trans. G.E.M. Anscome. New York: Macmillan, 1958

3. Religious Studies

Buber, Martin. *Good and Evil.* New York: Charles Scribner's Sons, 1953.

Curran, Charles. *Themes in Fundamental Moral Theology.* Notre Dame, IN: Notre Dame University Press, 1977.

Delarenzo, Talal. *Book of Morals and Manors of Imam Bukharis.* Beirut: El Sadawi Publications, 1997.

Fakhry, Majid. *Ethical Theories in Islam.* Leiden: E.J. Brill, 1991.

Goodman, Lenn. *On Justice.* New Haven: Yale University Press, 1991.

Heschel, Abraham.

Maguire, Daniel. *The Moral Revolution.* New York: Harper & Row, 1986.

Mayer, Ann. *Islam and Human Rights: Tradition and Politics.* Boulder, CO: Westview Press, 1991.

Niebuhr, Reinhold. *Moral Man and Immoral Society.* New York: Charles Scribner's Sons, 1932.

Polkinghorne, John. *One World: The Interaction of Science and Theology.* London: SPCK, 1986.

Ramsey, Paul. *Basic Christian Ethics.* New York: Charles Scribner's Sons, 1953.

Tillich, Paul. *Morality and Beyond.* New York: Harper Torchbooks, 1963.

Wogaman, J. Philip. *Christian Moral Judgement.* Louisville, KY Westminster /John Knox Press, 1989.

CHAPTER 3

The Family as Moral Context

Filial Piety is the root of all virtue, and the stem out of which grows all moral teaching.

—Confucius

The world has been abnormal for so long that we've forgotten what it's like to live in a peaceful and reasonable climate. If there is to be any peace or reason, we have to create it in our own hearts and homes.

—Madeleine L'Engle

The moral person portrayed in folklore and legend is often presented as a heroic, virtually self-made individual usually with little or no reference to family background: the Biblical Sampson; Deborah; King Arthur; Robin Hood; Joan of Ark, and on down to the rugged Hollywood stereotypical cowboy or underworld sleuth. Emil Brunner observed that such heroes may have the quality of a Robinson Crusoe, exemplifying the individual solely in the light of his or her own personality.[1]

The fact remains, however, that such persons, even fictional ones, were seldom the products of isolated wolf packs like Romulus and Remus of Roman legend, Mowgli of Kipling's *Jungle Book,* or the Tarzan of Edgar Rice Burroughs. The historically grounded persons of moral strength and courageous deed were for the most part raised in families with values and customs, many of which derived from their own complex environments. These are helpfully detailed in Urie Bronfenbrenner's "Ecological Theory of Development," suggesting five distinct, interacting levels of environmental influence.[2]

These levels include (1) the microsystem: the immediate family of parents/guardians and perhaps siblings and grandparents. It also includes peers, the neighborhood, churches, schools, and available health systems: (2) the mesosystem: the realm of dynamic interaction between the microsystem, and (3) the *exosystem:* friends of the family (which may involve diverse ethnic, religious, and racial groups), extended family members, the educational system (which may encompass several schools beyond the one attended by the person in question and which sometimes produces "cross-town

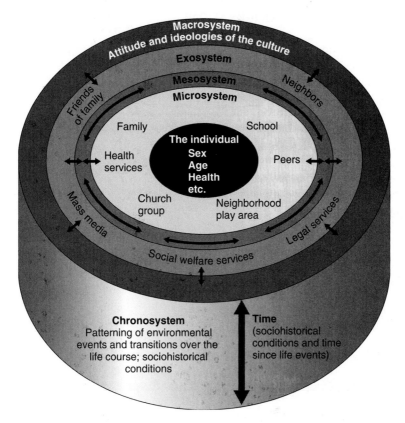

Figure 3.1   Bronfenbrenner's Ecological Theory of Development

rivalries" but also enriches social and scientific endeavors), legal services, government social welfare agencies, and the mass media; (4) the macrosystem: the broad attitudes, prejudices, cultural and religious beliefs, and various political and economic ideologies; and (5) the *chronosystem:* the patterning of events (e.g., how soon after parents' divorce do its negative effects reach their most severe impact in the lives of the child and or children? The chronosystem also evokes questions such as in the course of a married woman's family life, is it wise to return to school and/or seek a job or career?

The myth of the "self-made" man or woman seldom considers the multitude of influences, which, as Bronfenbrenner's proposal suggests, have shaped the personality of the person in question. Other influences must also be considered, such as the political/economic conditions experienced by such persons, their families, and the community at large. The stock market crash of 1929, the Great Depression, and World War II as well as the wars that followed radically changed the status of countless families, bringing poverty to some and to others opportunities for education, career development, professional leadership, and, of course, family building if such a choice were available. All of these events and family alterations must be considered in any assessment of how each individual develops.

A. SOME HISTORIC CONFIGURATIONS

Anthropologists, historians and sociobiologists are not of one accord as to just when the human family developed or when marriage became the event by which the family was formally recognized. It is fairly easy to trace familial structures through the literature of the major religious traditions where the sacredness of the family bond is secured as in the Qur'an,[3] in the expressed ontological bond in the Christian wedding before that,[4] the still earlier familial customs among the Hebrews,[5] and Confucius' declaration quoted at the beginning of this chapter, going back to the seventh century B.C.[6] Hinduism finds its guidance in the *Upanishads,* sacred documents that could have been created as early as 2000 B.C: "Love and respect must reign in the home. This is commanded because every member of the home circle is a soul, and as a soul is worthy of love and respect.[7] More impressively, burial sites of the Neanderthals, where the cherished dead were buried by their families with food and tools, suggest the contiguity of family structure as early as 50,000 B.C. Legal historian Ian Baxter claims that marriage rites may have been formally acknowledged as early as half a million years ago.[8]

Researchers in the social science community have explored the origins and purposes of family life among lower species, where the "safety in numbers" principle creates family groups for mutual protection as a natural, biological function.[9] Others have suggested that some kind of family structure was required from the earliest times of homo sapiens' appearance on the scene because food, clean water, and shelter were the urgent needs of females during pregnancy, labor, and nursing. "This was a new and unique bond between man, woman and child. It was an economic bond."[10]

Still others insist that the source of family organization was in the helplessness of the newborn and the need for a dominant and protective male parent to complement the female. "Natural selection doubtless operated to kill off those stocks in which the male refused this protection and care, and to 'select' those for survival in which (care and protection) was rendered."[11] There is much support for this in the relatively new discipline *sociobiology,* of which E.O. Wilson has been a chief expositor[12] and its perhaps more successful successor in academia, *evolutionary psychology.* Both are drawn largely from Darwin's evolutionary hypothesis. Wilson has asserted that nature operates to sustain physical attributes and behaviors that provide "survival value" and to eliminate those that do not. Fraser Watts lecturer in natural science at Cambridge in England, is uneasy about the paucity of laboratory evidence for either school of thought.[13]

As tempting as these speculations are, a certain caution must be encouraged. It should be noted that natural selection clearly did not operate to "kill off" all of those species, "those stocks," whose sire refused to provide protection. Newly hatched fish and turtles are virtually defenseless, but this fact has not created a family spirit among the parents or the protective oversight of the male adults.

Among apes, the social aggregate is of more importance than the biological "family," which in time disperses without evidencing a lasting emotional bond. Human families, on the other hand, grow emotionally closer with passing months and years, often with great affection and even reverence between younger and older generations. In her famous research among chimpanzees, Jane Goodall notes that the male adult, except for his function as sire in conception, actually plays no part in the offspring's development. "This exclusion of the male from responsibilities is perhaps one of the major differences between human and chimpanzee societies."[14]

It is always questionable when behaviors observed in nature are assumed to be "natural" to all species. By nature, the black widow spider kills her mate after copulation. A hungry male lion sometimes devours its young. Human societies have never, so far as history records, tolerated either such behavior. Some biological and social preconditions may have evoked responses among members of early human groups that shaped their evolution in such way as to establish behaviors that appear "native" to our species. Humans, like many kinds of birds and mammals, exhibit the "herd instinct," which combined with the phenomenon of infant helplessness and the female parent's need for protection, may have generated the occasion for establishing family units. This instinct is known to occur among swans and elephants that may be responding unconsciously to what Wilson calls *genetic determinism*. This, however, provides no warrant for assuming that humans who make conscious choices and plan for lifetime attachments are acting simply in response to blind determinism.

Many questions remain unanswered, and while we address some of them presently in more depth, it is useful at this point to consider the emergence of the monogamous, nuclear family arrangement. Historians have found the nuclear family to have existed as early as Hammurabi and his code (c. 1750 B.C.) when the marriage of a man and woman was required to be recorded in an official contract.[15] Saxon states, "The function of the nuclear family is so essential that it occurs in some form in all known societies. As the chief agency of socialization the family reproduces cultural patterns (and) profoundly shapes the child's character."[16]

Some have seen bigamy, polygamy, or some form of legal "harem acquisition" as natural and preferable alternatives to the nuclear family and certainly worthier of choice than adultery, which has been forbidden in every known culture. The Biblical King Solomon, for example, had many wives (perhaps several hundred) but was not rebuked for it because some kind of marital bond must have been established; none of his contacts was "extramarital." His father King David, on the other hand, was fully condemned for his extramarital affair with Bathsheba. Adultery always has an element of deceit and a tearing of the fabric of trust, not infrequently creating serious mental and spiritual disruption for the disregarded spouse. Bigamy (having two lawful spouses), polygyny (involving one husband with multiple wives), and polyandry (one wife with two or more husbands) purport to represent a spiritual commitment of mutual care and a heart-to-heart bond.

The Islamic tradition accepts polygamy but condemns adultery. Perhaps the severe psychological damage suffered by those with close ties to the adulterers invoked the condemnation in the Ten Commandments and in the annals of other faith traditions.

Ancient texts abound with references to monogamous marriage not only as the natural state for humankind but also intended to be so by a creator deity or (as in Buddhist and Confucian literature) as being simply the natural way of things. The Dammapada of Buddhism states, "The home should be a place of mutual love, of chastity and faithfulness,"[17] while Confucius noted, "The home, with its atmosphere of love and respect, should be the model for the entire world."[18]

The fact that many homes are not models "for the entire world" is reflected in the many laws and customs in virtually every nation governing matters of divorce, property ownership, and regulations about alimony and return of dowry. Even the way words are constructed reflect the domestic condition, whether tranquil or discordant. The Chinese pictographic word symbol for *peace,* for example, is a roof housing one wife:

The word for *chaos* is written with the symbol for the roof housing multiple wives:

Despite the ongoing debate about the prospects for the nuclear family to remain the standard (or even to survive), its antiquity is itself a strong support for its continuance. Every generation in every culture seems to go through stages of accepting the nuclear family, finding it too constraining and inimical to personal freedom, straying from it, rejecting it outright, and rediscovering its benefits in terms of enriching relationships, resolving conflicts that extramarital affairs created, learning the grace and discipline of forgiveness, and, finally, returning to defend it. Nena O'Neill, who with her husband George wrote *Open Marriage,* acclaimed in its time (1972) as the strongest of arguments for comarital sexual arrangements. It was finally concluded after five more years of research that the most stable marriages are based on couples' faithfulness to each other: "Infidelity is an extremely threatening situation."[19]

B. LIGHT FROM SIX MAJOR RELIGIONS, EAST AND WEST

A simple caveat is in order in this part of our study. It is important to remind ourselves that none of the major religious traditions has remained static from the time of their origin. "Early" Hinduism, as we note, differs from "later" Hinduism and even more from some modern forms of the religion. The same can be said for Buddhism and perhaps to a lesser degree Confucianism. It is not uncommon to find contemporary members of any given religion explaining, "We don't quite hold that position anymore." This represents a challenge that can create tensions and uneasiness but is part of the reward of open and honest discussion.

1. Eastern Traditions

Hinduism.   In about the middle of the second millennium B.C., as noted in the first chapter, a group of Indo-Europeans arrived in India bringing unique tribal customs that gave rise to new religious beliefs and social structure. These traditions came to be identified as early **Hinduism.** Here the family was central to the social life with the father (*pitar,* a word with the same root as the Latin pater) holding title to property and through whom descent was reckoned. The wife and mother (*matar,* as in the Latin *mater*) held authority over the domestic life, including the education of the children. By the end of the seventh century B.C., Aryan social organization prevailed with a grouping of clans that had a central council of chieftains called *rajahs,* and a distinct caste system emerged. Folktales, hymns, poetry, and rituals took shape comprising the Vedas, perhaps the most important and lasting being the Rig-Veda, an anthology of some thousand hymns in ten volumes that also give us a brief glimpse of family life in that era.[20] The principle *dharma,* or moral law for women, was to encourage large families, giving birth rights especially to sons. "The five traditional purposes of marriage in Hinduism include not only producing children, but also pleasure, companionship, sacrificial service and spiritual bliss."[21] The Code of Manu explicitly states that while she has rights, a "woman is never fit for independence" and her "husband must be constantly worshipped as a god by a faithful wife."[22]

This does not mean that a woman was devoid of honor despite being subordinate to her father, later to her husband, and then to her sons if their father died. In later Hinduism, the emergence of *the Upanishads* (sacred documents, meaning "discussions on ultimate wisdom,") clarified that "men of all classes and even women are dramatized as taking part in the discussions and ably as, if not sometimes more ably than the Brahmins (members of the highest caste) themselves."

Hinduism has always centered in the home. As Arvind Sharma reminds us,

> The deities were receptive primarily to the family, whose minimal definition included husband and wife. The presence of a wife was necessary for the presence of the gods, and a home was considered auspicious (*subha*) only with the presence of both.[23]

Hinduism has a rich and copious literature dating back more than three millennia, encompassing hymns and rituals as in the Rig-Veda, philosophical commentaries found in the Upanishads and legends collected, in the Bhagavad Gita and Mahabharata. Of special importance for our study is a collection of eighteen books, the Puranas, which form a kind of encyclopedia of the Hindu tradition. "Everything is to be found in them—theology, history, mythology, ethics, songs and high idealism."[24] It clearly states that the home is where the framework of faith, life, and work are to be nurtured and taught: "The parents of a child are but his enemies when they fail to educate him properly in his boyhood." (Note the stress on the male side of the family although indeed the mother was to share in the educative process for children of both sexes.) "Knowledge is the best treasure one can horde up in life . . . the holiest of the holies; shorn of it, one is but an animal."[25] In addition to emphasizing that the four major castes (and innumerable subcastes) were ordained by Vishnu, the first and highest of all were the Brahmana (priestly, intellectual, and noble). The second were the Kshatriya, the warriors, whose greatest duty was to protect and conserve the earth. Third were the Vaisyas, members of the merchant caste whose duties included feeding livestock, and maintaining agriculture in general along with commerce. The lowest caste was composed of the Sudra, the servants who attended to the needs of the upper three.

The home was the place where all duties and satisfactions of caste membership were reinforced. It provided the *ethos,* the distinguishing habit and attitudes that must nurture the ethical system of Hindu life, stressing everything from proper etiquette at mealtime to hospitality to strangers, to prohibition of cleaning one's teeth or blowing one's nose "without covering the mouth," and gambling. Above all, one should avoid becoming a slave to the quest for pleasure and strive to attain emancipation from the material world and attain the likeness of God.

> Final emancipation is in his grasp who is sinless towards them who commit mischief by him, who speaks amicably to them who use harsh words and whose soul melts with benevolence. The earth is upheld by the truthfulness of those who have controlled their passions . . . who are not sullied by desire, covetousness and anger.[26]

Buddhism.   As noted in Chapter One, *Buddhism* marked a departure from many of the customs and rules that had guided the Hindu population. It originated as a Hindu sect in the sixth century B.C., a fertile time for religion when Taoism, Confucianism, Zoroastrianism, and the establishment of the prophetic movement produced much of Hebrew scripture although each arose independently of the other. The beginning of Buddhism was as a kind of reformation rather than an outright repudiation of Hinduism. Siddhartha, a son of wealth, renounced all of his to-be-inherited riches and abandoned his wife and child to seek refuge from the vanities and what he perceived to be the corruption of the world through enlightenment and self-discipline. Siddhartha was to become the Buddha, "the enlightened one."

To address the question of the role of the family in promoting a moral foundation on which to build a global ethic, it would be misleading simply to point to the fact that the first Buddha abandoned his family to seek relief from the ills of the world. He had little positive to say about women in general, but as for their role in family life (marriage often being polygamous): "The relationships of women with their families were ones of marked subordination," and for those who are anxious to fulfill their duty, the husband, whether he is endowed with good qualities or not, is a visible God to them.[27]

The Buddha organized his converts into a monastic order, but only at the instigation of his disciples did he find a place for women in the community of faith as nuns. It would not be for several centuries (c . 350 A.D.) in China that monks were encouraged to marry "as a sign of their sharing the burdens of ordinary peoples."[28] Then, as with all familial relationships, the wife in the home became half the man, "better than his best friend, the root of Law, Profit, and Love. This is the reason why marriage is sought by man, where a husband finds a wife for now and eternity."[29]

While it is true that the Buddha departed from much of traditional Hinduism, there is no evidence that he repudiated the Puranas with their rich elaboration of the duties of families to inspire and educate. He did point out, however, that in the end, we should not become so attached to family members, household possessions, and so on that their loss would destroy our appreciation of the fact that "the living world, whether about us or within ourselves is constantly in flux." Nothing is fixed and permanent; we must accept that as true, the only reliable "fact."[30] Meanwhile, the most helpful environment the family can provide is one in which children are not conditioned to desire the things of this world, the loss of which produces pain and disillusionment. The key to ultimate contentment and satisfaction is in a compassionate embrace of the world as we find it. "Creative life is devoted entirely to transcending the individual self by continually reaching beyond the limits of space and time in pursuit of the universal self,"[31] yet the family remains the context in which the highest values are to be exemplified and taught and the creative life to be fostered so that the quest for identify with the universal self may be fulfilled.

Confucianism. This tradition affords a valuable insight into what is arguably the most powerful social and religious influence to emerge in China at about the time the Upanishads were being formulated in India.[32] *Confucianism* also provides insight into the role of Chinese cosmology in shaping both religious and political thought of the Chinese people. Furthermore, it serves as a corrective to the conclusion of eighteenth century British philosopher David Hume, who was powerfully influential in the writings of other historians, that "early man" was too much the "barbarous, necessitous animal" to have any interest in either religion or natural phenomena.[33] In point of fact, as modern paleontologists inform us, Peking Man (Synanthropus) employed "ritual treatment of the dead" many centuries before the era of Confucius. Such rituals occasionally could have included cannibalism "to acquire the good qualities and powers of the deceased."[34]

As early as 1000 B.C., before Confucius came on the scene, a fairly sophisticated cosmology was practiced; it involved the two primary "energy modes" of all things in existence: the *Yin* and *Yang*. The Yin involves female qualities: mysterious, secretive, dark, cold, wet, negative. The Yang is masculine in character: warm, dry, bright, procreative—in short, the positive qualities that counterbalance the Yin. All things in nature rely on these two, almost always in conjunction, to bring forth new creations. As might be anticipated, the roles of male and female are set by the qualities as noted: men are yang: positive, energetic, and "celestial." Women, on the other hand, are negative, passive, and earthy. Children cannot be born and families cannot be created without the interaction of the two genders. But the woman occupies a secondary role. Richard Guisso has summed the implications of the Yin qualities for the domestic life, which are quite explicit in the canonical texts of early Confucianism: "The female was inferior by nature, she was dark as the moon and changeable as water, jealous, narrow minded, insinuating. She was indiscreet, unintelligent, dominated by emotion. Her beauty was a snare for the unwary male, the ruination of states."[35]

To put this admittedly negative attitude in context, it will be helpful to mention the personal experience of Confucius and his drawing on the cosmic order of things to frame his teachings. He was born in the province of Shantung (c. 551 B.C.), the youngest child and apparently the only able-bodied son among ten siblings. When he was only three years old, his father died, leaving his widow in financial straits. Chinese society had already acknowledged a generally recognized statewide commitment to social justice and to governmental responsibility for the welfare of its citizens. This was based on the previously mentioned quasi-religious cosmology, with its triad of heaven, earth, and human orders. Confucius' great gift was to set forth these orders in written form, emphasizing that the human orders have their foundations in the family. "The call of the human community is not to worship Heaven and earth, but to learn from them, imitate their behavior, and thus form a human order modeled upon the cosmic order."[36]

Perhaps the most striking difference between the Confucian view of humankind's relation to the natural order of things was in the insistence that harmony rather than competition or conflict be its hallmark. Everything in life is relational; there was to be no abuse or exploitation of the natural order or personal relationships for reasons of pride or profit. Beginning in the home and moving outward to the community, everything should be done decently and with deference and "polite form." Thus, a peaceful, cooperative, and mutually supporting atmosphere will prevail.

The Yin aspect of womanhood within the family is given special attention. The woman was subject to "three obediences": her father, then to her husband, and then to her oldest son. When she is married, the wedding, although joyous, had its serious side in the fact that the bride (not the groom as in Jewish and Christian traditions) must "leave father and mother and cleave unto . . ." her husband and his family. The Confucian calling to the woman was "the wifely way" (*fu tao*), and, interestingly, the word symbol for "wife' in Chinese is a woman with a broom. Service to her husband, however, must go beyond deference and obedience; she has a responsibility for his moral character.[37] "Husbands are not always perfect in what they say and do, and need their wives to keep them on track, just as a good ruler needs a vigilant minister to keep him doing the good all the time."

In an interesting parallel to certain Western prejudices, pregnant women believed that the thoughts and experiences of an expectant mother influenced the character of the child she was carrying. She must therefore guard her attitudes and behavior. Even if the mother simply witnesses something frightening, the child could suffer disfigurement. The physical environment of the newborn was also considered of great importance so that, among the biographies of *exemplary women,* which all young ladies were encouraged to read, is the revelation that the wife of the outstanding philosopher Mencius persuaded him to move three times until they could find a home near a school where the atmosphere was suitable for their child's upbringing.

For all his emphasis on family life, we have almost no direct information about Confucius' own experience except that he was married at nineteen. No reference to his wife is found in any Confucian scriptures except for the fact that "Confucius reprimanded his son for mourning the death of his mother,"[38] yet in his teaching and writing, he frequently used the term *Hsiao,* which meant piety toward the spirits of ancestors, including parents, both living and dead. In translating the *Analects of Confucius,* Arthur Haley concluded that the growth of the concept's importance continued to increase until, by the end of third century B.C., "*Hsaio* became, at any rate in certain Confucian schools, the summit of all virtues."[39] It remains so to our own time.

2. Western Traditions

Judaism.   The Hebrew people (*habiru*) are presented as a nomadic family under the leadership of one Abram. Probably about 1800 B.C., they moved from a region we know as Babylonia near Ur of the Chaldees to the northern verge of the Arabian desert. They were in search of a place to occupy and call home. In time, the people came to be called *Jews,* their religion *Judaism,* and Abram's name lengthened to Abraham.

Family life was distinctly patriarchal in those formative years: as in the description of Jacob's family, women and children were often left out in the counting of family members. It is also to be noted, however, that when Hebrew scriptures were formulated, the role of marriage and family life was profoundly ontological, that is, scriptures acknowledged that from the beginning of the human race, the two sexes were created with the assurance that God created man in his own image . . . "male and female he created them." (Genesis 1:27) And God blessed them and said "Be fruitful and multiply." In the marriage union, the two shall "become one flesh." To be sure, one can argue that Jewish tradition differs from the Christianity that followed in that the "one flesh" expression did not mean an ontological identity that must never be severed on pain of sin. The rabbis allowed divorce for what today might be called "irreconcilable differences," yet despite the fact that divorce is not a "sin," it is nevertheless a cause for deep sadness, and, in fact, until very recently, divorce was was rare among Jews.

Compared to those in the Eastern religions, Hebrew scriptures may appear to have given little attention to family life. From the very beginning, however, we encounter Adam's family as a lesson in dysfunction with the bloody feud between Cain and Abel; Abraham's inner torment as he misperceived God's requirement for a blood sacrifice; Jacob's anguish over his sons' treatment of their brother Joseph and the overwhelming relief when he extends forgiveness and reconciliation to them; Jephthah's heart-wrenching vow before God and his daughter's gracious insistence that the vow be honored although it cost her life; and David's adultery with Bathsheba and his public humiliation and then his utter desolation over Absolom's death. These and many more stories are a veritable treasure for an exploration of the meaning of marriage and family life in the creation of Hebrew culture. Much that we find in the Eastern religions seem rather more hortatory than instructive in comparison.

Positive parallels can be found, however. The role of women in both Eastern and Western cultures during the period from 700 B.C. to the beginning of the Christian era, for example, was clearly one of submission to the authority of men. Though sometimes praised for their virtues, women were required to eat separately from the men and even to worship apart from them.

As for instruction about how to raise children, the often quoted injunction, "Spare the rod and spoil the child," is frequently misrepresented. The Revised Standard Version translation, "He who spares the rod hates his son," (Proverbs 13:24) is very probably the most abused passage of scripture. The word *rod* has several meanings in the Bible: a scepter of a king's authority to secure peaceful relations, a weapon used to protect sheep from predators, or as in the Twenty-third Psalm, a device for guiding the sheep safely along steep and rugged paths. It was never used as a stick for beating the sheep. The Twenty-third Psalm couples "thy rod" with "thy staff" as sources of protection and comfort. Whatever discipline may be involved, it is linked not with punishment but with coaching and guiding, literally *discipling.* With youth it was preparation for discipleship. In this sense, the passage from Proverbs provides a new level of insight; a father must truly hate the child whom he refuses to protect, comfort, and teach.

Hebrew scriptures contain several exhortations to education and the gaining of wisdom both inside and outside the family, but this belongs in the discussion in the next chapter. Meanwhile, it is instructive to note that references to "families" in Hebrew scripture often relate not to individual households but to the whole people of Israel. In Genesis 12:2–3, God proclaims, "I will make of you a great nation . . . and by you all the families of the earth will bless themselves." Psalm 133 proclaimed the brotherhood of Israel, "Behold how good and pleasant it is when brothers dwell in unity." Furthermore, note that parents have a number of duties in Jewish law including teaching their children Torah and a trade as well as how to swim. According to the Babylonian Talmud, the father is required to circumcise his son and to prepare him for marriage. Conversely, children have filial duties, which include honoring their parents and caring for them in times of illness, infirmity, or financial stress.

Human nature being what it is, these virtues were not always observed, and the prophet Amos reports God (Yahweh) as saying: "You only have I known of all the families of the earth," but because of the people's failure to heed God's commandments, adds, "Therefore I will punish you for all your iniquities." Their punishment, echoed by Isaiah and other prophets, was to be sent into exile in Babylon. After their long banishment from their homeland, they were forgiven and were restored and returned to "the land of Israel" (c. 538 B.C.).

The people relapsed from the ethical Yahwism they had previously known. After attempting reforms and placing major authority for a technocratic state in the hands of the priestly class, a long period of moral backsliding, warfare, restorations, more backsliding, and a return of disasters, invasions, and occupations followed. By 322 B.C., Alexander the Great had seized the Holy Land on his way to conquering Egypt and the land of Israel became Hellenized. Greek language and customs lured the people of Israel into Greek ways, and the ancient faith became increasingly compromised. Family life was a scene of tension as "the younger generation" was tempted to discard family traditions and loyalties. The last book of the Hebrew scripture concludes with the direst of warnings regarding the consequence: "Behold I will send you Elijah the prophet, and he will turn the hearts of the fathers to their children, and the hearts of children to their fathers, lest I come and smite the land with a curse." (Malachi 4:5f.)

Christianity. It is difficult to understand the emergence of *Christianity* apart from certain complex historical events, such as the Maccabean revolt (c. 165 B.C.) that turned a battle for Jewish national recognition into an all-out cultural conflict. It will be helpful here to review briefly these matters before directly addressing the immediate concern for family life in the early Christian communities and how that concern set the stage for what followed.

The king of Syria had demanded total absorption of Israel into his own realm and went so far as to prohibit observance of the Sabbath and made the possession of Hebrew scriptures punishable by death. One Judas Maccabeus led the battle against the king, recapturing Jerusalem and sending the Syrian army into retreat.

Jewish independence lasted until 63 B.C. when, in a tragic reversal, the Maccabean successors overreached themselves. The clerics had become the party in power, and the high priest without authority seized for civic as well as religious leadership.[41] He was, as John B. Noss expresses it, "in most respects archbishop, prime minister and foreign secretary all in one."[40] From the ranks of clerics there emerged the Pharisees, a powerful party to which most rabbis and scribes belonged and who advocated a rigorous obedience to traditional Jewish law, belief in the coming of a Messiah, and resurrection of the dead followed by a last judgment. A second group, the Sadducees, rejected what they regarded as rigidities of the Pharisees and won the support of the successors of the original Maccabean rulers. This triggered a violent conflict that resulted in a bloody massacre. The Roman general Pompey, who had previously been recalled from Spain to put down the revolt of the famous Spartacus, was invited to settle the growing dispute between the Pharisees and Sadducees that threatened to become a virtual civil war. He did so (c. 63 B.C.) and in the process took over the Holy Land as a Roman province.

Christianity was born into this chaotic atmosphere. Herod, and later his son, held ruthless but ultimately ineffective kingship only by permission of Rome. The Jewish high priest and other officials were likewise beholden to Herod.

This review is an admittedly overly compacted and perhaps tedious bit of history, but it informs the understanding of the world into which Jesus came: why Caesar Augustus wanted a census taken of the new Palestinian province, which brought Joseph and Mary from Nazareth to Bethlehem; the place of origin of Joseph's family; why Jesus was asked whether he was the Messiah predicted by Isaiah or the resurrected person of Elijah (predicted in Malachi 4:5–6); and a host of other points of interest.

The whole story of Jesus' life, teaching, popular support and rejection, crucifixion, and resurrection as well as the development of his church (which grew from a mere dozen disciples to nearly 2 billion followers today) is centered on the concept of family. This may seem a puzzling and even contrary statement because he never married or had a family of his own. The "Holy Family" theme has arisen because of the exceptional events surrounding Mary's pregnancy; the subsequent emphasis on the birth depicted in Nativity scenes, crèches, paintings, dramas, oratorios, and celebrations in almost every community in every nation. Each of these attests to the fact that family life played a central role in who Jesus was and how he is remembered.

Jewish families were proud to have a large number of children to nurture, and the family of Mary and Joseph grew after Jesus' birth, to include at least four brothers who are named in Mark 6:3 as well as an unspecified number of sisters. Doubtless Joseph and Mary heeded the injunctions of Genesis 1:28 ("Be Fruitful and multiply") and Proverbs 22:6 ("Train up a child in the way he should go, and when he is old he will not depart from it.") Boys were expected to undergo special education to prepare them for the *bar mitzvah* by their thirteenth birthday. This ceremony celebrated by the entire community included reading from scripture in the presence of the congregation, so literacy was mandatory.

Eager to fulfill all requirements of Jewish family life, Mary and Joseph presented the infant Jesus at the temple for circumcision on the eighth day and acknowledged the tradition that the first born son be dedicated to God. They were astonished at the prophesy of Simeon that in Jesus he had "seen God's salvation . . . a light for revelation to the gentiles, and glory to Thy people Israel." (Luke 2:25–32). The escape into Egypt to avoid Herod's murderous plot to kill the child, the return to Nazareth, and the subsequent return to the temple when Jesus was twelve were all accompanied by Mary. We hear no more of Joseph after Jesus began his mission, but Mary was on hand on the occasion of his first miracle at Cana and was at the foot of the cross when Jesus urged that she and "the beloved disciple" (perhaps John) be as mother and son from then on. Her very presence at the crucifixion attests to the powerful family bond Jesus shared and to her great courage. He was, after all, being executed as an enemy of the state. Our last glimpse of Mary is in the company of Jesus' disciples taking part in a prayer meeting after the resurrection and ascension. (Acts 1:14)

In many religions and cultural traditions, women and children are almost ancillary. As noted, they were often not even counted when a family was described. The gospels tell of the time when the disciples' irritation by the presence of children while Jesus was teaching caused him to interrupt their complaint with, "Let the children come to me . . . for to such belongs the kingdom of heaven." The mention of this in all three "synoptic" gospels (Matthew, Mark, and Luke) illuminates the importance of this statement. On another occasion, he declared that unless we can receive the Kingdom as little children, in all their innocence and capacity for love, we will never enter it. (Matthew 18; 1–4) This declaration introduces a new motif that the family and the home are all revealed as the context for faith and life. It is fascinating to note how so many of the early churches established by Paul and the others were identified: "Greet the church that is in thy house." (I Corinthians 16:19) No fewer than seventeen times were the apostles' letters addressed to women in those churches, a dramatic departure from the denigration of women in so many other religions. In her book *Family: A Christian Social Perspective,* Lisa Cahill refers to the family as a "little Church," tying together the concept of the identity of individual Christian and families "in Christ" and their several roles of mutual service and service to the world's needs. Congregations comprised the "body of Christ" at work in the world.[42] As enablers of change, the earliest Christian families set the example. The famous remark of the astonished Roman Tertullian, "See how these Christians love each other," reflected the realization that for Christians love was not merely a sentiment but the determining principle of their ethics. The very practical nature of this love attracted Romans to abandon the age-old practice of selling girls to the husbands by parental arrangement and of infanticide when unwanted babies were abandoned to wolves and other predators outside the cities or buried alive. Sexual experience was to be limited to marriage; in Christ, women were equal to men, concubinage and prostitution were to be abolished, and divorce was to be limited to grounds of unchastity.

After discussing some criticisms leveled at the identification of the Christian family as a metaphor for the church down through centuries, Lisa Cahill refers to the Puritan tradition: "The genius of the Puritans (was) to see that society can be transformed, that civil institutions at the grass roots can be enlisted as agents of change, and that cultural symbols, especially religious symbols and narratives, are necessary enablers of change."[43] In time, mercy hospitals and countless service organizations would be created to meet the needs of the poor and the helpless, giving rise to today's Salvation Army, Red Cross, Goodwill, Masons, Rotary and Lions clubs, Boy Scouts and Girl Scouts, Church World Service, and so on. It was the prayer of all Christians that one day faith, hope, and love would characterize all homes, families, communities, and nations and thus establish the foundations for a global ethics.

Islam. It could be argued that no religion in human history other than *Islam,* has had such a dramatic effect on the institutions of marriage and family life in so brief a time after its founding and with such widespread international impact.

It is instructive to remember that when Muhammad was born into a leading tribe in Mecca (c. 570), social conditions in Arabia were chaotic and violent:

> People felt almost no obligation to anyone outside their tribes. Scarcity of material good made brigandage a regional institution. Drunken orgies were commonplace, the gaming impulse uncontrolled. The prevailing religion . . . an animistic polytheism . . . peopled the sandy wastes with beastly sprites called *jinn* or demons. They inspired neither exalted sentiments nor moral restraint. A smoldering undercurrent erupted in sudden affrays and blood feuds, some of which extended for half a century. The times called for a deliverer.[44]

Philosophers and psychologists have argued as to just what impulse calls forth a Buddha, a Lao Tse or Confucius, a Jesus, or a Muhammad to buck the times and arouse diffident populations to transform whole cultures often against enormous opposition and threat of death. However this debate is resolved, these leaders have changed their worlds. In Muhammad's case, his followers within a single century became rulers of an empire that reached from Spain to China and was more powerful than Rome dreamed of becoming. As Huston Smith reminds us, however, Islam began not with Muhammad in sixth century Arabia but with *Allah* in the minds and hearts of its adherents. The expression Allah means *the God* (i.e., the one and only God). Muhammad would take no credit for any great insight as his own. Only God could have initiated the writing of the Qur'an and brought about such consequences. Indeed, it had always been admitted that Muhammed was himself illiterate and so spoke the words to a scribe as God spoke directly to him. He was so determined that he himself should not become an object of worship that neither the place of his birth or burial was ever to become a shrine. That would be idolatry, which he abhorred.

What we know of Muhammad's attitude toward family life and what he did to influence it must be drawn from the Qur'an, Muhammad's teachings, and recollections preserved by his successor, Abu Bekr. Muhammad's childhood was marked by the tragedy of a succession of deaths; of his father before he was born, his mother when he was six, and his grandfather who cared for him after his mother's death but only for two years until he too died. Happily, Muhammad had an uncle, a caring guardian for whom the boy worked as a shepherd. This pastoral life was an insubstantial fence between himself and the lawlessness and cynicism of his contemporaries whose excesses in every form sickened him. At the age of twenty-five, he was introduced to the caravan business and enlisted in the service of a wealthy widow, Khadija. Impressed by his maturity of judgment and sheer honesty, she, who was fifteen years older than he, eventually fell in love with him. He reciprocated this love and their marriage was more than a happy one. Tradition has it that through the stressfilled ensuing years announcing his new faith, she stood by him even when it seemed his mission must fail and "God comforted him through her."[45]

In sharp contrast with the scriptures of some other religions that relegate women to the status of subservience to and total dependence on their husbands, the Holy Qur'an states clearly that men should "reverence the wombs that bore you" and by extrapolation reverence all women whose wombs would bear the coming generations. (S. iv, I). Men are forbidden to "inherit" women against their will, but if marriage should ensue, "live with them on a footing of kindness and equity." (S. iv, 19). Detailed instructions are provided concerning whom one may or may not marry, including women their fathers had married: (S. iv, 22); "Your mothers, daughters, foster-mothers (who gave you suck), foster sisters; your wives' mothers; your step daughters . . . ." (S.iv. 23). Again in contrast to some other cultures, all children, male and female alike are to be welcomed into the family. "To God belongs the dominion. He creates what He wills. He bestows (children) male or female according to His Will."[46] (S. xlii.49)

C. CHANGING FAMILIES, CHANGING MORES

Some historians have suggested that in the ancient world, "the family existed in reality but not in concept." That is, procreation took place and family "members" lived together for mutual protection, but there was no philosophical framework for establishing clear patterns of moral or ethical behavior.[47] Others disagree, noting that "ancient" is too vague a term to provide a workable frame of reference. In fact, family life in Egypt centuries before the Christian era was cohesive, and the roles of its members well defined.[48] Indeed, cultural anthropologists remind us that Neanderthal society 100,000 years ago had established family identities. As noted, family grave sites in which bodies were almost always in east-west orientation are evident, indicating that the burials were not haphazard. Frequently, flowers were added, indicating a relationship of affection and perhaps even reverence.[49]

Nevertheless, it can hardly be refuted that as generations became centuries and then millennia, family relationships changed in accordance with the needs of the communities in which they interacted. It is worth recalling that in the Hindu culture where women were regarded as coauthors with men of the sacred Upanishads,[50] the family as a sacred creation was affirmed. The Vedic literature (c. 1,500 B.C.) reflects the complementarity between husband and wife, and the Rig-Veda makes explicit that the presence of the wife is essential to the presence of the gods in the home.[51] About that same time, Hebrew scriptures reveal a very different relationship of wives to their husbands. Among Israelites, the word for family, *bayit,* included wives, concubines, children, and servants, all presided over by the patriarch. The authority of the father extended to killing wives and children "without mercy" if they sought to influence adversely his loyalty to the faith. (Deuteronomy 13: 6–10).

Nevertheless, both Hebrew and early Christian writers regarded marriage and family life to be part of the God-ordained nature of things, and nothing in the scriptures of either tradition supports the practice of marginalizing women or treating them as a subservient. Even the oft-quoted line in Paul's letter to Titus about women being "submissive" to their husbands (2:5) should be put in the context of a well-managed home. The word for *submitting* is translated from the Greek word *upotassomenas,* which is better interpreted as '*assisting.*' Jesus made a special point of stressing the unity of husband and wife as of God's ordaining: "He who made them from the beginning made them male and female . . . and the two shall become one." (Matthew 19:4–5). The bond is ontological, but this was historically obscured with the rise of an all-male priesthood eager to use sacred texts to bolster its power.[52] This may account for the gradual marginalizing of women in many of the world's leading religious and political systems.

Perhaps the most striking of contrasts in the changing of family mores is in the attitude toward premarital sex. In early Hebrew history, if a man had intercourse with a virgin, the expected outcome was marriage to the girl and payment of a fine to her father. (Deuteronomy 22: 28) If, however, he engaged in the sex act with a virgin already betrothed to another man, he would be stoned to death because betrothal was tantamount to marriage, and his affront was the same as having violated his neighbor's wife. Consensual sex outside of marriage or betrothal was forbidden on pain of death by stoning. This so-called Mediterranean legacy still applies in some countries; as recently as the fall of 2003, a young woman in Saudi Arabia was condemned to death for giving birth to a child without having been married.[53]

In stark contrast to the Mediterranean legacy is another, the Nordic legacy.[54] As the name suggests, it began centuries ago in Scandinavia where there has been less emphasis on marriage as the exclusive passport to sexual freedom. There betrothal represents the real commitment of the man and woman to each other, and their sociosexual interaction is thereby legitimized. Furthermore, "it is the young women, not their parents, who decide whether to invite the young men" to share their favors. Indeed, in today's Holland, in the town of Staphorst, a woman cannot be married in the Reformed Association Church unless she is already pregnant.[55]

Infanticide was not uncommon in many parts of the Roman world for economic reasons; male domination rendered girls virtually useless outside of marriage, so baby girls were considered an unnecessary burden. The adult male–female ratio in such societies was as high as 4:1.[56] In contrast, Jesus urged that all children be loved and cherished, "for to such belongs the Kingdom of Heaven." (Matthew 19:14) The Christians, once set free from Roman persecution by order of Constantine (315 A.D.), managed to persuade the Roman government to abolish infanticide throughout the empire in 374 A.D.

In the Medieval world, when the majority of European families lived in cramped, walled cities with multiple families often competing for limited resources, there was little opportunity to develop anything like the modern nuclear family with a father, mother, and children in a single unit. In many situations, however, the extended family evolved something similar to a nuclear center with additional relatives and perhaps in-laws. This made raising the children more complex but also potentially more rewarding.[57] "In some communities, entire villages functioned as a family in establishing and enforcing moral codes, protecting orphans, and distributing wealth."[58]

Between the Middle Ages and the Reformation, an era of religious wars and unstable economic conditions, people in lower income levels had little time for developing close, warm relationships within families.

The mortality rate among children was high, as much as 50 percent. The surviving children were expected to work alongside their parents in the home and the shop or out in the field, whichever the man of the house decided.

When mining and manufacturing industries developed into the Industrial Revolution, children as young as six and seven were put to work in mine tunnels, mills, and sweat shops, as the novels of Charles Dickens, Victor Hugo, and others illustrate. Economic class structures, clearly apparent in Medieval and Renaissance communities, evolved during this period into new social configurations. The influence of religion was still fairly strong in the child raising of middle and upper social classes; church attendance and daily prayers were "givens." Illiteracy was high among the lower, middle, and impoverished classes, however, and teaching the rituals in Latin, not the vernacular, made religious training foreign to most people. It is important to recall that centuries before the Christian era, however, the Hebrews emphasis on learning had been prominent, and provided a powerful cohesion for both individuals and family groups, which set a pattern for Christians later. "Wisdom is the principal thing: with all your getting, get knowledge" was the admonition of Proverbs 4:7. The Christian and to some extent the Muslim world would in time be shaped by this distinctive insistence on learning.

From Augustine to Muhammed, Maimondes, Luther, Calvin, and on through their active followers came innumerable written guidelines for Jewish, Christian and Muslim families. Indeed, the Holy Qur'an reveals that Muhammed was keenly aware of both Jewish and Christian teachings and practice. (See, for example, Sura ii. 122–137; iv. 153). Lisa Cahill makes the case that in early Christianity, homes and families became virtual churches in many communities. Her observation, addressed to the Christian part of the triangle of faiths, is that "identification of the Christian family with the church is one way of transforming important formative institutions of civil society-family, to educate for Christian values and practices"[59] Jews and Muslims will find this true in their own institutional histories.

As family structures change with the evolving social, political, and economic realities, so do the mores. Today,

> there is no town so small that it does not have a "wrong side of the tracks" and a "right part of town." In rural areas some farmsteads are "nice," others are "slummy." People clique together. The banker's daughter is more likely to marry the lawyer's son than the telephone lineman's boy.[60] Probably nothing better illustrates the changing of mores than comparing early Christianity's moral stance, especially with regard to property ownership with twenty-first century Christian practice. It was, for example considered immoral to be preoccupied with gaining wealth in first-century Christian homes while the needs of the poor went neglected. Thus, it was a test of one's faithfulness to Christ; to meet the

needs of the homeless, the sick, and the imprisoned (Matthew 25:31–46). Giving up property and all personal wealth (which otherwise might have been inherited by one's children) to meet the needs of the community at large was mandatory. All personal and family possessions were to be given to the apostles for equal distribution. This was literally communistic, in which all possessions were held in common. (Acts 4:32–5:6).

This holds special importance for contemporary life. We have witnessed a marked change in the United States in the past several generations, as especially prominent among religious fundamentalists in their condemnation of anything resembling such social "liberalism," as Acts 4:34–35 explicitly requires. A newspaper editorial by a Harvard University law professor insists that Americans find greed and hording one's property quite acceptable. "Coveting is as American as apple pie. Our entire market system encourages us to covet our neighbor's wealth."[61] Such values are not taught formally in classrooms but informally within the family and reinforced in the surrounding society.

Conflicts across religious lines provide another example of changing mores. Religious wars, to be sure, are by no means as strident and lethal in most parts of today's world as they were, for example, during the medieval Crusades. Conflicts across religious identities (Jewish vs. Christian vs. Muslim) now are often no more acrimonious than conflicts within those traditions (e.g., Catholic vs. protestant; Orthodox Judaism vs. Reformed Judaism; Shiite vs. Sunni Islam). These conflicts occur most often over social, racial, cultural, and political traditions rather than purely religious ones. A graphic illustration is the insistence on female circumcision by some Islamic tribal groups that other Muslims condem because there is no support for the practice in the Qur'an. The ritual has been absorbed from some pre-Islamic cultures, especially in Africa, and carried down many centuries.

As families from these various traditions move about, migrating into regions where there are rigidly held biases and patterns of behavior, the consequences can be heartwrenching. When a family collectively feels it has been disgraced by a member who has, for example, become pregnant out of wedlock or "left the faith" for some other set of affiliations, the penalty for the person may be death at the hands of family members.

In light of altered relationships within or between families, changes, often severe, occur in the mores that characterize these relationships and the instruction passed along to the oncoming generation. Meanwhile, every couple who plans to marry must make crucial family-related decisions.

D. PARENTING ISSUES: TO BE OR NOT TO BE

Decisions concerning pregnancy, childbearing, nurturing, and the education of children are far more complex than many young couples anticipate. Newlyweds are left to ponder whether to become parents at all: "Are we prepared to deal with the economic, educational, recreational, religious, protective and affectional needs of children?"[62] To be sure, industry is seldom found in the home as in crofters' or peasant farmers' homes historically, so the economic support has been shifted from parents and children sharing the burden to parental employment outside the home. Education, too, has been largely transferred from homes to schools. Recreation has become commercialized, as any soccer mom or little league dad can testify. Religious instruction is seldom a regular part of family life, but is under the supervision of church and Sunday or Sabbath school if it occurs. Even mealtime and bedtime prayers, if observed at all, are usually memorized phrases. As for protection, most homes are equipped with locks and many with alarm systems, and cautions are expressed about staying out of trouble. Much of the protection of children—indeed, of the family as a whole—is left to outside professional law enforcement and department fire fighters. Finally, with an inordinate amount of time being spent outside the home and much of family time being taken by television watching, children's needs for affection get short shrift and are sought in social and sexual encounters at earlier and earlier ages.

Given these challenges, it is perhaps not surprising that sociologists and family therapists have increasingly expressed alarm about our social instability, "dysfunctional" family life, and countless young couples who are deciding not to become parents at all.

1. The Sex–Gender Tug of War: Religious Perspectives

There has been a long-standing dispute as to the appropriate designation of the terms *sex* and *gender,* revealing as much as anything the persistent issue of dominance between men and women. In Western traditions, God has been referred to as "he" and "him" until very recently. It is also the case that *gender* has simply designated the masculinity or femininity of the person in question. *Sex* has been a more proactive term, referring to the phenomenon of reproduction or, more commonly, the expression of sexual desire. A husband or wife does not ask "would you like to have gender?" instead of "sexual intercourse." The terms are still confused in popular and even professional parlance, suggesting that the tug of war continues for purposes of dominance. We now attend to how this contest has played out historically, drawing on the major Eastern and Western traditions to which we have already given special attention.

Perspective of Hinduism. Recalling the Hindu Code of Manu, which explicitly states that "a husband must be constantly worshipped as a god by a faithful wife," it seems clear that the temptation to exploit the wife sexually has long been present. The art of India is notorious for its phallic symbolism. Sculptures of the penis to be anointed with oil by worshippers and graphic depictions of intercourse keep sexuality uppermost in the consciousness of both men and women. Knowing this, the wife can only rebel, risking punishment and possible banishment or submissively accept her husband's advances however rough, risking the likelihood of pregnancy again and again. Thus, it seems that religion's rules often set up households for a tug of war.

It is surely obvious, however, that this is not inevitable, first because Hinduism is not limited by the Code of Manu countless adherents to Hinduism are influenced by the Upanishads and other sacred writings advocating greater self-determination for women. Second, other religions emerge, offering alternatives as did Buddhism, attracting great numbers to hold women on a parity with men.

Perspective of Buddhism. While *Buddhism* never supplanted Hinduism and eventually moved to China and Japan where it has enjoyed enormous popularity, the influence of Buddhism in India was not totally eclipsed by Hindusim. Other movements within Hinduism did provide for increasing parity between men and women. The Bhagavad Gita encourages increased autonomy for women, and the Tantric literature emphasizes the female principle of the universe represented in Kali, the wife of the god Shiva. Hinduism's caste system, which tended to solidify the dependant role of women, underwent scrutiny and disparagement during British occupation of India in the nineteenth and twentieth centuries. Caste was a major target of Muhatma Ghandi, whose prominence in India was largely responsible for outlawing discrimination against women in its 1947 Consititution. However, the tensions continue at all levels of Hindu society.[63]

While proclaiming in principle the equality of women with men, Gautama Buddha did little about making the idea operational until a group of his students virtually forced him to. Among them was a woman, called Maha-Pajapati, the Gotamid, who approached Gautama Buddha and said, "Pray, Reverend Sir, let women retire from household life to the houseless one, under the Doctrine and Discipline you announced." After some discussion, it was agreed that if a woman accepted "certain weighty regulations" set forth by the Buddha (among them that she must not reprove priests officially lest she herself might be reproved), then "let it be reckoned to her as ordination" as a priestess."[64]

Perspective of Confucianism's Reign. *Confucius* had little interest in equality for women or the problem of sexual conflicts in marriage and the family. His focus was on tradition and stability, and inasmuch as he could identify the "Five Constant Relationships" (between parent and child, husband and wife, elder sibling and junior sibling, elder friend and junior friend, and ruler and subject), he felt honor bound to preserve them.

> Confucius was all but obsessed with tradition, for he saw it as the chief shaper of inclinations and attitudes. He loved tradition because he saw it as a potential conduit—one that could funnel into the present behavior patterns that had been perfected during a golden age in China's past.[65]

The subservient role of women was a part of that golden age, and Confucius simply was not interested in altering it. It should not be concluded from this, however, that the role of a woman was the kind of subservience implied in Hindu custom. Indeed, by the Han dynasty in China (206 B.C.E.–220 C.E.), women were writing popular treatises on the appropriate interpretation of those "Five Constant Relationships." Among the most influential was *Instructions for Women* (Nu-chieh). (116 C.E.) by Pan Chao, a highly educated woman. In it she emphasized that "To obtain the love of one man is the crown of a woman's life," but to obtain this, Pan Chao stressed that one must not stoop to flattery and "cheap" methods. "The relationship must go beyond obedience and deference, and the woman must be responsible for the man's moral character. She guides his understanding that they owe each other mutual respect and warns him of the danger of too much familiarity, which can lead to lust and loss of respect. In this fashion she may avoid the "tug of war" that prevails in too many households.[66]

The Perspective of Judaism.   The inequality of women in respect to men in historic *Judaism* is suggested in the beginning of Genesis (1:27), when God created both sexes "in his own image," a unifying phenomenon. Yet it is the woman who sinned first by tempting Adam to eat of the fruit of the forbidden tree. Jacob Neusner offers an explanation for early Hebrew denigration of women by pointing to God's establishment of marriage between himself and man being the "active principles" while the woman, like earth, was a passive principle. Masculinity was the "normal" form of humanity; femininity was a deviation. The Mishnah, a digest of laws created by some rabbis who took over the care of the scattered Jews after the Diaspora (70 C.E.), excluded women from the centers of holiness. They could not even participate in sacred liturgy.[67] Where marriage was concerned, they had few "rights" regarding sexual activity but were to comply with object of men's needs as (for carrying forth the family line) and desires. However, the rabbis and the Torah (Exodus 21:10) made it clear that if a husband failed to satisfy his wife's sexual needs, she could take him to court, offering the option of divorce.

The inequality of Hebrew women in respect to men is strongly suggested by the fact that while prostitution was tolerated and a man's committing adultery with a prostitute was usually not punished, a married woman's act of adultery was punishable by death. On the other hand, Deuteronomy 22:22 imposes the death penalty on both men and women if they are apprehended in adultery.

If a wife failed to perform her duties to her husband's satisfaction, even including the "scandal" of appearing in public without a head scarf, he could easily divorce her. A woman's right to divorce was severely limited, however, and grounds could not even include the man's desertion, although one reason for which she might be successful was his refusal to have sexual relations "for it is her right."

Modern Judaism has moved light years away from many of the inequities suffered by Jewish women in ancient times. Changes to make women equal in all areas of faith and Jewish practice were brought about over the centuries by the medieval scholar Maimonides and movements such as Kabbalism, eighteenth-century Hasidism and nineteenth-century Reform Judaism, which emerged in 1846. Judaism, both Conservative and Orthodox, appears to be moving more slowly in these directions, and the battle of the sexes appears to be fading.

The Perspective of Christianity.   Central to *Christianity's* message to the world is "For as many of you as were baptized into Christ . . . there is neither male nor female, for you are all one in Christ Jesus." (Galatians 3:27–28)

The inclusiveness of the early church is perhaps its most characteristic hallmark and is especially clear in breaking down barriers between the sexes. The Gospels make clear that God's intention for the Christ to be born was first announced to Mary, not to the (male) leaders of the synagogue or to her father or even to her betrothed, Joseph. Among Jesus' closest friends were Martha and "the other" Mary; his miracles were not initially to the (male) pious elite, the priests and Pharisees, but to the poor and socially outcast and to foreigners who would not have been welcomed by most

Jews of the time. His self-disclosure became particularly dramatic "when it occurred to a woman with a flow of blood, a widow, a Samaritan woman." As women of these despised groups, they formed the bottom of the existing hierarchy of religious privilege." It is precisely these outcasts who are to be "first in the Kingdom of God."[68] As noted earlier, many of Paul's pastoral letters were addressed to women who were leaders in the earliest home churches.

How did it come about, then, that the New Testament has so often been portrayed as a male-dominated apology for a patriarchal Christianity? The answer appears to be twofold. First, Paul had been a member of the Pharisees who were vigorously engaged in persecuting the Christians and brought some of the baggage of his old orientation with him into his early work as an apostle. Thus, "The women should keep silence in the churches, for they are not permitted to speak, but should be subordinate" (I Corinthians 14:34). and "Train the young women to love their husbands and children to be sensible, chaste, domestic, kind, and submissive to their husbands." (Titus 2:4)

Such instruction would seem to be more at home in the Judaism that Paul eventually felt he had outgrown as he saw how immensely creative and helpful the women were in the churches. As to women being subservient with regard to their husband's sexual advances, Paul recognized the value of an active sex life for both partners and urged both: "Do not refuse one another except perhaps by agreement for a season, that you may devote yourselves to prayer. But then come together again, lest Satan tempt you through lack of self-control. (I Corinthians 7:5).

The second reason for the shift to a patriarchal Christianity is in the all too familiar reach for dominance and power on the part of the male apostles. Their creation of a hierarchical priest class drew on the spurious claims of Biblically supported feminine subservience. Many of the efforts at early reform sought to redress such practices: in second century, the Montanists, who sought to establish the rights of two women converts; Pricilla and Maximilia, to claim prophetic authority; the Culdees of Scotland in the ninth century; and the Waldensians in the thirteenth century. Then, of course, the integrative work of the Hussites, Martin Luther, John Calvin, and a rising host of reformers who made the Reformation one of "the hinge[s] of history" in no small measure by acknowledging the rightful leadership role of women in the church.[69] A major legacy has been a host of women who have in their own way molded a whole civilization: Helena (255–330), mother of Constantine who influenced the Christian transformation of the Roman Empire; Marcella (c. 325–410), founder of the first religious community for women in the Western church; Monica (331–387), mother of St. Augustine; Joan of Arc (1412–1431); and Vittoria Colonna, inspirer of Michelangelo as well as Clara Swain (1834–1910), the first medical missionary to the women and children of India. Literally hundreds of other women have made profound changes in history through the faith tradition that granted them equality and fraternal partnership with men.[70]

The Perspective of *Islam* has more to say than most of the other major religious traditions, and in graphic terms, about the rights and roles of women as related to their sexuality. After cautioning against marrying "unbelieving women," (Sii 221) the Qur'an goes directly to the question of what a woman's "courses" (menstrual period) mean in relation to sexual intimacy:

> They ask thee
> Concerning women' courses.
> Say: They are
> A hurt and a pollution.
> So keep away from women
> In their courses, and do not
> Approach them until
> They are clean.
> But when they have
> Purified themselves,
> Ye may approach them.
> In any manner, time or place
> Ordained for you by God."
> (S ii. 222)

Note that there is no suggestion here that the woman has any voice in the matter of being required to comply, but the man in question may require sexual favors "in any manner, time or place." presumably "ordained by God." The next paragraph (or Sura) begins by assuring the man "Your wives are as a tilth to you" (a piece of cultivated field ready to be fertilized). The wife then would appear to be viewed as her husband's property, and the Qur'an repeats: "So approach your tilth when or how ye will." Nevertheless, the Qur'an used the word *tilth* as a metaphor to indicate care and loyalty, not simply property or ownership. It is a misrepresentation to take the injunction as a husband's right to approach his wife sexually without her consent. He is instructed:

> do some good act
> For your souls beforehand;
> And fear God,
> And know that ye are
> To meet Him (in the hereafter). (S ii. 223)

Sexual intercourse, then, should not be demanded callously. Every act will be accounted for in God's judgment,

> For God is One
> Who heareth and knoweth
> All things. (S ii. 224)

Furthermore, if a wife's behavior is objectionable to the husband so that he decides to divorce her,

> If their intention
> Is firm for divorce,
> God heareth
> And knoweth all things. (S ii. 227)

The husband may relent and decide to take her back, especially if she is pregnant. Women may not "hide what God has created in their wombs," but the husband is strictly advised:

> . . . do not take them back
> To injure them, (or) to take
> Undue advantage. (S ii. 227)

Yet the Qur'an acknowledges that inequities will undoubtedly be displayed and that

> Men have a degree
> Of advantage over them. (S ii. 228)

The passages in the Qur'an dealing with marriage and the rights of men and women represent a major achievement over the coarse behavior in so many cultural and religious settings. The "sexual tug of war' continues, it seems, unabated.

2. Children and Youth: Preparation for Life

Most marriage counselors, whether trained primarily in psychology or sociology, would probably agree with Thomas Lickona's address to parents:

> You want them to be fair and honest and trustworthy.
> You want them to respect the rights of others. You want them to
> respect legitimate authority, rules and laws.
> You want them to be responsible for their own behavior.
> You want them to feel a decent measure of concern for their fellow
> human beings.
> You want them to be able to stand on their own feet and resist
> pressure to go with the crowd.
> You want them to be capable of generosity and love.
> Of all the tasks of parenting, none is as important, or as difficult, as
> raising good children.

To this list, Lickona is quick, however, to add a most important caution: "We may also want our children to be smart . . . good at sports, artistically talented. But they are no less persons, no less human if they do not possess (these) qualities."[71]

In his sociocultural theory of development, Russian psychologist Lev Vygotsky takes special note of an often overlooked condition: "The development of individuals occurs during the early formative years and has a specifically historical character, content, and form; in other words development will be different depending on when and where you grow up."[72]

This statement seems at first to be self-evident. Consider a child born in poverty without toys or books and even without a bed of his or her own, who has known little but physical and emotional abuse from one parent while being ignored by the other, and who attended a substandard public school before joining a street gang. He or she will develop with a quite different set of values from one raised as an only child in a loving, highly educated, professional family in an extremely affluent area. When an argument concerning the youth's background is raised in the court trial of a youth offender, however, the rejoinder of the prosecutor and sometimes even the judge is often that we are getting "soft" on crime or "making excuses for criminal behavior."

The correlation in the moral development of children and youth between those living in poverty and those with comfortable to affluent families has been studied by a growing army of researchers in recent years. Among other features studied has been the rise in numbers unwed mothers. "Single adolescent mothers constitute 30 percent of all single mothers. It is a phenomenon that has no counterpart in terms of magnitude anywhere else in the major countries of the Western world."[73] Most are unprepared for the multiple tasks of motherhood, contrary to the sentimental popular view that mothers, in general, are "by nature" ideal caregivers. "If mothers were by nature the best caregivers, why would an army of social workers be needed to watch over those hundreds of thousands of children abused or neglected?"[74]

Even when married, young couples face problems of being increasingly unable to cope with the needs of a young family. In 1994, the government estimate for the "threshold" or cutoff point before a family of four reached poverty was $15,000, but a Roper Survey in 1995 revealed that a U.S. family of four needed $25,000, or $10,000 more than the government had established. But the government's "poverty line' was actually based on 1950 needs! That was when housing was far less costly and life in general was less expensive.[75] Add to this situation the "comfortably" low unemployment rate in 1990 (about 4 percent) but by 1993 had risen to 7 percent over all. Between 1990 and 2004, 2 million jobs were lost, and unemployment for black males rose to 14 percent. Exacerbating this financial dilemma has been the fact that the United States is the only Western country that does not provide universal health care.[76] Given these conditions, it is clear that poverty has costly results for society in poorer health care, ineffective child-raising practices, the dread of homelessness, increased divorce rate, parental alcoholism, and on rare but tragic occasions incest and increased risk for sexual victimization[77] and teen suicide.

Teen suicide is one of the most devastating experiences a family can endure but is tragically familiar in a home in which an unwed pregnant teen, especially one living in a "culture of poverty" (for example, in some government housing project where family frictions and violence are the daily condition), succumbs to utter despair. "Some appreciation of the tragic circumstances is indicated by the high rate of suicide (among teen age single parents)—a rate that is ten times that of the general population"[78]

Following Vygotsky's perception that the development of children will be different depending on where and when they grow up, we must then ask what the optimal conditions for a healthy, morally sensitive childhood and youth are. Most of the theorists who have developed scenarios to depict how children make moral choices have given detailed and helpful guidelines.

Sigmund Freud, for example, published that all children go through four basic stages: Oral, Anal, Phallic, and Latency. Between birth and 18 months, children are self-centered (biologically, for self-preservation), demanding, and easily traumatized. Freud insisted that many adult misbehaviors stem from the child's *oral* behaviors for coping, (e.g., the frustrated need for breast feeding can lead to smoking, problems with alcohol, nail biting, and talking too much). Between eighteen months and about three years of age, the child's need for toilet training leads to forms of rebellion that root in the *anal* stage. Explosive angers, preoccupation with rules, compulsive neatness and miserly "retention" of money echo enforced cleanliness during childhood. The *phallic* stage is characterized by preoccupation with sexual pleasure seeking via masturbation (for which she or he is punished, and thus left with conflicted feelings of frustration and hostility toward parents whom she or he must also love). During the *latency* stage (age six to puberty), the child is a participant in formal schooling and takes a detour developing academic sporting and social skills. A time of sexual reawakening occurs during puberty (*genital* stage), and the person is en route to a mature life. Successful resolution of these conflicted stages is necessary for maturation to adulthood.

A number of other theorists including Erik Erikson, Jean Piaget, and Lawrence Kohlberg offered alternatives to Freud's presentation. Erikson exended the psycho-analytic model but developed it into eight stages, and where Freud had little to say about development beyond the teen years, Erikson encompassed the whole life span. His *stage 1* revealed general trust in caretakers and the environment as well as the potential for distrust as the surroundings were often threatening. The trust versus mistrust theme might well color all the rest of the stages through old age and pro-duce an optimistic or pessimistic personality. Much of the remaining seven stages was devoted to approaching and completing adulthood and showing a polarity between integration of selfhood versus despair in the face of mortality.

Piaget was primarily concerned with continual interaction between the child and the environment and wrote of a *sensorimotor stage* (birth to two years); a *pre-operational stage* (capacity to employ symbols, mathematics, and language, two to seven years of age); a *stage of concrete operations* (beginning of rational activity, seven to eleven years of age); and a final *stage of formal operations* (involving the ability to deal with abstractions, including scientific thought).

Kohlberg, whose work was discussed ealier, proffered three basic "levels," each of which can be further subdivided. For example, *I, the preconventional level,* ranges from birth to age seven during which the child's moral reasoning is egocentric; social or moral conventions are resisted between birth to two years of age "I do what pleases me." At two to three, "I'll do what I can and still avoid punishment." At ages four to seven, "I'll do what benefits me." Level 2, *The conventional level* (ages seven to twelve) is character-ized by "Avoid disapproval, and obey the rules" (*e.g.*, the Boy Scout Oath: "On my honor I will do my duty . . ."). Level 3, *the postconventional* level (ages twelve to fifteen): "I will implement my own (existential) principles and be a responsible adult." Dr. Kohlberg long resisted going beyond the level of personal existential choice. The present author had the opportunity to discuss with him the possibility that moral choices might some-times be guided from a transcendent, universal source as in the affirmation of religious prophets such as Isaiah, Jesus, Muhammad, Schweitzer, and Mother Teresa. Shortly before his death, it came as a particularly gratifying disclosure that Dr. Kohlberg had concluded, "What is moral is not a matter of taste or opinion—there is a universal morality."[79]

Some researchers have objected to these theories, stating that nothing about making moral choices at any given "stage" of life is preordained. Some people "grow up" faster than others, and some reach a fairly high plane and then "backslide." The whole stage concept is artificial, this is the basis on which William Damon declared,

> I reject wholly environmentalist or social-cultural positions on children's moral-ity. The truth is less simple and more encompassing than any of these extreme positions. It is the process of development that transforms the child's nascent pro-social orientation into a full-fledged moral perspective.[80]

As to charges of gender bias in the research particularly to Kohlberg, "it is not unusual for conclusions to be drawn about females' attitudes and behavior from research conducted with males as the only participants."[81] Gender bias has been a particular concern of Harvard's Carol Gilligan. According to Santrock, "Researchers have found support for Gilligan's claim that female's and male's moral reasoning often centers around different concerns and issues."[82] Eliminating biases of one form or another has always been a concern in every field of research. Beyond that, there remains the question of the family's role in nurturing the qualities of life most desirable for our children. So far serious divides exist among advocates and opponents of this role.

3.   The Nuclear Family: Obsolete?

For at least the past half century, much has been written about an impending crisis in family solidarity and stability. In the early 1950s, philosopher Elton Trueblood wrote of Karl Marx' *Communist Manifesto* (published in 1848) in which Marx denounced "the bourgeois claptrap about the family and education, about the hallowed co-relation of parent and child." Trueblood reflected on "the really frightening thought . . . of the degree to which we are more like the Russians than we realize. We are doing by neglect much that the Marxists have done by social planning."[83] By 1981, theological ethicist Stanley Hauerwas declared,

> One of the few issues on which there is a consensus today is that the family seems to be going through some kind of crisis. . . . Divorce statistics, examples of wife and child beating, the rates of delinquency, the demands of Women's liberation and rising sexual immorality are cited as evidence that the family is in deep trouble.[84]

The "family" popularly referred to is almost always the "nuclear" family system, each composed of two or more persons, held together by bonds of loyalty and affection. These people function as an organic whole but traditionally with one member (e.g., a mother or father) carrying primary responsibility for protecting and nurturing the family members. "Each such family is part of the 'glue' of the community of similarly organized units."[85] As these families interact and grow by expanding contacts and the birth of new generations of children, they may evolve into an "extended family," often encompassing two, three, or more generations. "Such families may benefit from other resources, such as the help of their relatives and the presence of a large community of parents' friends and colleagues who contribute to stimulate children's intellectual development, and serve as individual role models."[86]

Historically, however, the nature and multiple roles of individuals and family groups have undergone constant changes as the external social environment changed. One has only to reconsider what happened to family structure during the Industrial Revolution as noted earlier when countless young men and women left their rural or small town communities to move to the inner cities where factories and jobs beckoned.

The nuclear family concept survived nevertheless and forged new relationships. The apparent hunger in human nature for the security and enrichment of the heterosexual, monogamous nuclear family (however romanticized and short of historical reality) has been a powerful spur to recreate what was believed to be the character of family life at its best. Nuclear families often joined to form extended families living in one household with shared obligations and responsibilities. Historically, this situation is not as novel as we might imagine. A fascinating variation was "the corporate family," which reached its greatest development during the Ch'ing Dynasty in China (1644–1911), containing as many as seventy or eighty people living together in a walled compound of several buildings."[87]

There are, however, many variants in the typology of families, and it will be helpful to consider them, albeit briefly.

TYPE	DESCRIPTION
Unions	
Legal marriage	Legally/religiously sanctioned unions, generally heterosexual but may in time include same-sex partners
Common-law marriage	Union not legally sanctioned but socially acceptable
Monogamy	Legal marriage or cohabitation involving only two partners
Serial monogamy (or serial polygamy)	Sequence of spouses or partners over time as in the sequence of marriage, divorce, and remarriage, spouses succeeding each other
Polygamy/Polygyny	Multiple partners or spouses at the same time
	a. *Polygyny:* One man married to more than one woman at the same time
	b. *Polyandry:* One woman married to more than one man at the same time
Families	
Nuclear	At least one parent and one child living together
Conjugal	Husband, wife, child(ren)
	Male and female cohabitants with child(ren)
Single parent	One parent with one or more children
Grandparent	One or more grandparents with grandchild(ren)
Reconstituted	Remarried spouses or cohabitants with at least one of whom has a child from a former union
Extended Family	All the members of a family: child(ren), parents, grandparents, great-grandparents, and other ascendants: uncles, aunts, and cousins (by blood, adoption, or marriage)
One household	At least one parent and child(ren) and other relatives living together
Multiple households	All members of a family including relatives (by blood, adoption, or marriage) living in separate dwellings but interacting or a regular basis.[88]

The varieties and complexities of alternative marital styles appear somewhat daunting, but in fact most are subsets of two major family configurations, the nuclear and the extended. The definitional distinctions are not unimportant for reasons of accuracy and because they carry family policy implications. Anne-Marie Ambert points out that

> one often reads that children are born more and more "outside" of the family. Such a statement is accurate when a traditional definition is applied, but is inaccurate as soon as one accepts a mother and her child as a type of nuclear family. Furthermore, in terms of policy if a same-sex couple and their (adopted) children are not accepted as a family, they will not benefit from tax exemptions meant to help low-income families.[89]

The current state of affairs is one in which "only about 7 families in 100" now conform to the nuclear family stereotype of the father providing the sole financial and social support to the mother and children. In most families, both husband and wife work, providing a dual income,[90] suggesting to some critics that the "traditional" family is a myth and moving toward extinction. "The solution to contemporary problems will not be found in some lost golden age. In short there is no point in giving in to the lure of nostalgia."[91]

There is no gainsaying the fact that in the context of nuclear families, there has been a shocking rise in abortion, child abuse, divorce, drug and alcohol consumption, illegitimacy, and a host of other social cancers. These challenge such idealized portrayals of home life as the *Ozzie and Harriet* and *Father Knows Best* series of 1950s television. Nevertheless, in the face of often strident "antitraditional" criticisms, a new phenomenon is appearing. Mary Eberstadt, a research fellow at the Hoover Institution, notes that

> there has been a sea change in the way our secular cultural elites now write and talk about nontraditional heterosexual households. Just two and a half decades ago arguments for experimental family life were all on the offensive. Today, by contrast, most people in the public square have been recognizing the truth of this proposition: the traditional nuclear family, despite its problems, is nonetheless the best arrangement yet contrived for raising children—if only by default.[92]

Stanley Hauerwas, writing as a leading theological ethicist, states,

> I am less concerned with the question of the shape of the family—whether it is communal, extended or nuclear—or whether children are or are not in day care. We need an ethic that trains us to know what kind of relationship we are in. In this respect the ethic of self-fulfillment is a formula for self-deception.[93]

Furthermore, he states, our preoccupation with *self*-fulfillment is often at the expense of other members of the family, especially the children who are allowed to grow up without any form of real moral guidance. To be more specific, Hauerwas flatly declares, "It is a false and bad-faith position to think that if we do not teach them values, our children will be free to make up their own minds." In fact, the children are left in an amoral environment with no foundation on which to make up their minds. "What must be said and said clearly, is that the refusal to ask our children to believe as we believe, to live as we live, to act as we act is a betrayal that derives from moral cowardice."[94]

What of the effects of family participation in formal religious services? Ambert points to the supplemental force of the religious community to reinforce the family's values and provide life-long moral guidance. "Religion constitutes one of the most important cultural domains in any society."[95] A Canadian study of 10,000 citizens revealed in a 1996 survey that "overall, weekly attenders (of church services) hold more traditional family values and adopt better health practices. For instance, only 18 percent of weekly attenders aged 15 to 35 smoked, compared to 38 percent among those who never attended." Other studies have revealed that children of parents who attend religious services tend to follow suit. "Religiosity serves as an internal and external agent of social control so that religious commitment lowers health risks such as alcoholism, drug addiction and precocious sexual activity, and may serve to prevent depression."[96]

Hauerwas' judgment against parents who do not openly share their values, although perhaps less harshly expressed, may be reinforced by more recent studies that reveal a remarkable downscaling of family participation in institutional religion. "Each week anywhere from 30 to 40 percent of Americans attend religious services. Half the percentage of the 1940s."[97] However one may wish to rationalize this sharp decline (e.g., the increasing secularization of society via the media; the disillusionment over the apparent reluctance of churches, synagogues, and mosques to speak out on critical social issues such as war and political corruption; the economy's precariousness making it necessary for both parents to work—"we just don't have time for church") the future does not seem to invite optimism. Still, it remains true that "parents are more successful at passing on their beliefs within the context of a supportive religious climate." Their marriages tend to be measurably more secure, their children better able to live creatively even in an often chaotic social structure. "Children, on average engage in less risky behavior. Overall religious involvement seems functional in terms of health, psychological well being, marital stability and happiness, as well as child socialization."[98]

E. IMPLICATIONS FOR GLOBAL ETHICS

When Hans Kung used the word *family* as a metaphor for all humankind, he was moving beyond the poetic to some very down-to-earth tasks to be completed and goals to be achieved. "We are interdependent," he wrote in his proposal for the Declaration of the Parliament of the World's Religions. "Each of us depends on the well-being of the whole, and so we have respect for the community of living beings, for people, animals and plants and for the preservation of earth, air, water and soil."[99] The breathtaking scope of Kung's proposal might have been rejected as Utopian except for the impact on the 6,500 delegates from leading nations East and West. It was the first such meeting (1993) since the seed for such a Parliament was planted a century before.

"We consider humankind our family," Kung continued and underscored specific aspects of the interconnectedness:

> We take individual responsibility for all we do; we must not live for ourselves alone but should also serve others, never forgetting the children, the aged, the poor, the suffering, the disabled, the refugees and the lonely. We shall not oppress, injure, torture or kill other human beings, forsaking violence as a means of settling differences. We must strive for a just social and economic order.

The sweep of recommendations that follow is rooted in the recognition that "our world is experiencing a crisis in global economy, global ecology, and global politics. Hundreds of millions of human beings on our planet suffer from unemployment, poverty, hunger, and the destruction of their families."[100]

One wishes not to find fault with such evaluations of our current conditions; these declarations and many like them arising from similar organizations are undoubtedly "right on target." What is missing is not the hortatory "We must—" and "We ought to—" suggestions but a serious set of proposals as to how to create specific blueprints for accomplishing. It is clearly not enough to tell people to "listen to your parents," "heed your teacher's instructions," or "follow the admonitions of your pastor, rabbi, or priest" or even enroll in and attend the reading of papers at such-and-such a conference. It may be quite true that, as Kung insists, there is an irrevocable, unconditional norm for all areas of life: families and communities, races, nations, and religions.

It is now our task (and hopefully pleasure) to move forward to the roles of formal education and its place in supporting the family in providing the foundations for community and ultimately national and international cooperation to achieve what otherwise remains exhortation and wishful thinking.

NOTES

1. Emil Brunner, *The Divine Imperative,* trans. Olive Wyon (Philadelphia: The Westminster Press, 1947), 294.

2. Urie Bronfenbrenner, "Ecological Theory," in Santrock, John W., *Lifespan Development,* 9th ed., ed. John W. Santrock (New York: McGraw-Hill, 2004), 55.

3. *The Holy Quran,* Sura ii 228–232; 236–237; 241. The reference S. iv, 1, 2, for example, signifies sura (or chapter) four, verses 1 and 2.

4. In nearly every Christian wedding ritual, protestant or Roman Catholic, these words are incorporated: "These two shall be made one in this holy estate; whom therefore God has joined together, let no one put asunder." Matthew 19:19; Mark 10:19; Ephesians 6:1–4.

5. Exodus 20:12; Leviticus 19:3; Deuteronomy 5:16; Ecclesiastes 9:9.

6. See *The Analects of Confucius,* trans. Arthur Waley, (New York: Vintage Books/ Random House, 1938), 38–39.

7. The Brihad-Aranyaka Upanishads, 2-4-5 quoted in S.E. Frost, *The Sacred Writings of the World's Great Religions* (New York: McGraw-Hill, 1972), 397.

8. Ian Baxter, "Family and Marriage," *Encyclopedia Britannica.* (Chicago: William Benton 1974), 155. vol. 7.

9. Boyce Rensbrger, "On Becoming Human," reprinted in *Human Development* (Guilford, CT: Dushkin Publishing Company, 1984), 20–21.

10. Joan Berg Victor and Joell Sander, *The Family: The Evolution of Our Oldest Human Institution* (Indianapolis: Bobbs-Merrill, 1978), 10.

11. Willystine Goodsell, *A History of Marriage and the Family* (New York: AMS Press, 1974), 3–4.

12. Wilson, E.O., *On Human Nature*. (Cambridge: Harvard University Press, 1978), 55.

13. Fraser Watts, *Theology and Psychology*. (Burlington, VT: Ashgate Publishing, 2002), 18. He notes, "There is a surprisingly modest amount of technical scientific work underpinning the popularization of either sociobiology or evolutionary psychology. The popularizations seem to have run ahead of the research."

14. Jane Goodall, *In the Shadow of Man* (Boston: Houghton Mifflin, 1971), 185.

15. Charlotte Allen, "Some Folks Just Shouldn't Get Married," *Los Angeles Times,* November 23, 2003, M3.

16. Lloyd Saxton, *The Individual, Marriage and the Family,* 5th ed. (Belmont, CA: Wadsworth, 1982), 408.

17. The Dhammapada: 109 ("The Way of Virtue") was accepted in 240 B.C. by the Council of Asoka as the authentic collection of the sayings of Gautama. Shu King 4.4.2 ("Book of History") is the oldest of the Chinese classical known, containing historical documents from the period 2357 B.C. to 627 B.C. See Frost, *The Sacred Writings,* 145–146.

18. Confucius, Shu King, 4.4.2. See Frost, *The Sacred Writings,* 402.

19. Nena O'Neill, *The Marriage Premise* (New York: Evans, 1977), 199.

20. For a helpful explication of the evolution of early Hinduism and the Vedic Age into the sixth century B.C. and "later Hinduism" with its emphasis on religion as the basis for social behavior, see John B. Noss, *Man's Religions,* 4th ed. (London: Collier-Macmillan Ltd., 1970), 88–110, 190–233.

21. William Young, *The World's Religions, Worldviews and Contemporary Issues* (Upper Saddle River, New Jersey, Pearson Education, 1995), 129.

22. Sarvepalli Radhakrishnan and Charles A. Moore, eds. Princeton, NJ: Princeton University Press, *Source Book in Indian Philosophy,* quoted in John A. Hutchison, *Paths of Faith* (New York: McGraw-Hill, 1981), 148.

23. Arvind, Sharma, *Women in World Religions* (New York: State University of New York Press, 1987), 61–62.

24. Lewis Browne, *The World's Great Scriptures*. (New York: Macmillan, 1946), 120.

25. Ibid., quoting The Vishnu Purana, p. 129.

26. Brown, Lewis. *Ibid.,* 125.

27. J.M. Mehta, G.H. Bhatt, Vaidya, et al., quoted in Roderick, Hindery, *Comparative Ethics in Hindu and Buddhist Traditions* (Delhi: Motilal Banarsidass, 1978), 265, 270.

28. Hindery, Ibid., 243.

29. Ibid., from The Mahabharata, 270.

30. The Udana VIII.3, in John B, Noss, *Man's Religions,* 4th ed. (London: Collier-Macmillan, 1970), 136.

31. Daisssaku, Ikeda, *A New Humanism* (New York: Weatherhill, 1996), 8.

32. Noss, *Man's Religions,* 249.

33. David Hume, quoted in Annemarie De Waal Malefijt, *Religion and Culture* (Prospect Heights, IL: 1968), 35.

34. Hume Ibid., 107–108.

35. Teresa Kelleher, "Confucianism," *Women in World Religions,* ed. Arvind Sharma (New York: State University of New York, 1987), 135.

36. Kelleher, Ibid., 136.

37. Ibid., 148.

38. Max Muller, ed., *Sacred Books of the East,* vol. 27 (Oxford: 1910), 122 (n. 22), 131 (n. 2).

39. Arthur Waley, trans., *The Analects of Confucius* (New York: Vintage Books/Random House, 1938), 38.

40. Noss, *Man's Religions,* 405.

41. To protect the "Virgin Birth" narrative, some traditions insist that Mary remained a virgin all her life, and so substitute the term "cousin." There is no warrant for this, especially since the Greek word *Adelphos* is quite unequivocal, and it was considered the glory of womanhood to have a large family. *Cf.* Frederick C. Grant, "The Gospel According to St. Mark," *The Interpreter's Bible in Twelve Volumes,* vol. 7 (New York: Abingdon-Cokebury Press, 1951), 727.

42. Lisa Cahill, *Family: A Christian Social Perspective* (Minneapolis: Fortress Press, 2000). See especially Chap. 3, beginning 48.

43. Ibid., 79.

44. Huston Smith, *The World's Religions* (San Francisco: HarperCollins, 223.

45. *Ibid.,* 224.

46. Reference to passages from the Holy Qur'an are from A. Yusuf Ali *The Holy Qur'an, Text, Translation and Commentary,* Brentwood, Maryland, Amana Corporation. 1983.

47. Schuster, Clara Shaw, and Ashburn, Shirley Smith, *The Process of Human Development* (Boston: Little, Brown, 1980), 4.

48. Christiane Desroches-Noblecourt, *Tutankhamen.* New York: Doubleday, 1965, 78, 173. See also Veronica Lons, *Egyptian Mythology* (Middlesex, U.K.: Hamlyn Publishing Group, 1968), 66, 90–91.

49. Rod Macleish, "On the Durability of Love," *The Guilty Bystander* (Philadelphia: Fortress Press, 1971), 35–36.

50. Surendranath Dasgupta, *History of Indian Philosophy,* (Cambridge: Cambridge University Press, 1932), 33–35.

51. Sarvepalli Radhakrishnan, *Indian Philosophy,* 2nd ed., (New York: Macmillan, 1948), 233.

52. Robert B. McLaren, "The Ontology of Gender Equality" vol. 1 (paper presented at the *Parliament of the World's Religions,* Chicago, Ill., August 1993).

53. The execution order was rescinded under pressure from the United Nations and several oil-dependent nations on "humanitarian grounds."

54. Saxton, *The Individual,* 161.

55. *Ibid.,* 162.

56. L. deMause, quoted in Clara Shaw Schuster and Shirley Smith Ashburn, *The Process of Human Development,* 3rd ed. (New York: J.B. Lippincott, 1992), 6.

57. Saxton, *The Individual,* 329.

58. Schuster and Ashburn, *The Process of Human Development.*

59. Cahill, *Family,* 4.

60. Boyd R, McCandless, *Children; Behavior and Development* (New York: Holt, Rinehart and Winston, 1967), 576. See also Barbara Forisha-Kovach, *The Experience of Adolescence,* (Glenview, IL: Scott, Foresman, 1983), 272–273, and John W, Santrock, *Life-Span Development,* 9th ed. (New York: McGraw-Hill, 2004), 410–224.

61. Alan Dershowitz, *Los Angeles Times,* September 14, 2003, 1 (Op. Ed.).

62. More than half a century ago, Harriet Mowrer wrote of this extensively and with remarkable prescience in *Personality Adjustment and Domestic Discord,* which was quoted in Vergilius Ferm, *Encyclopedia of Religion* (New York: Philosphical Library, 1945), 272.

63. Young, *The World's Religions,* 129–31.

64. "The Admission of Women to the Order," quote in Henry Clarke Warren, *Buddhism in Translations* (Cambridge England: Atheneum, 1970), 441–445.

65. Smith, Huston, *op. Cit,* pp. 168–169.

66. Arvind Sharma, *Women in World Religions* (State University of New York Press, 1987), 144–48.

67. Jacob Neusner, "The Case of Mishnah's Division of Women," *Method and Meaning in Ancient Judaism* (Missoula, MT: Scholars Press, 1979).

68. Sharma Arvind, *Women in World Religions,* 210.

69. The term "hinge of history" is borrowed from Charlotte Waterlow, *The Hinge of History* (Cirencester, Great Britain: A One World Trust Book); see in particular Chapter 5 in which she traces the role of women in various societies from ancient Egypt, Mesopotamia, China, Japan, Greece, Rome, Africa to the modern-day United States.

70. For 120 others who made dramatic changes in human history via their faith and work from women who were welcomed into an inclusive Christianity, see Edith, Deen *Great Women of the Christian Faith* (New York: Harper & Brothers, 1959).

71. Thomas Lickona, *Raising Good Children* (New York: Bantam Books 1984), p. 3.

72. L.S. Vygotsky *Mind in Society* (Cambridge: M.I.T. Press 1978). Quoted in James W. Vander Zanden, *Human Development,* 7th ed. (New York: McGraw-Hill, 2000), 57.

73. Anne-Marie Ambert, *Families in the New Millenium* (Boston: Allyn and Bacon, 2001) 127; see also 160–61.

74. Vygotsky, *op. cit.* 162.

75. Ibid., 165.

76. Ibid., 16.

77. Ibid., 418.

78. Lloyd Saxton, *The Individual, Marriage and the Family,* 5th ed., (Belmont, CA: Wadsworth, 1980), 372.

79. James W. Vander Zanden *Human Development,* 7th ed. (New York: McGraw-Hill, 2000), 290.

80. William Damon, *The Moral Child* (New York: Free Press, 1988), 50.

81. John W. Santrock, *Lifespan Development* (New York: McGraw-Hill, 2004), 69.

82. Ibid., 344.

83. Elton Trueblood and Pauline Trueblood, *The Recovery of Family Life* (New York: Harper & Brothers, 1953), 23.

84. Stanley Hauerwas, *A Community of Character* (Notre Dame, IN: University of Notre Dame Press, 1981), 155.

85. Clara Schuster and Shirley Ashburn, *The Process of Human Development* (New York: J.B. Lippincott, 1992), 38–9, 624–26.

86. Ambert, *Families,* 337.

87. Saxton, *The Individual,* 329.

88. Ambert, Anne-Marie, *Families in the New Millenium,* London, York 6–7. A great debt of gratitude goes to Dr. Ambert for her careful delineation of categories and her discussion with me of their relevance to the overall study.

89. Ibid., 8.

90. Arlene Skolnick and Jerome Skolnick, *Family in Transition.* 11th ed. (Boston: Allyn and Bacon, 2001), 1.

91. Ibid., 12.

92. Mary Eberstadt, "The Family: Discovering the Obvious," *First Things* (New York: Institute on Religion and Public Life, 2004), 10–11.

93. Hauerwas, *A Community of Character,* 173.

94. Ibid., 166.

95. Ambert, *Families,* 226.

96. Ibid., 227–32.

97. Ibid.

98. Ibid., 236.

99. Hans Kung, *A Global Ethic The Declaration of the Parliament of the World's Religions* (New York: Continuum International 1993), 14–15. "Almost" first of its kind because this was in fact the second such Parliament in a hundred years, but the first produced no such document.

100. Ibid., 14–17.

CHAPTER 4

Can Schools Create an Ethical Society?

If you ask what is the good of education the answer is easy: that education makes good men, and good men act nobly.

—Plato

The idea that an educated electorate can create a more just, enlightened, and ethical society is at least as old as the Hebrew prophets, antedating Plato by more than three centuries. A brief tour of the stages of the rise of formal education from its domestic beginnings to the complex and politically potent force it has become will provide a perspective by which to understand not only its history but also its potentials for the generations ahead.

A. THE EVOLUTION OF FORMAL EDUCATION

The Athenian historian Thucydides (460–400 B.C.) cited Pericles' celebration of the broad education of Athenian citizens, which enabled them to bring Athens to the height of the times in the arts, philosophy, and sciences. Pericles commented in his famous funeral oration (c. 431 B.C.): "I say that as a city we are the school of Hellas."[1]

1. The Graeco-Roman Era

All Hellas (Greece) as Pericles declared was blessed by Athenian citizens' enthusiasm for and building of the city's educational system. He could not foretell but would not have been surprised that the teachings of his contemporary, Socrates, whose informal "peripatetic" style would inspire Socrates' pupil Plato to create the famous *Academy* that would flourish and outlive the Roman Empire,[2] or Aristotle's *Lyceum,* also called peripatetic by his students. Although the Stoic's equally informal school founded by Zeno of Citium would eventually attract such powerful Roman leaders as Seneca, Epictetus, and the emperor Marcus Aurelius,[3] Pericles' intuition was validated. Athens with its citizens' enthusiasm for learning did indeed become "the school of Hellas" and, made into formal institutions, helped shape the whole of Western civilization. Plato's idealism, Aristotle's scientific realism, and the Stoic contention that a godlike "Universal Force" pervades all reality inspired and guided followers to live ethically, raise well-educated children, and prepare them to achieve a spiritual grounding for the training of the mind and to hold to the ideal of freedom for all citizens.

Higher education, which early moved beyond the rudiments of the "Three Rs," fostered the philosophical disciplines of ethics, logic, politics, mathematics, and aesthetics balanced by the "hard" sciences of physics, mechanics, geography, and astronomy. A great boost in fulfilling their ambitions for classifying and organizing the vast array of subjects was the financial support of Alexander the Great. The emperor was especially helpful to his former teacher Aristotle by providing both money and a small army of "grad assistants" to travel with the army across the expanding empire to gather plant and animal specimens, as well as scientific data on climatology for Aristotle's classification and recording.

Meanwhile, less academically demanding forms of education, such as the rhetorical schools of Isocrates, were also becoming formalized. Their goals, as the name suggests, were more modest but still quite rigorous in preparing students for promoting democracy through rhetoric, argumentation, and public debate.

Neighboring Rome, which according to legend was founded about 753 B.C., began to exert itself as a state ruled by the privileged patrician class. Historians have often portrayed Rome's climb to greatness as resulting from riding roughshod over surrounding Latin states. The Romans admired and then copied Greece's culture, having developed only an impoverished one of their own. British historian, novelist, and critic H.G. Wells wrote with amused sarcasm that while the Greeks treasured formal education and made it a conduit for the transmission of philosophical ideals, religion, ethics, and the sciences, the Romans actually reduced education (except for military training and a modicum of architecture and engineering) to the responsibility of the father in each household who also had the authority of life and death over his children. The Romans, Wells insisted, exhibited a "monumental incuriousness" about science.

> "Impossible was any further development of the astronomy and physiography of Alexandria" (the city in Egypt founded in 332 B.C. and heavily endowed by Alexander the Great). Alexandria was eventually to house the most extensive libraries and museums of the ancient world. But already by 146 B.C. Rome overtook, and for all intents occupied Greece.

The most remote countries of the ancient world were ransacked to supply the pomp and grandeur of Rome, which collectively was content to feast, exact, grow rich, and watch its gladiatorial shows. "Science was still-born into a suffocating atmosphere of wealth and military oppression. . . . Political and social science never had a chance to germinate."[4]

A more objective history would surely have to acknowledge the developments of architecture and engineering exemplified by the great viaducts and aqueducts, the Coliseum, the vast extension of Roman roads that bound together all of the known world from India to Spain and to the British Isles (the latter admittedly for the convenience of the military). Perhaps above all were the great contributions to law, jurisprudence, and the judicial system that would continue directly to influence Western law into the present time. The names of Cicero and Seneca still resonate in the minds of historians of jurisprudence, although almost countless other names might be recalled. One example of the lasting influence of Roman law would be on the issue of equity. "Equity," as Rene Wormser reminds us, "is a vital part of our own legal system, and we have the Romans to thank for having laid the broad groundwork for our own equitable principles."[5] In the United States, for example, the same laws are applied to aliens as to citizens and the precedents for this are in ancient Rome.[6] Aliens cannot vote and are denied a few other privileges, but in general their rights are the same as those of any citizen.

Clearly, much that we find in Roman society could not have been achieved if access to formal education had not been available or if the caricature of life in Rome as presented by H.G. Wells and some other historians had been the whole story. Indeed, it is recorded that "children from ages seven to ten or twelve, girls as well as boys, were taught to read and write Latin, and to count."[7] The schools were private and voluntary with little supervision by the state, and they were available only to those whose family could afford them. In time, secondary schools arose to provide more sophisticated general education, and Julius Caesar as well as his successor Augustus gave franchise and rights of citizenship to many foreign teachers and physicians who had come to Rome. It remains true, however, that "in all its foundation elements the education to be obtained in Roman schools was basically borrowed from Greek Education."[8]

The most dramatic changes to education came when, after three centuries of persecution against the Christians, Constantine liberated the Christians in 325 A.D. and virtually adopted their religion for the empire. In 381, one of his successors issued a decree requiring the establishment of schools in all towns and villages for the free instruction of all children. This latter innovation was a turning point in educational affairs, which would have far-reaching consequences for many centuries to follow, long after the empire had fallen—and fall it did because of a host of problems that are at the very root of Roman culture. Financial resources of the empire were strained beyond endurance to maintain its far-flung colonies, senators distrusted each other, and the army was constantly at war within its own ranks. Meanwhile the jurists, the pride of the greatest legal system yet known to mankind, were muzzled and in many cases assassinated by the emperors' commands for challenging their lawless rule. Of fifty emperors on the throne in the three centuries prior to the Christian era, thirty-five were either assassinated or committed suicide. The common people were kept under control by the simple device of *panem et circenses* literally bread and circuses (i.e., free food and gladiatorial entertainments). These events further fanned their blood lust. Slaves and captives often died by the score in a given week, torn asunder by wild beasts in the arenas to amuse applauding crowds.[9]

Into this world of dehumanizing extremes, Christianity brought a new vision to mankind in which brotherhood and love of neighbor (and, even of enemies—known in few other religions) that eventually struck a chord in the heart of the nation. Perhaps Will Durant expressed it best: The Romans finally "turned from Caesar preaching war, to Christ preaching peace; from incredible brutality to unprecedented charity, from a life without hope or dignity to a faith that honored their humanity."[10]

2.   The Dark Ages, Reformation, and Beyond

There is no unanimity among historians as to what the popular terms "Dark" Ages or "Middle" (or Medieval) Ages mean, or what specific time frame they represent. There seems to be a general consensus that they comprise the period between Rome's fall and Columbus' discovery of the New World. "Dark" is thought to have been coined rather disparagingly during the Renaissance by scholars of a more intellectually stimulating period. They looked back to the centuries of Norse and other invasions of Europe that destroyed countless monks, monasteries, and their libraries. The constant wars among Bulgarian, Hungarian, and other ethnic forces left whole cities slaughtered and in ruins. It has even been suggested that the term derived from *Bulgar-man* "bugger man" or "bogey-man" an eleventh century word used to frighten children into submission.[11]

It should be remembered, however, that those centuries marking the era between the founding of the first Christian school of higher learning in Alexandria, Egypt (mid-second century A.D.), and the voyage of Columbus in the late fifteenth century, witnessed Charlemagne's establishment of the palace school in Aachen. In time, his idea for schools staffed by scholars from all over Europe (e.g., Alcuin of Britain and Peter of Pisa) inspired an extensive network of schools. Giovanni Villani's *Chronicle* (published in 1348) estimated that by the middle of the thirteenth century, upward of 10,000 children had learned to read in Florence, Italy. Advanced schools for instruction in arithmetic, grammar, and rhetoric as well as religion and ethics were spreading from the British Isles to the Mediterranean. Meanwhile, the era witnessed the rebuilding of ruined cities and extensive trade with Muslim businesses in Jerusalem before the tragedy of the Crusades. The Age of Cathedrals came into being, accompanied by the great universities of Bologna, Oxford, Cambridge, Paris, and Heidelberg.

However, despite emphases on morals and ethics in all elementary and "higher" schools, it is interesting that "there were relatively few students of theology per se in medieval universities. A prescribed theological training for the priesthood came only with the Counter-Reformation.[12] Meanwhile, the once violent hordes of Iron Age tribes from the North Sea to the Danube were tamed during these supposedly "dark" ages and were taught the rudiments of individual liberty and national self-government. The Imperial Library at Byzantium created by Constantine during the fourth century did much to preserve Greek and Roman literature. Although libraries, both private and public, were almost wholly destroyed by Germanic and Viking invasions in the fifth century, as noted, fragments of the cultural heritage of Greece and Rome were preserved in churches and monasteries from which later emerged the culture of the Renaissance.[13] Meanwhile, the Magna Charta was accepted (1215), present-day Western languages were shaped and the British Parliament was founded.

It must not be overlooked that while people and institutions of Medieval Europe were struggling to find their bearings, people of the Islamic faith were advancing in the arts, sciences, and other intellectual endeavors. Among them, Al-Kindi (800–870) was the first to embrace mathematics as the key to all the sciences. He also wrote about music, physics, medicine, and psychology. In the year he died, Al-Farabi (870–950), who was to be called "the second Artistotle," wrote extensive commentaries on both Plato and Aristotle and the logical necessity of a creator.

The three greatest philosophers among the Arabs, however, are generally conceded to have been Avicenna (980–1037), Al-Ghazali (1059–1111), and Averroes (1126–1198). Avicenna was a thorough-going dedicated Artistotelian at a time when the Christian world knew hardly anything of the latter's philosophy or science. Avicenna wrote an eighteen-volume encyclopedia and a canon of medicine that ran to a prodigious million words.[14]

Al-Ghazali held a professorship in law in Baghdad but relinquished it to pursue answers to questions that rational thought and philosophy alone could not provide. He pondered deeply the prospect that humankind can know nothing except through the senses but that sense impressions must always be checked by reason. He concluded that both sense and reason fail us at too many points, so within us, some innate guide to truth with which we have been endowed by Allah must exist. Both Jews and Christians also read with zeal his book, *Revival of the Science of Religion,* which created a link that would remain for centuries in some parts of the world a beacon of hope for a practical, global ethic and for peace.[15]

It was Averroes, however, who gained the highest respect among Jews, Christians, and Muslims alike, in large part because of his astonishing versatility. He studied optics and wrote on the function of the retina. His *Encyclopedia of Medicine* became the standard text in European universities as soon as it could be translated into Latin. Averroes was first to discover the possibilities of smallpox inoculations five centuries before Edward Jenner's first inoculation experiment in England. He wrote extensively on law and became for a time chief justice at Seville and later at Cordova.[16]

In 970 A.D., the followers of Islam established al-Azhar University in Cairo, Egypt, which in time became a teaching center for the entire Muslim world for more than a millennium.[17] With the Holy Qur'an as the central focus for its extensive curriculum in the arts, astronomy, geography, mathematics, medicine, physics, and even pharmacology, a strong emphasis on morality and ethics was also included:

> It is not righteousness (whether) you turn your faces to the East or West, but it is righteousness to believe in God and the Last Day and the Angels, and the Book, and the Messengers; to spend of your substance, out of love for Him, for your kin, for orphans, for the needy, for the wayfarer, for those who ask; and for the freeing of captives; to be steadfast in prayers, and practice regular charity; to fulfil the contracts which you made; and to be firm and patient in pain (or suffering) and adversity and throughout all periods of panic. Such are the people of truth, the God-conscious.[18]

It may be argued that universities, one of the major gifts of religion to Western culture, were not only the source of intellectual leadership but also of foment against the power of the Christian churches, and were heralds of the Renaissance and the Protestant Reformation.

3. The Assumed Moral Mandate

When Plato began his Academy about 387 B.C., it was with the conviction that "the direction in which education starts a man will determine his future life." (Cf. *The Republic*, Book IV) Accordingly, in addition to philosophy, science, and mathematics (Theatetus, Plato pupil's in the Academy, founded solid geometry), the Academy gave great emphasis to morals, ethics, and character and how law embraced them. In many centuries that followed, Augustine, Charlemagne, Aquinas, Luther, Calvin, and Helvetus repeated the theme that "education made us what we are." Schools could indeed create a moral society. In more recent history, Hebert Spencer wrote, "Education has for its object the formation of character," (Social Statics, 1850), and Ralph Inge, dean of St. Paul's Cathedral, insisted, "The aim of education is not knowledge of facts but of values." (Cf. Cambridge Essays on Education, 1917, Ch. 2)

It will be useful to track this theme more closely, resuming where we left off at the junction between the Middle Ages and the Renaissance. Much as the label Dark Ages was the product of a backward glance by Renaissance scholars at the thousand or so years following the fall of Rome, so *Renaissance* was a made-up designation by nineteenth century historians for the period of fourteenth to sixteenth centuries in Europe. Among the most prominent historians was Jules Michelet (1798–1874) who used the term *the Renaissance* as the title of volume 7 of his *History of France*. Also included among this group must be the Swiss historian Jacob Burckhard (1818–1897), who scorned Michelet's antipathy for the Middle Ages "as if during the Middle Ages all cultural life had been sleeping as though dead." He reiterated some of the items noted earlier here as singular accomplishments during the medieval period including the conviction that formal education was a means of preserving traditional morals and providing the framework for their implementation through clearly stated ethical codes.

The Renaissance, as the name suggests, was a time of the rebirth of classical culture, science, and philosophy inherited from Greece and Rome. In large measure, the rebirth was made possible by Jewish and Arab scholars who had translated newly discovered Greek materials into Arabic and Latin. Much of the classic literature, destroyed by Norse and other invasions that ravaged Christian monasteries and their schools after the fall of Rome, came into their possession again, thanks to the growing interaction of Jewish, Christian, and Muslim scholars. "By the middle of the thirteenth century, Christianity was once more in possession of careful literal translations of Aristotle's scientific works on biology, physics, metaphysics, ethics, politics and poetics."[19]

One may recall that in the Hebrew tradition, the role of the rabbi has always been held in highest esteem. Not an official authority in the earliest days, a rabbi was nevertheless assumed to be a teacher above all else who always prepared to lecture, discuss, and instruct whether from the pulpit or classroom. The curriculum for instruction was based primarily on the Torah (first five books of the Hebrew, or Old Testament, scriptures), although it also referred to oracles as well as the literature of the prophets on the demands of Yahweh.[20] Prophetic warnings of doom to come because of the unfaithfulness of the people are spoken of as oracles (e.g., Isaiah 17:1) "An oracle concerning Damascus. Behold Damascus will cease to be and become a heap of ruins. . . . For you have forgotten the God of your salvation. "

Without doubt, the most influential Jewish scholar of the Medieval world was Moses Maimonides (1135–1204), affectionately called *Rambam* (an acronym for rabbi). Born in Spain under predominantly Islamic governance, he moved with his family to Morocco where he excelled in rabbinical studies, Greek philosophy, and medicine.[21] The Crusades were underway, and historians have debated why, after he distinguished himself as an outstanding physician and the opportunity arose, he did not become physician to King Richard I of England. Perhaps his Jewish tradition, which had occasioned persecution in Spain, North Africa, and especially in Jerusalem was the reason. Instead he immersed himself in the Arabic medical texts of Hippocrates, Galen, Razi, Avenzoar, and Avicenna and became a highly reputed physician. He was eventually elevated to the position of chief physician to the Sultan.[22]

Despite his sense of having been cheated out of a formal education in his homeland, Maimonides pursued knowledge diligently in the three fields in which he excelled: He was to have a profound effect on subsequent generations of educators in these fields. There is, as his biographer Lenn Goodman reminds us, a family of qualities known by different names in many cultures. The Greeks called them virtues (*aretai*) and mentioned courage, wisdom, justice, self-control and generosity of spirit as prominent among them. The Christians valued charity especially, and humility; the Hindus *ahimsa* or reverence for life; the Arabs patience and forbearance; the Hebrew prophets, uprightness and loving kindness. Are such qualities the fruit of an awareness of or propinquity to God? Can they **be**? Our study of Maimonides can answer this last question, at least.

> The world depends for its existence, according to Maimonides, upon the act of God, a necessary Being . . . who totally transcends that to which He has given being. Despite transcendence, it is possible for this Being to be known—for the determination of the world's finitude is the expression of what we, from our perspective would call God's will or mind. . . . We are cognizant of that expression itself in the order and array of animate and inanimate nature, in the immanent rationality of the cosmos, and in the reason principle immanent in the mind of man. This is what Maimonides as a Rabbi taught and what would influence other rabbis and students for centuries that followed.[23]

Having its roots in the Hebrew scriptures, the Christian tradition, especially those parts dealing with morals and ethics, would quite naturally draw much of its educational curriculum from the same resources as had the rabbis. Jesus was in fact referred to as a rabbi, (John 1:38; 20:16) and his dire warnings in Matthew 25 and Mark 13 might well be examples of extending the Hebrew reference to oracles. In addition, the Gospels and Epistles of the New Testament contained teachings such as the Beatitudes and the sermons of Jesus (as well as the "enacted" messages in his miracles of feeding the hungry, healing the sick) on which to build classroom discussion. The pupils would be transmit into their homes and invite family reinforcement.

Morals and ethics occupied the attention of the leaders in Christian thought throughout the medieval period, including Boethius, Cassiodorus, and Alfred the Great heading the list of those who brought together the great ideas of Greek and Roman thought, both religious and secular, and made them available to the church. Alfred translated into Anglo-Saxon the works of Augustine, Boethius, and Gregory and during what is sometimes called "the Carolingian revival," paved the way for the expansion of school curricula incorporating what Charlemagne envisioned in creating the Holy Roman Empire. Two chief categories of classical learning had been termed the *Trivium* (grammar, rhetoric, and logic) and the *Quadrivium,* or the four liberal arts (arithmetic, geometry, astronomy, and music, all recognized to be ultimately mathematical concerns). They were also considered avenues to the truth, the most basic quest of learning. Because truth is established by God and grounded in eternal reality, it is simply *discovered* by, not established by, human effort. Thomas Aquinas (1225–1274) emphasized that humankind has been given intellect as a means for discovering truth but because our reason is corrupted by worldly preoccupation, intellect must be guided by faith, revelation, and grace. These are spiritual matters, so education must also be guided by faith, revelation "reason is a whore" and grace. Without these, as Martin Luther was later to declare at the beck and call of every wayward thought of lust or ambition.

Among the major contributions of the church to the conflicted age of the Crusades and interstate warfare throughout the empire were the rules of chivalry. Intended primarily for the upper classes for whom knighthood was the ultimate ideal of manhood, these rules spread to the middle and lower classes because of the immense popularity of the legends of Camelot and King Arthur. The rules included honor, mercy for the fallen foe, protection of the weak, and loyalty to the Christian faith.

For those not preparing for knighthood, there were three secular levels of learning. The first for *apprentices,* which involved mastering various crafts, often was based on a written contract, or indenture. The master promised to teach each boy the skills of the trade, look after his morals and religion, give him his keep and perhaps a small stipend, and teach him whatever reading and writing might be needed to carry on a trade. The period of apprenticeship varied considerably and might last from three to ten or twelve years.

In the second level of training, termed *journeyman,* the accomplished apprentice might travel, literally journey from place to place, town to town. Journeymen worked for different masters in their shops, were provided hospitality and, if acceptable by the *guild,* were paid a small stipend. If the journeyman proved his worth, he might then present his "masterpiece" to the guild of his choice as a demonstration of his mastery in the chosen skill and then be graduated to *master craftsman,* the third level. He was then a full-fledged member, his advancement being attended by appropriate ceremony, and he was permitted to set up his own shop. He might then begin training newly arrived journeymen in his turn, becoming their host and mentor.

Although this was a medieval curriculum, it continued to be practiced during the Renaissance for those who had no interest in going beyond elementary education to the university. The guild system in some disciplines continued for many centuries down to the twentieth. Many journeymen wore a distinctive gown or other apparel by which to be identified (e.g., the baker's or chef's puffed white hat still seen today at a few selective restaurants). The modern labor union owes much to the guild system of old.

While this was taking place across Europe, Islamic scholarship was effecting some powerful changes. This was remarkable because Muhammad (570–632) was almost totally illiterate and had to have a scribe take down his words as he received them during meditation from the will and mind of Allah. Islam became the most thoroughly advanced culture in Greek philosophy and science at the time. Education for all of his followers was the prophet's passion. One consequence was that while learning to translate Greek writings into Arabic, Muslim scholars absorbed Hindu, Jewish, and Christian thought. As these teachings, especially Jewish and Christian, came into contact with Arabic culture in Spain, Sicily, and Syria, a zeal to translate all of these materials from Arabic into Latin arose. Thus, Maimonides reconciled Aristotle with Jewish religion while Avicenna and Averroes reconciled Aristotle with Islam. As these writings flooded Europe, Aristotle had to be reconciled with Christianity, a task to which St.Thomas Aquinas and others addressed themselves in the thirteenth century.

Curiously, in the midst of this vibrant interaction after the time of Al-Ghazali (1058–1111), philosophy and science receded, and *fiqh* (Islamic jurisprudence) and theology became dominant. John Bowker writes,

> It is fair to say that the philosophical tradition of Islam is dead at the moment. . . . We have not had one for the last five centuries. But I think it is there. There are passages in the medieval and early Arab philosophers, people like al-Ghazali, al-Kindi, ibn Rushd (Averroes), which are philosophical in the modern sense of the word, not just in the Eastern sense of 'full of wisdom'. The importance of recovering that Islamic integration of understanding and character is that it would, in the Muslim view, contribute to prevailing philosophies of education a dimension which is at present disastrously missing; it would include within the educational domain as a matter of its concerns, the religious character of human beings and of the universe. As to ethics, including global ethics, "If the same values are embodied in all religions, it follows that there could be no Muslim objection to learning about all, or at least some other religions. We do not want (our children) to convert to any other religion, and we have no intention to convert other people to ours. They will be better citizens with each other after that."[24]

The early days of the Renaissance were a heady time for scholars, and the conviction grew that through sharing knowledge, diverse religious traditions with education as the key could resolve many old conflicts. This education had a moral mandate. Simultaneously, the Renaissance witnessed a rise in original thinking and a willingness to challenge old authorities including the established church. John Wycliff (1328–1384), an Oxford professor of theology, protested the worldliness and immoral practices of some leaders of the church and called for a reformation of the church. He was condemned for this by his superiors but later historians called him the "Morning Star of the Reformation." Wycliff died peacefully in his bed, but other reformers, including John Huss (1369–1415), Girolamo Savonarola (1452–1498), and William Tyndale (1484–1536), were executed as were countless others.

In an era when the Society of Jesus published an official directive that a professor who was "too liberal" in departing from Aristotle would be dismissed "unless something occurs which is opposed to the orthodox faith,"[25] Copernicus, Kepler, and Galileo were born. These men overturned the anthropocentric Aristotelian world view, and "it remained for Isaac Newton (1642–1727), to establish once and for all the superiority of science in the realm of natural knowledge . . . although there is nothing inherently anti-Christian or even anti-religious about science."[26]

Yet all had at least some influence on two great educators whose names became almost synonymous with the Protestant Reformation, Martin Luther (1483–1546) and John Calvin (1509–1564). Both insisted on the primacy of elementary education in every person's life; both urged that schools be made available to all children as a universal right and that schools should stress religion, morality, and ethics.[27]

B. FAMILIES, CONGREGATIONS, AND SCHOOLS IN INTERACTION

Only seven years after Martin Luther launched the Protestant Reformation, his work was so impressive that he was able to address The Councilmen of All Cities in Germany; That They Establish and Maintain Christian Schools. As a pastor with an economically diverse congregation, he was aware that a large segment of the membership had been raised without formal education, a fact that troubled him because its lack perpetuated economic as well as intellectual, moral, and spiritual disadvantages. Having met the traditional disclaimer ("We already have too many claims on our limited resources, and it would cost too much money"), he replied in writing;

> My Dear Sirs, if we have to spend such large sums every year on guns, roads, bridges, dams, and countless similar items to insure the temporal peace and prosperity of a city, why should not much more be devoted to the poor neglected youth—at least enough to engage one or two competent men to teach school?[28]

Having refuted the Roman Catholic claim that marriage is a sacrament (while denying it to the priests), Luther declared that a minister cannot fully understand the myriad problems of families while remaining celibate. Consequently, he married a like-minded nun and enlisted her insights to help him be a better parish pastor. Setting up a school in his own parish, he enlisted the support of parents throughout the community for schools that all children (especially those boys who might otherwise simply become apprentices in some shop or other) could attend. That his efforts were met with success is reflected in the fact that not only were schools established across Germany but also within three short, tumultuous years of the Reformation's beginning (1517), the Danish King Christian II brought a Lutheran pastor to Denmark. In a generation, Lutheran congregations and schools were beginning to appear as far east as Finland and as far west as Norway. In 1555, after severe political and military clashes, the Peace of Augsburg granted Lutheranism full legal establishment throughout Germany.[29]

The first Lutheran groups to come to America were from Sweden in the seventeenth century; they settled along the Delaware river, and a second came from Germany, mainly to New York. A third immigration, also from Germany in the eighteenth century, became by far the most conspicuous element in colonial Lutheranism until the 1830s. Then great waves of immigrants arrived from Norway, Denmark, Sweden, Finland, and Iceland. They tended to move past those who had settled on the east coast and moved to the upper Midwest, Illinois, Missouri, Wisconsin, Iowa, Minnesota, and the Dakotas.

As they moved, these immigrants also founded synods, councils of churches for given regions, which helped retain the languages and regional worship styles of the nations from which they came.[30] Of special interest is the parish churches, creation of schools that would train children in a more formal way what their parents believed and practiced. This created certain perhaps obvious problems as language differences plus diverse theological emphases tended to isolate these newly settled communities from each other. The German language gradually became the common tongue, and "not until the threshold of World War I did the predominant language for worship in their congregations shift from German to English."[31]

Despite diverse cultural identities that might otherwise have caused frictions, the slogan about being "loyally Lutheran" provided a sense of cohesion, so their elementary and secondary schools flourished, and their colleges and universities excelled. A sterling contemporary example is St. Olaf College, founded in 1874 in Northfield, Minnesota, which gained a national reputation for seriousness in teaching morals and ethics with its slogan, "St. Olaf does not *have* a religious program, it *is* a religious program." During the 1920s through the 1950s, the recordings and global concerts of St. Olaf's music program won worldwide acclaim. Yet, as James Burtchaell's book, *The Dying of the Light,* cautions, clinging to a reputation as a moral and ethical guide reinforced by compulsory attendance in Biblical classes and chapel services is a fragile undertaking. This fragility was reflected especially after World War II when the G.I. Bill of Rights provided a federal aspect to campus life, virtually outlawing compulsory religious activities. Today, in many if not most church-related schools, "chapel attendance is at an all-time low. At St. Olaf's it is less than 10 percent of the student body."[32]

Like Martin Luther, John Calvin (1509–64) was trained for the priesthood. Both also enjoyed great success in the study of the law. It was the opinion of each that formal education is a unique opportunity to change the course of people's lives and to train pupils in the basic disciplines of mathematics and forms of communication and to deepen their spiritual lives and commitment to God's laws of moral and ethical living. Undergirding Calvin's curriculum was the conviction that human nature has been fatally corrupted by worldly ambition and hostility to God; humans are inherently evil despite all of the outward show of good manners and protestations of following the Golden Rule. Salvation from all this is entirely in God's hands as the ultimate gift of his love and grace. The supreme value of education is to enable us to read, and thus to "relate" to, the "word of God" in its written form and in the person of Jesus Christ, "the Word made flesh." Union with Christ, the Word, enables humans to rejoice in the promise of the Resurrection when we shall be raised with Christ from death.

While Calvin believed that the church had a major educational task to fulfill, he believed it was up to the city fathers to provide universal education for all citizens and that biblical knowledge must be a part of every curriculum. "The liberal arts and good training are aids to a full knowledge of the Word." He advocated a system of elementary education in the vernacular for all including reading, writing, arithmetic, grammar, and religion. He also held that such training was critical for ecclesiastical leadership. Perhaps Calvin's greatest achievement in educational development was the establishment in 1555 of the Geneva Academy, eventually to become a major university. Given the dangers of travel in those days, especially for converts to Protestantism, it is remarkable that more than a thousand students from all over Europe enrolled to hear Calvin lecture. Among these was John Knox, who became the key figure in the Scottish Reformation.

The arrival of the *Mayflower* Pilgrims in 1620 was key to the coming of Calvinism to the New World, although "Calvinism" is not as accurate a label as is "Lutheranism" which represented in a number of different denominations with such distinctive names as Baptist, Congregationalist, Presbyterian, and so on. Plymouth Colony's establishment included the plan to build a schoolhouse for the few children who arrived. Sixteen years later with great foresight and support of the families, the Pilgrims founded the first college in the new world, Harvard, which eventually became one of the great universities in the world. Named for the Puritan pastor John Harvard, he bequeathed his library of several hundred volumes and half of his estate to the college. With a single frame house, one "master," and seven "scholars," its charter proclaimed the college's primary goal to be training clergy. Its curriculum was nevertheless so broad and thorough that all of its first students to graduate were admitted to universities in England for advanced study.[33] Among graduates of Harvard have been a number of U.S. presidents, court justices, congressional leaders, and such literary luminaries as Emerson, Holmes, Thoreau, Frost, and Eliot. Scientific investigations not only into the traditional sciences but also experimental psychology grew in prominence.

As the United States increased in population and people began moving westward, it seemed that, as one historian expressed it, every time the covered wagons settled for the night, a school had sprung up by morning. While the majority of middle and lower classes in many parts of Europe had little opportunity for formal education, especially at the higher levels, U.S. families were pressing for universal education. Predictably, where the families were active in local churches, the schools provided a strong emphasis on moral and religious instruction. Of the first nine pre-Revolutionary colleges, eight were founded by major Protestant denominations.[34] Today there are hundreds of church-founded or church-related colleges and universities. As noted earlier, however, concerning those following the Lutheran tradition, a majority of denominational schools have weakened or severed their relations with parent church bodies.

The Reformation opened the way for a number of changes in the lives of people and whole populations, migrations to the New World being perhaps the most conspicuous. Luther and Calvin, for all of their efforts in the direction of freedom of conscience and the right to break from centuries of Roman Catholic authority and exclusivist, were rigidly authoritarian in their own treatment of those who differed from them. Puritans, Separatists, and Presbyterians came under close scrutiny while the Arians (later to become Unitarians, embraced by Thomas Jefferson) and Quakers were roundly denounced. Significantly, the first state in the colonies to grant complete freedom of religion while it was still solidly Roman Catholic was Maryland. The Quakers, never a majority, nevertheless affirmed the goodness of humans and translated their ideals into action for helping the poor and underprivileged and opposing all forms of warfare or physical violence. "Thus they resurrected the simple spirit of Christ and like him, had love for their neighbor and even for their enemies."[35]

It is valuable to recognize that both George Washington and Thomas Jefferson continued the Puritan legacy of concern for the education of children; they were convinced that the future of democracy depended on an informed and rational citizenry. Jefferson (1743–1826) especially was influential in the development of the public school system. While serving in the Virginia legislature, he introduced a measure that would have established free public education for the state. This bill, however, was defeated, for most members of legislature regarded this as a radical measure.[36] Bringing Jefferson's dream to fruition, would be up to Horace Mann (1796–1859) half a century later adding his own strong convictions to its establishment. "Without undervaluing any other human agency," he wrote as secretary of the Massachusetts Stated Board of Education, "it may be safely acclaimed that the common school, improved and energized as it can easily be, may become the most effective and benignant of all the forces of civilization."[37] Mann has been widely credited for establishing the public school system in Massachusetts. Others followed in their own respective locales: Henry Barnard (1811–1900) assisted in founding a state board of education in Connecticut and persuaded Rhode Island to follow suit. William T. Harris (1835–1909) became U.S. commissioner of education (1889) and was instrumental in expanding the public school movement to include the kindergarten. John Dewey (1859–1952) was a staunch enthusiast for public education although he shared Ralph Waldo Emerson's misgivings about its becoming stereotyped and bland. He also warned that private education often created snobbishness and narrow loyalties, especially to religious institutions that sponsored them.

In retrospect, the contributions of religious commitment to education have been significant in perhaps unexpected ways. While "nonpublic" may not always imply sectarian or religious affiliation, it is true that when seen together as compared to public schools, as Frederick Mayer points out, (1) students in nonpublic schools have higher achievements than students in public schools, (2) nonpublic schools provide a safer, more orderly environment, (3) except for Catholic schools, nonpublic schools are smaller, have smaller class sizes, and encourage more student participation than do public schools, (4) nonpublic schools require more homework and have better attendance, and (5) superiority in school, climate, and discipline (e.g. homework, attendance) account for the higher achievement of nonpublic schools."[38]

State and federal funding for education in recent years has put a strain on the capabilities of public schools, necessitating increasing class sizes while reducing the number of teachers and library resources. This situation has led some to declare that disgruntled parents should have recourse to send their children to private schools at public expense through "vouchers." That would, in the opinion of others, further reduce the availability of government funds for those same public schools against which complaints have been leveled. The debate is expected to continue, probably in the courts.

This section has focused primarily on the effects of the Renaissance and Reformation on education in the Western world and almost exclusively on the U.S. experience. We must turn now to consideration of a more global nature in light of pluralism in its several aspects.

C. RELIGION AND EDUCATION IN A PLURALISTIC CULTURE

Ours is not yet "one world." Not only are there competing religious and political factions, but also there are cultural and language differences that make strangers of many who might otherwise wish to find common ground. Still others fight against attempts at fraternizing or "watering down" their distinctive identities. There is a not-so-secret "members-only" syndrome that actively adheres to the exclusive path, which has been just as true in the scientific community as in the arts and religious affiliations. For example, the hostility against the "germ theory" in medicine drove Ignaz Semmelweis (1818–1865) to a nervous breakdown. In seeking frantically to reduce deaths from puerperal fever, he simply tried to get fellow physicians to wash their hands before surgery. From Plato to Galileo and to Darwin and Einstein, one can find examples of heated opposition to any challenge to traditional wisdom, to suggest the possibility of a plurality of views and theories on any given subject that might broaden our outlook. Plato, the ultimate seeker after truth, was so committed to the universe being the product of intelligent design that "he recommended executing any citizen who refused . . . to acknowledge that mere matter cannot produce organic form and function."[39] (Plato, *Laws*, 909a)

1. One approach to dismantling at least some of the barriers that divide humankind is to acknowledge that nearly every major religious tradition has fostered education and that the leading figures almost without exception saw education as a way to bring about commitments to common goals, especially those ethical in nature. As in the opening chapter of this book, we confine the discussion primarily to three Eastern and three Western religions.

2. Another, simpler, way to bring down barriers is to seek some statement of faith and commitment, for example the Golden Rule that is common to all major traditions; fully and wholeheartedly adopted, it is capable of binding us together in a unique way. At this point, focusing on the leading representative religions of East and West holds the most promise for understanding and meeting the challenges of our increasingly pluralistic culture. At the risk of some redundancy, we return to these traditions.

1. Eastern Traditions

1. Hinduism.   As previously noted, Hinduism emerged from the Indus Valley area   about 2500–1500 B.C. It is not possible to fix the dates more precisely because no written texts from that period have been found. However, during the period from 1500 B.C. to 400 A.D., the Vedas, a vast number of writings, came into being, suggesting that some generation-to-generation transmission of wisdom and information must have been taking place. Whether in formal schools or, more likely, in less structured community gatherings, legends, lessons, and more than 250 hymns with references to a host of deities, especially *Indra* were shared.[40] All of the many deities mentioned in early and later writings were presented as manifestations of the one essential power at the heart of the cosmos, *Brahma*, the "All." In this sense, despite all of the deities written about, sung about, and prayed to, Hinduism at heart is a monotheistic religion except for the difference that Brahma is an impersonal all-transcending *atman*, or spirit.

In the quest for the morally perfect life, which leads to full self-realization, unity with Brahma, and thus salvation, one writer of the Upanishads asked in anguish, "Why have I not done the good? Why have I done evil?" not unlike the statement of St. Paul of Christian tradition. (Romans 7:19). To the Hindu, the answer comes in the revelation that "whoever knows 'I am Brahma,' becomes (one with) this All."[41] Recognition of this is considered the ultimate goal of all education. It happens that one of the great gifts of British colonization from the Victorian period onward was the system of education that made it possible. Clearly, however, the educational system was not focused exclusively nor even today emphasizes religious beliefs and practice. This has been brought home with a shock as American students in our U.S. universities find that students from India are often far better equipped for graduate studies in business, economics, and the hard sciences. Indeed, the United States as a whole has fallen behind India (and China!) in the production of computers and related specialties.

2. Confucianism. It is not without importance that the tentative monotheism of Hinduism has an echo in *Confucianism*, although paradoxically any specifically theistic affirmation is absent in both. That is, although neither tradition has a personal god, it has a sense in which the universe is governed by a "spirit" (*atman* in Hinduism and *Tien* an impersonal moral power in Confucianism) "rewarding good people and punishing bad people."[42] "Schools of thought" were common in China at the time of Confucius, although not in our contemporary sense of formal, government-supervised schools. These "schools" were for the most part loosely organized fellowships established by itinerate preachers and scholars who gathered disciples around them by sheer charismatic attraction. Confucius' ability to articulate the need for social reforms attracted groups in ebbs and flows, not infrequently with hostility because he seemed to threaten the political establishment. This is noteworthy because Confucius firmly believed in tradition and in the necessary hierarchy of social standing. Significantly, "two thousand years before Magna Charta, and the Rights of Man in China, Confucius and his disciples built the Right of Revolutions solidly into their political philosophy."[43]

At the time of his death, however, Confucius concluded that he had been a failure: "There is not one in the empire that will make me his master," but he underestimated his contributions and impact. Many followers mourned his passing in 479 B.C., and one student remained near his grave for six years. Confucius' writings continued to be copied and circulated, and his veneration reached a burst of enthusiasm when the emperor of China offered sacrifices to him at his tomb in 195 B.C.

Today, nearly 7 million people identify themselves as followers of Confucius. In major population centers in China where the state education mandates and closely monitors education, students and teachers are increasingly well informed about life across Asia, Europe, and the Americas. The media in all its varied forms, including line and cell phones and the internet, are virtually omnipresent. In addition, as increasing numbers of Western manufacturing and other businesses are "outsourcing" jobs and workers to the East, interest in all phases of social, scientific, and religious life as well as business is rapidly increasing.

3. Buddhism. Another tradition that has been difficult to label a religion because it disavows belief in a personal deity is *Buddhism*. Rather, it offers itself as an ethical and moral guide. His Holiness the Dalai Lama, has written numerous books, one in 1999 titled *Ethics for the New Millennium*. In it he stated, "I have observed that religious belief is not a precondition either of ethical conduct or of happiness."[44] Indeed, during a conference in South Africa that the present author attended, His Holiness made the pointed comment that belief in a personal God does not matter.

What did matter to Gautama, the original Buddha, was the establishment of teaching orders among his followers. Having received enlightenment while meditating under the bhodhi tree, he was eager to share the insights gained such as achieving freedom from all desire and from anxieties that foster frustrated greed (which leads to more anxieties and suffering). "Knowing neither satisfaction nor dissatisfaction, is the consummate purity of poised equanimity and mindfulness."[45] Education was clearly a priority, especially in regard to the extensive poverty, warfare, and suffering he witnessed throughout his native land. With his first five converts, Gautama established the first Buddhist Order and soon added to the little college of apostles some sixty members of his own Kshatriya caste and provided a curriculum called *the ten precepts,* a succinct, down-to-earth list of rules to follow and to teach others: (1) Refrain from destroying life, (2) do not take what is not given to you, (3) abstain from unchastity, (4) do not lie or deceive, (5) abstain from intoxicants, (6) eat moderately and not after noon, (7) do not look at dancing, singing, or dramatic spectacles, (8) do not affect the use of garlands, scents, unguents, or ornaments, (9) do not use high or broad beds, and (10) do not accept gold or silver.[46]

As the Buddhist movement grew, it needed an expanded "curriculum." Because metaphysical speculation had little appeal to Gautama, the *four noble truths* were added to the ten precepts:

1. Life is *dukkha,* suffering, from painful birth through successions of sicknesses and failures, finally culminating in death.
2. The real cause of life's grief's is *tanha,* the anxious yearning for personal fulfillment.
3. The cure for item 2 is suppression of such craving.
4. The cure is a sort of course of treatment like a physician's prescription called *the eightfold way,* involving (1) right views (of life, ourselves, problems to be solved), (2) right intention, (3) right speech, (4) right conduct (harking back to the ten precepts), (5) right livelihood, (6) right effort, (7) right mindfulness, and (8) right concentration.

Further elaborations to the curriculum were required as the movement grew, leading to lengthy discourses on *the law of karma,* a supreme power at work in the universe that leads to rewards and retribution for moral failure (perhaps the closest Buddhism comes to the Hindu and Confucian concepts of a cosmic moral order); *transmigration* of the self to another form after death (e.g., the rebirth of the Dalai Lama in a new person at the time of the current one's death); and *nirvana,* "the highest happiness" that may be achieved in a transcendent realm beyond this life.

Perhaps not surprising, the early appeal and rapid growth of Buddhism was due to its leveling of social distinctions across caste lines and its implication of equality for women and men. The Buddha had said, "Do not accept what you hear by report, do not accept tradition, do not accept a statement because it is found in our books nor because it is in accord with your belief. Be lamps unto yourselves."[47] Eventually, however, these hallmarks of Buddhism also served to limit the growth of the movement in India where the Buddhist rejection of the caste system, certain rites and rituals of Hinduism, and the near sacred authority of the Brahmin caste were deemed heretical.

The gradual diminution of Buddhism's influence in India was offset by its effectiveness as a growing influence in Ceylon, Burma, and Southeast Asia, reaching into China, Korea, and Japan. Ironically, the leadership of Emperor Ashoka (who ruled India from 268–233 B.C.) transformed Buddhism into a missionary faith and shifted its base to countries outside India. He was determined to change the world through the power not of the sword but moral law. His devotees exercised a zeal that resulted in a centuries-long evolution during which Buddhism as a philosophy became more intensely deep and better focused. His expression of the Buddhist life, called *Theravada,* was highly individualistic:

> By ourselves is evil done;
> By ourselves we cease from wrong,
> No one saves us but ourselves.

By contrast, the second major form of Buddhism, Mahayana, proposed that the fate of everyone is linked to all of life here and throughout the cosmos. The cultivation of compassion is at the core of the faith: "A guard I would be to those who have no protection, a guide to the voyager, a ship, a well, a spring, a bridge for the seeker of the other shore."[48] For our purposes here, it is enough to note that Buddhism had adherents numbering 359,092,100 by the year 2000 (5.7 percent of the world's population): 279,000 in Europe and 578,000 in North America. Of the totals, 56 percent of Buddhists are Mahayanists, 38 percent Theravadists, and 6 percent Trantrayanists (members of an early sect that opposed monasticism and offered a quasi-feminist argument for roles of adherents.[49]

2. Western Traditions

Moving toward a more Western orientation, a tradition in Judaism based on the Talmud states that when one stands before the gate of Heaven, three succinct questions are asked: Did you raise believing children? Were you honorable in business? Did you find time daily for serious study?

Judaism.   The Hebrew tradition, as historians usually call the early period of Jewish development, promoted the most vigorous efforts to be found in any religious tradition at the time of its founding. This was a conscious effort to provide a rigorous and systematic program of education. Among the advocates, of education, the program was never simply "learning for learning's sake" but an effort to prepare people to flourish in a constantly changing world. Beginning with the concept of creation itself, the writer of Proverbs declared: "The Lord by wisdom founded the earth" and Proverbs 3:19 advises, "The beginning of wisdom is this: Get wisdom, and whatever you get, get insight. Prize her highly and she will exalt you." (Proverbs 4:7). Author(s) of the Ecclesiastes adds, "The protection of wisdom is like the protection of money; and the advantage of knowledge is that wisdom preserves the life of him who has it." (Ecclesiastes 7: 12)

If we accept the dates for Abraham's birth (c. 2167 B.C.), the fact that his son Isaac was born when Abraham was 100, and Jacob appeared sixty years later,[50] these events can be placed considerably before the time of the Babylonia King Hammurabi (c. 1600 B.C.) and well before the classical ages of Greece and Rome as well as the appearance of Hinduism and Buddhism in India or Confucianism in China. It is remarkable then to find a structure for the education of children and youth being implemented at least as early as the Hebrew's exile in and exodus from Egypt (c. 1200 B.C.). Memorization was the primary, if not the exclusive, tool for learning. At least four periods for advancement appear to have been enforced. In the first, up to the age of six, schooling was conducted in the home, primarily by the father, with emphasis on moral attitudes, basic ritual, and the telling of tales about the glories of their culture.[51] Second, from ages six to ten, instruction shifted to the synagogue where boys and girls alike were taught to read, write, and do arithmetic. Religious instruction was intensified under the instruction of a scribe. Third, for ages between ten and sixteen, the rabbi taught the pupils a course on mastery of the law. Hebrew culture became highly legalistic over several centuries, with every detail "jot and title" observed. Finally, at age sixteen, when most girls had dropped out to be married and start a family, boys engaged in more advanced learning or what might today be termed "higher education." Lively intellectual exchanges of ideas, especially as pertained to the law, were encouraged, and students found themselves associating more with their teachers as disciples. The names of master teachers such as Gamaliel and Hillel are still revered today.[52]

Despite, or some might insist because of, the rigorous adherence to the Torah (the whole body of Jewish religious literature, including the first five books of the Old Testament), Judaism has exhibited a remarkable resiliency among the many cultural changes that have occurred in the societies in which the Jewish people have lived. The *Diaspora,* or dispersion of the people of Israel that began with the destruction of Jerusalem in 586 B.C.E. (before the common era). Their subsequent exile in Babylon and the return of a few to Jerusalem in 539 (but further scattering the majority during the reign of Alexander the Great) tested Jews' resolution to avoid being simply absorbed as they settled into Alexandria, Antioch, Rome, and, indeed, most of the major cities of the Greco-Roman world. Tradition rooted in faith proved a powerful cohesive. Among the leading and truly scholarly voices to be heard from Alexandria was that of Philo (20 B.C.E.–50 C.E.), a devoted Jew who sought to persuade all who would pay attention that the same God who spoke through Greek philosophy spoke also from Mt. Sinai. An admirer of Plato, he published his belief that mankind's inherent goodness would prevail in the midst of the moral laxity and thoughtless polytheism of the time. He led a delegation to Rome to plead the Jewish cause before Caligula, but to no avail. He did not live to witness the horror of the next diaspora when Roman soldiers sacked Jerusalem in 70 A.D. and crucified thousands who failed to escape.

Little written material about the fate of scattered Judaism survived until Islam burst upon the world scene in the seventh century with its astonishing expansion across Europe. Contrary to popular writers even today, the Arabs did not "spread Islam by the sword" but in fact insisted on freedom of religion for all (cf. The Holy Qur'an S ii 256; X 99 and 1480) and offered a new cultural as well as spiritual ideal. "The general rule of Muslim Arab civilization from Babylonia to Spain was a freedom and toleration which permitted the Jewish people to build the new forms of faith and culture of a Judaeo-Islamic age."[53] Saadia ben Joseph (882–942) was generally credited as the founder of Jewish scholasticism during this time of new freedom, he was a product of Greek, Muslim, and Jewish education. Under his guidance, philosophy, biblical studies, and other forms of scholarship flowered and many illustrious careers were launched, the most notable doubtless being that of Moses Maimonides.[54] Tragically, many of the advances made through the interaction of Jewish, Christian, and Muslim scholars, among them architects and scientists, came to an abrupt halt during the Spanish reign of Ferdinand and Isabella and the infamous Inquisition. This is particularly ironic because it was due in large part to Isabella's intervention that Christopher Columbus' initial voyage was made possible and set in motion many of the dramatic changes that would advance the eras of the Renaissance, the Reformation, and the subsequent Enlightenment.

Across Europe, Jewish social separation from the mainstream of European society was largely enforced by "Christian" political regulations, resulting in the Jews' being "ghettoized." Education for Jewish youth was a closely regulated process under a rabbi's determination, and to a greater or lesser degree formally enforced almost through the nineteenth century. As a young scholar in Berlin, Moses Mendelssohn (1729–1786) wrote a treatise on immortality that surprised non-Jews with its familiar tone; his translation of the Torah into German made Jewish thought more accessible, and his book *Jerusalem* began, at least among Christian scholars, the slow correction of old misunderstandings. "More than anyone else, Mendelssohn led Judaism away from the closed community of medieval Europe toward the open, free, and religiously pluralistic society of modernity."[55]

Perhaps the most striking feature of nineteenth century Judaism was the formation of the Frankfurt Society of the Friends of Reform, which wrote into the very "constitution" of the new "denomination" of Judaism: "A Messiah who is to lead back the Israelites to the land of Palestine is neither expected not desired by us; we know no fatherland but that to which we belong by birth or citizenship."[56] This statement met with great opposition by Jews of both Conservative and Orthodox persuasion but took root quickly in the United States; when in the 1840s and 1850s a wave of immigrants, from Ireland, Scotland, and other nations fled a prolonged famine. The most able spokesman for reform was Rabbi Isaac Meyer Wise (1819–1900), who was responsible for the founding of the Union of American Hebrew Congregations, Hebrew Union College, and the Central Conference of American Rabbis.

With the availability of public education, most Jewish children and youth enrolled and participated in virtually all forms of studious and social aspects of school life. Yet while few expected the local temple or synagogue to fulfill all public education roles most Jews viewed it as an invaluable educational institution. There youth underwent a rigorous preparation for the bar mitzvah (for boys and men) and bat mitzvah (for girls and women), "son (or daughter) of the commandment." Sermons directed to every social level in the congregations were expected to be of a scholarly quality. In every aspect of temple or synagogue life, the members were reminded of the central value of respect for wisdom, learning, and social justice. It has been often acknowledged that Jewish contributions to science and the arts is out of proportion to their numbers in the population.

Christianity.   Rome was already a pluralistic culture when Christianity entered the scene in the relative quiet of an obscure manger. Or, more accurately, one should say Rome was a multinational culture without real effort to weld the state into a functioning pluralism. Dozens of nations across Asia from Mesopotamia, Bythinia, and Judaea to Egypt and Libya had been conquered or otherwise swept up into Rome's rule. Each was permitted to continue its own languages and religions as long as it paid taxes to Rome and burned a pinch of incense in Caesar's honor.

The followers of Jesus were given an unprecedented challenge to "go into all the world and preach the gospel to the whole creation," (Mark 16:15) but the gospel ("good news") was not to be exclusive as was the case with so many religions of the time: "Peter said . . . I perceive that God shows no partiality, but in every nation anyone who fears Him and does what is right is acceptable to Him." (Acts 10:34f.)[57]

Education for discipleship to equip all Christians to carry this "good news" to the world required a special kind of curriculum and well-trained teachers. The Christians looked first to the parents as did their Jewish kin, and then to persons the congregations selected to be teachers. The pupils were called *catechumens;* the catechism itself was a curriculum of church history, doctrine, creeds, and practices of respect for teachers, for each other, for strangers, and even for enemies. By Augustine's time (354–430 A.D.), classical literature from Greece and Rome might be included but only cautiously to avoid compromise with Christian doctrine.[58]

In time, as the church multiplied in both numbers and size, the most prominent pastor in a given region (e.g., Jerusalem, Alexandria, and Antioch) was given the title of bishop, and his church was called a *cathedral* (or "chair" of the bishop). Both girls and boys were invited to the church or cathedral schools, and in time young men and women were enrolling from all parts of the Empire. After centuries of intermittent persecution, the Emperor Constantine adopted Christianity as virtually the official religion of Rome and called a council meeting in Nicaea in Asia Minor in 325 to clarify key issues of the faith. Some 300 bishops and "hundreds of lesser clergy and lay folk" attended to create one of the greatest historic documents of the church, the Nicaean Creed.[59] Eventually, Constantine declared that only Christians could teach in any of the schools of Rome.

The fortunes of the Roman Empire rose and fell in the next two centuries as segments of the army were sent as far east as Byzantium and northwest as far as Scotland. Its "fall" (unnoticed for the most part by most of the common people) was due to a number of complex reasons, not the least of which were the expense of maintaining the army over such a vast area and the fact that political intrigues tore away the heart of the stabilizing forces of government. Educational opportunities followed the missionaries who, in many cases, helped establish monasteries and libraries.

When Charlemagne ascended to power in the eighth century, he created a palace school as a focal point for the revival of education and culture throughout the newly proclaimed "Holy Roman Empire."[60] The palace school and its imitators, however, seldom went far beyond the basic curriculum begun in the first and second centuries of Christianity except in a few centers such as those in Baghdad, Toledo, and Alexandria where Muslim scholars had brought the fruits of their own astonishing research. "There the works of Aristotle, Galen, Euclid, Ptolemy, and Plato; Neoplatonic works and masterpieces in Judaic, Syriac, Coptic, Chinese, Hindu and Persian were made available for study by scholars who flocked there from all corners of the world."[61] The rest of Europe had to await the rise of universities.

The primary goal of universities in their beginning was not limited to the scholarly enterprises we have come to expect from Oxford, Cambridge, the universities of France, Germany, and Italy; of Harvard, Yale, Princeton, and California–Berkeley in the United States. Initially, universities provided professional training for lawyers, physicians, theologians, and artists, but such a high level of preparation as these professions required could not be met by the basic skills in reading and figuring customarily offered by lower-level education to "the trades." The universities, then, had a profound effect on the development of elementary and secondary schools (although it would not be until 1874 that U.S. secondary schools came into being as state-sponsored institutions).[62] They also taught students to challenge old customs and traditions required by the church or entrenched sciences and set the stage for pluralism in Western culture with a vengeance.

Travel became vastly extended after the voyages of Columbus and Magellan. New frontiers beckoned, and as disaffected citizens across Europe moved to the New World, they brought their languages, customs of food and dress, and school curricula with them. All would now need significant modification.

In 1660, only two decades after the founding of Harvard College, a textbook, *The New England Primer* appeared; it has been called one of the most important textbooks in all American educational history.[63] Utilizing visual references, it began with the alphabet, "A is for apple" with a picture of an apple and the pictured verse "A is for Adam, in Adam's Fall we sinned all" showing a scantily clad man and woman under a tree. It became a model for textbooks at the elementary level for two centuries until the publication of the McGuffey *Eclectic Readers*. These admittedly Puritan-inspired books, which embraced curriculum material for all eight elementary grades, became the national standard from about 1844 until the first quarter of the twentieth century.

With a conviction made explicit that religious faith, patriotism, and morality were essential for the success of a democratic society, the McGuffey Reader had the largest circulation of any book in the world, second only to the Bible by 1919.[64]

It is worth reiterating that the earliest elementary schools in the United States were coed with the exception of private schools for the children of the upper economic bracket who planned to attend a college or university. Institutions of higher education such as Harvard, Yale, and Princeton, were for men only. This pattern continued until the founding in 1833 of Oberlin College in Ohio, which, with its founders' opposition to slavery, was both coed and interracial.[65] Interestingly, when Harvard was founded, although not coed, it was interracial, inviting Native American "Indians" to enroll.

It is perhaps not an overstatement to say that education in all of its forms from kindergarten to colleges and universities has historically been driven by religiously committed leaders. From Plato to Einstein and Whitehead, they were convinced that not only the curriculum but also the whole atmosphere of learning—what Earl Pullias of the University of Southern California called "spirit of place"—would have deep emotional, moral, and academic consequences.[66] From the Renaissance to the Age of Enlightenment and to recent opponents of public, tax-supported schools and proponents of separation of church and state, such notions have had fierce adversaries. The most recent opponents have sometimes expressed harsh criticism of teachers for wearing religious symbols, whether in the form of jewelry or head scarves (resulting in the legal prohibitions of wearing these scarves in Paris, France, in March 2004) or even having a Bible or copy of the Qur'an on their desks.

For the most part, these are minor irritations but can become costly when, for example, a school in southern California risked losing millions of dollars in state school finance for initiating a faith-based ban on youth who declared the right to identify themselves as members of their perceived gender rather than the one biologically determined at birth.[67] Much larger issues have emerged, however, on the global scene.

Several attempts were made during the eighteenth and nineteenth centuries when missionaries from a host of denominations competed for converts in countries around the world, and had to pool resources and share programs to provide "foreign" populations' medical, agricultural, and spiritual needs.

In this regard, it is helpful to remember that the first colonial empires in the New World were founded by the Roman Catholic nations of Spain, Portugal, and France. Their mission history sparkles with the names of self-sacrificing missionaries and martyrs, the greatest perhaps being Father Francis Xavier, Apostle to India and Japan (1506–1552). Among those first to labor in the West Indies and South America, the most prominent would undoubtedly be Bartholome de las Casas." Among Protestant missionaries who became pioneers in education, medical science, and sometimes industrial organizations, the most prominent names would be William Carey (1761–1834) and David Livingston (1813–1873). Their work with their colleagues helped to advance nurses' training and studies in sociology and ethnology as well as knowledge of geography.[68] With his extensive travels across Africa, Livingston alone, plotting maps along the way, probably did more to link this strategy with religious mission activity than any other single figure before Albert Schweitzer (1875–1965).

With increasing cooperative activity among diverse missionary groups, a greater appreciation for each other's religious integrity began to dawn. By the close of the nineteenth century, many would have agreed with Huston Smith's more recent observation: "The historical religions have largely abandoned their earlier missionary designs on the 'heathen' as they were once disparagingly referred to."[69]

Out of this cooperative spirit grew one of the most exceptional events in human history, the dawn of religious pluralism in the form of The Parliament of the World's Religions. First meeting in 1893 in conjunction with the Columbian Exposition, sixty representatives gathered from what was then considered "the ten great religions of the world": Hinduism, Buddhism, Jainism, Zoroastrianism, Taoism, Confucianism, Shintoism, Judaism, Christianity, and Islam. Ironically, the United States, hosting the event, would not under "normal" circumstances have welcomed some of the delegates because of the Chinese Exclusion Act of 1882. Indeed, systematic exclusion policies were enforced to the extent that most Americans would not have heard the voices of Hindu, Buddhist, or Shinto traditions except for the Parliament.[70] Such was the outpouring of popular enthusiasm for this parliament that the directors had to seek a new venue to house the overflowing crowds.

Sadly, plans to guarantee the continuance of the parliament had not been put into place with sufficient organizational skill. The creation of other groups such as Salvation Army, YMCA, Boy Scouts of America, and countless regional church counsels highlight the period. Add to this the innumerable inventions with global impact including the telephone, automobile, airplane, motion picture, and electric light to say nothing of the effects of World War I, the Great Depression, and the buildup to World War II. Nevertheless, that initial parliament inspired many ecumenical organizations such as a national council of churches in many countries and laid the groundwork for the World Council of Churches created in 1948.

By 1990, the spark to hold a centennial celebration of the parliament in Chicago in 1993 had been ignited. "If in 1893 the world *came* to Chicago, today the people of the world *live* in Chicago: there are 80,000 Hindus attending 17 temples; more Muslims than Jews; more Thai Buddhists than Episcopalians." These religions in addition to representatives of more than 150 other religious bodies and organizations including seminaries and other educational associations became cosponsors of the parliament.[71] These meetings in 1993 drew nearly 8,000 people from around the world representing every major religious and some less well-known traditions including Earth Spirit Community and Wicca. This time future international gatherings were scheduled; one was held in South Africa in 1999, and another was in Spain in 2004.

Islam.   Islam, which had a prominent voice in the parliament, has a long history of creative involvement not only with other religious traditions but also with education. "At the heart of the community of those who accepted Muhammad's message stood the religious scholars, *Ulama,* men learned in the Qur'an, Hadith (a body of traditions from the time of Muhammad, and which constitute the *sunna* or standard of Muslim orthodoxy) and Law.[72]

There is a bit of irony here in that, although Christianity was deeply involved in educating children and youth from the beginning of the church and advancing the studies of mathematics, astronomy, grammar, rhetoric, logic, and music at higher levels, the early church shied away from the natural sciences and the philosophies of Greece and Rome until the Renaissance. They deemed the natural sciences and philosophies pagan and therefore distracting from the paths of discipleship. The Jewish and Islamic scholars were the ones who explored these subjects, and eventually, during their interaction with the Christians in the Middle Ages, stimulated among some a hunger for broader knowledge. The already established universities provided a launching platform for the advanced scholarly pursuits. Before this development, however, the Muslims had already established tuition-free schools and colleges in many major cities: Baghdad, Mecca, Damascus, Cairo, Cordova, Seville, Granada, and Toledo. There the world's first pharmaceutical schools were developed to service a growing medical profession. Faculty and students worked with trigonometry and learned to survey the land and to chart the seas and the heavens. All of these gifts would eventually come to the Western world, principally by way of the crusaders, and included such devotional objects as the rosary, votive candles, and the game of chess.[73]

So earnest were the Muslims in the quest for learning that the doctors of law who developed and preserved the consensus of the community were the nearest equivalent to a teaching authority in Sunni Islam, and it was essential for them to make sure that the understanding of *fiqh* (the authoritative theology and cannon law of Islam) and its bases was fully transmitted from one generation to another.[74]

By the fourteenth century, the fortune of Islam as a major power arose to its highest reach in the formation of the Ottoman Empire. Osman I, a Muslim prince whose successors were called *ottomans,* took possession of most of southeastern Europe. By the fifteenth century, the major part of the Muslim world was integrated into three empires: Ottoman, Safavid, and Mughal. In 1453, the Ottomans conquered Constantinople and within another century had absorbed a large portion of Hungary and most of the Middle East and North Africa. In the great Arab cities, education continued to focus on history, biography, the sciences, and compilations of the works of *fiqh* and *hadith.* The political struggles with former leaders of conquered regions and of Spain, Austria, and Russia, however, threatened the empire's stability. Suleyman "the Magnificent" came to power in 1520, but by 1566, it was evident that the Ottoman Empire was in serious decline. With the close of the eighteenth century, its borders had been seriously pushed back, and the empire was about to lose control of Egypt and the Balkans. After World War I, the Ottoman Empire lost its Arab provinces, and in 1921, Ataturk (Mustafa Kemal) declared it to be the State of Turkey. All semblance of Islamic rule was abolished in a wave of nationalism and antisectarianism. Turkey, after receiving much needed economic aid from the United States, declared itself "westernized."

It must be understood, however, that the decline of the Ottoman Empire, disruptive though it was to government affairs in the Middle East, did not diminish the loyalty of most of the peoples of the Arab world to their religious tradition. Today the world has 1.2 billion Muslims, a number that has more than doubled in the past forty years, making it the second fastest growing religion in the world.[75]

Common Affirmation.   As suggested earlier, a simple yet helpful way to find common ground among the major religions of the world is to identify one affirmation on which all can agree that might serve as a kind of passport to fellowship with kindred spirits of diverse religious, national, racial, and ethnic backgrounds. The Golden Rule has often been proffered, as discussed in Chapter Two.

Pluralism and Globalization.   As pleasant as it is to review some basic commonalities among the major religions, it is easy to recognize a certain hortatory, almost rhetorical, quality among these "golden" suggestions (they do not really qualify as rules). It seems painfully easy for earnestly devout practitioners of any of religion to give nodding assent to them, while for politically motivated excuses launching a pre-emptive strike against an assumed enemy. In the name of national security, these devout practitioners punish assumed enemies by locking them in prisons without formal charges against them and without access to legal counsel or even visits from family members. What then can be said for such "golden" exhortations?

Perhaps the most solid ground for optimism is in the recognition that, despite the conflicts seemingly global in extent, the effort to respond creatively to the religious and cultural pluralism that exists in fact, not just in wishful thinking, is growing. This is strikingly evident in the realms of religious growth, business and economic enterprise, and—even more especially in recent years—formal education. We have today an unprecedented opportunity both to reach out and to draw in.

In terms of reaching out, the missionary movements of early Buddhism from India to China, Japan, and neighboring regions set the pattern in motion. Western civilization, on the other hand, was identified with Catholic and Protestant churches. Samuel Huntington declares that "Western Christianity . . . is historically the single most important characteristic of Western Civilization."[76] As evidence he notes that while the Jews were persecuted and dispersed across Europe and North Africa by the Romans, Judaism was without signs of significant growth. Christians, even while being persecuted, grew rapidly in number and built schools and social structures while interacting with peoples of other faith traditions. By the eighth century, Islam experienced a within the vigorous expansion context of growing enthusiasm for globalization. "Historically Western Society has been highly pluralistic. What is distinctive about the West is the rise and persistence of diverse autonomous groups not based on blood relationship or marriage."[77]

Today such pluralistic phenomena are even more widepread. They are global in scope and more energetic, a fact not overlooked by either business entrepreneurs or educators. The world of business has a number of problems with both the pluralistic and global engagements, not the least of which is the issue of outsourcing goods and merchandise and the impact of such policy on domestic employment. Indeed, Amy Chua, a professor at Yale Law School, asks whether globalization is perhaps the "suicide of free market democracy."[78] We will return to this issue. At this point, however, our focus will be on the ways in which educational institutions are responding to the twin challenges of pluralism and globalization.

The Roman Catholic Church, founded most, if not all, of the great medieval universities, and the Protestant Reformation brought into being more universities, but none of them showed any interest in admitting students who were not of their religious identity. Pluralism was simply not in their lexicon. In the New World, university enrollment was almost entirely limited to men until 1833 when Oberlin College opened in Ohio with the published intent to accept women as well as men and "members of the colored race." Pluralism was clearly in evidence at Oberlin and was followed by Vassar in New York in 1865; Wellesley in Northampton, Massachusetts, in 1875; Park College near Kansas City that same year; and, in rapid succession, a host of other such schools. Many of these schools enrolled the sons and daughters of missionaries who had had wide exposure to different racial and ethnic groups as well as religious affiliations.

The University of Southern California, founded in 1880 under the auspices of the Methodist Church, had three founders, one a Protestant, one a Roman Catholic, and the third a Jew. Open admission to all races and all faiths was written into the university's charter. The current chaplain is a woman rabbi who monitors a complex of programs, study groups, and ecumenical gatherings of 57 distinctive religious traditions on campus. These represent what Diana Eck, a Harvard religious scholar, calls "this new neoreligious reality." Pluralism is not simply a static tolerance of differences among people but also an evaluative theory of how interaction can lead beyond mere tolerance to an enactive appreciation of those differences and a celebration of each others' celebrations: Christians celebrating Chanukah with Jewish friends, Ramadan with Muslim friends, Oban with Buddhist friends, and inviting these friends to share the joys of Christmas and Easter in a Christian context. John Kekes describes this interaction as "a theory motivated by a concern for human beings actually living good lives. Consequently pluralism is at once descriptive and evaluative. It offers a description of some conceptual and factual features relevant to good lives."[79]

These represent ways in which people of diverse religious, political, economic, ethnic, and racial traditions can be brought together on campuses, in churches, and in other social entities comprising a metaphysical counterpart of multiculturalism. And what of efforts to move outward from those organizations to involve and even embrace such diversity at the global level?

In 1991, the *Yearbook of the Association for Supervision and Curriculum Development* opened with the observation that

> Although there is a growing number of global education projects across the United States, most educators and most lay people understand neither the need for global education nor its promise. In fact many people are frightened by the changes occurring in the world; they seem to distrust even the term *global education.*[80]

As early as 1976, R.G. Hanvey provided a working definition that should have allayed many fears:

> Global education involves learning about those problems and issues that cut across national boundaries, and about the interconnectedness of systems—ecological, cultural, economic, political and technological. Global education involves perspective taking—seeing things through the eyes and minds of others—and it means realization that while individuals and groups may view life differently, they also have common needs and wants.[81]

Bill Clinton strongly advocated the importance of global education more than a decade later when, as governor of Arkansas, he noted:

> Our economic, political, social, and environmental systems have become interconnected to such a degree that we must develop a world awareness. . . . In an

increasingly knowledge-based economy, in which almost one in every four dollars made by Americans is tied to world trade, a good education fostering global thinking is more important than ever before.[82]

In the mid- and late 1980s, as Kenneth Tye points out, however, "global education in the United States came under attack, and was labeled unAmerican by various right wing individuals and groups."[83] Nor were such attacks unique to the United States. "In many nations of the world today, schooling is still seen as a major force in the building of national loyalties."[84] To understand the reasons behind the acceptance or rejection of trying to implement globalization in the schools of 52 countries, Kenneth and Barbara Tye devised a questionnaire. Of forty responses received, fifteen emphasized that globalization was not an acknowledged part of the curriculum; thirteen identified lack of resources as a major barrier to acceptance; ten pointed to nationalism; and only one cited religion as a problem. The surveyors had made clear ahead of time that they had no interest in just creating another class on international affairs, but the response to the questionnaire was that too many teachers were just too busy to care about it.

Among the more encouraging aspects of several similar studies was the indication that rejection of globalization rested on a misunderstanding of the goals and techniques of the teaching/learning environment. A student need not be studying things foreign or international (though, of course, involvement in exchange programs or Peace Corps assignments would suggest themselves as being highly conducive). "There are ways in which a student can be studying his or her community and be just as much involved in global education as when he or she is studying a community in another part of the world."[85] The prospects and promise appear almost limitless.

D. IMPLICATIONS FOR GLOBAL ETHICS

In the preface to his admirably objective and otherwise secular *History of Educational Thought,* Frederick Mayer declared "we cannot understand the history of educational thought without understanding its religious foundations."[86] He points to the teachings of the Buddha, who spoke of human equality even amidst the ravages of the caste system; to the instruction of Confucius, who placed the family and its faith in the decrees of Heaven at the center of the education venture; to the Hebrew prophets, who insisted on educating children in "the way in which they should go," emphasizing the command of Yahweh to "do justly, love mercy, walk humbly with God"; to Socrates, "the gadfly of Athens," who inspired by his stress on eternal ideals; to Jesus, who was to be extolled as "the great teacher and healer" and whose teachings later inspired the building of schools and universities across Europe and America; to the advocations of Muhammed, a master organizer who translated his theology into the foundation of advanced mathematics, cosmology, medicine, and translations of Greek and Roman thinkers.[87]

Given the fact that almost all religions of the world propose some variation on the Golden Rule, and that parents and teachers have generally tried to educate each new generation with moral commitment and ethical practice, one might view their work optimistically as the seed from which a global ethic might grow. Educational reformers such as John Comenius (1592–1670), Johann Pestalozzi (1746–1827), and Friedrch Froebel (1782–1852) envisioned unified educational systems from kindergarten through the university everywhere. While it is true that their ideals were based largely on Christianity and "Western" ideals, all were open to inclusive studies appealing to what they believed to reflect the inherent idealism in all humankind. Similarly, during the Age of Reason in the eighteenth century, philosophers such as Descartes, Pascal, Spinoza, Locke, and Newton sought to maintain their stand somewhere within religious orthodoxy while struggling with new concepts of science.

How, then, did it happen that all of their work seemed to come unraveled in the flames of revolution when the oppression of the wealthy and powerful over the masses of unemployed and hungry (e.g., Louis XV, who declared in 1776 that "supreme authority is rested in my person alone,"[88]) ignited deadly rebellions. Even some well-educated scientists were executed during the Reign of Terror in France, where the already world-renowned chemist, Lavoissier, was put to death with the judges' verdict; "The Revolution has no need of scientists." The so-called Age of Reason, especially in France, the cultural capital of all Europe, was dead. Platos idealism, which had been handed down through two millennia proposing that education was the single most important means of revealing the innate goodness and creativity, was replaced by the materialism and opportunism of Niccolo Machiavelli (1469–1527) who believed that humans are essentially motivated by self-interest. In large numbers, philosophers and political leaders adopted his posture of detachment from judgmental moralizing, which earned him (inaccurately) the reputation of being unscrupulous, promoting wickedness in the name of efficiency, and justifying war in the interest of guaranteeing the power of the state. In reality, Machiavelli was not interested with issues of good and evil and ejected most religious views, especially those of Christianity, as endangering political effectiveness. His writings soon became popular in Italy (although they were placed on the Index of the Roman church), France, and England. Among his admirers were Mably, Rousseau, and, in nineteenth and twentieth centuries, von Ranke, Nietzshe, Hitler, and Mussolini.

Meanwhile, however, the older, traditional views rooted in antiquity appear to have followed the patterns of the Hebrew, Athenian, Roman, and Medieval cultures. These societies viewed education as a major conduit for knowledge of God (or other deities), rational enlightenment, and citizenship. When Charlemagne established his cathedral school at Aachen in 800, he brought together the leading scholars of the time, including theologians, to encourage other cultural as well as religious disciplines. During the Medieval and Renaissance periods (and through the work of missionaries in China, India, and the Middle East), ethics, the sciences, and religious faith were at the core of the curriculum. On the U.S. frontier, Harvard, Yale, Princeton, and the other six colonial universities established in the seventeenth and eighteenth centuries offered strong coursework in moral philosophy and religious practice while, as the nation expanded, church-related schools, colleges, and universities became a distinguishing feature of the U.S. landscape. To be sure, "Many observers have questioned whether this unplanned, helter-skelter mutiplication of colleges did not go too far. Yale, which helped to found at least sixteen new colleges, became a mother of colleges."[89] Other universities followed suit, enriching the prospects for keeping alive a spirit of optimism for the future.

A burning question keeps smoldering beneath the seeming certainty of a better world through education, however. If today masses of humanity can read, write, drive cars, and enjoy the fruits of industrial civilization, are they now torn in all directions in what some call an age of violence? It is not an altogether new situation when we think of how "the glory that was Greece" was deflected into wars by the likes of Heraclitus, who in 480 B.C. advocated that war is precursor of all important changes and good things, and of early Hebrews writers who called God "a man of war." (Exodus 15:3). Both Zarathustra and later Hebrew prophets tried to resolve the inner conflicts that prompt a warlike stance against enemies—real or perceived—holding that humankind is at odds with the creator's intended destiny for it. Education has held the promise of a utopian order but also taught us to create and manufacture weapons that put the whole human species (and some think the planet itself) at risk of annihilation.

We can hope that at the heart of the educational venture, the inherent striving for peace and brotherhood common to all the major religions, will prevail. The benefits in terms of keeping alive a sense of both spiritual and academic preparation is beyond calculation and remain both a model and challenge as we consider further movement toward consideration of global ethics.

"Hope" may seem a frail container into which we may place our expectations for the future, but in Tennyson's words: "It is our mighty hopes that make us men." For Jurgen Moltman perhaps most of the scientifically minded, "natural theology" is a better receptacle. Theologically, it is

> a necessary part of reflection upon nature and human existence; it is not that from which we come but the light to which we are going. The *lumen naturae* is the reflection of the *lumen glriae* . . . assigning revelation to this age, but natural theology to the age to come, a foretaste and advance intimation of the promised universal glory of God.[90]

If this seems a bit too visionary for modern ethicists, it may be helpful to recall the words from Proverbs 29: "Where there is no vision, the people perish."

NOTES

1. Thucydides, *History of the Peloponnesian War,* trans. Richard Crawley (London: J.M. Dent and Sons Limited, 1910), 121f–122.

2. Plato's Academy was founded around 387 B.C. and survived until it was dissolved in 529 A.D. by Justinian. Rome "fell" in 476 A.D. when Odoacer, the German conqueror of the western part of the empire deposed the last emperor, Romulus Augustus. Thus, the Academy outlived the Roman Empire by more than half a century.

3. The word *stoic* came from the Greek *stoa,* a covered walk or portico on a public building where Zeno and his informal "faculty" gathered their students.

4. H.G. Wells, *The Outline of History,* (Garden City, NJ: Doubleday, 1971), 413–15.

5. Rene Wormser, *The Law* (New York: Simon and Schuster, 1949), 123. Some would argue that the Patriot Act, approved by the U.S. Congress and signed by President George W. Bush in the wake of the World Trade Center attack on September 11, 2001, violates the principle of equity (e.g., imprisoning suspects without formal charge and with no access to legal counsel or even family visitation). This has yet to be resolved; we have not yet applied the principle of ius gentium ("the law of foreigners" as developed by the Roman jurists, much less the dictum of Abraham Lincoln that "all men are created equal" and entitled to humane treatment.

6. R. Freeman Butts, *A Cultural History of Western Education* (New York: McGraw-Hill, 1955), 85–86.

7. Ibid., 86.

8. Ibid.

9. Robert B. McLaren, *The World of Philosophy* (Chicago: Nelson-Hall, l983), 48.

10. Will Durant, Caesar and Christ, (New York; Simon and Schuster, 1944), 667.

11. "The Buggar man will get you if you don't. . . ." See *Webster's New World Dictionary.* (Cleveland: World Publishing Company, 1964), 191.

12. Charles Homer Haskins, The Rise of Universities (Ithaca, NY: Cornell University Press, l967), 34.

13. *The New Encyclopedia Britannica Macropedia,* vol. 10 (Chicago: Encyclopedia Britannica, 1974), 857.

14. Majid Fakhry, *The Oxford History of Islam,* ed. John L. Esposito (New York: Oxford University Press, l999), 275–76.

15. McLaren *The World of Philosophy,* 72.

16. Albert Hourani, *A History of the Arab Peoples* (Cambridge: Harvard University Press, 1991), 167–76.

17. *The New Encyclopedia Britannica Micropedia,* vol. 6. (Chicago: Encyclopedia Britannica, l974, 457.

18. *The Moral System of Islam* (Chicago: The Institute of Islamic Information and Education). Reprinted with the permission of World Assembly of Muslim Youth, Riyadh, Saudi Arabia.

19. Butts, *A Cultural History,* 144.

20. It should be noted that "oracles" in Hebrew thought did *not* refer to semidivine persons, diviners, seers, or "mediums" believed to be in communication with the deity or deities (as in Greek and Roman religions). The Holy of Holies in the Jewish temple might itself be called an oracle; it was the holy place where the spiritual wisdom might be attained. (Cf. I Kings 6:16–37)

21. Butts, *A Cultural History,* 157.

22. Lenn Goodman, *Rambam, Readings in the Philosophy of Moses Maimonides* (New York; Viking Press, 1976).

23. *Ibid.,* 217.

24. John Bowker, *What Muslims Believe.* (Oxford, England, One World Publications, 1998), 146–47.

25. Jacobus Dominicus, *Ratio Atque: Institutio Studiorum Societatis Jesu,* (January 8, 1599), quoted in James W. Noll and Sam P. Kelly, *Foundations of Education in America* (New York: Harper & Row, 1970), 87–88.

26. William M. Kirtines and Jacob L. Gewirtz, *Morality, Moral Behavior and Moral Development* (New York: John Wiley, 1984), 17–18.

27. Frederick Mayer, *A History of Educational Thought,* 3rd ed. (Columbus, OH: Charles E. Merrill, 1973), 384.

28. Martin Luther, *To the Councilmen of All Cities in Germany, That They Establish and Maintain Christian Schools.* From Walther I. Brandt, ed., *Luther's Works,* vol. 45 (Philadelphia: Muhlenberg Press, 1962), quoted in Noll and Kelly, *Foundations of Education,* 67.

29. Williston Walker, *A History of the Christian Church,* 3rd ed. (New York: Charles Scribner's Sons, 1970), 342–43.

30. James Tunstead Burtchaell, *The Dying of the Light: The Disengagement of Colleges and Universities from Their Christian Churches* (Grand Rapids, MI: William B. Eerdmans, 1998), 460.

31. Ibid., 461.

32. Ibid., 512.

33. For the students to be admitted was a signal achievement because in England, colleges and universities were not accredited unless founded by the king, which although in a British colony, Harvard was not so founded.

34. The following lists the original school name, founding group or founder, and the date it was established:

Harvard College—	Puritans and Congregationalists—	1636
College of William and Mary—	Anglicans—	1694
Yale College—	Congregationalists—	1701
Princeton College—	Presbyterians—	1746
College of Philadelphia, now the University of Pennsylvania—	Benjamin Franklin—	1755
Rhode Island College, now Brown University—	Baptists—	1764
Queens College, now Rutgers University—	Dutch Reformists—	1766
Dartmouth College—	Congregationalists—	1769

35. Frederick Mayer, *A History of Educational Thought,* 3rd ed., (Columbus Ohio: Charles E. Merrill, 1973), 200–1.

36. Ibid., 345.

37. Horace Mann, *Twelfth Annual Report to the Massachusetts State Board of Education,* quoted in Mayer, ibid. *A History,* 347.

38. Allan C. Ornstein, and Daniel U. Levine, *An Introduction to the Foundations of Education* 3rd ed. (Boston, Houghton-Mifflin, 1985), 548.

39. David Depew, "Intelligent Design and Irreducible Complexity," *Rhetoric and Public Affairs* vol. 1 (East Lansing, MI: Michigan State University Press, 1998), 571–72.

40. William A. Young, *The World's Religions* (Englewood Cliffs, NJ: Prentice-Hall, 1995), 105.

41. Swami Nikhilananda, *The Upanishads* (New York: Harper & Row, 1962), 54–55; see also *Thirteen Principle Upanishads,* trans. Robert Hume (Oxford, England: 1959), 83–84, 289. (*Cf.* Hume ibid, 26-27)

42. Charles L. Manske, and Daniel N. Harmelink, *World Religions Today* (Irvine, CA: Institute of World Religions, 1996), 16. However, note the commentary of Ninian Smart, *The World's Religions* (Englewood Cliffs, NJ: Prentice-Hall, 1989), 106. He points out that *Tien* became a personalized god whose cult was that of the emperor. See also Arthur Waley, *The Analects of Confucius,* 181 Concerning the "bad end" to which a legendary hero was called, presumably because he violated the will of *Tien.*

43. Huston Smith, 182.

44. H. H. the Dalai Lama, *Ethics for the New Millennium* (New York: Riverhead Books, Penguin Putnam Inc., 1999), 220.

45. Lord Chalmers, trans., *Further Dialogues of the Buddha,* from the *Majjhima Nikaya* Chalmers (London; Oxford University Press, 1926), I.p. 15 (1.22)

46. *Buddhist Scriptures,* trans. Edward J. Thomas, Wisdom of the East series (London: 1913), 52.

47. E.A. Burtt, *The Teachings of the Compassionate Buddha* (New York: Mentor Books, 1955), 49–50, quoted in Smith, 94.

48. Quoted in Smith, 122–123. Cf. see also Hans Kung, *Christianity and the World Religions* (New York: Doubleday, 1986), 334–339.

49. Manske and Harmelink, *World Religions,* 18.

50. H.H. Rowley, "Chronology of the Old Testament," *The Interpreter's Dictionary of the Bible,* vol. 1 (New York: Abingdon Press, 1962), 580–99.

51. Mayer, *A History,* 88.

52. Ibid.

53. John A. Hutchison, Paths of Faith, (New York: McGraw-Hill, 1981), 340.

54. Ibid., 341.

55. Ibid., 346.

56. George F. Moore, *History of Religions, vol. 2* (New York: Scribner, 1948), 103.

57. The "fear of the Lord" is not simply an expression of primitive dread of a deity. The word *fear* as used in Acts 10:35 comes from the Greek *phoboumenos,* which in early Christian thought reflects more a sense of reverential awe toward the creator of the universe who calls us to live together in mutual love and peace. See R.J. Knowling, "The Acts of the Apostles," The Expositor's Greek Testament, vol. 2 (Grand Rapids, MI: William B. Eerdmans), 259.

58. S.E. Frost Jr. and Kenneth P. Bailey, *Historical and Philosophical Foundations of Western Education* (Columbus Ohio: Charles E. Merrill, 1966), 108–11.

59. Kenneth Scott Latourette, *A History of Christianity* (New York: Harper & Brothers, 1953), 153–157.

60. Frost and Bailey, *Historical and Philosophical Foundations, op. cit.* 136–37.

61. Ibid., 140.

62. In Boston in 1821, an English classical school, later to be called an English high school, was established and was so successful that in 1827 Massachusetts passed a law requiring the building of such schools in every town of 500 or more families. Over the fierce objections of private school operators, these schools multiplied until

there were more than 600 of them across the country. In 1874 the famous *Kalamazoo School* case was handed down by the Michigan Supreme Court that made possible through taxation the creation of public secondary schools, by 1900, there were 6000. cf. Frost and Bailey, *op. cit.,* pp. 425–432.

63. Ibid., 274.

64. Thomas Lickona, *Educating for Character* (New York: Bantam Books, 1992), 7, 233–35.

65. John S. Brubacher and Willis Rudy, *Higher Education in Transition* (New York: Harper & Row, 1968), 68.

66. Earl V. Pullias and James Douglas Young, *A Teacher Is Many Things* (Bloomington and London: Indiana University Press, 1968); see in particular Chapter 11, "A Teacher Is an Inspirer of Vision."

67. "Gender Definition Ok'd," *The Orange County Register,* April 20, 2004, Page 1. See also the Orange County Section of *The Los Angeles Times,* April 27, 2004, B1.

68. Lars P. Qualben, *A History of the Christian Church* (New York: Thomas Nelson), 392–94, 407.

69. Smith, Huston, *The World's Religions,* 280

70. Richard Hughes, Seager, ed., *The Dawn of Religious Pluralism* La Salle IL: Open Court, 1993), 3–10. Fifty-nine articles, speeches, and presentations given at the 1893 Parliament are included in this invaluable text.

71. Dirk Ficca, *Making the Connections: A SourceBook for the Community of Religions,* Joel D. Beversluis, Project Editor, (Chicago: The Council for the Parliament of the World's Religions, 1993), 19–20.

72. Albert Hourani, *A History of the Arab Peoples,* 158.

73. McLaren, *The World of Philosophy,* 68.

74. Hourani, *A History of the Arab Peoples,* 163.

75. John L. Esposito, *The Oxford History of Islam,* (Oxford: Oxford University Press, 1999), Ix; 608–9.

76. Samuel P. Huntington, *The Clash of Civilizations: Remaking of World Order,* (New York: Touchstone/ Simon and Schuster, 1997), 70.

77. Ibid., 71.

78. Amy, Chua, "A World on the Edge," *The Wilson Quarterly* vol. 26, no. 4, (2002): 61–62.

79. John Kekes, *The Morality of Pluralism* (Princeton, NJ: Princeton University Press, 1996), 10.

80. Kenneth Tye, Introduction to *The World at a Crossroads, The 1991 Yearbook of the Association for Supervision and Curriculum Development* (Alexandria, VA: ASCD Press 1990).

81. R.G., Hanvey *An Attainable Global Perspective* (Denver, CO: Center for Teaching International Relations).

82. Bill, Clinton, foreward to *Global Education: A Study of School Change,* by Barbara Benham Tye and Kenneth A. Tye, (Orange, CA: 1992).

83. Kenneth Tye, "Global Education: A Worldwide Movement," New York: The American Forum for Global Education *Issues In Global Education* no. 150 (n.d.).

84. Ibid.

85. Tye and Tye, *Global Education*, xvi–xvii.

86. Mayer, *A History of Educational Thought,* 3 viii.

87. Ibid., 3–4, 167–69.

88. McLaren, *The World of Philosophy,* 146.

89. John B. Brubacher and Willis Rudy, *Higher Education in Transition* (New York: Harper & Row, 1968), 62.

90. Jurgen Moltmann, *Theology of Hope, as theologie der Hoffnung.* (New York: Harper & Row, 1965), 90; originally published.

CHAPTER 5

The Just Society

*Let Justice roll down like waters, and righteousness as a
mighty stream.*

—Amos 5:24

*Justice is the first virtue of social institutions, as truth
is of systems of thought. A theory, however elegant and
economical, must be rejected or revised if it is untrue;
likewise laws and institutions no matter how efficient
and well-arranged, must be reformed or abolished if
they are unjust*

—John Rawls

"Bring them to justice!" is often the cry of victimized citizens concerning treatment
of those suspected of crimes. What is usually meant is confirmation of guilt with
punishment to follow. But justice is far more complex. Huston Smith expressed it
well:

> It is to a remarkable group of men whom we call The Hebrew Prophets more
> than to any others, that Western civilization owes its convictions that (a) the
> future of any people depends in large measure on the justice of its social order,
> and that (b) individuals are responsible for the social structures of their society
> as well as for their own direct personal dealings.

Eastern cultures appear similarly persuaded.[1]

A. THE NATURE OF JUSTICE

In philosophical discourse, at least two major forms of justice are identified: procedural and substantive. The first, *Procedural law,* refers to fair and unbiased processes
for judging people. In bringing Saddam Hussein to trial in 2005, for example, it was
one of the tasks of defense attorneys to ensure their client's right to be assumed innocent

until proved guilty, be guaranteed a "fair" trial, and be eligible for bail (or if denied bail, given an explanation for its refusal, and on what definitive grounds). It also embraces the modus operandi for establishing one's rights and to starting a lawsuit and proceeding with it.

Substantive law has more to do with such nitty-gritti of arguments presented as to what rights one has against a thief, the justice of who acquires a man's savings and other belongings and investments after his death, and whether and how "the punishment fits the crime."

Most of the major religions and cultures have developed some notion of standards of justice that undergird the written regulations, the law behind the laws. This is true even of traditions, such as Confucianism, that do not hold to a personal God. One of the most remarkable challenges to this idea is found in the Torah, Exodus 18, where God declares he has chosen Abraham to be the man by whom all the nations of the earth will be blessed. But God knows Abraham needs clarification about God's righteousness and thus sets up a test case in which Abraham is allowed to challenge: "Shall not the judge of all the earth do right?" What follows reveals God's mercy as well as his justice in withholding the threatened destruction of Sodom (although it was in fact later destroyed because of its stubbornly persistent corruption).

Since Aristotle's dictum that justice must be rooted either in divine law or some "primal order" (*phusai dikaion*), those who followed him accepted the proposition that a just society can be sustained only by laws and enforced order. But if such governance is imposed by tyrants who scorn the notion of sacred origins of law and the people have rejected divine guidance as a myth (as happened in the eighteenth century's Age of Reason) where will justice be found? Are the roots of its opposite, injustice, to be found in some perversity of human nature or in warped social structures?

Oliver Wendell Holmes conceded that justice derives from the law but that laws are simply what the courts decide. Is this a sufficient conclusion? What if entrance-level or lower courts' decisions conflict with each other? Appellate courts (modeled after the *appella* of ancient Rome), literally courts of appeal that may lead all the way to the Supreme Court, may be the only recourse until even the current Supreme Court's decision is overturned. This occurred when the Supreme Court of the United States in 1954 found it necessary to overturn its predecessors' nineteenth century rulings on racial segregation. The "separate but equal" determination of that earlier Supreme Court provided, according to the 1954 court, a distorted justification for segregating pupils of different races, thereby supporting a social practice inherently unequal.

Justice may be satisfied in some cases with compensation for lost property (as with insurance claims) or for rights illegally denied. Compensatory justice may also involve rendering rewards or punishment according to what is perceived as "due" or merited.

Justice may also be identified as "distributive" (i.e., treating people as equals acknowledging Lincoln's affirmation that "all men are *created* equal") [emphasis my own]. This has been adopted in the United States as the procedural presupposition of justice.[2] Judgments may also be guided by need when the necessities of life (health care, education, adequate income, police and fire protection, safe roads, etc.) are distributed to guarantee society's well-being. Aristotle suggested a somewhat mechanical theory of justice, as the *mean* between two extremes. This might occur in the form of a jury's proposal of *excess* punishment (or compensation) or inadequate punishment or compensation. It effectively leaves the final decision to the judge who then might decide on the basis of some personal consideration of a political, religious, or "public-spirited" nature. The judge might also base the final disposition on an effort to "fill in the gaps" when no clear law or rule has been established. Again, the judge might base the decision on precedents set by previous cases.

Plato proposed a metaphysical support for a natural law theory of *rights* as God given and/or achieved by "right reason" and therefore to be deemed justly assigned. Some form of natural law theory seems to be at the root of most legal decisions; we like to say (at least) that we believe in certain basic human rights, which, according the natural order, no minority should be denied. America's Declaration of Independence clearly justifies these rights on the concept of natural law as celebrated in the days of John Locke and Thomas Jefferson.

Of special concern for Western religious believers is the inherent righteousness of God who maintains and is faithful to his God's covenant relation with the established order of creation. To be just is to be as God is ("be ye perfect as your heavenly Father is perfect," Matthew 5:48) and to fulfill perfectly the strenuous charge "to do justly, to love kindness and to walk humbly with your God" (Micah 6:8). This also accords well with what we discover in the Eastern traditions.

B.   RELIGIOUS SOURCES OF JUSTICE

In Hindu thought, the just person is one who has so identified with Brahma that he or she can comprehend *Atman,* the soul, which is akin to the cosmic mind. One of the cardinal principles for the knowledge of Atman is the practice of ethical virtues.

> These ethical virtues are at the root of justice, and are, according to the Upan-
> ishads, truthfulness, non-injury, forgiveness, good conduct, non-appropriation
> of another's property, control of the senses, absence of anger, equanimity, detach-
> ment from the world, charity and continence.[3]

These virtues are incorporated into objective legal ethics dealing with social welfare with a view to creating an ideal environment for the peaceful pursuit of the spiritual life.

Among the literary treasures of Buddhism is the *Dhammapada* (the Way of Virtue), which the Council of Osaka adopted in 240 B.C. as being the authentic sayings of Gautama. They include: "Hasty judgment shows no man just. He is called just who discriminates between right and wrong, who judges others not hastily, but with righteousness and calm judgement, a wise guardian of the law."[4] Gautama, having been raised a Hindu, broke from that tradition and became not an atheist (one who actively denies the reality of a deity) but a nontheist. With His Holiness the Dalai Lama of today, he would doubtless aver:

> Whether a person practices religion or not, the spiritual qualities of love and com-
> passion, patience, tolerance, forgiveness, humility and so on are indispensable. At
> the same time, I believe that these are most easily and effectively developed within
> the context of religious practice.[5]

Confucius might agree with Gautama in doubting the existence of a personal God but gave credence to some divine reality in his reference to Heaven: "The Master said, "Heaven begat the power (*te*) that is in me. What have I to fear?"[6] S.E. Frost translates this, "Heaven produced the virtue that is in me," and continues "He who lacks faith will not succeed. One must hold to faith at all times. Heaven makes great demands upon one's faith, but God is with man and he should never waver in his faith."[7] This indwelling virtue is what makes justice possible, although justice as such is not further elaborated in *The Analects*.

In Judaism, justice takes on a complex nature unlike anything in those Eastern traditions where God is not regarded in personal terms. In Hebrew thought, the very essence of God is his personal righteousness: "All His work is done in faithfulness; He loves righteousness and justice" (Psalm 33:4–5). "Righteousness and justice are the foundation of His throne" (Psalm 97:2). "If a man is righteous, executes true justice between man and man, walks in my statutes and is careful to observe my ordinances, he is righteous (and) shall surely live" (Ezekiel 18:5–9). Altogether Hebrew scripture has 28 direct references to "justice" along with 41 more indirect ones that use the word *just* as meaning fairness. There are more than 450 words for *judgment* implying dependence on justice, and nearly 600 words that equate justice with righteousness.[8] A culturally agreed-upon concept of justice (although nowhere specifically defined) is declared to be "the foundation" of God's throne. It is also the foundation of Hebrew faith and social life.

The meaning of justice in Western religious traditions including Jewish, Christian and Islamic religions appears to have evolved in at least three stages. These emerged early with the prophets of Israel (the word *prophet* meaning one who speaks for another, in this case on behalf of Yahweh), later with Jesus (regarded by some disciples to be the reincarnation of Elijah or Jeremiah (Matthew 16:13–14), and lastly Muhammed, proclaimed in Islam as the final great prophet of Allah.[9]

The first stage involved a kind of prophetic guild, not unlike the soothsayers, seers, and shamans in other cultures. Some of them traveled in groups singing and dancing, often into a state of ecstasy during which they were thought to be conduits for the spirit of God. Although they seldom spoke directly to matters of ethics or justice, in their rapturous utterances, they illuminated their hearers as to God's being and intent. Such a revelation occurred during a meeting with Saul, who was destined to become the first king of Israel, thus fulfilling their prophesy. In the first book of Samuel, chapters 9 and 10, the prophets are not named except for Samuel, who identified himself only as a "seer" (I Samuel 9:19), yet they represented a turning point in the history of their little nation.

Saul is portrayed as dependent almost totally on Samuel who anointed him king but then as violating his relations with the seer by overstepping Saul's rightful authority in the matter of a sacrifice before battle. Saul did so again some time later, in refusing Samuel's order to slaughter the enemy without mercy, men, women, and children (I Samuel 15:3). However one interprets Samuel's brutal command in terms of morality, the writer of I Samuel clearly wants us to understand that Saul's behavior included acts of insubordination in refusing to follow Samuel's orders. This would result in the end of Saul's reign and was a major turning point in the history of their nation. Saul's successor, David, sent Bathsheba's husband to his death in a "rigged" ambush in order for David to possess her. David's successor, Solomon, was a spendthrift who virtually bankrupted the country. These conditions reveal how unjust conditions in a nation can start a progressive unraveling of the whole ethical and even legal fabric.

Ethics and a struggle with issues of justice appear in the second stage of the prophets' appearing, which introduces the "pre-writing prophets." Here their names are clearly established: Elijah, Elisha, and Nathan among others. These received inspiration from God and exhibited astonishing courage in facing down kings (e.g., Elijah versus King Ahab and Nathan versus David) who had committed unjust, sometimes murderous acts. The kings had the power to have the prophets executed for confrontations but were apparently so struck by the prophets' fearlessness that they refrained. (Cf. I Kings 21 and 2 Samuel 11 and 12). These prophets too, left no writings of their own of which we have any record; we know them only through the stories and legends handed down, although these are certainly more fully "fleshed out" than during the first stage.

The third stage introduces the writing prophets whose names include Amos, Hosea, Micah, Isaiah, Jeremiah, that is "the major prophets." These prophets attacked injustice not only at the personal level but also at the political, social, and national levels of Hebrew life. The prophets lived in a time when extremes of wealth and poverty were protected by laws and sheer fiat so that the poorest citizens could be bought and sold like sheep and, as Amos declared in evident disgust, needy debtors could be traded for a pair of sandals (Amos 8:6). Speaking on behalf of God, he roars "The Lord says, 'I hate, I despise your feasts, and take no delight in your solemn assemblies'" (Amos 5:21 RSV). "I abhor the pride of (Israel), and hate his strongholds, and I will deliver up the city and all that is in it" (6:8). The fate of many of these prophets was death at the hands of the king's henchmen (e.g., Isaiah was sawn asunder). Centuries later, Jesus lamented over "Jerusalem . . . killing the prophets and stoning those who are sent to you" (Matthew 23:37). The surviving prophets warned of Israel's imminent collapse and predicted that its people of the already divided kingdom's northern part would go into exile. This occurred in 721 B.C.E. The southern region was taken over by Babylon in 587, and the captured peoples were plunged into despair as in Psalm 137:4: "How shall we sing the Lord's song in a foreign land?"

Their sense of hopelessness was gradually assuaged by the Messianic anticipation, in effect a fourth stage of prophesy. "Comfort my people says your God," wrote Isaiah. "Speak tenderly to Jerusalem and cry unto her that her warfare is ended, that her iniquity is pardoned" (Isaiah 40: 1–2). King Cyrus of Persia invaded Babylon in 538 and seemed almost to embody the liberating Messiah they hoped for. Many responded positively to Cyrus' emancipation and to Isaiah's directive to return to Palestine, rebuild it, and become "a light to all nations" (Isaiah 42:6). However, many refused to return and instead dispersed across the Eastern world and as far south as Egypt and as far north as Russia. Those who did return were not of one mind; some actually tried to rebuild the city, especially the ruined temple under the direction of Era and Nehemiah. But others contented themselves with simply replacing lost houses and properties. Ezra, having brought with him a copy of the Torah, "the book of the law of Moses," was able to bring these two factions together and begin the building of a new Jerusalem. Time and space do not accommodate us in trying to trace the succession of new failures, occupations of the land again by foreign powers, climaxing with Rome. But we can look briefly again at the Messianic expectation that prepared the way for Christianity.

This expectation took different forms, the first being the coming of one who would serve as God's vice regent, a heroic figure effecting a new order: "The government shall be upon His shoulder, and his name shall be called wonderful, counselor, Mighty God, Everlasting Father, Prince of Peace" (Isaiah 9:6). The second form of the expectation was in the assumption that the new Messianic age would essentially restore the old order, reestablishing Israel's past glory conceived in rather utopian "good-old-days" imagination. A third form looked forward to an altogether new order that would shake the foundations of the world and replace it apocalyptically in the "End of Days," with the ultimate gift of super natural, eternal fellowship with God for those who have made a full affirmation of their faith in him.

The emergence of Christianity in the person of Jesus, born into a Jewish family, is bracketed by the concept of "the just person." Before his birth, Jesus' mother was found already pregnant "before they came together" (presumably on their wedding night since Joseph is called "her husband"). In Jewish society of the time, a young woman in that situation might well be stoned to death or at the very least put aside in disgrace. But we are told that Joseph, "being a just man and unwilling to put her to shame, resolved to divorce her quietly" (Matthew 1:19). The writer could have used a different word, such as "a fair man" or "a good man" but instead chose to translate *Dikaios* as "*just*," with its undertones of faithfulness and affection.

Three decades later, at the climax of Jesus' trial before his crucifixion, the concept of "the just man" again appears, this time in direct reference to Jesus. Pilate disavowed any guilt for passing judgment in view of the clamor of the crowd: "I am innocent of the blood of this just man."[10] The word *just* as well as its cognate *righteous* appears 74 times in the Gospels and in writings of the apostles. It was clearly also in the mind of Jesus when in his teachings, as exemplified in the famous "golden rule," he pointedly commanded his listeners to care for the just needs of their neighbors and even of their enemies. This last, of course would be grounds for the charge of treason in many societies that forbid giving "aid and comfort to the enemy." It is nevertheless a central concern of Christianity if there is to be peace among neighbors and nations.

To those who would emphasize faith in Christ as the only means of salvation, his response is: "Not everyone who says to me 'Lord, Lord' shall enter the kingdom of heaven, but he who does the will of my Father who is in heaven" (Matthew 7:21). And what does the will of the Father require? "By this all men will know that you are my disciples, if you have love for one another" (John 13:35).

In the final judgment, the focus is not on piety, but whether we fed the poor, clothed the naked, sheltered the homeless, and—in short—met the just deservings of fellow human beings. Here Jesus tightened the screws: "I was hungry and you gave me no food; I was thirsty and you gave me no drink; a stranger and you did not welcome me, naked and you did not clothe me, sick and in prison and you did not visit me." Then they will answer "Lord, when. . . .?' And he will answer, 'as you did it not to one of the least of these, you did it not to me. And they will go away in to eternal punishment" (*Matthew 25 : 42–46*). The apostle James may indeed have had the last word on this: "Faith apart from works is dead" (James 2:26). And those works are efforts toward justice in a world where injustice seems omnipresent.[11] But such negative messages are not at the heart of the gospel, which means "good news." Indeed, the upside of these same words emphasizes the blessings that will come to those who do feed the hungry and care for the sick and imprisoned. When Jesus completed his teaching on one occasion, some of the people exclaimed, "This is really the prophet." Others said, "This is the Christ" (John 8:40–41).

The Western world owes a special debt to Islam for resurrecting many of the Greek and Roman classical philosophers during the Dark Ages and bringing their works into the curriculum of education at about the time of the founding of the medieval universities. Both Jewish and Christian scholars were invited to share these resources. The results provided the Western conception of justice that lasted well into the Age of Reason, a period roughly bracketed by the birth of Galileo (1564) and the outbreak of the Seven Years' War (1756). Justinian (483–565) had long since codified Roman law, and Aquinas (1225–1274) reconciled Aristotelian philosophy with Christian theology elaborating Justinian's *Corpus juris civilis* as *jus naturale*. This achieved a synthesis in what was one of the greatest achievements in the history of philosophy.

Because the Holy Qur'an is central to the Muslim concept of justice, it is appropriate to note a few passages that hold this claim before us. In the fourth chapter, we find: "God doth command you that when ye judge between man and man ye judge with justice" (S iv. 58). To those who ask how justice is to be discerned comes the response: "If you differ in anything among yourselves, refer it to God and His apostle." But many do not know how to ask God or to hear his response. The reply came clearly:

> "We have sent down to thee the Book in truth, that thou mightest judge between men as guided by God. So, be not used as an advocate by those who betray their trust, but seek forgiveness of God; for God is oft forgiving, most merciful. (iv 105–106)

Some will say that, even with the book in hand, they find it hard to achieve a godly point of view. "Say [to them], My Lord hath commanded justice, and that you set your whole selves to Him, at every time and place of prayer, and call upon Him making your devotion sincere, as in His sight" (vii.29). So far, so good, but what are the practical consequences of all this? "God commands justice, the doing of good, and liberality to kith and kin, and He forbids all shameful deeds and injustice" (xvi. 90).

Such a dialogue might well be climaxed with a passage from Chapter Lvii. 25 in which God says to us:

> We sent aforetime our apostles with Clear Signs, and sent down with them the Book and the Balance (of Right and Wrong) that men may stand forth in justice; and We sent down iron, in which is material for Mighty war as well as many benefits for mankind, that God may test who it is that will help.

Three things are presented here as gifts of God: the book, balance, and iron. The symbols here are of tremendous importance for the just society. *The book,* as Ali explains, represents *revelation,* "which commands Good and forbids Evil." *Balance* symbolizes "*justice* which gives to each person his due, and the strong arm of the Law which maintains sanctions for evil doers." *Iron* is

> the most useful metal known to man. Out of it is made steel . . . and implements of war, as well as instruments of peace: ploughshares, bricklayer's trowels, architects and engineer's instruments. Iron stands as the emblem of strength, power, discipline, law's sanctions, etc. Iron and steel industries have also been the foundation of the prosperity and power of modern manufacturing nations."[12]

The focus here is clearly on the providence of God, who supplies spiritual and moral sustenance, as well as our physical, social, and even capacity for technological development. It is a providence that extends to the protection of the natural habitat, where conservation protects the just needs of all creatures. In this latter sense, "All Human beings whether they are conscious of it or not, or whether they accept it or not, are *khalifas* (stewards) of God."[13] To guarantee natural, inherent rights in our person-to-person interactions as well as our social, international, and even ecological endeavors is an act of justice. To obstruct them is injustice.

C. SOURCES OF INJUSTICE: RELIGIOUS REFLECTIONS

Religious histories suggest that sinful acts from lying to outright murder involve offense against both divine holiness and human decency; all involve some breach of justice, sometimes committed by religious groups themselves by way of persecutions and "holy" wars.

The story of the prodigal son (Luke 15:25–32) provides a more familial illustration, wherein a young man demands of his father whatever inheritance he will one day receive and then wastes it all "in riotous living." Stunned by his consequent poverty, "he came to himself" (a remarkable aside, reflecting discovery of his self-violated psyche) and went to his father with the confession, "I have sinned against heaven and before you; I am no longer worthy to be called your son." His father's love redeems him while the jealous rebuke of the older brother reminds us that one injustice may breed unexpected twists and turns and more injustice.

In Hinduism, we find this latter conclusion when the Lord Krishna in the Bhagavad Gita explains the reason for his repeated incarnations: "When-so-ever the law fails and lawlessness up-rises . . . then do I bring myself to bodied birth. To guard righteousness, to destroy evil doers, to establish the law, I come into birth age after age" (Lesson 4:7–8). Does Lord Krishna ever show love or at least forgiveness for fallen sinners? "Come not to me for refuge (those) besotted workers of evil, basest of men. Being bereft of knowledge, they come into daemonic existence" (Lesson 7:15). Indeed, even for good mortals, Krishna has no special affection: "I am indifferent to all born beings; there is none whom I hate, none whom I love" (Lesson 9:29). As noted briefly in our first chapter, Krishna assured Arjuna that he need not feel remorse at killing others in war since a cycle of rebirth awaited them all (Lesson 2:17–27), but if he failed to wage war against evil doers he would be guilty of a greater transgression against justice (Lesson 2:33).

The Lord Krishna assures us that those who "drink the soma [a plant-derived juice and a favorite libation of the Vedic gods] and are cleansed of sin and worship me with sacrifices. They [will] taste in heaven the heavenly delights of the gods. [But] when they have enjoyed the wide world of paradise, they re-enter the world of mortals [and] win but a going and coming" (Lesson 9:19–21).

And so the cycle repeats. Ultimately, our own choices are at the root of injustice and of all other sins that keep us from heaven, yet there is a shadow of hope: "Be assured that none who is devoted to me is lost" (Lesson 9:31).

Buddhism has many scriptures, but the Dhammapada has been a favorite for over two thousand years as a book for meditation. While much attention is given in Buddhism to the eradication of selfhood and all traces of egocentrism, the Dhammapada opens with a tribute to the human mind. "Mind it is which gives to things their quality, their foundation and their being; whoso speaks or acts with impure mind, him sorrow dogs as the wheel follows the steps of the draught-ox."[14] And while Buddhism's virtual denial of selfhood might seem to denigrate the issue of volitional choice, Buddhism, like Hinduism from which it sprang, places responsibility for all injustice squarely on us, making no excuses on grounds of our merely "doing what comes naturally" or on some metaphysical concept like original sin. "If a man is a great preacher of the sacred text, but slothful, and no doer of it, he is a hireling shepherd who has no part in the flock."[15]

When asked about the achievement of virtue, **Confucius** is reported as replying: "He who could put the Five [virtues] into practice everywhere under heaven, would be Good: courtesy, breadth, good faith, diligence and clemency."[16] Such sentiments seem more oratory than substantive, and at times Confucius' disciples seemed to demand more substantial evidence of human goodness and reasons for some doing evil. Is it simply due to a lack of trying? The philosopher Mencius, an enthusiastic disciple of Confucius (though some 200 years later), sought to extract an answer from what few writings of Confucius survived, and stated, "The great man need make no effort to be sincere in his speech, nor be resolute in his acts: he simply does as his conscience prompts him." But given that human nature is common to us all, a student asked, "How is it that some are great men and some are small men?" Mencius replied, "Human nature is disposed toward goodness just as water flows downward. Those that follow their higher nature are great men; those that follow their lower nature are small men."

Challenged as to why some men choose the higher nature and others the lower, Mencius answered,

> Thought is the function of the mind: by thinking it achieves; by not thinking it fails to achieve. These faculties are implanted in us by Nature. If we take our stand on the higher part of our being, the lower part will not be able to rob us of it.

Doubts still lingered. Is the choice of the higher way versus the lower simply a matter of rationality? And what sort of reward or punishment awaits us when our choices are evaluated? To this Mencius answered, "Heaven confers titles of nobility as well as man. Man's titles of nobility are duke, chancellor, great officer. Those of heaven are benevolence, righteousness, true heartedness and good faith."[17]

In sharp contrast to Confucian optimism that mankind is basically good, the scriptures of Judaism declare bluntly, "Surely there is not a righteous man on earth" (Ecclesiastes 7:20). The King James version translated this, "There is not a *just* man on earth." Is human nature then corrupt by nature? No. "God created man in His own image . . . male and female he created them. And God blessed them" (Genesis 1:27). Things went wrong when humankind tried to tinker with inventions and take control of everything, with or without God's approval. "God made man upright, but they have sought out many devices" (Ecclesiastes 7:29). Humankind, self-corrupted, is thus the original source of injustice in the world, hence the concept of "original sin." While this was never made official doctrine in Judaism, the Torah does affirm an inherent inclination to be self-serving, yet it also affirms yearning to be "other-serving," so one might conclude that if some defect called "original sin," exists, so does "original virtue" in that we are all created in God's image (Genesis 1:27).

Long centuries after the events recorded from the time of Abraham, Joseph, the Egyptian bondage, invasions of "the promised land," and repeated failures to create a just society, the prophet Isaiah (c. 742 B.C.) addressed the people of Israel with harsh criticism:

> Your iniquities have made a separation between you and your God, and your sins have hid his face from you so that he does not hear. For your hands are defiled with blood and your fingers with iniquity; your lips have spoken lies, your tongue mutters wickedness. (Isaiah 59:2,3)

Jeremiah echoed the charge: "The sin of Judah is written with a pen of iron. I will make you serve your enemies in a land which you do not know" (Jeremiah 17:1,4). The prophets' charges against their injustices included these: "No one enters suit justly, no one goes to law honestly; they rely on empty pleas, they speak lies, they conceive mischief and bring forth iniquity (Jeremiah 17:4). Hosea sounded a similar condemnation:

> You have ploughed in iniquity, you have reaped injustice . . . therefore the tumult of war shall arise among your people and all your fortresses shall be destroyed. Thus it shall be done to you, O house of Israel because of your great wickedness (Hosea 10:13–15).

The consequence was exile.

"Exile," as Lenn Goodman has observed "is the fruit of faithlessness." But God does not leave the matter there. Faith must yield a vision of return, forgiveness, and restoration. "The life of exile is not to become a mere waiting for return" (Jeremiah 29:1–14). It must be full, reflecting and still projecting the values that gave substance to life in the land: "Build houses, plant gardens and eat their fruit, take wives and raise sons and daughters." The life of an integrated community remains an orienting norm. . . . The idea of redemption fuses here with the ancient Biblical theme of divine providence working through, rather than despite nature."[18] This divine providence is born of God's love because "the Lord set His heart in love upon your fathers" (Deuteronomy 10:15), and "the Lord loves the righteous" (Psalm 146:8). "So you, by the help of your God, hold fast to love and justice, and wait continually for your God" (Hosea 12: 6).

A major tenet of Christianity holds that love and justice must always be maintained in balance. Sources of injustice are often evident in social interaction but go virtually unnoticed because of the lack of love. In Jesus' story of the Good Samaritan, for example (Luke 10:25–37), "a certain man was going down from Jerusalem to Jericho" (a twenty-mile sloping journey known as the "Bloody Pass") and was attacked by thieves who beat him and left him for dead. A priest saw the victim, but avoided contact and "passed by on the other side." Next a Levite passed by, and he too went on his way without offering aid.[19] "But a certain Samaritan," a virtual half-breed with whom Jews refused to associate, was moved with compassion, bound up the victim's wounds, took him to an inn where he could get care, and paid the innkeeper's fee. Jesus asked his listeners, "Which of the three proved a just neighbor to the stranger, who had suffered a grave injustice?" The answer was obvious: "the one who showed mercy." So Jesus, without belaboring the story by appending a "moral," simply added, "go and do likewise."

Other parables reveal Jesus demonstrating how loving concern addresses injustices, including unjust stewards (Luke 16:1–9); the unjust treatment of debtors (Matthew 18:21–35); determining just wages (Matthew 20:1–16); the willingness and even eagerness to forgive another's folly (Luke 15:11–24) versus the unjust withholding of forgiveness out of spite (Luke 15:25–32); and at least a dozen more. To these must be added God's love for the world, which prompted sending his son into human society to demonstrate a truly godlike life (John 3:16). The tragedy of human reviling of God's gift, and Jesus' refusal to condemn his tormentors but instead praying for their forgiveness (Luke 23:34), and restoring the frightened run-away disciples to full fellowship after the Resurrection (Luke 24:36f.) demonstrate a balancing of love and justice. Jesus' teaching and healing works were directed at overcoming social injustices such as slavery, political imprisonment, and confinement on false grounds; the crippling consequences of war; and even "natural injustices" where "nature" has robbed the sufferers of food, shelter from storms, sight, hearing, and even life itself.

Emil Brunner, a Swiss theologian writing in the midst of the Great Depression of the 1930s, traced the failure of the Christian world to achieve social justice not only to the sins that Luther, Calvin, Wesley, and other reformers emphasized but also to the philosophical shift away from theism. A morally sterile rationalism was spawned in the eighteenth century. What, he asked, had gone so terribly wrong that unjust, greed-driven business dealings of a few could bankrupt whole nations? What made it possible, for example, in Germany, once the home of the greatest literary artists, musicians, and scientists of the world, to be taken over by one man, Hitler, and his Nazi henchmen, and threaten a whole civilization? Justice no longer meant "the just shall live by faith," as proclaimed in both Hebrew and Christian scriptures (Habakkuk 2:4; Romans 1:17). First, the divine law of nature was reduced to the subjective law of human reason. Then the "nature" in the natural law theory was interpreted in a thoroughly biophysical sense devoid of divine guidance. Justice became a matter of social changes codified and merged with positivism. "The denial of the metaphysical dissolved the idea of justice by proclaiming the relativity of all views."[20] Brunner notes that if there is no divine standard of justice, there is no criterion for the legal system set up by the state. If there is no justice transcending the state, then the state can declare anything it likes to be law; there is no limit to its arbitrariness save its actual power to give force to its will.[21] It was, wrote Brunner, precisely this freedom to "give force to its will" that helped establish the power of the fascist state under Adolf Hitler.

Today, many "social" diseases are contracted by drugs, sexual exploitation, and alcohol addiction and passed along to children and others so that whole communities, indeed whole nations, are facing, for example, epidemics of AIDS. One can no longer blame God or nature. The fact that thousands are left crippled or dead yearly as the result of careless highway driving or other crimes and that warfare kills tens of thousands, even millions, can be attributed to disregard for the rights of others to have good health and long lives. The Christian response to this is not alone in building houses of worship, schools, and colleges, mercy hospitals, and enterprises like the Salvation Army, YMCA, Church World Service, and so on. Christianity has a history of planning for social as well as spiritual involvement, which has contributed to its becoming the largest single religious tradition in the world with 2,130,000,000 members (33.56 percent of the world's population).[22]

Islam, the second largest religious tradition, with 18.25 percent of the world's population, by no means lag in advocating justice. As we have already noted, the Qur'an is quite explicit: "God commands justice, the doing of good, and liberality to kith and kin" (S. xvi, Section 13, 90). Some westerners unfamiliar with such statements are apt to be dismissive, regarding the words as mere platitudes. A common target for complaint is what they regard as unjust Islam's treatment of women, requiring them to cover themselves from head to foot in concealing clothing, and to accept a subservient relationship to men.

It will be helpful to see what the Qur'an actually teaches on these subjects, as well as related topics *vis a vis* women's rights. We can do this by examining six areas: human rights, civil rights, social rights, political rights, economic rights, and domestic rights. It will also be helpful to be reminded that what is written in the Qur'an is addressed to both men and women, with a reference to the 21st Sura, "All men and women of God form one united brotherhood" (xxi 91-93).[23]

D. THE ISSUE OF HUMAN RIGHTS

1. The first verse of the 4th sura of the Qur'an is addressed to men, in particular, reminding us that we were created "from a single soul, and from it its mate, and from them both have spread abroad a multitude of men and women." Arising from the same essence, they are equal in their humanity. Neither gender can be deemed superior because it would be a contradiction of equality.[24]

2. *Civil Rights*. A woman has the same basic freedoms as men. First, she is and shall be free to choose her religion (2:256). She is to be reverenced (iv. 1), free to choose her husband, and even to keep her name after her marriage.[25]

3. *Social Rights* "The Prophet(s) said, 'seeking knowledge is a mandate for every Muslim male and female' This includes knowledge of the Qur'an and the Hadith (traditions). Men and women both have the capacity for learning and understanding. Since it is their obligation to promote good behavior in all spheres of life, women have a right to acquire an education in accordance with their natural talents and interests. If she has the skills to work outside the home for the good of the community, she may do so as long as her family obligations are met. "Concerning motherhood, the Prophet said 'Heaven lies under the feet of mothers.' This implies that the success of a society can be traced to the mothers that raised it. The first and greatest influence on a person comes from the sense of security, affection and training received from the mother. A woman having children must be educated and conscientious in order to be a skillful parent."[26]

4. *Political Rights.* God guaranteed women the right to vote 1400 years ago. On any public matter, a woman may voice her opinion and participate in politics (Qur'an 60:12) She may hold important positions in government.[27]

5. *Economic Rights.* Islamic women have a legal right to be financially supported by their husbands, but the Qur'an recognizes, "By the creation of male and female, verily the ends you strive for are diverse" (923–4). Women therefore are also free to engage in commerce, own property, enter into legal contracts, and manage their assets in any way they please.[28]

6. *Domestic Rights.* Generally, the Qur'an upholds the concept that women are entrusted with the nurturing role and men with the guardian role. Some kinds of work are more suitable to men than to women (e.g. heavy lifting, working with dangerous machinery, soldiering). Marriage is a special gift from God. The Qur'an states, "Among His signs is that He created for you mates from among yourselves that you may live in tranquility with them, and He has put love and mercy between you; verily, in that are signs for people who reflect" (30:21).

Many of these directives from the Qur'an will meet with surprise among those who know of Islam only through movies and misinformation gleaned from some negatively slanted media.

To be fair, it must be acknowledged that many travelers' exposure to Islam in different Arabic countries have fostered negative images and raised questions that demand answers. Why, for example, are there so many rules and regulations to keep women in lowly subservience to male domination, and why does the practice of female circumcision persist among some Muslims? The facts reveal that in the Qur'an, women are by no means relegated to subservience, as noted briefly, and female circumcision (a widely expressed criticism) is not in the Qur'an and is not practiced in the great majority of Arabic societies.

The situation is not unlike that in medieval Christianity when great numbers of "converts" were illiterate and knew nothing of the New Testament's insistence on love of neighbors, including enemies. The Crusaders brought their bloody practices of warfare from their previous cultures into play. Painted on shields and other devices the cross was hardly more than a superstitious emblem supposed to deflect weapons of war and even what Shakespeare called "the slings and arrows of outrageous fortune." Many terrorist practices, including butchery "in the name of Allah," have been transferred into Islam from other cultural traditions.

E. THE PRIMACY OF HUMAN RIGHTS

It might be assumed that because issues of justice and injustice are so often related to the violated "rights" of victims, the whole concept of rights should be the bedrock of justice. However, justice is almost universally concerned with laws, primarily those to maintain social controls. As one definition of justice, "fairness" is easily abrogated in times of national security or other crises, and "the divine right" of kings and dictators almost always reserves the power to suspend whatever civil or human rights have been previously taken for granted. "Let justice be done" is the inevitable cry of the demagogue against those who threaten her or his power or the freedom of her or his powerful supporters to exploit and control unwary populations.

How has the notion of human rights evolved from early time? How are such rights to be identified? How can we safeguard them in times of alarm when they are threatened to be sacrificed?

As we have noted, while the concern for justice can be traced to many ancient religious traditions, agreement about human rights has been more recent and more problematic. One sticking point has had to do with who or what agency bestows uniquely human rights. Plato, Aristotle, and a number of their contemporaries were clearly absorbed in issues of justice and discoursed about the relation of divine law to natural law. Human rights were expressed more clearly in plays by such dramatists as Aeschylus (525–456 B.C.) and Sophocles (496–406 B.C.). The latter's *Antigone* contains a particularly compelling exchange between the condemned girl and King Creon, determined to have his will acknowledged as law: "And didst thou," he demanded, "dare to disobey these laws?" Antigone answers:

> Yes, for it was not Zeus who gave them forth,
> Nor did I deem the edicts strong enough
> That thou, a mortal man, should'st overpass
> The unwritten laws of God that know not change.
> They are not of today nor yesterday
> But live forever. . . .[29]

From the classical Greek and Roman periods and the medieval world there emerged various forms of anarchy and absolute monarchies in which "rights" were granted the masses only piecemeal and grudgingly if at all. Not until 1215 did a monarch ensure personal liberty and individual rights. After losing most of his continental holdings to the French, King John of England (1199–1216) was forced by his barons into signing the Magna Charta. Not a statement of abstract ideas, it is quite specific in requiring, among other things, "No taxation without representation," (a stipulation made famous in the New World by the Boston Tea Party more than five centuries later). In what is often called the cornerstone of English common law, the Magna Carta also guaranteed "due process of law to all freemen and affirmed the right of all, without regard to wealth or social position, to resort to the judicial process."[30]

The Magna Charta did not fully address basic human rights, but through it, in small incremental steps, the English parliament gained power over the budget and the power to impeach offending royal officials and even depose a king. Overtime, England became for all intents and purposes, a parliamentary democracy.

King James I ascended the throne in 1609 and challenged the whole structure of governance, declaring himself absolute monarch by "Divine Right." All rights assumed by anyone were regarded an affront to the throne unless explicitly granted by the king. No one had the right to address challenges or even questions to the king: "You know I will never give a plausible answer, for it is an undutiful part in subjects to press their king, wherein they know before hand he will refuse them."[31] This was the same King James who ordered a new translation of the Bible (1611) and made life in England impossible for the Puritans. Charles I, son of King James I, continued his father's clear challenge to the Magna Charta and so enraged both the British and Scots that the ensuing crisis brought on a civil war and ultimately the execution of Charles, "condemned of high treason" in 1649.

The seventeenth and eighteenth centuries were convulsed by efforts to establish clear statements of human rights. The "immemorial rights of Englishmen" became the slogan that resulted in the English Bill of Rights of 1689. The American Revolution a century later produced its own Bill of Rights ratifieds (1791). French philosophers of the Enlightenment (Diderot, Voltaire, Rousseau, etc.) stimulated ideological debates among the Americans (Thomas Paine, Thomas Jefferson, Benjamin Franklin, etc.) who in turn inspired the French to formulate their own Declaration of the Rights of Man and of the Citizen (1789), which helped foment the French Revolution.

Rights are often assumed to imply powers, such as the *political right* to voice support or dissent concerning government actions and the *civil right* to be free in selecting a marriage partner, the right to work and own property, and the right to be secure from arbitrary arrest. Both forms of rights are rooted in prior commitment to some theory of rights such as those *endowed by God* or by *Nature,* which cannot be legally violated. Another form is the *contract* theory in which some agreement between two or more parties or the state itself grants certain privileges of action or possession that cannot be taken away. A third form is simply *utilitarian;* these rights depend on the general welfare. Still another is *totalitarian,* variations of which hold that no individual really has any rights at all except those granted by the civil power, which is the sole source of all rights.[32] All of this must be understood in the context that rights in themselves do not really guarantee the power of enforcement. A person may have rights but be powerless to enforce them if the courts are corrupt or opponents are too powerful to risk offending.[33] Indeed, it is not necessarily that the courts are corrupt in dismissing rights based on the will of God or on natural law if the government declares such laws to be invalid on grounds of enforced separation of church and state. Nevertheless, citizens have the right to challenge such rulings on grounds that blocking rights because they are deemed religiously based is a violation of a basic legal tenet (i.e., "State officials cannot control the religious life of their subjects or attempt in any way to regulate the distributions of divine grace—or for that matter, of ecclesiastical or congregational favor and encouragement."[34]) The debate over whether human rights are unalienable "endowed by the Creator" as a "self evident" truth that carries eternal validity will doubtless rage on.

The period from 1791 when the American Bill of Rights began to function until the United Nations adopted the Universal Declaration of Human Rights in 1948 was fraught with high aspirations and idealistic proclamations, as well as heartless conquests and bombast.

The era began with Napoleon's rise to seemingly unlimited power over a shattered France, crowning himself emperor in the presence of Pope Pius VII in 1804 and being declared king of Italy in 1805. He subsequently overwhelmed Austria, and the Treaty of Tilsit (1807) with Russia and Sweden (1808) enabled Napoleon to dominate virtually all of Europe. His apparent megalomania quickly unraveled, with his defeat, in his foray into Russia in 1812. His Grande Armee. Napoleon's abdication and expulsion to Elba two years later, followed by an abortive effort to regain power, ended in disaster at Waterloo, and he spent his exile at St. Helena, where he died of cancer in 1821.

Louis XVIII of France ascended to leadership as a constitutional monarch and presented a new charter declaring: "All Frenchmen are equal before the law, whatever may be their title or rank."[35] People on both sides of the Atlantic were relieved that decades of pain and bewilderment seemed over and tuned their thoughts to more creative ventures.

The nineteenth century became a time of optimism for the many who emigrated to the New World where declarations of rights were made by virtually every organization that could produce a constitution from church congregations to school boards, businesses, and political parties. Unprecedented inventions began to emerge: steam engine, and cotton gin, telegraphs, telephones, cameras, motion pictures, and by 1903 airplanes.

Rehearsing these technological triumphs cannot conceal the fact that it was a profoundly unsettled era in which capturing and importing slaves was still a harsh reality in much of the world; serfdom enslaved millions of Russian peasants; Karl Marx, "brilliant and erudite, expounded [in 1848] the form of socialism that has passed permanently into the tradition of Western Civilization";[36] a civil war to terminate the slavery system in the United States; the Thirteenth Amendment. Meanwhile the Native American population was denied a truly safe haven in their own country and were required to live in 314 reservations. Large numbers of Indians—men, women, and children—were simply slaughtered outright, perhaps the most infamous being the Battle of Wounded Knee in 1890.[37]

Where were the religious institutions during those tumultuous decades of the nineteenth century? They were by no means inactive. Numerous interreligious federations were formed, from the Holy Alliance in 1815 to the Federal Council of Churches in 1908. High on their agendas was the establishment of schools, hospitals, and even agricultural stations to serve the needs of regional populations. Many were actively involved in antislavery movements, and some championed the cause of labor unions to secure safe working conditions and provide medical help (whereas previously a person injured on the job was simply dismissed). Many member denominations supported foreign missions; and missionary names such as William Carey in India, Robert Morrison in China, David Livingston in Africa became almost legendary. The "social gospel" movement, beginning toward the end of the nineteenth century and continuing into the Great Depression, emphasized that the business of the church was "to labor for the promotion of justice, the reign of peace and the realization of human brotherhood." Youth organizations such as the YMCA, the Epworth League, Young Men's Hebrew Association, Christian Endeavor, and so on were created to prepare youth for the strenuous challenges ahead in supporting human rights wherever they were threatened.

One wishes it possible to report that when all these grand ideals were finally adopted as part of the Universal Declaration of Human Rights by the United Nations in 1948 (thanks in no small measure to Eleanor Roosevelt), we could relax and begin to enjoy the fruits of so much effort. The declaration codified freedom globally for the first time, proclaiming, "All human beings are born free and equal in dignity and rights." It embraces "everything from the right to one's opinion, privacy, education, security, judicial recourse, migration, employment and fair wages to the right to leisure and marriage by choice, while it condemns abuses ranging from slavery, torture, and discrimination based on language, sex, religion, opinion, origin and race."[38]

Anyone alert to current affairs living though the twentieth century knows that these "rights" have been violated in every society and on every continent countless times. If one cannot expect the people in the Western world to abide by the Declaration, perhaps it is not surprising the *Los Angeles Times* editor wrote "Mention human rights in Asia and what typically comes to mind are the *Tien An Men* massacre in Beijing, or Nobel peace laureate Aung San Suu Kyi under house arrest in Myanmar." The support for such incidents is sometimes, ironically, rooted in religious tradition: "To Singaporeans raised and educated in a society that reveres Confucianism and its emphasis on strict law and order, the sacrifices of personal freedom in the name of national prosperity are often justified."[39]

The preceding statement was published more than a decade ago, but our more current situation illustrates that little, if anything, has changed. Indeed, it may have worsened as torture and violent death in "detention facilities" are justified in the name of "national security." The once hidden but later widely publicized episode of prisoners being stripped naked, beaten, and handcuffed to each other in an obscene, helpless pile on the floor of the Abu Ghraib prison in Iraq (spring 2004) is coupled with the Pentagon's report that at least thirty-seven prisoners died in prison of severe beatings.[40] This comes on the heels of the instruction of Donald Rumsfeld, then U.S. secretary of defense, to military intelligence that wartime prisoners have no rights. "Take the gloves off."[41] Dr. Mohammed Alazmirili, an Iraqi scientist, learned before his death in prison that a person can be arrested by the U.S. military without any charges, handcuffed, hooded, and while incarcerated for weeks or month, denied legal council. By what definition of justice can this be acceptable?

With a plethora of human rights violations mounting in open transgression of declarations and laws (going back more than eight centuries), we are likely to ask what to expect next. Anthropologists and psychologists debate with biologists as to whether the human brain is actually programmed to distrust "others" as a survival instinct.[42] Are we prewired to hate, or do socializing forces including religion give hope that we may overcome our violent tendencies and create viable systems of justice in which courts can operate and by which individuals can monitor our own compliance with rules of that justice. If the latter, how should we respond when, against our better judgment and religious training, our elected political leaders give us "reason" for suspending the rules of justice for national security or profit motive? We are told that for our own good and the stabilization of international efforts, we must temporarily forgo the luxury of human rights. Exhortations in sermons as well as classical and contemporary plays, and novels and the emphasis in education on moral development seem to rise in waves and then subside in the face of what Bertram Gross calls "friendly fascism."

Gross notes that as early as 1933, Adolf Hitler began "publicly promising full employment and prosperity. He kept his promise to the unemployed (as many as six million men) who did not seem desperately concerned with the loss of political freedom." Hitler thus assured himself of the support of the working class even as he was courting the largest industrialists with the pledge: "Private enterprise cannot be maintained in a democracy."[43] This has often been the position of nationalism and right-wing extremism deceptively backed with smiling promises. It is also the path toward what Amaury de Riencourt, in the aftermath of World War II, called the era of "the coming caesars," warning us that as Julius Caesar too was a great "internationalist" who attempted to carry out the dream of unifying of the world "in which all worthy men would be citizens with equal rights."[44] We must be wary because kings, dictators, and even democratically oriented presidents are, at least for public consumption, eager to overthrow foreign governments so they can set up "democratic" structures.

Can democracies be effectively imported? It took more than two centuries for democracy to become a reality in the New World. de Reincourt warns that U.S.-style democracy has no validity in Singapore or anywhere else in the developing world because the promised checks and balances often interfere with governing in countries where executive action must be swift to forestall disorder. "The irresistible Americanization, like the Romanization that preceded it, arouses bitter resentment, sometimes envy. European critics forget that America is the Old World's offspring.[45]

So where do such dour reflections leave us—or lead us? Is there anything in the fractured picture of modern commerce and warfare to encourage the development of an ethical foundation that provides the framework for a system of justice on an international scale to which all nations could (and would) subscribe? And what role can organized religion play in such deliberations?

F. IMPLICATIONS FOR GLOBAL ETHICS

As far back as the study of history reveals, the distinction between the lower animals and the human species has been made that the so-called lower animals have no real concept of justice but are motivated by the need for self-preservation so "the fittest" may survive. For humans, the need for justice is especially demonstrated when some person's acknowledged rights ("rights" being almost instinctively a part of that person's very being) have been violated. The response is inevitably, "That's not fair." The ancient Greeks identified *lex naturae,* the law of nature, with a divine order, that was in fact a divine necessity. Such necessity established order to the whole cosmos, both physical order as well as moral order expressed not only as part of the *lex naturae* but also for revealing the practical consequences of just or unjust behavior. Among primitive peoples, ancient Greeks and Egyptians, and our contemporaries, physical and moral orders are so inseparable that just as we might say that the laws of gravity will be strictly enforced so too will be the laws of morality. As mediators in court, judges have been almost reverenced as is evidenced by fact that many wear ecclesiastical-styled robes.

Since the writings of Hugo Grotius (c.1625), equating natural law with divine law has been challenged. Certainly not an atheist, he nevertheless asserted in his *De jur belli ac pacis* that natural law would be valid even if there were no god because it was rooted in reason. This philosophy, inspiring politicians and philosophers, opened the Age of Reason, which began a movement from proposing a religious foundation for the idea of justice to affirming a transcendental (but not theistic) foundation, asserting purely naturalistic and secular grounds, a reinterpretation of justice as a fictitious idea providing an instrument of self-preservation, and then proclaiming the rights of those with political and economic power.

Partly for this reason, John Rawls virtually identifies justice with "fairness,"[46] but this definition is by no means static. He does not isolate fairness alone as being the foundation for justice: "Each person is to have an equal right to the most extensive scheme of equal basic liberties compatible with a similar scheme of liberties of others." Second, "social and economic inequities are to be arranged so that they are both (a) reasonably expected to be to everyone's advantage and (b) attached to positions and offices open to all." Justice, then, requires a careful investigation into both fairness and equality. (p. 53)

Some very basic concerns remain, however; one having to do with the relation between justice and equality, another with the paradoxical relation between justice and inequality, and a third with the dangers of a religious foundation for justice. These were explored memorably half a century ago by Swiss theologian Emil Brunner.

"Equality" Brunner wrote, "was the great word of the French Revolution."[47] Jean Jacques Rousseau (1712–1778) began his revolutionary treatise on *The Inequality of Man* (!). Brunner noted that ironically equality is also the ideal of the socialist-communist social ordering of society which would undermine all that makes for equality and that, which Karl Marx embraced. France and Russia (and elsewhere in oligarchic Europe) had an oppressive social structure with the aristocratic and wealthy holding down the masses of the uneducated, jobless, starving, and wretchedly housed poor. The great strategy of the wealthy was to own as much land as could be obtained on which farming, mining, and industrial endeavors could flourish while keeping the wages of the poor at the lowest possible level. The "fairness," to which Rawls refers as a definition of justice would have been seen as a naïve concept. Hope for genuine equality arose on the U.S. frontier as it did in France and Russia with revolutionary zeal. One major difference was that the French and Russian peasants had also felt the sting of their religious leaders' siding with the oppressors, the wealthy and the powerful. The French Reign of Terror did away with the religious persons, much as Lenin, Trotsky, and Stalin advocated in Russia in the early twentieth century.

With cooperation from major businesses, religious and humanitarian groups in England succeeded in getting Parliament formally to forbid slave trade in 1807. Denmark, Holland, Sweden, and France quickly followed suit, all decades before the United States achieved abolition of slavery in 1865 at the staggering cost in lives and property of a civil war. In the United States, forces in opposition to freeing the slaves continued in a variety of ways from intimidating black laborers and segregating black families from white communities though local and/or state laws. These laws were often enforced by intimidation, arrest, and localized violence by such groups as the Ku Klux Klan. Lynching, a form of mob violence that included torture and execution without trial under the pretext of justice, resulted in the deaths of 3,437 mostly black people between 1882 and 1951.[48]

Enforced segregation of those who had been slaves from the white population became another major problem after Abraham Lincoln's Emancipation Proclamation. It took many forms such as denying "negroes" access to many services in restaurants, hotels, theaters, and parks, as well as the "freedom" to build homes in certain "districts" where real estate developers managed to have restrictions enacted into law. Even some public services organizations like public schools, hospitals, and perhaps most conspicuously the military services where black soldiers were assigned to "units" defined according to race—were off limits to blacks. Then came the fruition of the Civil War and long decades of public debate and litigation, when the Supreme Court ruling of 1954, outlawed all forms of racial discrimination in any setting public or private.

Clearly, the conviction that "all persons are created equal" is not honored the world over. Slave trade is still a reality in some parts of the world, and women do not share equal social or religious status with men. Traditional loyalties often nullify the "equal treatment" of all people. This is especially evident in religious settings, such as the practice of the Roman Catholic Church to bar Protestants from receiving Holy Communion regardless of the invitation enunciated by the same Lord whom they both worship. Can we seriously contemplate organizing a global ethic among an effort by the leaders and followers of religions including Hinduism, Buddhism, and Confucianism that effectively deny the reality of a personal deity and of the subscribers to Judaism, Christianity, and Islam, for whom worship of a creator God is absolutely central to the faith?

It is the hope of the present writer that such an effort can at least be tried without accusations that those who make the effort are merely giving way to religious or ethical minimalism. One of the major obstacles to success may be, as George Weigel cautions, a spiritual malaise that haunts Europe:

> Over the last 150 years or so, the makers of European culture and politics have convinced themselves that, to be modern and free, Europe must jettison its Judaeo-Christian heritage; that part of its culture formed by faith in the God of Abraham, Isaac, Jacob and Jesus.

To illustrate this point, Weigel points to the delegates (intellectual and political leaders) to the European Union who in 2004 seemed determined to prevent any acknowledgment in the Constitution for Europe of Christianity as one of the roots of contemporary Europe's commitment to human rights and democracy. "That is why," Weigel says, the 70,000 word "European Constitution awaiting ratification could not find room in it for one word—Christianity."[49]

One can only hope that this malaise is not funguslike, infecting other parts of the world from which must come those who work together in search of a viable global ethic.

NOTES

1. Huston Smith, *The World's Religions* (San Francisco: Harper, 1991), 288. *Cf.* Lewis Brown, *The World's Great Scriptures* (New York: Macmillan, 1946), 209.

2. An exception to the "all men are equal" policy has sometimes been expressed in times of war, as the insistence of former Secretary of Defense Donald Rumsfeld that captured enemy combatants "have no rights."

3. Swami Nikhilananda, *The Upanishads* (New York: Harper Torch, 1963), 61.

4. The Dhammapada quoted in S.E. Frost, ed., *The Sacred Writings of the World's Great Religions* edited by Frost, S.E., (London, New Delhi: McGraw-Hill, Book Company, 1972), 149.

5. His Holiness The Dalai Lama *Ethics for the New Millennium* (New York: Penguin Putnam, 1999), 220.

6. Arthur Waley, trans., *The Analects of Confucius* (New York: Vintage Books, 1938), 127. In Book VII, 6, Waley translates *te* as moral power.

7. Frost, *op. cit.*, 396. This particular citation is not a direct translation of a specific quotation of the *Analects* but Dr. Frost's effort to encapsulate the essence of this portion of the work.

8. These figures are based on the *Analytical Concordance to the Bible* ed. Robert Young 21st American ed. (New York: Funk and Wagnalls n.d.).

9. These are especially well presented by Smith *op. cit.*, 288–96.

10. The Greek word as used by Pilate may be translated "this just man" *tou dikaiou toutou* (King James Version) or "this righteous man" (American Standard Version).

11. Karen Lebacqz plunges a needle in to our usual pattern of defining justice in philosophical language when "there is reason to think that attention to injustice is an important beginning point for a theory of justice." She provides a homespun example, hard to elude: "My first cup of coffee each day represents a decision to accept the benefits of unjust labor practices in the so-called third world." Other illustrations crowd in when we read in the morning news about more than a million people displaced and homeless in the African Sudan because of business and governmental greed and of countless other injustices on every continent. See Lebacqz, *Justice in an Unjust World* (Minneapolis: Augsburg Publishing), 10 f.

12. A. Yusuf Ali, trans. and comm., *The Holy Qur'an* (Brentwood, MD: Amana Corporation, 1983), 1505.

13. John Bowker, *What Muslims Believe* (Oxford, England: Oneworld Publications, 1998), 67

14. The Dhammapada, *op. cit.,* 145.

15. Ibid.

16. Waley, *The Lin Yu,* (also called *The Analects) op. cit.,* 210.

17. Frost, *The Meng-Tze, op. cit,* 117.

18. Lenn Goodman, *On Justice* (New Haven, Yale University Press, 1991), 175. See also Martin Buber, *Good and Evil* (New York: Charles Scribner's Sons, 1953), especially Part Three where he deals with the "truth of the myths."

19. Priests and Levites were both ministering officers with holy orders, but nowhere in the Old or New Testaments is there evidence that a Levite was an exact equivalent of a priest; he was unique only in being of the tribal lineage of Levi. The debate as to the distinction continues among historians. See "Priests and Levites," *The Interpreter's Dictionary of the Bible,* vol. 3 (New York: Abingdon Press, 1962), 887–89.

20. Emil Brunner, *Justice and the Social Order,* trans. Mary Hottinger (New York: Harper & Brothers, 1945), 6f.

21. Ibid., 7.

22. Charles L. Manske and Daniel N. Harmelink, *World Religions Today* (Irvine, CA: Institute for World Religions, 1967), 34.

23. Ali, *op. cit.,* 833.

24. Mary Ali and Anjum Ali, *Women's Liberation Through Islam* (Chicago: Institute of Islamic Information), 1.

25. Ibid.

26. Ibid., 2.

27. Ibid. It is instructive to compare the right to vote being accorded to women in Islam 1400 years ago with the U.S. experience of less that a century ago when women had little or no access to voting polls.

28. Ibid., 3.

29. Sophocles*, Antigone,* antistrophe II, lines 484–91.

30. Milton Viorst, *The Great Documents of Western Civilization* (New York: Barnes and Noble, 1994), 113–116.

31. Ibid., 118.

32. John E. Smith, "Rights," *Dictionary of Christian Ethics,* ed. John Macquarrie (Philadelphia: The Westminster Press, 1967), 300–1.

33. This line of argument is more fully carried forward in Stanley I. Benn, "Rights," *The Encyclopedia of Philosophy,* vol. 7, ed. Paul Edwards (New York: Macmillan and The Free Press, 1967) 195–99.

34. Michael Walzer, *Spheres of Justice: A Defense of Pluralism and Equality* (New York: Basic Books, 1983), 283–84.

35. Viorst, *op. cit.,* 213 f. Students of history will, of course, recall that Napoleon tried to return to power but was defeated at Waterloo and was exiled on the Isle of St. Helena where he died in 1821.

36. Ibid., 233.

37. Kevin Fedarko, "This Ride Is About Our Future," *Los Angeles Times,* May 16, 2004, 4f (Parade section).

38. Robin Wight, "Defining Heroes and Villains," *Los Angeles Times,* February 28, 1993, M1.

39. Elizabeth Lu, "When Rights Are Surrendered Voluntarily in Favor of Prosperity," *Los Angeles Times,* February 28, 1993, M2

40. Alissa J. Rubin "Suspicion Surrounds Death of Iraqi Scientist," *Los Angeles Times,* May 28, 2004, A.1

41. Richard A. Serrano, "Prison Interrogator's Gloves Came Off Before Abu Ghraib," *Los Angeles Times,* June 9, 2004 A 1.

42. Sharon Begley, "The Roots of Hatred, " *AARP Magazine,* May–June 2004, 43f.

43. Bertram, Gross, *Friendly Fascism* (Boston: South End Press, 1983), 14.

44. Amaury de Riencourt, *The Coming Caesars* (New York: Coward-McCann, 1957), 334f.

45. Ibid., 291.

46. John Rawls, *The Principles of Justice* rev. ed. of Harvard University Belknap Press, 4th printing, 2001.

47. Emil Brunner, "On Ethical Nihilism," *Christianity and Civilisation,* New York: Charles Scribner's Sons, 1948 p. 109 f.

48. Encyclopedia Britannica, Micopedia *op. cit.* p. 416

49. George Weigel, "The Spiritual Malaise That Haunts Europe." *Los Angeles Times,* May 1, 2005, M5.

CHAPTER 6

The Community of Culture

All religions, arts and sciences are branches of the same tree.

—Albert Einstein

Developmental psychologists and philosophical realists as well as theologians have long insisted that far from developing in a social vacuum, our beliefs and values are molded and shaped in large measure by the icons, artifacts, spiritual and aesthetic experiences, and scientific theories of our particular culture. Earliest cave paintings, the pyramids of Egypt, the soaring cathedrals of the Middle Ages, the artistic and literary endeavors of the Renaissance, present day culture have inspired human values. Thus, in agreement with Einstein's observation at the beginning of this chapter, students of the humanities, religion, and the sciences may concur with the seventeenth century astronomer Johannes Kepler who, contemplating celestial mechanics, discovered "that marvelous harmony, that order of things like to the order of music that heals the soul and harrows sin from the world."[1]

Our contemporary John Polkinghorn, a Cambridge Anglican priest and physicist reaffirms that the sciences, arts, and diverse religions have evolved in similar ways, yet we are not to conclude that the three are purely social constructions.[2] There is a spiritual as well as an aesthetic element in the way religious and scientific advances are mutually enhanced, inspiring a sense of wonder that Einstein believed to be essential to progress in every social and intellectual endeavor. The affirmation of common ground for these endeavors suggests the need to explore the concept of purpose in the natural scheme of things, of fulfilling teleological goals.

Culture is often defined in terms of the patterns and products of learned behavior. Comprised of language, activities, and artifacts that are distinctly of human origin, culture takes on a life of its own and includes the development of individual personalities, of family and community values comprising their societies. It also involves endowing language, acts and created objects from artists' and musicians' studios to laboratories with symbolic as well as practical value and meaning. Consider, for example, the verbal expression, "Honor thy father and mother." What is it to honor someone and to affirm the sacredness of family bonds in a way unique to those relationships? This is just one of the essential elements of every society and civilization.

As to attributing special value to products of human invention, consider a flight around the world and in space with brief stops at the Taj Mahal, the Vatican library, a Tibetan monastery, a ballet by Moscow's Bolshoi, and the Hubble telescope in orbit. If visited by an extraterrestrial traveler, the experience would doubtless evoke a reaction of wonder and awe, a curiosity about what cultural conditions produced these places and these objects. In this chapter, we consider some traditionally treasured components of culture.

A. RELIGION AND THE ARTS

Students of the humanities or the history of religion are aware of ways the several arts have evolved in relation to religious faith and practice. Many sculptures found in the Indus Valley such as like the Cro-Magnon or Paleolithic Venus of Willendorf (Figure 6.1) can be dated as early as 28,000 B.C. and are considered to have been fertility goddesses or at least fetishes.[3]

1. Hinduism

Such works and the prevalence of carvings of the phallus as an object of worship or used in the worship of the Hindu god Siva reveals a very early connection between religion and art. Historian Heinrich Zimmer has pointed out that the history of India as we know it began much later than the paleolithic period, in fact with the Aryan invasions (2,000 to 1200 B.C.). Called *Hindu* in reference to their Indus Valley origin, the Aryans left in the Rig-Vedas written denunciation of the people they conquered because of their obsession with sexuality. Among the Vedic hymns are scornful references to "those whose god is the phallus."[4] Ironically, practices so early abhorred by

Figure 6.1 Venus of Willendorf (c. 28,000–25.000 B.C.)

Figure 6.2 Dancing Girl (c. 24,000–20,000 B.C.)

the Aryans somehow carried over when the various Hindu castes evolved and persist in Hindu religion to this day as the usual mode of honoring Siva.[5]

In India, the earliest sculptural figure to be found is identified historically simply as a Dancing Girl, (Figure 6.2) copper work. It would be inaccurate to link it directly to Hinduism, because it has been dated at about 2000 B.C., while the Indo-Aryans who eventually became Brahman (Hindu) priests, did not actually settle in India until 1400 B.C. Nevertheless, the stylized form appears to have carried over to the Hindu fashioning of other figurines of copper, terra cotta, and stone seals with vivid representations of ceremonial bulls and various deities. Important to recognize is that while the Venus of Willendorf figure is thought to have been fertility oriented and the copper dancer with her prominently cleft vulva may have been as well, art historians interestingly agree generally that many subsequent Hindu dancing figures were intended to be sensual but not pornographic (Figure 6.3). The figures also represent pristine, disciplined liturgical motifs. Every movement of the dancer has been choreographed with precise placement of hands, feet, body, and head intended to convey a drama that inspires lofty thought and devotion with each movement executed with exactitude and grace.

Primitive art that began as almost wholly secular themes was appropriated in substance and symbolism by religion to spiritual aspirations. Myers and Goetz agree that the sensate aspect of faith was never far from early Hindu thought, noting that the embrace of a beautiful, amorous woman was celebrated as the highest bliss to be hoped for on earth as well as in the lower heavens. Poetry elaborated female beauty in every detail, even as major literary works, such as the vedas and the oldest of Indo-European religious treatises contained hymns to the gods of the sky, sun, storm, earth, and sexuality.[6]

Figure 6.3 Dancing Siva (c. eleventh century)

In addition to the vedas were the Upanishads and two major epics, the Ramayana (tales of the god Rama's exploits on earth) and the Mahabharata, a vast collection of tales and a veritable tapestry of myths that dominate the arts of early Hinduism.[7] In the latter is the highly prized Bhagavad Gita, quoted in nineteenth century by Ralph Waldo Emerson, Henry David Thoreau and in the twentieth by physicist Robert Oppenheimer upon the explosion of the first atomic bomb in 1945. The latter was in pointed reference to "the potential for the destruction of all reality." Some of the Gita is set to music and dance, which has generated the largest television audiences in India."[8]

The Upanishads declared that the material world is an illusion as is very notion of the human "self." The early Vedic books tell us nothing about temples or figurative arts until after the rise of Buddhism. After them comes a somewhat slow-motion explosion of architectural, sculptural, and painted works that feature the gods and their interactions with mankind, portraying all manner of mythological and legendary occurrences.

2. Buddhism

Of special interest in this sequence is that although the emergence of Buddhism may have stimulated more artistic expression by the Hindus, the fact is that Siddhartha Gautama, the original Buddha, discouraged the creation of art works glorifying himself for fear it would instigate idolatry. Nevertheless, Buddhist art is actually anterior to Hindu art by six to seven centuries. The Buddha is quoted in scriptures as extolling the building of topes (shrines in the form of domes with a cupola) to enshrine relics. Buddhist tope art developed into India's most extensive and ancient artistic heritage. Furthermore, the popular impression among westerners that Mahayana Buddhism is responsible for *stupa* (stone columns, railings, and gates around hemispheric memorial mounds) and related art is chronologically inaccurate; the stupa at Sanchi (Figure 6.4) began much earlier, and those of Osaka are older still.

The Buddha created a monastic movement (c. 500 B.C.) in which members, both men and women (priests and nuns), sought sanctity by following the much quoted "eightfold path" of right views, right action, right mindfulness, and so on. Eventually (by the fourth century B.C.), this fairly ascetic form of Buddhism known as *Hinayana,* was replaced with a more rigidly organized hierarchy, *Mahayana,* in which the Siddhartha was deified and, in his honor, countless symbolic (but not naturalistic) depictions appeared on stupa. The great stupa at Sanchi is perhaps the most studied sculpted object to emerge from this movement.

The transition of representation from symbolic and stylistic to realistic did not occur until the first centuries of the Christian era when Bodhisattvas (Figure 6.5) were presented in classical Greek style with what Renaissance artists would have called "Christlike" features. The reason for this is clear when we recall that after contact with the Christian world, Bodhisattvas were viewed as heroic, saintly persons who died and, instead of moving on to an eternal life with Brahma, chose to return to earth to save other souls.[9] One result of the proliferation of Buddha and Bodhisattva images (given that these saintly persons literally became Buddhas) is that there are now more depictions of the Buddha than of any other human figure in history.

Figure 6.4 The Great Stupa at Sanchi and Eastern Gate (second to first century B.C.)

The Buddhist concept of divinity in its most perfect form may be seen in the caves of *Yun-Kang,* where the concept of the Buddha, a blend of conventional restraint and religious fervor, became human enough for popular recognition while remaining sufficiently idealized to carry the worshipper beyond the image to the abstraction it symbolized.[10]

Unlike the arts of India, which from very early times revealed their firm root in religious belief and practice, the arts of China reflect far more secularity. Religion

Figure 6.5 Bodhisattva
(fourth to fifth century)

appears to have been more a matter of ancestor worship than spiritual contemplation or the gathering of worshippers.

3. Confucianism

Confucius was born about 551 B.C. and died in 479; this was a time of the Chou empire's disintegration into a number of warring feudal states. Early in his youth Confucius was absorbed in trying to understand the violence of his conflicted world; he believed fervently that humankind is basically good and needs only education and paternal moral guidance to correct its ills. His contemporary, Lao Tsu, founder of what was to become the Taoist faith, was even more optimistic about humanity's innate goodness. In Lao Tsu's quasi-libertarian conviction, he insisted that it would be best to let people alone and they would be good without formal guidance. Taoism, without any formal structure, has always been in danger of subsiding into magic and superstitious practices such as the exorcism of evil spirits. It has never fully lost its appeal, however. With its *Sermon-on-the-Mount* tone of moral advocacy it is similar to the *Tao Te Ching*. Only 5000 words in length, it has inspired centuries of devotees and given rise to an extensive creation of poetry as well as a growing literature on environmental concerns, and guides to health. The latter includes the popular technique of acupuncture now adopted in numerous medical schools worldwide. In theory, the needles affect the restoration of balance between the Yin and Yang. Historians differ as to whether Lao Tsu created or "inherited" the practice because evidence indicates that it was practiced as early as 2500 B.C.

Confucian teachings, meanwhile, have sustained the power to lift people's spirits and have been credited with inspiring the emperor Shih Huang Ti (259–210 B.C.) to unify China by melting down weapons, standardizing laws, and, perhaps most impressively, building the Great Wall as protection against Tartar invaders.[11] Confucius was canonized as a "sage" by 492 A.D., and temples for worshipping him were ordered in almost all major population centers.

"Although the Chinese never regarded architecture as a major art form, the best are true works of art. The most famous is the Hall of Annual Prayer (Figure 6.6), which perfectly embodies the Chinese love of order and harmony." Hugo Munsterberg, *Art of the Far East* (Baden Baden, Germany: Holle Verlag, 1968), 206.

Regarded as a virtual deity, a designation which would doubtless have confounded the nontheistic Confucius, his veneration continued in China for centuries until the rise of Communism in the 1940s. At that point, most temples were ransacked and/or destroyed. The few remaining ones to Confucius—notably excluding the one associated with his burial in Shantung—have been taken for use as schools, offices, or military barracks.[12] Such objects as silk paintings, lacquered bowls, stoneware, porcelain vases and sculptures (for the most part bearing depictions of historic events, landscapes, memorable sages and warriors) were not objects of "religious" works in the sense discussed elsewhere, yet they deserve our attention because of the role of Confucianism in their creation. They have been popular acquisitions, however, for personal pleasure as home decor sold by art dealers and for museums and tourists. This observation is not meant as disparagement because the

Figure 6.6   Hall of Annual Prayer, Temple of Heaven, Peking (fifteenth century)

fact remains that some of the most graceful and meticulously rendered work to be found anywhere is here represented.

4. Judaism

In sharp contrast is the appearance of Jewish art on the world scene. Given the prohibition in the Ten Commandments proclaimed by Moses (c. thirteenth century B.C.E) against making "graven images, or any likeness of anything that is in heaven above, or that is in the earth beneath" (Deuteronomy 5:8), it may be surprising to discover that painted pottery with depictions of birds, flowers, and palm trees as well as ivory carvings of animals often decorated homes.[13] When the Temple of Solomon was erected (c. 960 B.C.E.), it contained "sculptured panels of wood brightened with gold inlays and composite creatures with human faces and wings."[14] The cherubim of the Ark of the Covenant (Exodus 25:18–20) were similar to the winged figures of Egyptian deities. The key to the apparent violation of the prohibition by the Jews probably rested on their interpretation of the reference to graven images as not rigid regulation but to prevent their actual worship. Hellenic, Roman, and Christian influences further stimulated realistic sculptural production: "Human and animal figures are common on the mosaic pavements of Palestinian synagogues of the fourth-fifth century."[15]

Jewish contributions in poetry and music rather than in the visual or tactile arts became widely respected. The books of Psalms and Proverbs are cases in point, and prophetic writings illustrate this fact. A glance at a Hebrew Bible in the original language will disclose that, for one example, the Book of Amos (a hard-hitting condemnation of social corruption) is so carefully crafted that it reads like an extended poem. What appear to be musical superscriptions within the text suggests that the lines were in fact set to music to be performed.

All students of religious history are familiar with references to King David playing the harp and some recall among Solomon's many wives an Egyptian princess who carried in her dowry a thousand musical instruments. Indeed, Jewish women figure prominently in music: when we remember Miriam, Deborah, Jephtha's daughter, and the women who hailed young David as a conquering hero (I Samuel 18: 6–7). Important events within families such as parties (Genesis 31:27) and banquets (Isaiah 5:2; 24:8–9) were accompanied by music. Even digging wells (Numbers 21:17) and planting vineyards were occasions for singing and dancing (Jeremiah 31:4–5). To be sure, solemn occasions such as death brought forth lamentation in musical expression (II Chronicles 35:25). Bells, cymbals, flutes, rattles, trumpets, lyres, harps, and that curious instrument called the sackbut were in popular use.[16]

Across the centuries, music and drama have played a powerful role in Jewish synagogues and temples in addition to family events. Chants, plain song, and more elaborate compositions have always been a hallmark of "being Jewish." In fact, the famous Dead Sea Scrolls provide instructions about instrumentation including explanations as to why one form was superior to another (e.g., strings as opposed to woodwinds). As Jewish people blended increasingly with Christian and Islamic communities and performances became more formal, more elaborate musical forms became prominent: chamber works, symphonies, and fully developed operas and ballets. Spanning the classics to operettas and popular "musicals" for stage and screen, Jewish composers, actors, and instrumental performers have made unprecedented contributions to emerging art forms.

5. Christianity

Christianity emerged in the context of the Jewish tradition, so it is not surprising to find that its earliest art forms reflect those roots, especially in the avoidance of anything that might appear idolatrous. After the expulsion of the Jews from Jerusalem (70 A.D.), this prohibition faded in the growing interaction of Christians with the surrounding Hellenistic and Roman cultures and wholly new cultures on the missionary frontiers from Africa to Scandinavia. This interaction developed in response to the command of Jesus to "go into all the world and preach the gospel" or good news that forgiveness, salvation, and eternal fellowship are God's great gift to all humankind (Mark 16:15; John 3:16).

The Christian arts of the early period are distinguished from pagan less by style than subject matter. After all, the Christians of the time were trained in the same crafts, were brought up in the same environment, and spoke the same language. Rather it [is] the product of an entirely new world view. To Christians, the empire with its exactions, cruelties, materialism, wars and false gods, became *regnum Caesaris regnum diaboli*— 'the kingdom of Caesar, the kingdom of the Devil.'[17] The Romans reaction was predictable; Christians were persecuted, forced to fight wild animals in the Coliseum for the amusement of vast crowds, and slaughtered in their villages in great numbers. Perhaps the most conspicuous monuments of the period were the catacombs, underground caverns tunneled by the Christians for their own dead, nearly four million of them.[18] The catacombs housed not only funeral sites but also *cubicula,* small rooms for chapels and places to hide during times of persecution. Ironically, they also served as the first Christian art galleries. Many of the rooms were vaulted and adorned with frescoes representing the dome of heaven or scenes from Biblical stories like that of Jonah, who was honored as a *prefiguration* (prophetic forerunner) of Christ "who rose from death as Jonah had been delivered from the belly of *ketos,* also after three days."[19]

While realistic frescoes and sculptures became more acceptable, early Christian art came into its own in the realm of church architecture. With his conversion to Christianity in 313 A.D.,

> Constantine the Great became the first emperor to sponsor the construction of churches in Rome. His generosity went well beyond providing land and erecting edifices. It extended to outfitting the interiors with costly alters, chandeliers, candlesticks, pictures, goblets and plates fashioned of gold and silver and sometimes embellished with jewels. The greatest of Constantine's churches in Rome was Old Saint Peters, probably begun as early as 319.[20]

6. Religious Architecture and Artifacts

Old Saint Peters, (Figure 6.7a & b) which was capable of housing three to four thousand worshippers, stood on the western side of the Tiber River where both Constantine and the Pope agreed to have been the burial place of Saint Peter. Interestingly, their decision has been supported by recent excavations revealing a second century memorial erected in Peter's honor.[20] The church was to gain special importance as the place where Charlemagne was crowned Emperor of the Holy Roman Empire in 800.

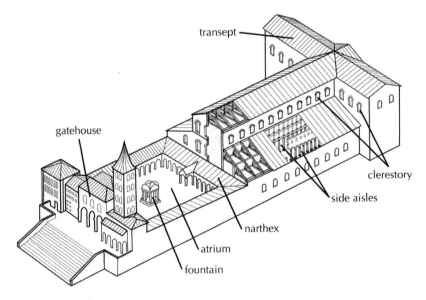

Figure 6.7a   Old St. Peters Cathedral, Plan and Section (c. 333 A.D.)

Figure 6.7b   Interior of Old St. Peters, Coronation of Charlemagne (c. 1480)

Christianity's rapid spread across Europe witnessed the building of greater and greater churches and cathedrals, many borrowing liberally from classical designs infused with Romanesque vaulted arches, unadorned block walls, and towering spires.

> An immense building enterprise that raised thousands of churches in western Europe . . . reflected a widely felt relief and thanksgiving that the conclusion of the first Christian millennium in the year 1000 did not bring and end to the world, as many had feared. The construction of churches became almost an obsession.[21]

Two major and divergent influences on church architectural design were the eastern Byzantine and the western Romanesque-Gothic. The hyphenation of the latter will be explained later.

Hagia Sophia, the Church of Holy Wisdom, built in 532–537 (Figure 6.8) remains to our own day the most magnificent place of worship of Byzantine legacy with its 108-foot diameter dome rising 180 feet above ground. In contrast to the dark gothic structures of western cathedrals, visitors were struck by the illusion of Hagia Sophia's vast dome floating on the air admitted by its forty windows.

The dome's apparent weightlessness gave a lift to the spirit while the richly appointed interior with multicolored stones from every corner of the known world in the floors and walls as well as in vast mosaics transformed the physical reality into a spiritual vision. The style influenced other places of worship, such as the magnificent San Vitale in Ravenna, (Figure 6.9) where it was greatly enhanced by masterly icons. These icons outlived the Byzantine period and prevail as spiritual expressions to our own time.[22]

Begun by William of Normandy in 1067, "most critics consider the Abbey Church of Saint-Etienne at Caen . . . a striking design rooted in the tradition of Carolingian and Ottonian westworks, but displays the increased rationalism of Romanesque architecture."[23] Durham

Figure 6.8   Hagia Sophia (c. 532–537)

Figure 6.9   San Vital, Ravenna (c. 526–547)

Cathedral in England (Figure 6.10) is perhaps the most splendid example of this with its vaulted structure and bold patterned columns becoming the standard for other churches and cathedrals in northern Europe. For casual tourists, the Romanesque is hard to distinguish from the Gothic style, which appeared in northern France only a century later, around 1140 (hence the hyphenated "Romanesque-Gothic" referred to earlier).

Critics of the time used the word *gothic* as a term of ridicule, a "monstrous and barbaric" invention of the Goths with their preference for tall pointed arches and darkly enclosed chapels with light filtered through stained-glass windows. Nevertheless, Gothic was exciting with its towers reaching heavenward, elaborately sculptured portals and stained-glass windows depicting Biblical stories providing an inspiring relief from the drab conditions of the streets outside. The cathedrals of Chartres and Notre Dame in Paris (Figure 6.11) became the standard references for devotees of the Christian faith as well lovers of art and beauty in general. Even small, wooden U.S. country churches can be found to emulate the narrow pointed arches of the gothic style.

7. Religious Music

Perhaps more than the paintings, sculptures, frescoes, and even the overwhelming architecture of churches and cathedrals, music is the art form that has most captivated the hearts and motivated the worship of Christians over the centuries. Music is of special

Figure 6.10 Durham Cathedral, England (c. 1093)

interest because leaders of the earliest churches held it in an ambivalent regard because the most popular forms were associated with public spectacles, deadly competitions, and Greco-Roman stage performances. These events were unsuitable for the church, which took as its responsibility to wean its rapidly growing numbers from their barbaric past. At first, only the human voice, not musical instruments, was admitted into worship services. The tongue was believed to be the only approved psaltery of the Lord. The oldest surviving example of the early church's music is a third century hymn of praise to the Trinity. The canticles of the Byzantine church so touched the hearts of worshippers that they remain today in the liturgy of the Roman Catholic Church.[24] "The basic proposition in the philosophy of the Church Fathers was that music should be the servant of faith. Only that music is good which, without obtruding its own charms, opens the mind to Christian teachings and disposes the soul to holy thoughts."[25] Despite the seeming disregard for music for its own sake, however, it was included in the required educational curriculum called "seven liberal arts" and in the mathematical *quadrivium* (along with arithmetic, geometry, and astronomy) of the schools being established across the empire.

This first stage of religious music came to an abrupt end with the advent of the Gregorian period. Educated as a Roman citizen, Gregory, who was to become Pope Gregory I (c. 540–604) is traditionally thought to have composed the entire body of liturgical chants at the bidding of the Holy Spirit. Some of the chants are now known to have been composed as recently as the seventeenth century, so calling the period Gregorian is not altogether appropriate. Nevertheless "the form of the chant (or 'plainchant'), performed without instruments, in unison and without a clearly defined rhythm, can represent some of the most subtle and sophisticated music in

Figure 6.11   Notre Dame Cathedral, Paris (c. 1163–1250)

our history."[26] Ironically, this becomes even more apparent as the improvised nuances were written down; musical notation encouraged an increase in formal composition. From the ninth century when Charlemagne encouraged a synthesis of Roman and Frankish liturgy through the twelfth century a fondness for elaboration in music mirrored the penchant for everything from "illuminating" manuscripts and translations to scholarly research in all academic disciplines and encouraged the rapid growth of universities in Bologna, Padua, Paris, Oxford, and Cambridge.[27]

Because the earliest universities owed much to their founding churches and, reciprocally, the churches owed much to the scholarly ferment in the universities, it is not surprising that the Renaissance and Reformation were indebted to both. Education and religion were explosive forces that ultimately reshaped both the churches and the schools of higher education and, in fact, the direction of Western culture.

This new era was triggered by the victory of King Henry V of England over the French at Agincourt (1415), which established the Duke of Bedford as Regent of France. Of special importance for our purposes is that the duke's secretary, John Dunstable, was the foremost English musician of his time. His music was to be found in over thirty continental manuscripts and had an incalculable influence with the first generation of Renaissance composers.[28] The Roman Church, meanwhile, retained much of its ambivalence about music except when rigorously controlled by liturgical standards. The leaders of the Reformation, especially those among the Swiss and Scottish churches, retained a similar reservation, noting John Calvin's caution that "one must always watch lest the song be light and frivolous; rather, as Augustine says, it should have weight and majesty."[29] The exception to this was Martin Luther's adoption of music from both inside the tradition of the Roman Church and secular songs. Adapting theologically appropriate words to the melodies, he is reported to have asked, "Why should the devil have all the best tunes?" Luther was an accomplished musician in his own right, providing what became the hallmark of the Reformation, "A Might Fortress Is Our God," and countless other hymns to build a fast-growing and enthusiastic following.[30]

The many positive aspects of the Reformation, especially in freedom of religion, have been well rehearsed elsewhere. In music, however, a "down-side" has been argued in terms of the Baroque departure from the churches' guidelines for musical integrity. Begun roughly in 1600 with Giulio Caccini (d. 1618) one of many claimants as the founder of "the new music," Baroque represented a revolt against classicism with its major and minor scales replacing church modes.[31] Considering anew the individual capacities of instruments and the human voice, it produced two principle forms: instrumental (fugue, sonata, concerto, and overture) and vocal (opera, oratorio, and cantata). Undoubtedly its most celebrated composers were J.S. Bach (1685–1750) and his contemporary G.F. Handel (1685–1759).

The Baroque moods—emotional but not without thoughtful control—gave rise to a still more elegant and graceful style called *Rococo*. Its chief medium was arguably the piano (invented by Cristofori in 1709) whose first major composer was Francois Couperin (1668–1733). Its introduction was certainly not to the detraction of its forerunner, the harpsichord. From this point in history to the present, churches have had decreasing authority on musical forms and presentation. Perhaps precisely because of the lessening influence of organized churches, religious musical expression has periodically found its voice with greater power. Surely the Neoclassical Period (roughly late eighteenth to the first half of the nineteenth centuries) with its spokesmen in Haydn, Mozart, Beethoven, and others cannot be minimized. Nor can the impressive exemplars of the subsequent Romantic period—Liszt, Chopin, Mendelssohn, Wagner, and Tchaikovsky—for whom the spirit of a work of art must be found behind and beyond its physical, sonic composition.

The highly disciplined and inspired composers and performers of our own recent century deserve better than simply "modern" designation. Meanwhile, the professional musician—the composer, performer, teacher, scholar—is also a listener, hopefully to a degree an amateur listening to music for the sheer love of it. The professional balance is difficult to define. Like a Medieval 'mean,' it is found somewhere between the free-wheeling "anything goes" and the punctilious "nothing is accurate enough." History, as Edith Borroff suggests, can chart the mean where religion and art find common ground, revealing many paths and many answers.[32]

8. Artistic Expression in Islam

In Islam, art and faith are inextricably bound, but within a rigorous set of regulations. Comparisons with either Western or Eastern art forms whether in painting, sculpture, architecture, or music must be carefully weighed because Islamic art is unique and unmistakably Islamic. "Anyone with the patience to follow the artist in Allah's service through the labyrinth of geometric decorations will become captivated by the beauty of its artistic logic. The axiom for Islam's essentially a-naturalistic art was laid down in the teachings of the great Prophet Muhammad, in which he counseled against the representation of men and animals."[33]

This is not to say that birds and animals and even human figures are never to be found in Islamic art. A beautiful floor mosaic depicting a lion attacking a deer is found in the palace of Khirbat al-Mafjar, in Jordan, built by Calif al-Walid about 743, a scarce century after the Prophet Muhammad's death in 632. A bare-breasted dancer is one of the oldest (c. 743) free-standing sculptures in Islamic art (Figures 6.12a and b).

Often colorfully depicted has been the famous Muhammed's night journey (Holy Qur'an, Sura XV11) depicting the Prophet's guided tour to Heaven with the Angel Gabriel, riding winged horse Buraq, to meet with Adam, Moses, Jesus, and others, and to have a direct encounter with Allah in the company of angels (Figure 6.13).

Although these and other representations indicate brief lapses in strict compliance with the Holy Qur'an, they illustrate the employment of art for religious purposes. The truth remains that the vast amount of Islamic art, including architecture, music, mosaics, and even household goods such as carpets, are designed in compliance with Muhammed's dictum that they be educational and inspiring but free of human or animal likenesses.

In time, verses from the Qur'an were added as artistic embellishments and inscribed on walls, urns, vases, and even jewelry with the most compelling artistic flourishes. But in the area of architecture,

Figure 6.12a   Floor Mosaic, Palace of Khirbat, Jordan (c. 743–744)

mindful of the ideas of the great Prophet, mosques were at first very soberly deco-
rated, the adornment consisting of a simple insartia (insertions) of colorful stones.
This technique was soon supplanted by mosaics with which, for example, the
Dome of the Rock and the Great Mosque of Damascus were richly embellished.[34]

The Dome of the Rock (Figure 6.14) is of special interest because of its employment of truly breath-taking artistic nuances. The influence of Byzantine design in the
Christian Church of the Holy Sepulcher in Jerusalem is said to have so overwhelmed

Figure 6.12b   Dancer, One of Oldest Free-
standing Sculptures in Islamic Art (c. 743)

Figure 6.13 Muhammed's Night Journey, tapestry (date unknown)

Caliph Abd-Malik that he had it moved from the place of the rock (a spot sacred to Jews and Christians as well) "lest it dazzle the minds of the Muslims," and then erected above it the magnificent dome that was to become the destiny of sacred pilgrimages for centuries that followed.[35] The dome itself was completed in 691–692.

It was not alone the mosques, however. Such brilliant and distinctive artistic achievements were not restricted. Palaces reflected unsurpassed mastery in the ornamental use of stone, brickwork, and stucco. Limestone facades were sumptuously adorned with zigzag friezes of upright and inverted triangles containing rosettes and acanthus leaves.

> The religious prohibition on using precious metals like gold and silver forced the craftsman into an awkward position. He found himself obliged to forge noble forms in base metals or alloys such as bronze. The true masters in this field were to be found in Persia, and the provinces of Khurasan and West Turkestan.[36]

These masters managed to hold their monopoly until the tenth century when first Egypt and later Mesopotamia succeeded in producing masterpieces of their own distinctive type.

Figure 6.14   The Dome of the Rock (c. 691–692)

9. Shared Art

Amid many confrontations and wars in the next two centuries, Jews, Christians, and Muslims learned to respect each other and began sharing their insights and skills. Thus,

> by the year 1000 a Europe recognizable to the modern world had taken shape. The clash between pagan and Christian, between barbarian and Roman, between nomadic and settled had ended. For four hundred years, great trading routes tied the various regions together. Schools flourished, regional styles of architecture arose and literary accomplishments and history were many.[37]

For most people of the three religious traditions, life and religion were one, and music reflected them both.

> Music enlivened the monasteries and the churches, the town halls and the banquet halls. It was sung under ladies' windows, at funeral services and in processions. It rang across battle fields; it echoed in castle court yards; it lent dignity to coronations and joy and sanctity to weddings. It gave color to the age. In experiencing it today, we can learn about the inner life of medieval Europe as in no other way.[38]

Tragedy struck in 1492, the same year that Queen Isabella of Spain (largely to irritate her husband) sponsored the exploration of Christopher Columbus to the New World. In that year, new laws were issued decreeing that Jews and Muslims could no longer hold either property or citizenship, and they were to be expelled.

Throughout the Mediterranean world, however, there were places where Jews, Christians, and Muslims continued to live in relative harmony; those who had been forced from Spain had at least safe harbor elsewhere. In Iraq, as just one example, lived a group called *Yazidis*, followers of a religion which had elements derived from both Christianity and Islam."[39] Here all three traditions were welcome, according to the custom of the hospitality of many regions throughout the Middle East, Egypt, and northern Africa.

> In the mountain valleys of Lebanon there was an ancient symbiosis between the main religious communities. A member of a local family, that of Shihab, was elevated by the Ottomans to be chief tax farmer, and the Shihabs had become in effect princes of the mountain, heads of a hierarchy of land holding families both Christian and Druze, between whom there were common interests, alliances and formal relationships.[40]

These common interests included births, rites of passage, weddings and funerals, and life events that neighbors could share and celebrate. In such communities, music and the other arts often cemented the fellowships that help create a culture. It has occurred even more recently. Ludwig Schneller, German theologian who spent his entire adult life in Bethlehem's Holy Land, wrote of this in 1889 in his book *Kennst Du Das Land? (Do You Understand the Land?)*. In it, he reminds us that

> David's psalms and harp were once heard here, and the song of everlasting love was sung here. That Holy Book, with its gripping songs of sorrow regarding human sinfulness, and his songs of praise of the heavenly love and home—from that land and its hills it rings for thousands of years.[41]

B. RELIGIOUS REFLECTIONS ON SCIENCE

It was not uncommon in the late nineteenth century to encounter statements to the effect that nearly all questions about the functions of nature had been resolved scientifically. Only a few puzzles remained, and they were destined to be settled within a very few years. Religious explanations, it was insisted by some, were as irrelevant as the deity(ies) they invoked. A famous nineteenth century atheist, Robert Ingersoll, expressed this at the grave of his brother in 1879: "Life is a narrow vale between the cold and barren peaks of two eternities. We cry aloud—and the only answer is the echo of our wailing cry." Is there then no God, he was later asked; no honest, compassionate Creator? He answered "An honest God is the noblest work of man."[42]

Nevertheless Ingersoll upheld the viability of religion in an age increasingly dominated by science during this period. At the very least, he affirmed it could be acknowledged that while both disciplines pursue different questions and have unique disciplines for resolving them, they do focus on some common interests. These include at least six major goals to be achieved: (1) providing a body of knowledge about the facts and processes of the natural order and the nature of "being" itself (the task of ontology, e.g. whether, and if so how all reality emerged from a Big Bang); (2) exploring for the most effective ways to understand these processes (the task of epistemology); (3) describing changes that have occurred from generation to generation or, at the cosmic level, eons to eons; (4) explaining these changes in terms of determinants (what factors guided the emergence of new adaptations needed for survival; (5) predicting changes that are seemingly destined to occur; (6) learning how to intervene in these developments and to control their probable outcome. An example of this last goal might be the prediction of a comet colliding with the earth and ways to halt or at least deflect it. This goal may become urgent as the discovery of the the the Smith-Tuttle Comet, discovered in 1872 and resighted in 1992, is predicted to collide with earth on August 14, 2116.[44]

Meanwhile, we may note that certain questions of metaphysics, such as the meaning and purpose of natural events, may be shared by the scientific and religious communities. At the 1893 Chicago World's Fair, although only a few score were anticipated to attend the first meeting of the Parliament of the World's Religions, excitement about the intellectual and spiritual level of the meetings was such that accommodations for hundreds had to be found.

Delegates and attendees at the parliament from all walks of life including the sciences, learned facts about other religions. Among *Hindus,* the universe was held to be the work of Brahma, the Maker of the universe, the Preserver of the world, the first among devas (sons of the sky father Dyaus). Brahma told His eldest son Atharva, about the Knowledge of Brahman, the Foundation of all knowledge.[45] Thus, despite the great number of lesser deities identified in their tradition, Hinduism is essentially a monotheistic faith that fit well with a tradition where cosmology, astronomy, and mathematics are combined to bring faith and scientific practice into meaningful dialogue.

Zoroastrianism noted that their *Magi,* Wise Men, had used their knowledge of astronomy to travel from Persia to Jerusalem to locate the birthplace of Jesus in Bethlehem, thus fulfilling a spiritual summons.

Buddhist cosmology posits vast cycles of beginnings and destructions of the universe, not unlike the "big-bang, big-crunch" cycles popular among some modern astronomers until fairly recent times. An adjunct to this interpretation is a very up-to-date expectation of multiple, perhaps a thousand million, universes.[46]

Confucius did not teach of a sovereign God to whom we should turn in times of joy and sorrow but spoke of the Great Unity behind the universe. This unifying force provides the *Yin* and *Yang,* the negative and positive universal principles in nature (perhaps an intuitive metaphor for electromagnetic forces). These in turn devolve into five dynamic elements that tear through mathematically probable combinations produce the familiar material things comprising the kingdoms of the created world: plants, animals, and minerals.

Hebrew thought expresses the conviction that all natural entities were brought into being by the purposeful design of a personal creator God and that all things and occurrences move toward destined ends called "the teleological argument." The sheer facts that order prevails in the organic and inorganic realms and that the emergence of living, thinking, value-seeking beings seem to go far beyond any possibility of random chance and to make the dialogue between science and religion inescapable. Add to this the conviction of the value-seeking mortal human's that there is profound personal fulfillment in dialogue with a good, forgiving, and loving Father God, which may at least tentatively affirm the teleological proposition.

The *Christian* view of cosmology does not actually begin in Genesis 1 with God's ordering the universe into being out of an apparently already established ground. ("The earth was without form and void." Gen. 1:2). Instead it begins, prior to such a ground, with the Word (John 1:1–2). The concept of a word (as in "I give you my word"), being the very essence of the person, is both metaphysical and pragmatic. When a person reneges on her or his given word (i.e., she or he lies, denying the integrity of her or his very being), that disruption of selfhood is not simply "metaphysical" but can be identified on a lie detector. The assertion in John's Gospel is that God's word is both God's essential self and is able to take on a dynamic of his own: both *with* God and *as* God, actively creating all things (1:3), and in time "became flesh and dwelt among us . . . as the only Son from the Father" (1:14). This highly complex idea challenges us to think ontologically, balancing our capacity to know both intuitively and counter-intuitively. There are no instruments, at present, by which to test or measure the truth of the assumption; the physicist cannot weigh, measure, or see the strings undergirding the "string theory" of the universe. Much has to be taken "on faith." This should not be taken as looking for a God who merely fills in the gaps in our knowledge. "Science and theology," as John Polkinghorne reminds us, "are responses to the way things are and both proceed by conjoining logical analysis with intuitive acts of judgment."[47]

The *Islamic* position is that "there cannot be any conflicts between the Qur'an and science, because both came from God. In Islam, religion and science complement each other."[48] What if a scientific hypothesis, such as Darwin's evolutionary process, contests the Qur'an's story of Adam and Eve being the first formed human at the time of creation?

> If it should prove to be a fact and be supported conclusively by scientific evidence, we need not be worried, because the Qur'an says that God has created man from earth. That is really describing whole stages of development. That is one interpretation. The other, which is a much older one, treated most of these (Biblical) stories as symbolic. They represent the relationship between man and God, and therefore Adam becomes the human race rather than just an individual person.[49]

The popular assumption that Islam began its intellectual pilgrimage through the classical writings of Greek and Roman philosophers during Western culture's "dark " ages is no longer so widely accepted. It would be more accurate to affirm that Islam "channeled" Indian mathematics, science, and literature to the West. What is often overlooked is the significance of this research in terms of understanding two foundational concepts of philosophy, ontology (the nature of nature, indeed of being itself) and epistemology, or ways of knowing. Pursuing mastery of these concepts, Muslims learned how all aspects of the natural order are interlated in an essential unity and how God relates to all realms of nature.

> The question of the Unity of the Divine Principle and the consequent unity of Nature is particularly important in Islam where the ideal of Unity (*al-tawid*) overshadows all others. It remains at every level of Islamic culture the most basic principle upon which all else depends.[50]

The assumption that there is a continuity between God and Nature is to avoid producing some form of pantheism or monism. We tread a fine line here, but of critical importance is that "there cannot be two orders of reality independent of each other. The formulation of Unity is the most universal criterion of orthodoxy." What is affirmed here is expressed in the daily prayer *La ilaha illa Llah:* "There is no divinity but the Divine, which in its most profound sense means there is no reality outside of the Absolute Reality."[51]

Can this be demonstrated empirically? It is widely affirmed among Muslims that at the beginning of time, Creation occurred, and this must have been initiated. "Caused creation" implies a Creator, what Aristotle suggested in the expression "the unmoved mover." The Kalam Cosmological Argument (KCA), explicated by Gustavo Romero, senior scientist of the Argentine Institute for Radio Astronomy in Buenos Aires, remains a basic premise among Muslim scientists. Romero notes that there are theoretical models, like "wormholes," which tunnel through the fabric of space-time. These were created at the time of the Big Bang. If traveled through, "such a trip would occur along a closed time-like curve (CTC) and could, theoretically, end before the Big Bang occurred. This astonishing prospect is not actually forbidden in general relativity but renders the factual existence of such wormholes ontologically improbable, proposing as it does that an astronaut on such a journey would emerge before the beginning of time. Nevertheless,

> an all-powerful Creator may have created the universe from a vantage point beyond space-time. Romero's proposal to search for wormholes through distinct gravitational lensing signatures seems viable. Their discovery would profoundly affect our understanding of physical reality in the universe.[52]

The discovery of wormholes would also illustrate the benefits (if not urgency) of correspondence between science and religion.

C.   SCIENCE AND RELIGION IN DIALOGUE

In a cave drawing from Paleolithic times variously dated from 15,000 to 50,000 years B.C., an unknown artist blended the diverse disciplines of religion, arts, and science in their most primitive forms and depicted the wisest person in the tribe, probably the tribal priest engaged in a ritual to bring the illusive spirit of an animal under the power of the hunters. Archaeologists generally agree that the artist's depiction was part of the "spell" of the sorcerer (Figure 6.15).[53]

It would seem that long before the division of the various disciplines into discrete, and sometimes jealously guarded, specialties, cooperation among them was virtually taken for granted. The rudimentary science of the primitive was one with his religion. Many of the myths and legends of early times have come to us simply as stories to be shared. Myths were not regarded as lies but as aids to visualizing what was already ancient history and beyond empirical verification. Many scholars attribute the two distinct stories of the creation of earth and the first human inhabitants in the opening two chapters of Genesis to an adaptation of the Canaanite version of a Babylonian myth. To read the two accounts as scientifically testable fact, we would have to overlook the obvious contradiction in the Old

Figure 6.15 The Sorcerer, cave
drawing (c. 50,000 B.C.)

Textament between Genesis 1:1-2 that Adam was created after the plants and other animals and the second telling (Genesis 2:4b-25) that Adam was created before them.

Science is not opposed to religion per se, but when religious followers oppose their story accounts to scientific data, a certain disjunction is inevitable. Nobel Laureate Arthur Compton, physicist and Presbyterian elder, expressed it well over half a century ago when the conflict was heating up: Science can have no quarrel with a religion that postulates a God to whom (mankind) is as His children . . . with free, intelligent wills capable of learning nature's laws, of seeing dimly God's purpose in nature, and of working with him to make that purpose effective.[54]

Science and religion have different functions. Albert Einstein put it with elegant simplicity:

> Science can only ascertain what is, but not what should be, and outside of its domain judgments of all kinds remain necessary. Religion is the age old endeavor of mankind to become clearly and completely conscious of these values and goals. If one conceives of religion and science according to these definitions then a conflict between them appears impossible.[55]

Science can be described in a number of ways as already noted: as a body of knowledge that can be exhibited in an array of equations, and so on. Perhaps of greater practical interest, science has been a potent force for good in the world through its contributions to enabling global communications, curing diseases, improving meteorological predictions, and fighting ignorance and superstition by providing evidence for their debunking.[56]

On the other hand, similar descriptions can be applied to religion as a way of knowing and thinking: serving agricultural and medical needs across the world; building the first major European universities in the twelfth century and sponsoring the first free public schools in the New World. Geologist Frank Rhodes points out that

> the original dependence of science on Christian theology is seen most clearly if we remind ourselves of the presuppositions of modern science. These are a belief in an orderly, regular, rational universe; a belief that this orderliness is intelligible, and a belief in a broad principle of causality . . . it was the philosophy, theology and outlook of a whole Christian civilization that provided the cradle of modern science.[57]

Had it not been for the medieval universities' provision for scientific speculation and the insistence of Roger Bacon (1214–1294) that the study of natural science was complementary to faith and must proceed by way of observation and experimentation, modern science as we know it might never have emerged.

It is clear that science and religion must remain distinct; neither is equipped to answer the other's questions, yet the two are not unrelated. People who work within their disciplines are sometimes forced to ask questions of each other. For example, if a scientist is asked by his or her government to use scientific means to achieve something the scientist considers immoral (e,g., to use sophisticated electrical or chemical techniques to torture and extract information from jailed suspects), the scientist must conclude that the issue arises from a value system outside the realm of science per se. Thus the exclamation of Robert Oppenheimer upon learning of the atomic bombing of Hiroshima: "Science has known sin, and that is a knowledge we dare not lose."[58] This was quoted in *The Bulletin of the Atomic Scientists* at a time (1966) when science was generally regarded as morally neutral. C.P. Snow refuted such a claim in his "two cultures" concept declaring that science cannot insist on such neutrality and certainly not on indifference.[59] Albert Einstein added his voice to the debate in noting "Science without religion is lame, religion without science is blind."[60]

A new attitude toward dialogue that had no precedent in modern history began to open in the 1960s. Charles Townes, after winning the Nobel Prize for his work on the masers, addressed this opportunity in his article, "The Convergence of Science and Religion": "They both represent man's efforts to understand his universe, and must be dealing with the same substance." He added that the fact both are so intimately related to mankind's decision making in every area of private and public life makes their cooperation all the more urgent. "Converge they must, and through this should come new strength for both."[61]

This attitude of openness reached an important milestone in the establishment of the annual Templeton Prize in excess of $1 million awarded annually for progress toward research or discoveries about spiritual realities. Recent winners have included the Rev. Dr. Arthur Peacock, biochemist; the Rev. Dr. John Polkinghorne; and the 2004 recipient, Dr. George Ellis, a South African cosmologist who is also professor of applied mathematics and president of the Royal Society of South Africa.[62]

Encouraging as these developments are, there is still another convergence to be considered which, in fact, has been underway for millennia, but still evokes both enthusiasm and dire warnings: It is to that end we now turn to the scientific contributions to technology, with its implications for globalization with its blessings and discontents.

D. TECHNOLOGY: BENEFITS AND CHALLENGES

Nostalgia aside, few of us would give up our ability to drive cars that far exceed early "speed limits," fly planes across oceans in a few hours and, as astronauts, travel at thousands of miles per hour to return to a time when a person could travel no faster than a horse could run. Most of us would be reluctant to return to a time when countless millions died of influenza, pneumonia, and other diseases for which there were no known cures; before aqueducts, giant dams, and pipelines could facilitate the transport of water supplies from distant mountains or rivers to teeming cities; before agricultural engineering *began* to make food production and distribution equal to the needs of great populations; before communication technologies enabled us to send critical information instantly to local police, national military headquarters, distant countries around the world, and even remote planets; and before sanitation technologies made cities livable with standard flush toilets in countless homes replacing outhouses located in back yards without adequate provision for sewage disposal. It was not uncommon for city dwellers to empty chamber pots out of windows onto streets below in the dark of night. These suggest only a fraction of the benefits of technologies that most of us would be loath to relinquish.

Yet many such innovations met with skepticism and even outright hostility when first introduced, however. Resistance has been omnipresent and often noisy from accusations of "man's overaching himself" like Icarus; "trying to play God" like Dr. Frankenstein; and the father of the Wright Brothers complaining, in 1903, "If God wanted us to fly, he'd have given us wings," Then there have been the outlandish parodies on the "mad scientist" theme in novels, movies, and television. Efforts to go beyond the ordinary in problem solving have often met with scorn. When Mark Twain refusing to invest in telephone stock because telephones "are only toys with no commercial value;"

In addition to being greatly influenced by science, technology, has become one of four major "environments" for us all, along with the cosmic, the earth-bound "natural," and the social. It deserves at least a cursory review to note its impact on and reaction from the social sciences and the population in general.

In its prehistoric infancy technology was represented by the point at which sticks and stones were recognized as inadequate for either tools or weapons, and were combined to fashion the hammer and the hand ax (c. 70,000 B.C.) It would be tedious to trace the evolution of the stone-tipped stick to the javelin, bow and arrow, gun, and all technical weapons that followed. It would be equally dull to trace in detail the evolution of information transmission from drums and smoke signals to cell phones, computer Internet, and satellite communications. The juncture between the sciences, which were presumed to embrace all knowledge, and technology, which was identified more with crafts such as tanning, dying, milling, and smithing, is less difficult to identify. One needs consider only that the science of astronomy would not have advanced without the combined vision and practical skills of Roger Bacon (thirteenth century), of Leonardo da Vinci, and others who followed.

The reciprocal relation between science and technology was curiously still being resisted in many leading American universities as recently as the early nineteenth century for fear that it would jeopardized. the traditional classical curriculum. The 1828 report to the Yale Corporation held that students who wanted to study chemistry or physics with their offensive test tubes and mechanical contraptions would do better to work in a factory. A prescribed list of courses featuring the thorough study of the ancient languages, mathematics, and philosophy was the only proper curriculum for a college. Failed efforts at innovation caused Francis Wayland to step down as president of Brown University in 1855, and Henry Tappan was fired from the presidency of the University of Michigan in 1863 by a hostile board of regents for his emphases on stricter academic standards and a curriculum that included more emphasis on the sciences and technology.

Ultimately, however, it was one of the great gifts to U.S. culture that some schools of higher education, such as the U.S. Military Academy (founded 1802) and the Rensselaer Institute (founded 1824 and by 1849 added courses in architecture, mechanics, civil, and mining engineering), began to be taken seriously, especially abroad. Some of the more visionary leaders at Yale, Harvard, Dartmouth, and the establishers of land grant colleges in virtually every state (thanks to Justin Morrill and Abraham Lincoln) enabled the United States to become a major player in science and technology. The country had entered the nineteenth century as a modest, still secondary nation, but by the end of the century, it emerged an industrial giant.

Yet there persisted voices of caution. Some of these came from writers as noted above in the Frankenstein novel of Mary Shelley (1818) and the depersonalizing effect of factory work with all their new hazardous machines, destructive especially with children. Later implications of alienation of people from society via technology appear in Jules Verne's *Twenty Thousand Leagues Under the Sea* (1870) and H.G. Wells' much imitated *War of the Worlds* (1898) and on through decades of warnings against run-a-way technology which continue popularity today. Few of these authors stirred such controversy as did Aldous Huxley in his *Brave New World* (1932) or George Orwell in his *1984* (published in 1949). At the edge of fiction and nonfiction was the movie *Modern Times* starring Charlie Chaplin depicting the dehumanizing effects of assembly line production in factories where at the end of the day a worker could not identify his contribution to the finished product.

A more direct attack on technology came as early as the early 1800s when the new factory system brought ways to substitute machines for people, leading to massive layoffs of workers. In 1806, Manchester, England had only one loom; by 1818, it had two thousand. Hundreds of workers, victims of the new technology, were laid off, and some became so desperate to feed their families that they attacked the factories and smashed the looms.

Parliament retaliated by establishing the death penalty for breaking a loom, and executions began to diminish the already starving populations. Factory owners refused to believe there could be starvation in England when they themselves were growing so rich.[63] Enchanted by new gadgets and the wonders of the steam engine's ability to move people and commodities from place to place, few wanted to hear

Ralph Waldo Emerson's warning that we were being seduced by novel *things:* "Things are in the saddle and ride mankind."

Among the things in addition to the looms in the mills were new means of extracting coal and other mined products. Mining operators discovered that they could hire women and children more cheaply than men, putting more men out of work and sending children into stifling underground tunnels.

> Children of both sexes were clad in male attire, naked to the waist in canvas trousers with an iron chain fastened to a belt of leather between their legs. They hauled tubs of coal up subterranean roads for twelve to sixteen hours a day . It was not unusual to find children of four or five years of age working in these conditions.[64]

Pressure from the churches in England for child labor laws finally brought this situation under control. In America, however, where these oppressive labor conditions were coupled with the practice of slavery, secure family life was in jeopardy in the industrial centers. This made migration to the "wild west" an arduous and often dangerous alternative. It is easy to disbelieve idyllic portrayals of family life in the eighteenth and nineteenth centuries.

Furthermore, it is important to remember that Eli Whitney's invention of the cotton gin, which was fifty times more efficient than the then current method of separating cotton seed from the fiber, that made slave labor increasingly profitable. This profitability increased the Southern plantation owners' resistance to the emancipation of slaves who had made the United States fourth among manufacturing nations in the world.[65] "The insatiable demand for cotton riveted chains on the limbs of the luckless Negro," a moral and political issue, which according to some historians, prompted the Civil War.[66]

By 1894, after the postwar reconstruction and a generation of technological triumphs that included the stock tickertape, telephone, telegraph, typewriter, automobile, electric lights, and motion pictures. America, among the manufacturing nations of the world, spurted into first place; it has seldom relinquished that leadership.[67]

Americans in general have never felt it necessary to apologize for its technological preeminence. After all, technology accompanied the nation through two world wars, an unprecedented Great Depression, subsequent economic recovery, smaller-scale wars, economic ebbs and flows, and agricultural development making possible an increase of food and water and their efficient distribution to some developing countries. All in all, popular wisdom has it, there has been a persistent upward trend. Certainly among the achievements celebrated "from sea to shining sea," must include the moon landings and exploration of the solar system to the very edge of space.

It is generally agreed that technologists cannot be expected to monitor the uses of their creations; that technology, if not morally neutral, is at least no better or worse than the people who use its products. However, we still need the writers Rachel Carson, Jacques Ellul, and William Barrett, whose books like *Silent Spring, La Technique,* and *The Illusion of Technique* (in the 1950s, 1960s, and 1970s) to alert the rest of us to the destructive effects of respectively, some of technology's hazards: pesticides, automobiles, overcrowding, unrestricted waste-disposal practices, poor land management, and reckless abuse of forests, lakes, and oceans etc. ad infinitum (it seems). The August 2004 issue of *Scientific American* announced the mounting death toll from arsenic poisoning in well water in Bangladesh, directly traceable to what had been hoped was a solution to a pressing need. This involved the installation (since the early 1990s) of 10 million "tubewells," low-cost technological wonders created to facilitate easier gathering of drinking water from deep wells (as opposed to collecting buckets of often contaminated surface water). The tubewell was "a rare success story in the otherwise impoverished nation" but has turned out to be a lethal device that destroys the lives it was designed to save.[68]

But it is not only the water that is so deadly poisoned. "Bangladeshis may be ingesting arsenic through a secondary route: the grain they eat two or three times a day. In dry months rice fields are irrigated with pumped underground water. Nor is it only Bangladeshi who are suffering. "Arsenic in drinking water could severely poison 50 million people world wide." The World Health Organization, notes that "The mineral occurs in the water supply of countries such as India, Nepal, Vietnam, China, Argentina, Chile, Taiwan, Mongolia and the USA.

The story of the tubewell could serve as a parable on how we as a species might become victims of our own technology, yet in the last analysis, it is no less naïve to blame our tools and machinery for our woes, than for the Victorians a century ago to laud technology as our sure savior from natural as well as manmade misfortunes. It would be worthy of Darwin to suggest that such anguish is simply the growing pains experienced in cooperating with nature to guide our evolution.[69]

Without a doubt, science and technology have made possible achievements that would have been impossible even to envision a generation or two ago. Advancing technology can and does place deadly tools and capabilities within reach of corrupt, violent and even demented political leaders. This is not the familiar dream among explorers to bring the wealth and power of the world into the domain of one sovereign nation. That even antedates the Romans Empire. But globalization seems a nobler ambition, which is to unite a fractured world with its clashing civilizations and increasingly deadly wars by developing the means for meeting all the needs of all inhabitants of the world! Science and technology have already begun to share their wisdom and powers to make this a reality.

The uniting of these resources however has more than a casual "downside." Multinational corporations such as General Motors and Coca-Cola make possible the building of networks for extensive business transactions and worldwide trade. They can create a global marketplace without geographical borders. Businesses and corporations are at liberty to move from one country to another without the historic restraints of loyalty to any given society or nation. Does this not threaten to humanize the most human aspects of social life?[70]

Translate this treatment of globalization from banks and legitimate businesses to the underworld of crime and "terrorist" organizations, and the ultimate nightmare of globalization becomes a reality—and all made possible by virtually unrestrained technology. Rajan Menon puts this in the starkest of terms:

> Both Al Qaeda and GM rely on high-speed transportation, computerized global banking networks and information systems that enable the marshaling of financial and human resources. Try to imagine Osama bin Laden and his terrorist network in a world without satellite phones, global positioning systems, fax machines, electronic banking, wide-body jets, web-sites, soft targets that dot the landscape of globalization: high rise office buildings, rock concerts and sporting

events attended by tens of thousands. In such a world, Bin Laden would be an isolated voice ranting in a cave, his millenarian ideology lacking in international constituency. . . . Bin Laden is dangerous precisely because he has turned globalization's principle assets into a deadly arsenal.[71]

Certainly, it is clear that neither technology nor globalization are going to go away. It is also clear that there is still substance in the old cliché that technology is only as good or evil as the people who use it. If there is to be a viable global ethic, it will require employing our best resources both intellectually and spiritually but also pedagogically so that the next generation which inherits the fruits of our follies will not repeat them.

E.   IMPLICATIONS FOR GLOBAL ETHICS

Reflecting on the 1999 Parliament of the World's religions held in Cape Town, South Africa, Gerald O. Barney, director of the *U.S. Government's Global 2000 Report to The President,* issued this statement:

> We find ourselves at a moment when people everywhere are coming to recognize that the world is a global village. The perils and promises of this new reality bring to mind several ancient understandings: that human beings are interdependent and responsible for the care of the earth; that we are each worthy of a meaningful life and obliged to help the human community toward a life of peace and dignity; that the choices shaping a just, peaceful and sustainable future are choices we must make together.[72]

Having explored, albeit in painfully brief form, the contributions of the arts, sciences, and technology to our evolving culture, the pithy response of Johann Sebastian Bach concerning the "secret" of his compositions comes to mind:

> In the architecture of my music I want to demonstrate to the world the architecture of a new and beautiful social commonwealth. . . . it is the enlightened self-discipline of the various parts—each voluntarily imposing on itself the limits of its individual freedom for the well-being of the community.

Little more than half a century later, Beethovan reacted to the horrific consequences of the Napoleonic wars as well as to his own career-threatening deafness by setting Schiller's *Ode to Joy* to music in the ninth Symphony: "Seid umschlungen millionen, Diesen kuss der ganzen Welt" ("Be embraced ye millions, here's a kiss for all the world").

This chapter has discussed some of the problems of relating faith to science and technology, in response to which John Polkinghorne of Cambridge University provides this engaging insight: "The experience of wonder is an authentic part of the scientist's experience. But where does wonder find its lodgment in the world as described by science? It is missing, as are our experiences of goodness, beauty and obligation."[73] The ethical demands of social and cultural life are insistent. Although neither the arts, science, nor technology appears capable of supplying an adequate formula on its own, Nobel Laureate Mother Teresa may have expressed a solution: "Es kommt nicht so sehr darauf an, wieviel wir tun, sondern wieviel Liebe wir in unser tun legen." ("It is not so very important how much we do, but on the contrary how much love we put into our doing.")

NOTES

1. M.G. Lord, *Los Angeles Times*, June 13, 2004, 9, James A. Connor, *Kelper's Witch* (SanFrancisco: Harper, 2004) quoted in.

2. John Polkinghorne, *belief in God in an Age of Science* (New Haven and London: Yale University Press 1998), 121.

3. Heinrich Zimmer, *The Art of Indian Asia*, vol. 1 (New York: Bollington Foundation, Princeton University Press, 1955), 22–24. Helen Gardner dates the Venus figure 15,000–10,000 and stresses the fact that, unlike animal figures, the creator of Venus did not strive for realism but symbolism of female fecundity. See Helen Gardner, *Art Through the Ages* (New York: Harcourt, Brace, Jovanovich, 1975), 6th Edition 34.

4. Ibid., 24.

5. Ibid. Zimmer declares that this practice of the wife of a deceased man with him continues today in some parts of India. "Through this it was indicated that she, in passing, having transcended the bondage of earthly life, had been released from the cycle of births and subsumed in the transcendental essence of the Great God's eternal being."

6. Bernard S. Myers, *Art and Civilization* (New York: McGraw-Hill, Book Company, 1967), 91 *Cf.* Hermann Goetz, *The Art of India* (New York: Greystone Press, 1964), 150–59.

7. Veronica Ions, *Indian Mythology* (London: Paul Hymans, 1968), 119–25.

8. William A. Young, *The Worlds Religions*, 2nd ed., (Englewood Cliffs, NJ: Prentice-Hall, 2005), 64.

9. Myers, *op. cit.*, 92.

10. Gardner, *op. cit.*, 832.

11. Myers, *op. cit.* 102.

12. *Cf.* Michael Sullivan, *A Short History of Chinese Art* (Berkeley: University of California, 1967), 180f.

13. According to archaeologist William Albright, the dating of the exodus should be around 1290 B.C.E. when the Jewish slaves would have only a primitive skill in the arts but would remember well the figurative sculptures and paintings of Egypt, which they proceeded to imitate. *The New Encyclopedia Britannica,* vol. 12 (Chicago: Encyclopedia Britannica, 1974), 487.

14. Georges Barrois, "Hebrew Art," *The Interpreter's Dictionary of the Bible*, vol. 1, (New York; Abingdon Press, 1962), 237–39.

15. Ibid., 240.

16. The "sackbut" is thought by musicologists to have been a kind of trombone, as is cited in E. Werner's "Musical Instruments" vol. 2, *Interpreter's Dictionary of the Bible, op. cit.,* 476.

17. Gardner, *op. cit.,* 246–47.

18. Ibid., 247–48.

19. Helen Gardner, *Art Through the Ages,* 11th ed. United States: Thomson/ Wordsworth, 2003), 234.

20. Ibid., 241.

21. Ibid., 342.

22. The four towering minarets distinctly a part of the Hagia Sophia today were actually added after the Ottoman conquest in 1453 when the Christian church became a Muslim mosque. Today, with the secularization of Turkey, the building is a museum.

23. Gardner, *op. cit.*, 349–50.

24. Donald Jay Grout, *A History of Western Music* (New York: W.W. Norton, 1960), 20–21.

25. Ibid., 31.

26. Jeremy Yudkin, *Music in Medieval Europe* (Englewood Cliffs, NJ: Prentice-Hall, 1989), 42.

27. Ibid., 203.

28. Piero Weiss and Richard Taruskin, *Music in the Western World* (New York: Schirmer Books, 1984), 79.

29. John Calvin, "OEuvres" (Geneva, 1543), quoted in Weiss and Taruskin, *op. cit.,* 107.

30. Weiss and Taruskin, *op. cit.,* pp. 104–05.

31. "Mode" refers to a pattern of arrangement of tones and half tones of a scale. On the piano keys, one mode might be described as only white keys from D to D, or from F to F. The pattern of whole and half tones from D to D would then be 1, 1/2, 1,1,1, 1/2 1. But from F to F it would be 1,1,1 1/2, 1, 1, 1/2. A melody composed in one mode and then transposed to another would thus be completely changed. The medieval "plainsong" had eight modes, four called *authentic* and four called *plagal;* the difference between them is in the range. *Cf. The Columbia Viking Desk Encyclopedia,* (New York: Viking Press, 1953), 826. See also Yudkin, *op, cit.*, 66–74.

32. Edith Borroff, *Music in Europe and the United States* (New York: Ardsley House, 1990), 746.

33. Carel J. Du Ry, *Art of Islam* (New York: Harry N. Abrams, 1970), 7.

34. Ibid., 30.

35. Ibid., 23. "The Rock" is, according to tradition, the site where Abraham went to sacrifice Isaac and from which Muhammed launched his night journey with Gabriel. It was also the location where Solomon's Temple was built (c. 966 B.C., destroyed by the Babylonians (586 B.C.), rebuilt (536 B.C.), but destroyed again by the Romans in 70 A.D.

36. Du Ry, *Ibid.*, 47–49.

37. Yudkin, *op cit.,* 13 Tragically, those centuries were also stained by the horrendous events known as the Crusades. This is not the place to critique that disruptive era, although one can note that, ironically, the interfaith and intercultural exchanges already initiated continued to benefit all three major religious traditions and their adherents in virtually all areas of the arts and sciences, higher education, medicine, and exploration.

38. Ibid., 17.

39. Albert Hourani, *A History of the Arab Peoples* (Cambridge: Harvard University Press, 1991), 96.

40. *Ibid.*, 277.

41. Ludwig Schneller, *Kennst Du Das Land?* Leipzig: Kommissionsverlag von H.G. Wallmann, 1892), 1. trans. Fred E. Rose (Belleville, IL: self-published by Dr. Rose. 1987).

42. These words, spoken at the graveside of Robert Ingersoll's brother, Ebon, in 1879; were repeated at the funeral of Luther Burbank in 1926 and are quoted in *Bartlett's Familiar Quotations* (Boston: Little, Brown, 1948), 602–3. A portion of it is in *The Oxford Dictionary of Quotations* (New York: Oxford University Press, 1992), 360.

43. Duncan Steel of the Anglo-Austrian Observatory announced this to delegates to the International Astronomical Union in Sydney after its rediscovery on October 15, 1992, predicting: "It would create an impact force of 20 million megatons, 1.6 million times the force of the first atomic bomb dropped on Hiroshima [and] would wipe out at least 75% of mankind, probably 95%."

44. Of the six major concerns shared by science and religion, the first two were proposed by Harold K. Shilling, *Science and Religion* (New York: Charles Scribners', 1962), 14ff; the other four were detailed by James Vander Zanden, *Human Development,* 7th ed., (New York: McGraw-Hill, 2000), 5f.

45. Swami Nikhilananda, *the Upanishads* (New York: Harper & Row, 1963), 109.

46. The recent discovery that the universe is not only expanding but accelerating in its expansion has cast doubt on the "big crunch" predictions of twenty years ago. *Cf.* Edwards, Harrison, *Cosmology: The Science of the Universe* (Cambridge, England: Cambridge University Press, 2000). See especially Chap. 14. Meanwhile, the concept of multiple universes is no longer a science fiction subplot. See "Origin and Fate of the Universe" *Astronomy,* (Waukesha, WI: Kalmbach Publishing, 2004).

47. John Polkinghorne, *Science and Creation* (Boston: New Science Library, 1989), xii. Noting the value of natural theology in locating the divine logic and evident plan of nature, Polkinghorne observes that "it will only at best be able by itself to bring us to the Cosmic Architect or Great Mathematician." The faith that makes a prayerful communion with God "is to be reached by other means. See also Polkinghorne, *The Faith of a Physicist* (Princeton: Princeton University Press, 1994), chap. 4.

48. John Bowker, *What Muslims Believe* (Oxford: One World Press, 1995), 152–53.

49. Ibid., 155–56.

50. Sayyed Hossein, *Islamic Cosmological Doctrines* (New York: State University of New York Press, 1993), 4.

51. Ibid., 5.

52. *Mike Martin,* "Islamic Argument for God's Existence May Be Testable," *Science and Theology News*, May 2004, 6.

53. Gardner, *op. cit.*, 6th ed., 32. Cf. Robert B. McLaren, *The World of Philosophy* (Chicago: Nelson-Hall, 1983), 3.

54. Arthur Compton, "A Modern Concept of God," *Man's Destiny in Eternity: The Garvin Lecture* (Boston: Beacon Press, 1949), 19.

55. Albert Einstein, *Out of My Later Years* (New York: Philosophical Library, 1950), 25.

56. Harold K. Shilling, *Science and Religion* (New York: Charles Scribner's, 1962), 15.

57. Frank H.T. Rhodes, *Christianity in a Mechanistic Universe,* ed. D.B. Mackay, editor, (London: Intervarsity Fellowship, 1965), 18.

58. McLaren, Robert B. "Science and Contemporary Theology, " in *Bulletin of the Atomic Scientists*, March, 1966, p. 25,

59. Charles P. Snow, "The Moral Un-Neutrality of Science," *Science,* 256.

60. Einstein, *op. cit.,* 22, 26.

61. Charles Townes, "The Convergence of Science and Religion," *Think*, March 1966, 7.

62. *Science and Theology News*, Brentwood, Tennessee, April 2004.

63. Brian Inglis, *Poverty and the Industrial Revolution* (London; Hodder and Stoughton, 1971), 100.

64. Robert McLaren, Christian Ethics, *op. cit.*, 159, quoting Gerald Hershey and James Lugo, *Human Development* (New York: Macmillan, p, 24–25. The authors added the editorial comment: "Conditions were so terrible that criminals today would certainly choose the death penalty rather than be forced to endure them."

65. Thomas A. Bailey, *The American Pageant*, 5th ed. (Lexington, MA: D.C. Heath, 1975), 319.

66. Ibid.

67. Ibid., 561.

68. A. Mushtaque Chowdhury, "Arsenic Crisis in Bangladesh," *Scientific American*, New York: Scientific American, Inc., 2004, p. 87.

69. Edward O. Wilson, *On Human Nature* (Cambridge, MA: Harvard University Press, 1978) 80, quoting Lionel Trilling's *Beyond Culture*, in which Trilling notes: "There is a hard, irreducible, stubborn core of biological urgency, and biological necessity and biological *reason,* that culture cannot reach and that reserves the right, which sooner or later it will exercise, to judge the culture and resist and revise it." It may also be argued, however, that the conscious, willing selves that we are can interact with our biological selves (what Trilling calls biological *reason;* italics his) to shape the direction of our evolution. *Cf.* Wilson, *op. cit.,* on the trajectory of history, 81.

70. Hopkins, Dwight, and Lorentzen, eds., *Religions/Globalizations* (Durham, NC: Duke University Press, 2001), 7–10.

71. Rajan Menon, "Terrorism Inc.," *Los Angeles Times,* August 22, 2004, M1, M3.

72. Gerald O. Barney, *Threshold 2000* (Ada, MI: CoNexus Press, 2000), 114.

73. John Polkinghorne, *The Way the World Is* (London: Triangle SPCK, 1983), 9.

CHAPTER 7

Value Conflicts in a Pluralistic Society

The measure of a civilization is how it respects the rights of its weakest members.
                                    —*Katherine Dowling*

A variety of conditions, from political and economic to religious, military, agricultural, and environmental, have motivated migrations of whole populations from one region of the world to another. On rare occasions it has been from continent to continent. It is important at the outset of this discussion to distinguish migratory movements from nomadic or simple commuting. A *migration* may entail a whole population moving with the intent to conquer and settle in or move on to further conquests. In this sense, the term "migrant farm labor" is a misnomer because the individuals, though they may move with large numbers, usually have no intention of making a permanent home. They simply "move with the crops," hoping to earn enough to return to their place of origin to survive until the next season. Migrant workers come closer to the nomadic or even a gypsy lifestyle, which makes little effort to be assimilated or to leave a lasting impression on the people among whom they have lived for a brief time.

Heterogeneous societies are often the product of diverse racial, ethnic, religious, and other groups, some of whom may have started out as invaders (the Romans, the Huns, the hordes of Genghis Khan) or simply as relatively benign visitors, as with the British settlers who created Jamestown, Virginia (1607), or the Puritans in 1620 looking for a safe place to call home in the "new world." Their reception or rejection by the indigenous populations determines their length of stay. If the newcomers are successful in becoming established, they may seek to pave the way for others to follow and give hospitality a new face. In this light, it is instructive to review the hospitable message on the U.S. Statue of Liberty:

> Give me your tired, your poor,
> Your huddled masses yearning to breathe free,
> The wretched refuse of your teeming shore,
> Send these, the homeless, tempest-tossed to me:
> I lift my lamp beside the golden door.[1]

By contrast, we may recall the expression of a white Southern politician during the 1950s Civil Rights movement, regarding the inclusion of the "homeless, tempest-tossed" blacks in white public schools: "Not as long as I have a breath in my body, or gunpowder burns." Consider the growing phenomenon in many European countries today. "Anti-immigration sentiment is spreading across a historically liberal northern Europe and Scandinavia, a region that worries about diluting national identities."[2] This was even more pointedly expressed in the Web site of the right-wing Danish People's Party platform: "Denmark belongs to the Danes." It is backed by laws that, for example, forbid a Danish woman who married an Egyptian to live in Copenhagen with her family. For economic reasons, she had to live apart from her husband and travel back and forth to Sweden where he could establish a separate residence.[3] The European Council in July 2004 criticized Denmark's legislation on immigrants as "a threat to human rights," but the phenomenon appears to be spreading.[4] The French have accepted black Africans, but in 1990, 76 percent of the French public said there were too many Arabs in France, and Interior Minister Pasqua argued in 1993 for "zero immigration." The German constitution, which had guaranteed asylum to people persecuted on political grounds, was amended to cut numerous benefits earlier offered to them. "Overall in the mid-1990s Western European countries were moving inexorably toward reducing if not eliminating immigration from non-European sources."[5] In 1994, California voters approved Proposition 187, denying health education and welfare benefits to illegal aliens and their children.[6]

Even within more homogeneous societies where immigrants have been fairly well assimilated politically and economically and are able to retain their cultural and religious identities, there are certain "hot-button" cultural issues that incite hostilities. We will attempt to cultural how the interaction of indigenous cultures and foreign, "outside" cultures shape new perspectives and decisions.

A. MIGRATIONS: RELIGIOUS AND CULTURAL PERSPECTIVES

The word *migration* is often associated with partial or whole human populations whose moving from place to place like great flocks of birds or herds of animals may be prompted by seasonal changes or an otherwise unstable or threatening environment. The designation may also be used in reference to some cataclysmic event such as the Neanderthals crossing the Bering Strait from Europe and Asia to Alaska (as long ago as 40 thousand to 70 thousand years) in response to massive climatic changes during the Ice Age. Such migrations did not always begin as mass movements. They followed a solitary explorer and perhaps a few of his former companions who brought back to the flock, herd, or community, by some form of communication, a route to safety and food. There were, of course those massive military migrations of Attila the Hun; the Viking invasions across Europe; the sweep of Genghis Khan's Mongols from China and Russia to Afghanistan. In most cases, the migrations brought major changes in the social and political environment they touched, and the migrants themselves experienced changes including a transformation of their political structures, folkways, and religious ideals.

1. Hinduism

Few examples of the mutual influences of migration can be more revealing than the Aryan invasion into the Indus Valley in India, about 1500 B.C. The rise of *Hinduism*, as we briefly traced earlier, occurred when the indigenous occupants, already diminishing in strength and population size because of a shift in the course of the Indus River (which threatened their city's extensive water system) were overwhelmed by the Aryans. Centuries of speculation as to how the transformation took place were corroborated in 1922, when archaeological excavations of giant mounds in Pakistan (*Mohenjo Daro*, mounds of the dead) revealed an extensive urban culture that had developed contemporaneously with Egyptian and Babylonian counterparts. They had a written language (pictographic), and their mastery of weaving cotton into fabric and fashioning kiln-fired brick reflect, a growing skill with technical processes.[7]

Of special importance to our study is the fact that the Aryans brought with them their sacred scriptures, the Vedas and the Upanishads. In contrast with the indigenous culture's pantheism and devotion to a mother goddess, the worship of the phallus (the most powerful symbol of fertility), and a belief in transmigration of souls, the Aryans held to the belief in one omnipresent, all-sanctifying world soul, *Brahman*. The Aryan emphasis on monotheism, however, was soon diluted with nature worship and other aspects of the previous Indus Valley culture. Possibly the product of intermarriage and other social accommodations, this dilution led the Hindus to adopt or create subdeities representing different aspects of nature and usually personified with distinctive names.

The Vedas, as noted earlier, are composed of four elements: Rig-Veda, or Psalms in praise of some seventy natural objects or "powers"; Yajur Veda, or sacred formulas; Sama Veda, chants; and Atharva Veda, "the knowledge of charms." So revered are these writings that they are believed to constitute the most ancient of religious documents in the world; indeed to have been created before the world itself. A critically important part of the revealed body of the Vedas is the Upanishads ("secret teachings"), concerned, among other things, with the meaning of sacrificial rites. The Upanishads gave rise to rich metaphysical concepts such as rebirth and the paradox of the God, Brahman being eminent in nature yet standing transcendently outside the whole Cosmos. In a real sense, the Upanishads present to the world the central concept of Hinduism, which is essentially monotheistic although it is important to note that the Upanishads do not literally speak of Brahman as a god.

As Ninian Smart cautions, "Even to talk of a single something called Hinduism can be misleading, because of the great variety of customs, forms of worship, gods, myths, philosophies, types of ritual, movements and styles of art and music contained loosely within the bounds of the religion."[8] Furthermore, until late in the nineteenth century, "Hindu" had no specific religious meaning outside India but in western texts referred simply to the people east of the Indus river. The British colonial authorities employed the word as a religious designation in 1871. Quickly, the word took on special importance in the growing agitation against British rule and today connates a Hinduism far removed from the bland toleration of "outside" religions that had long been its stereotype. This now implies among radicalized Hindu nationalists threatening severe civil and religious restrictions against Muslims and Christians (who number about 17 percent of India's population) and other religious traditions.

2. Buddhism

During the period around 500 B.C. when the priestly class of Hinduism was transforming the faith into a rigid system of ceremonies and class distinctions, *Buddhism* was slowly providing the alternative Siddharta hope. Buddhist monks expanded the peripatetic nature of what can be characterized as wanderers across India and Sri Lanka. Migration soon became a driving force that propelled the new Buddhist priest class to China and eventually Korea and Japan.

It is helpful to remember, however, that Buddhists did not seek to conquer other nations or peoples as was the case with the Aryans when they overwhelmed the Indus civilization. The object of Buddhism's teaching was simply enlightenment. The word *Buddha* is the past participle of the Sanskrit "to become enlightened." One of the most striking facts in religious history is the way in which Siddharta, who taught no doctrine of a divine person or deity and avoided drawing such attention to himself, was to become the object of worship.[9] Wherever he and his disciples traveled, they encouraged the establishment of a monastery or *sangha* ("community").

In the southern regions of India and eventually much of Asia, Hinayana *Buddhism* (the "lesser Vehicle," also called *Theravada*) adhered to the original message that Siddhartha was only a teacher of the way to escape the endless miseries of Hindu cycles of rebirth. In the north, *Mahayana Buddhism* developed a much more elaborate teaching of theological and ethical complexities (the "greater Vehicle") and proclaimed the Buddha as not merely a teacher but also a divine savior. Furthermore, Buddhahood was accessible to all who succeeded in obeying all of the many new rules and disciplines of the faith. The message carried to China, Japan, Tibet, and elsewhere throughout the world was that Buddhists came not to conquer but to enlist and to liberate.[10]

But to liberate from what? This question was crucial among populations where the Theravada Buddhist influence is seen by many (as in Thailand) to be a barrier to, rather than a help, in overcoming such grievous conditions as poverty, interreligious warfare, ethnic cleansings, and HIV/AIDS.[11] Even hunger must not divert one from seeking inner peace. (see note under section B below).

3. Confucianism

The word *Confucianism* is actually a Western designation; the Chinese are more accustomed to Ju Chiao, "teaching of the sage," referring to the man by his family name *Kung* and given name *Fu Tzu*. His beliefs were incorporated into a system of teaching in a manner quite unlike that of either Hinduism and Buddhism. Confucianism involved neither an invasion nor an international migration; it was more like the pilgrimage of an itinerant scholar. Confucius was the most promising of a family of seven children, and his mother instilled in him the love of learning that developed into a broad range of interests including literature, poetry, governance, and natural sciences.

At twenty-one, he started a school that eventually had to some 3,000 students. His special interest in government brought him to an understanding that China's history stretched back to a date that would have been about 2300 B.C. While not intending to found a religion, he noted that social justice and governmental responsibility for the common good had always been sustained through religious commitment. As scholar Mencius the later records, when Confucius was thirty-four, "The world [actually the State of Lu, where he was born] fell into decay, and principles faded. There were instances of Ministers (of state) who murdered their rulers and of sons who murdered their fathers."[12]

The resident prince was forced to flee, so Confucius accompanied him to a neighboring state and began urging the recovery of antiquity, asking such fundamental questions as What is old? How can we make it our own? How can we make it a reality? His fascination with things ancient that once held society together prompted him to declare, "I am a traditionalist, not one who creates new things. I am faithful. A lover of the old." Confucius was not simply one who rehearsed the past but who wove it into a new tapestry of ideas with the current strands of social life. He wrote, "A man born in our days who simply returns to the ways of antiquity is a fool and brings misfortune upon himself." What he advocated was not imitation of the past but "a reiteration of the eternally true."

At age fifty-one, he returned to his home of Lu, where his teachings were so effective that he was appointed chief magistrate. Obtaining peace and order and even the beginning of disarmament where previously there had been so much conflict, he became prime minister of Lu. The prince, however, ignored his counsels and at last Confucius resigned to become an itinerant teacher. He sought a government position unsuccessfully in another state and wandered about for twelve years from his fifty-sixth to his sixty-eighth years. He went from state to state in the hope that somewhere he would be allowed to put into practice his political doctrine that incorporated his general belief in the goodness of human nature yet emphasized that "He who overcomes his self and takes upon himself the restriction of the *li,* the laws of custom–he becomes a man."[13]

Despite Confucius' lament that he felt his life a failure, the impact of his teaching, urging virtue in place of evil under the mandates of heaven, was so great that in the year 195 B.C.E. the emperor of China offered a sacrifice at Confucius' tomb. Sacrifices were ordered four times yearly; a statue of Confucius was placed in the center of the Imperial College, and in 1068, he was elevated to the full rank of emperor.

For two thousand years, until 1905, Confucianism remained the basis of the educational system of China. During most of the twentieth century however, Confucianism suffered in China: first when the country looked to the West economically and culturally and second as a result of a campaign against Confucianism in the early decades of the People's Republic under Chairman Mao Tse–tung. Mao died in 1975, and in 1978, the constitutional guarantee of free private religious expression was re-introduced. Indeed schools dedicated to teaching Confucian values have been springing up all over China, some with government funding.[14]

What began in the itinerant, almost nomadic wanderings and teachings of a lone scholar and his few disciples with a zeal for social reform some 2,500 years ago has been joined by almost countless fellow migrants around the world. Confucianism has grown to 6,300,000 followers in Asia, 26,000 in North America, 2,000 in Latin America, and more than 4,000 in Europe and Eurasia.[15]

4. Judaism

Judaism is a tradition that began with a migration and in many respects has retained this characteristic throughout history. Its people have been perpetually "on the move" since the days when Abram (later called Abraham, in Genesis 17:5) felt called by God to go forth with his family and flock from the polytheistic religious environment of tribal Semites. The promised reward was, "I will give to you and to your descendants . . . all the land of Canaan, for an everlasting possession" (Genesis 17:8). From that point, Abraham proclaimed an ethical monotheism that eventually witnessed the rise of two other religious traditions, Christianity and Islam. From around 1700 B.C.E. to the time of Moses (c. 1200 B.C.E.), the people moved about, both changing and being changed by the religious and cultural traditions of native peoples. The Jews introduced ethical monotheism while, incongruously, joining in the worship of Baal, and a female goddesses called Ashteroth and adopting from the Zoroastrians a belief in angels and in the reality of Satan.

Migrations included the move a large group of Abraham's descendants, who included Joseph's family and descendants; to Egypt where they lived in relatively peaceful interaction with that government. After some 400 years among the Egyptians, a pharaoh arose who "knew not Joseph." (Exodus 1:8) and enslaved the "Habiru," a nomadic branch of the Hebrews (also called Israelites). Their delivery from bondage via God's prompting of Moses is too well known to need repeating except to note that the return of the Hebrews to "the promised land" brought major changes in the land, and re-introduced beliefs and practices that previously God had forbidden: "Judah did what was evil in the sight of the Lord . . . for they built for themselves high places and pillars, and Asherimon on every high hill and under every green tree; and there were also male cult prostitutes in the land. They did according to all the abominations of the nations which the Lord drove out before the people of Israel." (I Kings 14:22–24).

In accordance with warning of the prophets (Amos, Hosea, Micah, Isaiah, etc), the next migration would be (and was) at the points of swords and exile in Babylonia lasting from roughly 586–537 B.C.E. Given a reprieve under King Cyrus, only a few took advantage of returning to their homeland and instead became farmers and businesspeople in Babylonia and neighboring countries. Those who did return rebuilt the temple in Jerusalem and, refocusing on what they believed Judaism ought to be, instituted strict rules of orthodoxy in beliefs, ceremonial practices, and rituals. They enforced absolute obedience to God's commands as interpreted by the priests. Subsequent conflict with Greece, however, brought stress, migratory dispersion, and finally settling under the rule of Rome.

Among the most discriminated against ethnic groups in history, the Jews have suffered at least three catastrophic persecutions since the beginning of what is often termed the Common Era. The first was in Jerusalem in 70 C.E. when thousands were executed and the survivors fled in all directions (the diaspora). A second occurred in Spain in 1492 when Ferdinand and Isabella ended a five hundred-year era of creative interaction among Jews, Christians, and Muslims. Jews and Muslims were virtually outlawed in Spain while Christians were held to absolute obedience to the crown and the pope on pain of death as a result of the Inquisition. In marked contrast to Christ's forgiving those who sought to destroy him, the popes persecuted by the thousands those who even murmured against their rule. A three volume *Registre d'Inquisition de Jacques Fournier* reveals the ways trials, torture, and executions were conducted with not a single acquittal during the entire reign of Fournier as Pope Benedict XII.

Undoubtedly the most horrendous of the three episodes was the effort by Adolph Hitler's Nazi party to exterminate all Jews, not only in Germany but also in Poland, Czechoslovakia, France, Holland, and anywhere else they could be caught. This holocaust, which lasted briefly in the 1930s and 40s, claimed the lives of more than six million Jews and triggered an unprecedented migration of millions more to any countries where they could find sanctuary.

5. Christianity

Migratory *Christianity* is not a mere happenstance, a passive phenomenon, but, according to tradition, the response to a special insight initiated by God and spoken through Jesus, "His only begotten Son" (John 3:16). The disciples of Jesus were to "go into all the world" (Mark 16:15) to proclaim the Gospel message that God, the Creator of us all, is above all else a compassionate, loving, and forgiving Father who wants no one to perish but to have eternal life and fellowship with him.[16]

While Jesus engaged in limited travel, he did cover (presumably on foot) many miles from Jerusalem in Judea, through Samaria, and to Galilee. His first major journey was as an infant with his parents fled to Egypt to the escape the murderous wrath of Herod. Herod was reacting to the word from visiting "wise men," possibly Zoroastrians, that the child would eventually displace him on the throne. As a young rabbi, Jesus' itineration made major changes in people's lives, a fact that would ultimately put him at cross-purposes (literally, since it led to the cross) with the Jewish as well as Roman authorities. The problem was not a matter of evil men bent on Jesus' murder as so often portrayed rather it was what a group of ultraconservative leaders saw as Jesus' liberal approach to both religious and social affairs as well as a deeply rooted anxiety about Rome's impatience with unrest however instigated. If Jesus succeeded, the leaders concluded, the Roman government would do away with traditionally Jewish authority. This is made manifestly clear in the warning of the high priest and his insistence that for the security of Israel, Jesus had to be put out of the way. It was an intensely pragmatic decision.[17] Almost immediately after the crucifixion, the disciples received their "marching orders" from the resurrected Christ to "go and make disciples of all nations, baptizing them in then name of the Father and of the Son and of the Holy Spirit" (Matthew 28: 18–20).

Migrations, at first by way of missionary journeys, began almost immediately with the apostle Paul, a former Pharisee, setting the pace. Everywhere the disciples traveled, from Antioch to Perga, Cyprus, and across the mainland of Asia Minor, they established home-based family gatherings for worship, which would in time evolve into church congregations. Three such missionary journeys were completed by some fifty assistants who effectively served as convening pastors of scores of churches. It is remarkable to recount that despite persecutions from both a handful of dissident

Jews (who regarded Paul as a traitor to the faith) and massive Roman legions, by the time Emperor Constantine liberated Christianity in 325 C.E., there were over six million baptized Christians. By 350 C.E., the number exceeded 33 million. To achieve this number, the membership would have to have grown from the time of Christ's resurrection (c. 33 C.E.) at the astonishing rate of 40 percent per decade.[18]

Thanks to the genius of Roman technology, Roman roads were interconnected across the Mediterranean world eastward to Constantinople and north as far as Germany, Spain, France, and Great Britain. This facilitated travel so that not only missionaries but also whole Christian communities could migrate to distant locations. Interestingly, the last we read of St. Paul's journeys involved planning a trip to Spain (Romans 15:24–28). The Bible gives no evidence to support that martyrdom was imminent, so there is speculation that one day archeologists may confirm that Paul did indeed travel to Spain to continue his vital work of church building and spiritual, moral, and ethical instruction.

Although Christianity did not become the official state church under Constantine, it virtually became so when all Roman emperors (except Julian 361–363) placed themselves on the side of Christianity. They viewed the church as a great unifying force when pagan invasions threatened, and emigrating Romans warned of the growing instability of Rome. Missionaries moved across Europe and into Scotland, Ireland, and Wales, building schools, libraries, and teaching the virtue of human compassion by making hospitality a cardinal virtue (Acts 16:15, 18:27; III John 5–6). The word *hospital* has its roots in the word for hospitality; from the beginning, care for the sick and injured was an element of the earliest commandment of Christian ethics. At the time of his ascension, Jesus promised the ministry of healing to his disciples: "They will lay their hands on the sick, and they will recover" (Mark 16:18). Failure to make at least the effort to heal was a failure of discipleship: "As you did it not to one of the least of these, you did it not to me," and the fault barred the one who failed from eternal life (Matthew 25:45).

From the beginning of Christianity, too, monks in monasteries grew their own food and native populations began to share their rudimentary knowledge of farming and medical care, which led to the formation of hospitals and hospices. The gospel was seen as a profoundly practical expression of good news, tailoring spiritual disciplines to worldly needs no matter how modest or rustic. As more opportunities for Christian immigrants opened in northern Europe, they converted Teutonic tribes to Christianity, and Anglo-Saxons in Britain met Christianity through already converted Britons and Celts. In Africa, churches were being established in Egypt and Abyssinia (later Ethiopia).

The legacy of such migrations is at least in part demonstrated by the fact that what began as a reenergized dozen or so disciples after Christ's resurrection developed into today's overwhelming number of people comprising the largest religious body in the world: over two billion adherents, one-third of the world's total population.[19]

6. Islam

Meanwhile, Jews, Christians, Hindus, and Buddhists met a new challenge in the rise of *Islam*. "The fact that within a century of the death of prophet Muhammed in 632, Islam had spread across much of the known world, was for many Christians inexplicable, frightening and theologically incomprehensible."[20] But for the faithful Muslim, it is clear that everything is predestined by God's will (The *Qur'an* Sursora 40:67–68). God not only knows our fate but also guides and controls what is to happen. A popular expression, is *im shalla,* "if God wills," a monotheistic affirmation similar to the Judeo–Christian predestination that provided a profound sense of comfort not found in many primitive religious tradition amid natural and human-initiated disasters.

Briefly tracing the powerful migratory force of such a message is useful in understanding a truly astonishing period of mutual cultural and religious enrichment. Starting in Arabia, Islamic armies swept over Syria, Palestine, Egypt, and Persia between 633–651. By 707, had they subdued most of North Africa and then moved north to conquer Spain in 711. By 732, they were poised to overwhelm the army of Charles Martel ("The Hammer") with superior numbers and force it to retreat. They also apparently expected to be welcomed. In a suddenly dense fog, the Muslim forces became disoriented and scattered. In accord with their belief in predestination, they determined it was Allah's will that further incursions be forbidden, so they retreated and reorganized in Spain. There they initiated the Moorish culture that dominated Spain for more than seven hundred years.

The central authority for Islam meanwhile was moved to Baghdad (c. 750), which became a center of Islamic culture a remarkably large population of highly creative Jews, Christians, and Muslims working together.

> Their scholarship preserved the works of Greek philosophers and scientists. The Abbasid dynasty succeeded in spreading Islam to the East into India and ultimately into China. The predominantly Islamic civilizations of the Middle East brought about great advances in medicine, mathematics, physics, astronomy, geography, architecture, art, literature and history that were to have profound influence on Western. Culture.[21]

One aspect of Islamic thought often neglected although both influential on and influenced by Hinduism is mysticism. R.C. Zaehner quotes Nietzsche as saying of that France it is *Die Hauptschule der Geschmack* (the high school of good taste), so we might say that India is *Die Hauptschule der Mystik* for two reasons. It's theological thinking is first and foremost mystical. Second, Hinduism is bound by no dogmas as Islam is, and the mystic is thereby quite uninhibited in expressing any view he pleases."[22]

Like Judaism and Christianity, Islam denounces any form of spiritual experimentation that might violate the commandment, "You shall have no other gods before me." Among Hebrew scholars, however, there emerged around the thirteenth century the *Cabbala,* a system of mystical interpretation of scripture in which every word and letter has an occult meaning and the various names for god have magical powers. Mystical tendencies were also represented among the medieval Christian scholars, especially by Meister Eckhart (1260–1327). A German Dominican much influenced by neoplatonism, he held that the one thing that is real in all things is the divine. In the soul of every person is a spark of God; that is the true reality so that all aspects of self-hood that make us "individual" and unique should be laid aside. Eckhart's emphasis seemed to be too close to the Hindu absorption of the self into some cosmic All and both the church fathers and Islamic scholars condemned his proposition. His insistence that Christ is the one whom we should all emulate because he is the "pattern" in whom God dwelt in the fullness of what it means to be truly human, filled with love and righteousness, reoccurs however in almost every generation of Islamic as well as Christian and Jewish scholars.

Among the branches of Islamic faith (e.g., the *Sunni* and the *Shi'ite*) there is also *Sufism*, the line of thought and practice commonly identified as mysticism.[23] The Arabic equivalent to the word possibly derived from the robes of wool (*suf*) that the early followers wore. At first, they met with stern opposition from both the Sunni and Shi'ite who rejected the Sufis' rigid movement against "worldly" ambitions under the guise of being practical. Maintaining that Muhammed had taught a simple lifestyle, the Sufis harked back to Muhammed's long periods of meditation that made him receptive to Allah's words, which in turn comprised the Holy Qur'an. The Sufis also referred with profound reverence to Muhammed's ascension into heaven (the night journey), which was clearly a mystical experience. "It is now generally agreed that (Sufism) drew its inspiration from the Qur'an, A believer meditating on its meaning might be filled with a sense of the overwhelming transcendence of God."[24]

Interaction with other faith traditions brought new understandings and ways of relating to unfamiliar practices. One of the most dynamic periods in Islamic history occurred during the fading era of Christian monasticism and of asceticism. Muhammad discouraged monasticism as unnatural.

> Converts to the new religion brought into Islam their own inherited ways; they were living in an environment which was still more Christian and Jewish than Muslim. In fact however, the influence of Christian monks seems to have been pervasive. The latter's idea of a secret world of virtue, beyond that of obedience to the law, and their belief that abandonment of the world, mortification of the flesh, and repetition of the name of God in prayer might, with God's help, purify the heart and release it from worldly concerns to move toward a higher, intuitive knowledge of God.[25]

The many migrations of these religious groups and their sharing of ideas and ideals as well as scholarly and practical pursuits have challenged all faiths, strengthening some aspects and perhaps refining others. In the case of Islam, its successful growth has enabled the religion to become the second largest in the world today with more than one billion, thirty-three million members.[26]

B. MAJORITY RULE VERSUS MINORITY RIGHTS

Historically, when superior forces took over a country, they usually swept aside any "rights" the conquered minority had assumed were permanent. Any thoughts of democratic sharing of governance, if it even occurred to the invaders, would have been discounted as impractical and naive. An ancient Roman dictum held that "the strong do what they will; the weak suffer what they must." After all, even in a democratic society, the greatest number expects to win, not only in elections but also in the power that sheer numbers hold to set the rules of society. The development of checks and balances over the centuries that made democracies feasible is too complex to pursue here. It will be helpful, nevertheless, to inquire how human migrations, whether for military or other purposes, helped shape the distinctive features of the societies that evolved, making democratic rule appealing and attainable.

Human migrations and their often dramatic effects conjure up scenes of Genghis Khan's Mongol hoards overwhelming native populations of Iran, Russia, and China in the thirteenth century or perhaps the sixteenth century conquests of the Spanish conquistadors, whose zeal for power and wealth led to the exploitation of the human resources (in the form of enslaved populations) and natural treasures (e.g., gold and silver) of Puerto Rico, Jamaica, Cuba, Mexico, and Peru. In sharp contrast, we may think of the relatively benign Protestant pilgrims landing at Plymouth Rock in 1620.

The case of the Mongols and the Spanish, massive, brutal force often deprived the invaded peoples of their presumed rights to the very land they lived on and from which they derived an array of natural resources among other things. The pilgrims acknowledged their indebtedness to God's providence and to the native "host" peoples, and shared with them what harvest they gathered for a Thanksgiving celebration. They sought to make real for the native Americans many of the rights that as Christians the newcomers took for granted. What made the difference?

Seeking simplistic answers, some would say that the difference involves the contrast between *Hinduism* or *Buddhism,* in the adherence to polytheistic faiths that emphasize the individual's quest for moral enlightenment through meditation or "looking within." These are viewed as contrasted with monotheistic religions in which an authoritative god issues such moral demands as "thou shalt" and "thou shalt not." The Mongols under Genghis Khan, as just one example, lacked any compelling religious philosophy that could mediate a concern for the plight of the people of lands they invaded. In contrast, the dicta of the Jewish god protected even the rights of conquered people to their trees, which might have been their primary source of nourishment (Deuteronomy (20:19).

There may have been some influence on the Mongols from Hindu, Buddhist, and/or Confucian traditions, but warfare was viewed among the three as an inevitable part of human activity. For this reason, in Hinduism, a whole warrior class, the *Kshatriyas,* was established, according to their tradition, at the beginning of time by Lord Krishna. Krishna dissuaded Prince Arjuna from concerning himself with the fate of fallen soldiers; a future incarnation would either reward or punish each according to his or her karma (the accumulation of good and/or evil with its own built-in retribution earned by past action). Such moral quietism as ostensibly urged in Hindu tradition became a great embarrassment to Mohandas Gandhi, in the twentieth century.[27]

Buddhism, especially the Theravada form, urges compassion for the well-being of all people, but the emphasis on personal caring in the face of social conflicts or even regarding fighting off hunger, homelessness, and diseases must not be allowed to divert one from seeking one's own inner peace.[28] Furthermore, some Mahayana texts allow killing other humans "in constrained circumstances." "Ironically, over the centuries Chinese and Japanese military forces have used Buddhist symbols to empower their actions and intimidate their opponents."[29] Meanwhile, "Zen Buddhism contributed to the famed warrior culture. . .the idea that life and death are ultimately empty essence-less phenomena. This also helped develop a lack of hesitation (in killing)."[30]

In *Confucian* thought, the issue of human rights tended to focus on discipline (within the familial and social spheres) rather than on "rights" per se, on loyalty rather than on entitlement. The conquered foe had no rights.

It may be argued that in the absence of a personal God, Asian migrants includ-ing the Mongols and Attila's hordes lacked the moral imperative to acknowledge any-one's rights. Asian values in general, as Nobel Laureate Amartya Sen observes, might seem to Western theorists to offer "no quintessential values that apply to that immensely large heterogeneous population, none that would separate them out as a group from people in the rest of the world."[31] Would Genghis Khan's rampage and plundering of much of Eurasia have been less aggressive and destructive if his per-sonal ethics had been based on a monotheistic faith as opposed to the loosely struc-tured moral inclinations of polytheistic traditions?

It is of considerable historical interest that during Genghis Khan's reign, he arbitrarily broke alliances and attacked and sacked villages and whole cities includ-ing Peking, virtually causing China's complex governance to unravel. Because the name "khan" is the Turkish equivalent of the Qur'an's to unravel word for Sultan, there has been some debate as to whether Genghis Kahn was in some respect influ-enced by Islamic ideals.[32] There is no concrete evidence for this, although it is note-worthy that one of his generals (Mugali) who favored Buddhism and persecuted Islam was overthrown by another Mongol general, Jebe. The latter subsequently pro-claimed freedom for all religions, a basic tenet of Islam (*Cf.* the Qur'an, Sura ii 256), and forbade any massacre or plunder. Only later interaction with Buddhism, Islam, and Taoism stimulated the kind of humanistic political interest that would lead to consolidating Mongol tribal groups. This led a torturous path to a Mongolian state that fell to Manchurian forces in 1691, emerging as an independent monarchy in 1911, and finally proclaiming itself as the Mongolian People's Republic in 1924.[33]

It should not be forgotten, that the "western" traditions historically had their roots in the eastern part of the world and that Taoism, in particular, contains much that echoes the moral concerns of the western (i.e., Europeanized) religions. Con-sider the words of Lao Tsu of China (c. 700 B.C.) regarding minority groups whom one would help:

> Go to the people: live with them;
> Learn from them; love them.
> Start with what they know.
> Build with what they have,
> But with the best leaders.
> When the work is done,
> The task accomplished,
> The people will say:
> "We have done this ourselves."

This way, preservs the self-respect of the people.

When we examine the beliefs and practices of the three major Western and avowedly monotheistic religions of people who were often "on the move," we must ask whether their monotheism did indeed provide a clearer, mere authoritative and humane mode of acknowledging other peoples' rights than did their polytheistic (or nontheistic) eastern counterparts?

C. RELIGION: FREEDOM VERSUS IDEOLOGICAL COERCION

In the time of Moses (thirteenth century B.C.) , the moral authority of a loving, forgiving creator god seemed an appealing alternative to the violent image so often portrayed by polytheistic cultures and by tribal groups of the Middle East. The panoply of gods and goddesses of other religions seldom consulted on moral issues. According to the polythiotic cultures, the gods were too much embroiled in their own ambitions and squabbles to bother with humans except to demand obedience and sacrifices,

Most of the ancient religions appear to have begun with individual leaders or very small groups, but those that flourished sometimes evolved into overwhelming majorities in many parts of the world. An issue deserving serious consideration is whether these groups in the process safe guarded the rights and freedoms of the societies they displaced. One need hardly recall the woeful treatment of the immigrant Europeans from the seventeenth to twentieth centuries toward Native American Indians, who today find their own hegemony challenged by new minority groups from Africa, Asia, and Latin America. This is a matter of no small concern among the white populations of the United States (stridently expressed by White Supremacists) accustomed to being the ruling majority in regions where Asian and Latino populations have migrated and now outnumber them.[34] In a sense, the shoe is now on the other foot.

The authoritative decrees of the Ten Commandments infer certain obligations regarding other people's rights. For example, "Honor your father and mother," presupposes parents' God-given right to be honored through proper respect and care all through their lives. "You shall not kill" implies every person's right (even your captured enemies) to life. "You shall not commit adultery" underscores the right of a spouse to lifelong faithfulness of the partner in the marriage vows. "Neither shall you steal" protects the right of every person to hold property inviolable. " Neither bear false witness" incorporates the right of each person to hear the truth with nothing being withheld if asked for (Deuteronomy 5:6–22). These rights and others such as "life, liberty and the pursuit of happiness" in the U.S. Declaration of Independence do not depend on mere social agreement or even judicial mandate, but on the commandments of a deity who is their author. These rights are "endowed by their Creator," and cannot be put aside or in any way transgressed. The books of Leviticus and Deuteronomy are filled with such regulations that are presumably rooted in God's will. In a similar fashion, the teachings of Jesus are as authoritative as the Hebrew scriptures' "Thus saith the Lord" to the degree he is acknowledged to be the Messiah. "You are my disciples if you *do* the things I command you." Loving one's neighbor is a command, not a negotiable act of grudging tolerance.[35] It is *the* divine imperative, which is both a gift and a command.

Lenn Goodman notes in his perceptive treatise on monotheism that the divine imperative is not an external event, not an occasion outside the human mind but an event within the mind itself. We are created in God's image, so the human mind mirrors that of God.

> To moderns the Biblical imagery may be somewhat misleading in this regard, for it seems to represent the giving of the Law and Covenant in the manner of some ancient public legislation and oathing ceremony. It is as though God were standing here on some lofty mountain dais, the people here below, Moses in between, God announcing orders. Those assembled are told that they are standing in the place of all future generations of Israel. What is it that Moses cannot tell them but they must hear for themselves?[36]

Tragically, too often people hear what they want to hear or what their leaders demand them to conclude without reference to either the substance that came before or the context in which they are to hear and implement it. A startling example is found after the prophetic emphasis on God's holiness and love and no more killing, when we find God being "quoted," saying that when he clears the seven nations of Canaanites, Hittis, and so on: "You must utterly destroy them; show no mercy to them" (Deuteronomy: 7:2). Furthermore, than slaughter is to be complete. "In the cities of these people that the Lord God gives you, you shall save nothing that breathes, but you shall utterly destroy them." (Deuteronomy 20:16). And where is the fervently touted mercy of Yahweh concerning Israelite soldiers wounded in battle? How will they be honored? If their testicles are crushed or their "male members" are cut off, they will not be honored but instead barred from their communities and forbidden to enter the assembly of the Lord (i.e., to attend worship services (Deuteronomy 23:1). Meanwhile, what of children who suffer the stigma of being born out of wedlock? Will their neighbors comfort them and help restore their self-respect (Deuteronomy 23:1)? Not so: "No bastard shall enter the assembly of the Lord; even to the tenth generation, none of his descendants" (Deuteronomy 23:2). Other Deuteronomy passages like that in Psalm 137: 8–9, remind us of our almost universal penchant for perverting God's word when it serves some advantage. Being a monotheist per se is no guarantee against moral turpitude.

In all honestly, we must not neglect other aspects of Hebraic life required by the one god and recognize that these few aberrations do not represent the whole. From the smallest act of neighborliness such as helping a friend rescue a wounded ox (Deuteronomy 22: 1–4) to generously giving food and other necessities to a former slave now free (Deuteronomy 15:12–14), to lending to a brother whatever is needed without charging interest (Deuteronomy 23:19–20), these and countless other passages reflect the details of God's care for all creatures. Indeed, the Hebrew scriptures abound in passages including Psalm 141:1–4, Isaiah 56:3–5; Micah 6:8 that affirm the patience and love of God. When the people of Israel were sentenced to decades of bondage in Babylon for their apostasy and many failures to obey the commandments, God instructed them through the prophet Jeremiah how to atone and how to develop a pattern of life that would ultimately win the friendship of their captors and ensure their own restoration to nationhood (Jeremiah 29:4–14). They also lay the groundwork for two of the most urgent requirements of faith: to love God "with all your heart . . . soul . . . and might" (Deuteronomy 6:5) and "love your neighbor as yourself" (Leviticus 19:18). Of special interest to Christians is that Jesus declared in quoting these two passages: "On these two commandments depend all the law and the prophets" (Matthew 24:37–40).

The New Testament is a model for monotheistic expression, everything focusing on God, the creator, author of the human race and, in a unique way, the father of Jesus. Jews and Muslims traditionally object to this father–son relationship because it appears to mimic Greek mythology with its multiple deities begetting mortal children, thus introducing a form of idolatry. Refutation of such charges has been the work of theologians since the beginning of the Christian era and would be too distracting a detour for our present task. Just a brief comment might be helpful. When God, in Genesis 1:27, "created the heavens and the earth," humans were the only creatures declared to be fashioned "in the image of God." The Jews of that time had a saying that in the birth of every child there are three partners: father, mother, and the spirit of god. One New Testament version of the conception of Jesus written by a Jewish scholar relates that Joseph experienced a prophetic revelation: "That which is conceived in her (Mary) is of the Holy Spirit" (Matthew 1:20) Another version written by a Greek physician tells the story from Mary's experience of a similar revelation: "The Holy Spirit will come upon you, and the power of the Most High will overshadow you; therefore the child to be born will be called holy, the Son of God" (Luke 1:35) .

Of special interest is that Islamic scripture presents the story of the annunciation in this vivid way:

> Behold! The angels said:
> "O Mary! God giveth thee
> Glad tidings of a Word
> From Him: his name
> will be Christ Jesus,
> The son of Mary, held in honor
> in this world and the hereafter
> and of (the company of) those
> Nearest to God."

The Holy Qur'an, Sura III., 42–45
Ali, A. Yusuf, *op.cit* p. 134.)

The commentator A. Yusuf Ali, elaborates on this version: "Mary the mother of Jesus was unique in that she gave birth to a son by special miracle without the intervention of the customary physical means." Ali also makes it clear that there must be no coercion as to how Jesus is to be understood in relation to God in either Christian or Muslim communities as long as the essence of monotheism is preserved (Sura x 99, n. 1480).

Among the many images in Hebrew scripture of Jesus, who was to be revealed as God's gift to the world, were "Wonderful, Counselor . . . Everlasting Father, the Prince of Peace" (Isaiah 9:6). The accolade of "prince" not a common designation in the New Testament, but refers to Jesus the Christ as "first-born of the dead, and prince (*archon*) of the kings of the earth" (Revelation 1:5). The most costly aspect of this "prince of peace" depiction was its emphasis on Christ as the agent of reconciliation and, by extension, convert were also to serve such a role. Countless early Christians were executed for refusing to become soldiers in the Roman army. This aversion to military action continued through centuries of persecution and conflict almost to the time of the legendary King Arthur, who first appears in a brief reference (c. 600). The need for defensive measures against the Danes, Vikings, and the Muslim invaders in Spain, France, and middle Europe made arming for battle a virtual "given." After Charlemagne (c. 835), the military became an enterprise of honor.

The gradual alteration of Christianity's face to the world came at a high price. The popes of Rome began to spend more money during the eighth through tenth centuries on their private armies than on missions and launched wars and crusades that decimated cities and spread slaughter, famine, and pestilence in a way reminiscent of the horsemen of the Apocalypse. One pope during the Crusades ordered, "kill them all. God will know His own" to be certain that he had exterminated of all his enemies in a city known to contain more Christians than Muslims. The Inquisition that followed sometime after the Crusades was designed to search out and kill all who opposed or even questioned the absolute authority of the church.

What happened along the way was a fabrication of Christianity during which a growing hierarchy of power set up regulations and prohibitions incumbent on all members, denying fellowship with other more compliant members and preventing access to the sacraments for those who violated the rules. Thomas a Kempis' book *Imitation of Christ* has been called "a noble product of this simple period of mystical churchly piety." The actual situation outside the books and treatises on the ethics of the period reveal a time of vast accumulation of wealth amid growing poverty despite Thomas Aquinas' strong pronouncements against ownership of private property.[37] Bishops often became the largest landowners in their realms with palaces grander than those of kings. In a biting critique of what some would call "churchianity," Jacques Ellul declares that nothing has really changed since that time except in superficial details and that

> Christians have known what they were doing. They have voluntarily forsaken revelation and the Lord. They have opted for a new bondage. They have not aspired to the full gift of the Holy Spirit that would have enabled them to take the new way that He opened up. This is why the burning question is a purely human one: Why have Christians taken this contrary course? What forces have induced this subversion? Human aggrandizement and nothing else.[38]

It is clearly not enough to wear the label of Christian unless the Christian can accept the challenge of striving to be at one, ontologically, with God who is best understood as love incarnate in Christ (I John 4:8), who calls us through his spirit to be agents of reconciliation in all encounters with God's creation. This provides at least an element of hope for Christianity's participation in the development of a global ethic.

Is Islam significantly different? Rigorously monotheistic, Muhammed was very critical of polytheism and idolatry and emphasized that God was one and only God was to be worshipped. His expression of concern won for him few followers at first and great opposition in Mecca, especially from those who furnished shrines for pagan pilgrims who brought considerable revenue to the city. Opposition grew to the point that Muhammed's life was in danger, but by 622 he had gathered enough followers to set up the first truly Islamic community "the model for all later Islamic societies."[39] Opponents launched numerous attacks from caravan raids to all-out war, but the power of his message was such that by 629–630, his followers had conquered Mecca, and Islam was on its, way to becoming a major religion among the world's greatest; one billion thirty-three million second only to Christianity today.

Two major features of Islam that reveal its impact on the world was first that, in contrast to virtually all conquering forces that became the majority in power, Muhammed forgave his former enemies and not only became a model for fraternal relations but also granted to the conquered minority and other groups (including foreigners of other faiths) all the rights and benefits of Islamic society. Second, and in some regard even more astonishing, is that such a religious movement started by a semiliterate camel driver developed within its first century research and educational endeavors that advanced medicine, mathematics, physics, astronomy, geography, architecture, art, literature, and history. "Even the navigational instruments that were to make possible the voyages of discovery were developed by Muslim scholars. For eight hundred years Arabic was the major intellectual and scientific language of the world."[40]

In the minds of many who witness the turmoil in so much of the Islamic world today, something has gone awry. Islam's monotheism has never changed and thanks to early rules that the Qur'an be transmitted in exactly the same words across the centuries (and translations be rigorously inspected), its holy book is doubtless closer to its original text than is the case with any other religious tradition. However, the much publicized oppressions and restrictions on the common life of devotees, the alleged enslavement of foreigners, and dire poverty suffered in the presence of extravagantly wealthy Muslim families and dictators leave many bewildered and angry. A common charge is that they just don't know their own Qur'an.

A partial explanation of this situation might be in the often fracturing of Islam into contentious camps: Shi'ites, Kurds, and especially the Sunnis, all of whom have further subdivisions or schools of thought. The *Hanafites* are a scholarly group, indeed the most widespread school in the Muslim world that emphasizes not only the Qur'an and Suyhhah, but also "ra'y" human opinion. The Hanafite hold that the Qur'an is in fact God's word and, challenging the moral lassitude of the contemporary world, it orders those guilty of turpitude or heresy be punished by execution or by amputating their hands and feet (*Sura v. 33*). It must be noted however, that v.34 offers leniency to "those who repent."

The *Malikite* school with its roots in the eighth century seeks to gain the consensus of the community on any difficult interpretations of the Qur'an. An appeal to popular authority was given special hospitality in Egypt, North Africa, and Eastern Asia. In contrast, a much more rigidly conservative faction, the *Hanbalite*, demands that the Qur'an hold literal and unchallenged authority in all matters of private life, faith, and government. The conflict among these schools accounts for much of the internal hostilities in Islam (and their disconnect from other religions and societies) for the past millennium. When the mystical Sufism movement joins the mix, it is not surprising that schools of thought become warring camps.

It must be confessed that such diversity is certainly not unfamiliar in religious communities elsewhere—indeed, everywhere. Consider the divisions within Christianity with its Roman and Greek Catholics and its many Protestant denominations, Hinduism with its castes (still vigorously active despite governmental prohibitions), Buddhism with its Mahayana and Hinayana traditions, and so on. The need for an integrated and a well-funded educational system in which children might be indoctrinated with the elements of Islam has been considered. The existence of the Parliament of World Religions and other organizations devoted to studying religious ethics might prove both enriching and energizing for Muslim scholars who wish to see their traditions recover their former preeminence. The conflict among these schools accounts for much of the mutual hostility seen in the Middle East for the past millennium. When Sufism, the "Mystical Movement" is introduced with its quest for a central theme that would bind all traditions together, it is not surprising that schools of thought sometime become warring camps.

The cherished hope among Jews, Christians, and Muslims alike that monotheism would provide an authoritative voice commanding us to love our neighbors and pray for our enemies; to provide decent wages for employees, safe housing for the homeless, and adequate health care for all; and to eliminate warfare has not prevented the lust for power and sheer human ego from disregarding these hopes or, worse, using them to disguise political objectives. Identification of extremely expensive temples, cathedrals, extravagant dwellings, tax benefits available to the upper classes, and multimillion-dollar wage and benefit packages for corporate executives in contrast to low-paying jobs and grinding poverty for increasing segments of society can attest to this dichotomy.

The case for monotheism rests in large measure on the experience that confronting and being addressed by a personal creator God is more likely to sharpen an individual's appreciation for the gifts of life and to stimulate becoming an agent of reconciliation, healing, and zeal for the preservation of all forms of life. From the Western point of view at least, polytheisms appear to have been less effective in kindling such concerns. It must be acknowledged, however, that in times of greatest peril, such as experienced in the catastrophic tsunami that overwhelmed whole cities and killed tens of thousands of people in Indonesia, Thailand, and much of southern Asia in December 2005, the outpouring of prayers of people of all faiths and the hundreds of millions of dollars in aid from all major (and not a few minor) nations around the world gave testimony that a powerful spirit of both shared grief and generosity brought out the best of our humanity.

D. SOME "HOT-BUTTON" ISSUES

The expression "hot button" is not intended to cast aspersion on problems that may only trouble the sensibilities of one tradition (or even just a small section of that tradition). As an example is the much praised/maligned requirement that Muslim women wear the *hijab* (veil or headscarf). For many non-Muslims, the issue seems parochial and even trivial, but in Saudi Arabia and Iran where police as well as irate citizens have been seen beating women not wearing the veil, it is definitely a hot-button issue. The French government that has banned wearing such apparel as a violation of secular policy, was warned that in January 2005, French hostages in Iraq would be beheaded if the ban is not lifted. In Egypt, proud of its freedom-for-all-faiths policy, a judge received death threats for publishing a carefully researched book revealing that Islam does not require such a head covering. A Nobel Laureate was stabbed on a Cairo street for espousing similar views.

What follows are certainly not the only "hot-button," problematic areas for religious or moral consideration but are somewhat more widely debated than the *hijab* issue and have been selected to provide clues as to how devotees of the several major traditions seek to clarify such contentious issues and thereby challenge future generations.

1. Ecology's Impending Crisis

No one wants to play the buffoon and echo Chicken Little's hysterical cry, "The sky is falling!" In growing numbers, however, many would agree with research physicist Harold Shilling that "the pollution and destruction of the environment are religious and ethical problems that derive basically from irreverent and immoral attitudes toward nature, rather than from technological inadequacy alone."[41] He is joined by theologian Larry Rasmussen, who points to a host of global ills such as ozone depletion, deforestation, and pollution of water and the earth itself from which we draw our sustenance. He also emphasizes the greenhouse effect of carbon emissions causing polar ice to melt, which is predicted to cause the oceans to rise and to drown dwellings miles inland. He makes special note of the fact that in nature's economy, "Nature runs off current solar income" is increasingly jeopardized by heat-trapping carbon dioxide and rapid increase of particulates in the air. These lead not only to contaminating the air we breathe but also to blocking ultraviolet rays needed for plants (and our food) to thrive.[42]

The problem is not a new one. In 1872, the Massachusetts State Board of Health warned of pollution, especially in New England where mill towns were beset by conditions similar to those in England half a century earlier. Legislation was difficult to pass and harder still to enforce with corporate lobbying blocking effective implementation in the interest of profits. "In the end there was very little to be done about industrial pollution except to plead with manufacturers. If the manufacturer said he was doing all that could be done, that was the end of it."[43]

What has all this to do with religion? Daniel McGuire put things crisply: "If current trends continue, we will not (succeed via legislation.) And that is qualitatively and epochally true. If religion does not speak to (this), it is an obsolete distraction."[44] Former Vice President Al Gore has pointed out that many of the major religious traditions have a long history of concern for the earth's well-being, citing evidence from Jewish, Christian, Muslim, Baháí, and Native American sources.[45] Philosopher William Young quotes from a declaration proposed by the Parliament of the Worlds Religions that adds to those traditions noted by Vice President Gore Hinduism, Buddhism, Jainism, Daoism, Confucianism, Shintoism, and scores of "smaller" faith communities such several

African groups. The declaration calls for "pluralism, not exclusivism or inclusivism. We do not mean a global theology or a single unified religion beyond all existing religions, and certainly not the domination of one religion over all others."[46] A brief survey of some of these in their conceptions of earth, nature, and human proclivity to exploit both to the borderline of ecocide will be useful here.

Hinduism. This tradition celebrates the sacred in nature. One of the reasons for its apparent polytheism has been the tendency of its adherents to personalize various aspects of nature and create demigods or minor deities of forests, mountains, rivers, rain, and so on because these subdeity figures are ultimately conjoined in one supreme divine being, Brahma, and all nature is perceived as spiritual and eternal, there really is no ultimate ecological crisis. Hinduism proposed that all perplexities will eventually be resolved in the continuing cycles of life.

This position might lead the western mind to perceive it to be indifferent whereas to the Hindu it encourages faith in the integrity of creation and patience with the vicissitudes of life. Hindu thought does not separate nature, morality, and law. A large measure of the legacy of Mohandas Gandhi, Jawaharlal Nehru, and Indira Gandhi, among their many other achievements, has been to sustain the people's pride in their sacred environmental heritage.

Buddhism. In both of its "denominations,"—Theravada (also called Hinayana) and Mahayana—Buddhism takes a cautious but insistent approach to humankind's proper relation with the natural environment. Even more consistently than the Hindus who first gave the world the concept of *ahimsa* or nonviolence based on the recognition of the sacredness of all life, ecology might be considered a key element of Buddhist thought. Indeed, all living things whether human or nonhuman (which extends to insects and poisonous snakes and even nonliving things such as earth's natural resources) are deemed to deserve reverence and protection.

According to legend, in gratitude for the shelter provided throughout his meditation, Siddharta, the original Lord Buddha, looked at the bodhi tree for a week without blinking. A physical impossibility, this nonetheless symbolizes the heart of Buddhism: reverence for life. "Perhaps such a Buddhist teaching as 'destroy the forest of your derailments or passions, not the forest of trees,' stems from this original experience at the foot of the sacred tree."[47] The bodhi tree (*ficus religiosa,* which can live 4,000 years) under which Siddharta meditated awaiting enlightenment is said to have its roots fixed at the world's axis. The original tree still grows in India, and the current Dalai Lama writes of his great pleasure when groups of Buddhists and Christians "joined an historic pilgrimage of practitioners from both traditions for meditation and dialogue under [that] tree at Bodh Gaya in India."[48] Among the things honestly and earnestly discussed were the sense of interdependence to be discovered as the world's economy evolves and concerns for preservation of the environment and our world's ecological concerns.[49]

Confucianism. Whether one argues that confucianism is a religion, essentially a social philosophy, or even just an ethical system, a reading of its literature seems to indicate that an ecological crisis was the last thing on Confucius' mind. The tug of war between political tyranny and social anarchy was more likely to be debated. What had been an orderly world that sought peaceful resolutions under the Chou Dynasty (c. seventh century B.C.E.) that fostered a military organization that prided itself on a code of chivalry deteriorated into almost continuous warfare between baronies, slaughtering whole populations of 60,000 to as many as 400,000. Pleas from all quarters for solutions urged at one extreme a kind of Hobbsian "eye for an eye" retribution, to the other extreme a social philosophy called Mohism, after its chief spokesman, *Mo Tsu*, He insisted that the solution to China's bloody conflicts was not force but love.[50]

> Mutual attacks among the states, usurpation, mutual injuries are among the major calamities of the world. But whence do these calamities arise? Out of want of mutual love. Feudal Lords have learned to love only their own state and not that of others. Therefore all the calamities, strifes, complaints and hatred in the world have arisen out of want of mutual love.[51]

Support for each alternative was remarkably swift and enthusiastic, but most of the world of the time was not ready, and Confucius himself remarked, "By no means. Answer hatred with justice, and love with benevolence." His alternative was to adopt a more moderate way and urged a careful study of the classics of the past that had produced such rulers as these of the Chou dynasty and to adopt and nurture what he called the five positive relationships. These relationships would secure all conflicts of social life: those between parent and child, husband and wife, elder sibling and junior sibling, elder friend and junior friend, and ruler and subject.

What has all this to do with ecology or environmental concerns? At least two elements are in Confucius alternative worth considering. First, he was not simply indulging sentimentality in his devotion to the past. All societies have needs, natural as well as cultural, and these needs give rise to the poetry, drama, and legendary heroes who set the tone for each generation's striving. Reverence for historic exemplars should include respect and affection for the elderly of the present who will soon join their own generations in a realm that is beyond history. Veneration, however, must include not only the human or even just the living part of our world but also elements of nature in which we are embedded.

Second, Confucius considered earth and heaven as a continuum. While avoiding speculative discourse on metaphysical matters, he proposed that our ancestors watch what good or evil we commit here. These forefathers are positioned in a kind of heavenly amphitheater, cheering us on to finer achievements. Furthermore, being pleasantly disposed toward their descendants, the ancestors would naturally want to share with them knowledge of things to come."[52] "Because death is no more than promotion to a more honorable estate, our ancestors may provide occasional signs of warning against despoiling nature, or welcome us as we approach our own transition to a future life. The simplest, mundane activities will be evaluated by them, and here Confucius foreshadows a bit of a Scottish proverb worthy of the *Analects*: "If each of us cleans in front of his own home, the city will be clean." This accords well with Huston Smith's appraisal of Confucius' philosophy as "a blend of common sense and practical wisdom," This alone, however, would not explain its enduring power over so many centuries. For this we need to consider a certain dynamic in Confucius' view that the whole cosmos belongs to an organic whole. Our extensive natural environment deserves to be safeguarded. Our present space-exploring generation may come to include the moon, the planets, and even the stars in its natural environment.

The three monotheistic religions. Judaism, Christianity, and Islam (all of which originated in the Middle East and became regarded as western only because of their migrations and settlements across Europe) have come in for a great deal of criticism being cast as closet antienvironmentalists.

The popular impression is that since all three (including Islam) trace their origin to Hebrew scripture, especially the five books of Moses, it is to be believed that God commanded Adam and Eve to "be fruitful and multiply, and fill the earth and subdue it" (Genesis 1: 28). Many critics construe the expression "subdue it" as license to exploit nature without restraint. During centuries of time, charges of overgrazing, overfarming, overfishing lakes, rivers, and more recently oceans (as in whaling and massive pollution via industrial waste dumping), haphazardly destroying forests, despoiling the earth through strip-mining, and many more complaints have been aimed at the monotheistic religions, which have largely remained silent. There have indeed been countless cases of people using scriptures to justify violent acts including "subduing" the environment, and child abuse[53], killing members of one's own family suspected of heresy (Deuteronomy 13: 6–9), executing anyone suspected of witchcraft (Exodus 22:18), and war (Exodus 15:3; Deuteronomy 7:1–5; 16). Each of all these travesties can be included in the litany of abuses against human and natural ecology in the name of religion.

This is not the place to offer excuses. Anthropologists can cite research revealing how shamans and priests put words in God's mouth, and then had those words entered into holy writ. What is often overlooked, however, is that the people of Israel did in fact acknowledge the sacredness of the whole realm of nature. "The earth is the Lord's and the fullness thereof, the world and those who dwell therein" (Psalm 24:1). Lifting the eyes heavenward, the Psalmist exclaimed, "When I look at thy heavens, the work of thy fingers, the moon and the stars which thou hast established, what is man that thou art mindful of him?" (Psalm 8).

Our challenge to undertake the stewardship of the environment follows the acknowledgement of. Even in time of war, God insists that amid their attacks and destruction of buildings, the Hebrews were never to destroy a fruit tree or any of the enemy's vineyards (Deuteronomy 19:19–20). All humankind, like the natural environment which sustains us, must be acknowledged as sacred to God: "Thou hast made [man] little less than God, and dost crown him with glory and honor . . . and given him dominion over the works of thy hands. O Lord, our Lord, how majestic is thy name in all the earth!"(Psalm 8). A better translation might be "created him to have dominion," the purpose of which implies accountability. As God's vice regent, humans do not have lordship over creation but do share a mature responsibility for its well-being.

Although it emerged in the context of Jewish history, Christianity began with the eternal Word by which all things were made and that became incarnate and dwelt among us (John 1:1–3). The purpose for this unprecedented incarnation was to reveal

God's love for the world (John 3:16) by redeeming all of it—all nature as well as all humankind, reflecting that all of creation is sacred. The entrance of this eternal enfleshed Word is described in the Christmas story in Matthew (2:1–12) and Luke (2:8–20) in a way that brings the whole of creation together around the birthplace of the infant Christ: sheep and shepherds, learned men and angels, and the very stars of the heavens. This Christ (called as such in the Qur'an (Sura iii, 86) and the New Testament) came into the world to set free the whole of the natural environment "from its bondage to decay, and to obtain the glorious liberty of the children of God" (Romans 8:19–21).

"Christians," as Hans Kung reminds us, "have always regarded the world, in principle, as God's good creation: the world and humankind which can only exist as real beings insofar as they share in the Being itself *ipsum esse,* that is God."[54] Doubtless the twelfth century Dominican scholar and mystic Johannes Meister Eckhart would find an enthusiastic audience today among "green scene" advocates for contending that God creates the world and humanity in himself. God's being spreads itself out into all things so that in the "depths of the soul," the mystical can experience the underlying unity of everything in the existence of God.

Without unnecessary detours into the paradoxes of God being both imminent in all things natural yet transcendent over all of them, we can trace such reasoning through Thomas Aquinas, St. Francis of Assisi, the German idealists, Hegel's identification of God with the world, A.N. Whitehead's "process theology," and Kung's affirmation that "even though God is not the world, nor the world God, yet God is in this world, and this world is in God."[55] Parenthetically, we may also note that such affirmations are sometimes considered theologically dangerous and come at a price. Hildegard of Bingen was excommunicated at the age of 81 along with her entire convent; Francis of Assisi had his order snatched from him; Meister Eckhart was condemned on three occasions and, according to Matthew Fox, his name remains on the official condemned list; Thomas Aquinas suffered a nervous breakdown and his death in 1274 was precipitated by constant battles with church authorities before he was "safely dead" and posthumously canonized in 1323.[56]

It is temptingly easy for us to give assent to the theoretical sacredness of nature without fear of theological rebuke. Protecting the environment has become almost a mantra in the face of the widely publicized threats of environmental damage. We may feel we are positioned safe in confronting destroyers of forests and those who poison the lakes, rivers, and oceans. However, when legislation is proposed to curb ecologically destructive practices and when jobs, personal wealth, corporate profits, and political advantage are thereby threatened, we apply the brakes and either water down, shelve, or defeat outright any reforms. This is not to repeat the tired arguments against big business, that—given recent advances in communications, improvements in technology, and ease of travel—are almost surely to continue as a major engine of global interaction. It is rather to encourage more interaction among business leaders, religious communities, and scientific agencies to resolve such obvious problems as waste disposal, land management, medical and food distribution, and so on.

Fortunately, the volume of activity within and among religious communities, environmental agencies, and scientific endeavors has been growing. Councils of churches and interfaith organizations—the idea for which began in the late nineteenth century—can be found at local, national, and international levels in discussion groups, seminars, and full-scale conferences on religious, environmental, and scientific collaboration. In the United States, the National Council of Churches, like the World Council of Churches the British Society for Christian Ethics, the trans-European Societas Ethica, and the *Parliament of the World's Religions* are engaged, in sponsoring frequent dialogues on ecology issues. The Templeton Foundation provides an annual million-plus dollar prize for outstanding contributions to the science-religion dialogue and periodically publishes a journal, *Science and Theology News* that highlights interfaith meetings and publications on a host of issues relating to science and religion. It also highlights interfaith endeavors in environmental studies, by organizations, most of which had their beginning in Christian endeavors. Adding to them the proliferation of by secular organizations such as the Audubon Society, Sierra Club, Wilderness Society, National Wildlife Federation, Earth First! and almost countless others rules one reason for optimism.

John Polkinghorne, a Cambridge physicist and Anglican priest, expressed the range of this concern well:

> This phenomenon of human influence upon the course of the natural world has led Philip Hefner to speak of humanity as the created "co-creator," an idea which A.R. Peacocke reminds us goes back at least as far as the confident days of the Christian humanists of the Italian Renaissance—the thought recalls to us our human responsibility for the integrity and sustainable fruitfulness of the world which we inhabit"[57]

Polkinghorne also adds that we must guard against sentimentalizing nature; it does contain "enemies" (e.g., the streptococcus bacteria), while at the same time it providing our food. The Christian, he notes, really should protest where abuses occur as in the cramped confinement of factory-farming methods that inflict grievous suffering. Meanwhile, "we need to behold Behemoth, even as we remember that the Lord made him as he also made us."

The Hebrew Psalms and Proverbs reach poetic heights in extolling God's glory with reference to the creation. The Psalmist expressed it in Psalm 19:1:

> The heavens are telling the glory of God
> and the firmament proclaims his handiwork

We find a similar lyrical declaration in Islam in the Holy Qur'an S. XXIV, 41:

> Seest thou not that it is
> God Whose praises all beings
> In the heavens and on the earth
> Do celebrate, and the birds
> (of the air) with wings
> Outspread? Each one knows
> Its own (mode of) prayer
> And praise. And God
> Knows well all that they do.

The following verses proclaim that all the heavens and the earth, the clouds, rain and lightning, the mountains, night and day all belong to God, and God's fellowship is the final goal of all creation. The Qur'an even expresses the course of creation (God's word coming forth in a plural "we" as in the royal "we" of kings and queens):

> It is We who have set out
> The Zodiacal Signs in the heavens,
> And made them fair-seeming
> To all beholders.

The twelve signs of the Zodiac mark the solar path through the heavens month after month. Majesty, order, beauty, and harmony revealed in the heavens enable us to mark the seasons and understand nature's laws as they reveal the facts we need to comprehend meteorology, agriculture, seasonal winds, and tides.

Ali explains that mapping the constellations introduces us to "the marvellous facts of the heavens, some of which affect our physical life on this earth. But the highest lessons we can draw from them are spiritual."[58] The key to this tutelage is first to recognize that Allah is one, and alone is worthy of our worship. The underlying message is that the awesome beauty and holiness of nature imposes on humankind a requirement to employ the gifts of creation with respect and thanksgiving. In an almost whimsical aside, he adds, "If by chance any rebellious force of evil seeks to obtain by stealth a sound of that harmony to which all that make themselves consonant are freely invited, it is pursued by a shooting star, for there can be no consonance between good and evil."[59]

That humans are held accountable for despoiling God's world is made strikingly clear in *Sura* IV:19–20, in which God's providential gift of the earth to be our home "spread out like a carpet" brings with it "all kinds of things (such as 'means of subsistence') in due balance. Furthermore, as Iqtidar Zaidi underscores, whatever ecological imbalance exists is not attributable simply to "human dominance" but to the materialism and greed that characterizes so much of corporate culture. A society based on Islam accepts human control of nature but within the limits set forth by Allah. Muslim leaders have a responsibility to ensure that the programs of development necessary to better the conditions for humans do so in a way that preserves the environment."[60]

2. Gender and the Role Definition

We explored some of these issues broadly in Chapter Three and now must delve more deeply into them.

Hinduism. Inequality between males and females is by no means a recent phenomenon; it can be found in the epic poem *Ramayana* of ancient Hinduism. In it, Sita, the always faithful wife of Prince Rama, is abducted by an evil demon but is found by a friend Hanuman and restored to her husband. The prince demands an ordeal by which she could prove her faithfulness and then a second one that deeply offend her sensitive nature. She disappears until, convinced in her heart that her marriage to Rama would continue in heaven, she returns and they are reconciled.

Curiously from a Western point of view, the story did not have a "happily-ever-after" ending. Although he loves Sita dearly, Rama never really allowed her to be her own person and the climax of the story has been lost in antiquity. This tale reinforces the subservient role of the wife in Hindu tradition, amounting almost to servility, and has exerted a great influence on modern Indian culture, becoming a rallying point around which women have gathered to argue for equal rights. Spousal relationships have from time to time been polygamous (never polyandrous) and unequal to the point of idolatry.[61]

The most grievous evidence of the subjugation of Hindu women arises with reference to marriage, the now outlawed but still prevalent practice of the groom's family exacting an extravagant dowry, and the growing popularity of abortion, addressed in section 3 of this chapter.

Buddhism. It is remarkable that Buddhism, arising directly out of Hinduism, became a reform movement in the same sense that Christian Protestantism sought a reformation of the Roman Catholicism and return to the church's earliest character. In Buddhism, however, the reforms were more aggressively pursued. Siddhartha Gautama, called the Buddha, actively condemned the subjugation of women. It is true that in organizing his first monasteries to give his disciples a sense of identity, Siddhartha inadvertently omitted women from membership, probably because of his Hindu training. His followers reminded him of his own emphasis on the equality of all people. One result was the argument: "Since all human beings possess a sinful nature, the sole condition for salvation is faith alone rather than moral merit. Buddhist monks [were] to marry as a sign of their sharing the burdens of ordinary peoples."[62]

In addition, women could become buddhas in their own right. "On the spiritual path monks and nuns do the same things. They even look alike for they shave their heads and wear the same robes. In every way monks and nuns appear to be a single group among whom distinctions based on gender no longer apply."[63]

Confucianism. This tradition exalts family life above all other social organizations, so much so that when one considers that ancestor worship and filial piety are its key components, "the family emerges as the real religion of the Chinese people."[64] Given this point of view, it is paradoxical that in the canonical texts of early Confucianism, "estimation of women's nature was by and large a low one." Richard Guisso sums up the negative attitudes in the *Thunder over the Lake Classics*: "The female was inferior by nature, she was dark as the moon and changeable as water, jealous, narrow-minded and insinuating. She was indiscreet, unintelligent, and dominated by emotion. Her beauty was a snare for the unwary male, the ruination of states."[65] The paradox is immediately evident when we recall that "women played a central role in Confucianism by virtue of their place in the cosmic order and in the family."[66]

The fundamental optimism of Confucianism that life is good (and therefore human nature is good) derived from the concept of the connectedness to heaven, earth, and all humanity (i.e., the cosmic order). Everything in life is relational. Marriage is a vocation to which we are all called. As we all receive life through the marriage of our parents, we must accept our responsibility to pass on that life to successive generations. Confucius emphasized that, as our fundamental being is wrapped up in the existence of others, the virtue of *Jen* (variously translated benevolence, love, humaneness) is a central theme in the teaching of the cosmic order. The role of women is to mirror that order in educating their children.

The feminine force in nature is identified as *Yin* and, as discussed earlier, is characterized as yielding, passive, and lowly like the earth itself. It is the opposite side of the coin to *Yang,* the positive, aggressive, and creative masculine force. To prepare for such a life, boys were to begin formal education by the age of ten to enable them to fulfill *sheng-tao,* "the way of the sages."

It is perhaps not surprising that in time, the tension between the sexes would lead to an unraveling of Confucian authority; indeed, with the collapse of the Han dynasty around 220 C.E. Confucianism was nearly eclipsed by Buddhism and Taoism. Not until a thousand years had passed did a neo-Confucianism emerge, blending the more metaphysical interests of Buddhism with family-state allegiances. China as a nation however, was in decline. By the nineteenth century, poverty, overpopulation, and governmental corruption had taken their toll. The encounters with the imperialism of Western nations also undermined what integrity there was, and the role of women reached an all-time low. Examples of women's vulnerable status included the humiliating ritual of foot binding (literally crippling their feet to the point that they were almost unable to walk), female infanticide, and the sale and purchase of young women as sex slaves. Mao Tse-tung cited these and many other practices as justification for imposing Communist rule in the mid-twentieth century. "Indeed there are few Chinese women today who want to identify themselves with Confucianism."[67] Huston Smith reflects that "it may be that we are looking at a religion that is dying."[68] The denigration of any part of a society endangers the whole.[69]

Judaism. While Judaism has no comments about women as ungracious as those found in early Confucianism, it remains true that from earliest Biblical records to Talmudic times (c. sixth century B.C.E. to about 425 C.E.) and to a great extent in the present day, the male population in conservative and orthodox divisions of the faith, has enjoyed greater authority than women do.

Genesis pays an immeasurable compliment to both genders in declaring that both were created "in the image of God" (Genesis 1:27). This would seem to imply equality, but it was not to be. Patriarchal Jewish concern for stable family life evolved into a conviction that a woman's reason for being was motherhood and that girls should marry soon after puberty, but only after *proving* her virginity. If her husband were to conclude she had not been a virgin but had seduced him under false pretense, he could have her stoned to death. Almost paradoxically, the complementary relation between husband and wife made for true fulfillment of their humanity. "Indeed, Genesis intuits a basic equality between the sexes, and their equal share in human dignity."[70]

During what is sometimes called the "Biblical period" about 1200 to 200 B.C.E., roughly from Moses to the Maccabean revolt, the roles of women varied widely from virtual subservience to a praiseworthy status: "She is far more precious than jewels . . . her children call her blessed and her husband praises her" (Proverbs 31: 10, 28). Women's social roles ranged from one whose essential value was bearing male children, to the rare position of leadership (e.g., Miriam, Deborah, Ruth, and Esther). All this seemed threatened during the Talmudic period, the beginning of which is disputed to have been as early as the sixth century B.C.E.

The Talmud, a vast compendium of Jewish tradition including ethics, folklore, legal opinion, and medical and scientific theories, inspired a widening of education (for boys). Denise Carmody quotes from Jacob Neusner's research in the *Mishnah* revealing that "woman is considered an anomaly, something abnormal" who must not have access to sacred writings: "Let the words of Torah rather be destroyed by fire than imparted to women."[71]

This rigidity would, for example, forbid a man to engage a strange woman in conversation in a public place or to heal a leper by physical contact or anyone on the Sabbath. The influence of the Pharisees was a powerful molder of public opinion so that some practices, such as excluding women from worshipping with men in a synagogue, are still enforced today in the Orthodox branch of Judaism, that prohibits women from sitting next to men during prayer. According to the Roman historian Josephus (c. 37–110 C.E.), wrote that "the Pharisees thought of women as 'in all things inferior to the man' and 'evil.'" Maimonides (1140–1204) summarized the continuing legal view when he identified all women with the ignorant. A residue of Talmudic attitudes toward women formed most of Jewish culture until the nineteenth century. Misogyny continued unabated, and this negative attitude led to a generalized character assassination: "Women are gluttonous, eavesdroppers, lazy and jealous."[72]

Significantly, organized resistance to such attitudes and treatment was attributable to men in considerable measure. It began formally as early as 300 C.E. with Rabbi Abbahu of Ceasaria, and although it eventually dissipated, it had a lingering effect in the teachings of Hillel and a few of his successors. By the eighteenth century with the birth of the "enlightenment" era, a liberalizing of social distinctions became evident.

In 1787, United States, crafted its Constitution based, among other things, on principles of equality and freedom of religion. Four years later, the French National Assembly enfranchised all Jews in France. In Germany, Moses Mendelssohn led a humanist movement that spread to almost all of Eastern Europe and renovated the cultural life of the Jewish people. The movement also involved virtual assimilation within Christian society and laid the groundwork for what became Reform Judaism. The first Reform temple was built in 1810. A second, in 1818 in Hamburg, became the model for Reform synagogues throughout the world with special stress on revising the liturgy, worship in the vernacular, family pews, and, above all, confirmation of girls as well as boys.

The establishment of the Union of American Hebrew Congregations (1873), Hebrew Union College (1875), and a succession of other colleges formally recognized women as equals with men in and later the ordination of women to the rabbinate. The latter has not been fully recognized in the other branches and has been denounced in Israel, but optimism for the future gender inclusiveness within Judaism is still high.

Christianity.   A change from the Hebrew Biblical texts regarding the status of women is immediately apparent. Women figure frequently and prominently in Jesus' life in all four Gospels. Luke tells the birth narrative from Mary's perspective. The names Mary and Martha, Mary Magdalene, and "the other" Mary[73] as well an the unnamed woman at the well are inseparable from accounts of Jesus' life. The woman at the well is particularly interesting because of Judaism's early caution against a man being seen in public talking to a female stranger. In the post-Resurrection church, the early influence of his Jewish past caused Paul to urge that women should "keep silent in the church" (I Corinthians 14:34). His growing awareness of the gospel's inclusiveness, however, inspired him to declare that the old custom of gender separation be rendered null and void "in Christ" (Galatians 3:28) and that women be allowed to become deacons. That this transition was disquieting to Paul's erstwhile Jewish companions may be surmised in light of a traditional Jewish morning prayer in which the men thank God that "Thou hast not made me a Gentile, a slave or a woman." The morning prayer, still observed in some branches of Judaism, may be only a reflection of the position of womanhood in general in the older Jewish tradition.[74]

Newly ordained christian women deacons exercised considerable influence in the new and growing congregations. Under old Roman rule, such women deacons were sometimes dragged into prison along with the men for their religious activities (*Cf.* Acts 8:3, 9:2, 18:26; Romans 6:1–2; II Timothy 1:5). Nevertheless, with the emergence of an all male Christian clergy, vestiges of the Jewish patriarchal system survived. Women who sought the formal recognition of the communal religious life were shunted off to convents or abbeys. For centuries, women were not permitted to sing in church choirs. Instead, boys were trained in vocal music and then castrated before puberty to provide the desired high soprano voices. Protestant churches made castration illegal during the Reformation when women were encouraged to teach and serve on special committees devoted to charitable work—but not to be ordained as clergy (except in Unitarian churches).

Other Organizations. In 1848, the Seneca Falls Women's Convention in New England issued a demand for equality with men, pointing to what the U.S. Constitution presumably stood for: "that all men *and women* are created equal." The movement, broadly designated "feminism," has been called "the most profound and global shift in human relations in the modern era."[75] It has in response to the failure of both the churches and the secular world to fulfill the principle made explicit in the constitutions of both, that of full equality. The U.S. a giant stride was achieved by the end of World War I in guaranteeing the right of women to vote in all public elections. Equality in the work place has not yet been fully achieved, however; in the National Organization for Women reported that across the spectrum of employment, women still receive only 83 percent of men's salaries for the same work (for black women, the figure 79 percent). Although the teaching profession has made great progress: from kindergarten through graduate schools, salaries for the women and men are equal in virtually every state. The picture of the world-wide scene reflects the urgency for a greater global effort.

Islam At least since the Medieval crusades, Islam has been the target of recurring criticism for a number of its alleged infractions of human rights, most notably its subjugation of women to the desires and dictates of men (as made conspicuous in its dress code), its determination to convert unbelievers by force of arms if persuasion fails, and its "inherently warlike" posture.

The apparent murder of Dutch filmmaker Theo van Gogh in 2004, allegedly for his recent movie dramatizing the abuse of women in Islamic societies, underscores the urgency (made even more evident in light of the Middle-Eastern conflicts), that the record be clarified.[76]

Among the more visible symbols of apparent abuse has been the veil that women are required to wear. Different forms have evolved; one covers just the face below the eyes, another, the *burka* or *chador,* covers the entire body (including the face) with small eye slits that enable the wearer to see without being recognized. A personal friend of this author told of her scorn for Western women who are willing to bare everything to attract seductive attention. Muslim women, on the other hand, appreciate the modesty and privacy afforded by the veil, which her father, brother, or husband provides for her protection. The Qur'an expresses this in a manner that recognizes that the Muslim household is often multigenerational:

> Believing women . . . should lower their gaze and guard their modesty. Draw their veils over their bosoms and not display their beauty except to their husbands, their fathers, their husband's fathers, their sons, their husbands' (other) sons by another wife their brothers or their brother's sons . . . And oh ye Believers turn ye all together towards God, that ye may attain Bliss.

To be sure, the family may also include "small children who have no sense of the shame of sex."[77]

Those who are devoted to the tradition see in it no subjugation of women to the dictates of men. Furthermore, caused so many misunderstandings, there is a movement in most Islamic societies to drop the use of the veil—the source of many misunderstanding—because current of economic and political activities seem to require a form of frank openness toward co-workers and the public in general. The problems regarding the composition of the strict dress rules recently in Afghanistan relates to the fact that they were enforced by a power-hungry minority who simply failed to read or understand the Qur'an. While men in pre-Islamic societies treated women as chattel, the Qur'an leaves open the possibility of full equality of women with men. Women have a right to marry whom they will so that not even a Sultan can marry a woman without her consent, "Ye who believe! Ye are forbidden to inherit women against their will" (S. iv 19). A woman has a right to education, voting privileges, and a career of her own. Huston Smith reminds us that the most recent prime minister of Pakistan and the leader of the opposition party were both women, that since Mohammed's day, women have had the right to hold property in their own name. Women in the United States did not win that right until the twentieth century.[78]

With regard to a wife's sexual rights, there is room for dispute. The Qur'an emphasizes that a woman is a man's "tilth," a groomed field ready for planting. He is therefore free to "have his way" with her, except during her menstrual periods; "but when they have purified themselves you may approach them in any manner, time or place" (S ii 222). "So approach your tilth when or how ye will; but do some good act for your souls before-hand" (S. ii 23). This comes dangerously close to giving a man license to force unwelcome advances that the woman might well believe are as abusive. Furthermore, inasmuch as a man may have four wives at one time, "ill conduct" on the wife's (wives') part (open to easy misinterpretation, depending on the husband's temperament), opens the way for him first to "admonish them, next refuse to share their beds and last beat them (lightly)". In his translation of *S. iv 34.,* A. Yusuf Ali placed the word *lightly* in parentheses.

As to the charge that Muslims convert unbelievers by force, Qur'an (S ii:256) states, "Let there be no compulsion in religion." "If God had pleased, he would have made (all humankind) one people (people of one religion), but He hath done otherwise . . . Wherefore, press forward in good works. Unto God ye shall return." If some Muslims have used force in recruiting converts they were in clear conflict with the will of Allah as reflected in the Qur'an.

3. Abortion: Freedom of Choice?

Among the hot-button issues, few equal the arguments surrounding abortion.

Hinduism. While it is true that the traditional position among Hindus opposes abortion as contrary to Dharma, the Laws of Manu and the principle of noninjury (*ahimsa*), the fact is that since 1971, abortion has been legal throughout India. One reason is in the age-old preference for male offspring. With sophisticated medical procedures available to determine whether the gender of the fetus is female, termination of the pregnancy is increasingly common. One study of a New Delhi clinic in 1992 and 1993 revealed that 13,998 abortions had been performed; all of the fetuses were female. Female infanticide has dramatically lowered the ratio of men to women in India.[79] The primary reason for so many abortions of females appears to stem from the anticipated roles of girls and women and their drain on family's financial resources. Outlawed in 1961, the dowry traditionally demanded by the groom's family (or sometimes by the groom himself) was viewed to exploit and be demeaning of the bride to be. She was being regarded as no more than a means to unearned wealth. Her predicament often led to suicide or murder (e.g., failing to provide the demanded TV sets, cars, or even houses), of the bride by setting her on fire and then reporting her death as the result of a kitchen accidental. "At least two women are killed each day, in this manner, in New Delhi."[80]

Once "safely" married, the bride is a virtual servant to her husband and his family. Swami Ramsukhdas advises that if she is mistreated, including being beaten: "The wife should think that she is paying her debt of her previous life, and thus her sins are being destroyed and she is becoming pure . . . it is possible that her husband will start loving her."[81]

Buddhism. From the earliest days, Buddhists viewed abortion with abhorrence in keeping with their dedication to the concept that all forms of life are of equal value. "It is a moral ideal and the first principle of Buddhist ethics not to injure any living creature," but

> a well informed woman is the person who knows what is best for her: to give birth and socially to take the responsibility for the baby, or to have an abortion— to release herself from having a child at the time she is not ready—and to take the moral or psychological responsibility for it. A woman should have the right to make decisions about her own body because it is she who takes the consequent responsibility. Society as a whole should not make the decision for her."[82]

But what about the emotional anguish she may be unable to bear? Here the Buddhist response is in terms of compassion seldom made so specific by other religious or secular bodies: "For rape victims and for women who have had abortions, *Bhikkhuni* can perform religious rituals that help to reestablish them mentally and spiritually"[83] The ability of the *Bhikkhunito* to perform such a service derives from a cultivated empathy, *nying je,* which the Dalai Lama believes to be innate and can be nurtured to the ultimate level of *nying je chenmo,* the Great Compassion.[84] Such empathy is at the heart of Buddhism, reaching out to all who yearn to find peace and release from the pain of guilt, such as those who have undergone an abortion or performed other act such as those by the soldier in battle or police officer stopping a crime in the only measure available.

Confucianism   With the Confucian concentration on the family and its role in social relations, the omission of direct consideration of abortion is puzzling until we review the negative attitude toward women in general discussed earlier. With the advent of neo-Confucianism in 220 B.C.E., a more overtly religious atmosphere began to permeate the previously secular society, increasingly stressing self-discipline rather than following traditional rules and "correct" principles. "In family relationships," wrote Cheng I, a leading neo-Confucian (1033–1107) "parents and children usually overcome (such) principles with affection, and supplant righteousness with kindness."[85] Yet nothing in the earlier classical period matches the preoccupation with chastity found in neo-Confucianism. Its near fundamentalist Puritanism may have diverted attention from anything that would prompt interest in abortion except for the most urgent consideration and then kept as quiet as possible.

Judaism   In contract, Judaism, doubtlessly regarded abortion as a very grave matter although there are no recorded incidents of the practice. Humans are, after all, created in God's image (Genesis 1:27, 5:1–2) and even before we were formed in the womb, God knew us, not simply as biological organisms but as persons (Psalm 139:13; Jeremiah 1:5). It is probable that no such dangerous surgery or administering abortion-producing medication would lightly have been allowed to interfere in the birth and development of a child of God. Despite the religious implications of the issue, some still argue that because the word abortion is not specifically identified in the scriptures, the practice cannot be held as a religious issue. An obvious rejoinder would be to note that the Biblical scribes omitted many terms familiar to moral and ethical concern: by embezzlement, bootlegging, pimping, gambling, and suicide. The lack of discussion by no means removes it from the concern of those writers. From the moment of conception, in the Biblical view, we are dealing with human lives whose essential nature has been established by God's providence.[86]

Christianity.   With its roots in Judaism, Christianity is widely assumed to have continued to observe rules and customs derived from it. This is supported by the fact that the early church fathers continued to insist that God knew us even before we were conceived (as emphasized in both the Psalm and Jeremiah mentioned earlier) and guided our development. Paul expresses it well, and extends its importance to Christian understanding: "Those whom He foreknew He also predestined to be conformed to the image of His Son" (Romans 8:29). Abortion cuts irrevocably across that predestined path. The fathers of the early church concurred. Tertullian included abortion under the category of such irremissable sins as homicide.[87] The Council of

Elvira (c. 300) delivered a similar judgment, denying Holy Communion for any woman who had undergone abortion. Two centuries later Augustine was more lenient, simply assessing a fine for the first abortion but treating a second as an act of murder. Toward the end of the thirteenth century, Thomas Aquinas condemned the practice on grounds that it violated natural law.[88]

Protestant ethicists did not deviate significantly from the position of the Roman Catholic church in this matter almost to the twenty-first century, although Protestantism never quite equaled the sheer rigor of the Roman church in its condemnation of abortion. The Encyclical Casti Connubi of 1930, for example, forbid abortion on any grounds, and so strictly enforced it that nuns who were raped when the Russians invaded Germany in 1945 were forbidden to abort unwanted fetuses.[89] Daniel Callahan and James Gustafson representing Roman Catholic and Protestant views, respectively, share some central concerns of on the subject that are important for us to review.

Among the key arguments of the Roman Catholic relevant to abortion include these: (1) God alone is the Lord of life, (2) Human beings do not have the right to take the lives of other (innocent) human beings, (3) human life begins at the moment of conception, (4) abortion, at whatever the stage of development of the conceptus, is the taking of innocent human life. Callahan expresses some ambivalence to these, noting that while point (1) affirms that God alone is author of life, it does not solve the problem of how we are to derive our particular "right" to life or how other human beings are to respect that life or to balance a conflict of rights. As to the second point, the insertion of "innocent" is crucial. Traditional Catholic morality has defended the "just war" where the death of innocent civilians is not positively willed, but is reluctantly permitted as unavoidable. This does not seem particularly relevant to the issue of abortion until point (3) specifies that all human life begins at the moment of conception so that the final point affirms that abortion takes innocent human life at whatever stage of development of the conceptus. However, is the third point biologically defensible? Is the inclusion of *innocent* in the second point merely an escape route for the end justifying the means, as in killing in self-defense or cutting out a pregnant fallopian tube containing a nonviolable but still "living" fetus to save the life of the mother?[90]

Protestant positions on abortion range between to extremes. On one hand, there are the ultraconservatives employing what we might call a top-down authoritative body of regulations, urge legal controls that forbid abortion for any reason. Those described by the ultraconservatives as "liberals" in a most derisive manner take an opposite, permissive position, affirming that what a person feels is best is morally right.[91]

Between them are those bottom-up theorists, the religiously oriented counselors often trained in psychology or psychotherapy who first seek to understand the woman involved in the decision and her health, emotional condition, financial plight (e.g., is she a single mother who has two or three children to feed with only a part-time manual employment and no family to provide a safety net?). What has been her religious upbringing, that might have instilled in her the fear of eternal punishment? On what basis will the counselor give advice? Here James Gustafson is quite insistent: "The moralist himself is responsible for his decision: if he offers recommendations: if an abortion is induced, he shares moral responsibility for it."

Whether the moralist is willing to take such responsibility is a separate issue, but many believe that leaving the matter ultimately to the discretion of the woman is the choice that defines our humanity. The alternatives need not be between fundamentalism and anarchy. The Roe Versus Wade decision of 1973, which effectively has claimed the lives of more than 40 million human fetuses since the Supreme Court rendered this decision until the time of this writing, is still viewed by many as having interdicted the force of maternal love, which throughout history has represented nature's deepest bonding and culture's highest calling. Ironically, "the woman who pseudonymously gave the (Court's) decision its name has lamented its consequences, saying that women 'have literally been handed the right to slaughter their own children.'"[92]

It is perhaps not a surprise that the majority of Protestant pastors and religious counselors, refusing to be caught between right-wing fundamentalism and anarchy, have tended to gravitate to a position closer to that of Swiss theologian Karl Barth, who stressed, in agreement with the earlier description of the Roman Catholic position, that a definite no must be the ultimate presupposition.[93] Barth was reflecting on the fact that abortion had become so easy to obtain that many couples, especially the unmarried, used abortion as a virtual substitute for contraception. Anthropologist Margaret Mead struck a sobering note, however, when she urged, "If they are willing to plead for the rights of the just-fertilized ovum they should scrutinize their willingness to see a fellow adult who is surely completely human in the capacity to sin, suffer and repent, be hung or electrocuted"[94] She emphasized that abortion is a religious issue, however, and one from which the state should remove itself, agreeing only on laws that require no citizen to violate what he or she understands as the will of God. Meanwhile, the bottom-up thinker might ask whether we cannot simultaneously protect the rights of the unborn human beings *and* acknowledge the wrong headedness of capital punishment and, for good measure, preemptive wars. Such wars inevitably kill large numbers of innocent civilians including unborn children as well as those already born but who will never see adulthood.[95] Since *Roe v. Wade* in 1973, abortions have averaged 4,000 per day, destroying more lives than have been lost in all wars in U.S. history.

Islam.   The position of Islam on abortion is less easy to articulate because the Holy Qur'an, like the Jewish and Christian bibles, does not mention the word. Successive imams have been, for the most part, less inclined to argue about just when the new conceptus truly becomes a human person. In some respects, abortion may be classified with adultery and homosexuality, which the Qur'an does not mention. This may be surprising to many outside the Muslin faith because popular notion is that adultery is punishable by death for both parties. Although death sentences have indeed been carried out in some Muslim countries,

> it is really the (cultural, not religious) tradition. And although all the Muslim schools take the view that adultery is punishable by death, there is a school of law, which is not commonly known, which says that since there is no mention of this punishment in the Qur'an, we reject it.[96]

The abortion question, also fraught with difficulties due to the absence of specific pronouncement in the Qur'an, may be better comprehended in light of the authority of the Muslim judicial system.

An underlying concern of Qur'anic legislation is that of annunciating ethical principles in the form of moral exhortation that ought to be followed in the administration of justice. The Prophet's elaborations in communicating revealed guidance, and his own practice formed "the model pattern of behavior"—the *Sunna*—and was promulgated as the authoritative precedent for religious-moral prescriptions as treated by the *Sharia*, the virtual embodiment of the concept of justice. The function of the Sharia is to teach humans the way of salvation by virtue of which God's justice and other goals are realized.[97]

The dangers for those "guilty" of abortion whether physician or patient but also for the judges who try the cases are enormous, involving their very salvation. Among the most revered imams of early Muslim history, Ibn Babuya (d. *381/991*) cautioned, "Beware of *al-qada* (sitting in judgment).

As for judges, they are of four kinds: (a) A judge who executes a decision that is incorrect while knowing that he is wrong. Such a person is doomed to be in hell. (b) A judge who carries out a judgment that is unsound while not knowing that he is incorrect. He too will be in Hell. (c) A judge who judges correctly while not knowing that he is sound (in his judgment). He too will be in Hell. (d) A judge who carries out a judgment correctly, being fully aware that he is right will be in Paradise.[98]

The jury is still out with reference to a definitive judgment on abortion, but those who judge are surely forewarned.

4. Freedom to Choose? Homosexuality:

One of the formost hot-button issues is whether or how one's sexual preference may be expressed. It would be worse than trite to note that the relation of lesbians and homosexual males to the rest of society has become a thorny issue. It has actually been so for centuries and recurs as the focal point of concern not only for religious leaders but also politicians, research biologists, and a host of other academics not to mention anguished individuals and their families. It may be that the 2004 decision of the Supreme Court of Canada legalizing same-sex marriages nationwide will make the customary arguments against such arrangements seem merely quaint. The historic opposition even to contemplating such decisions must be examined if we are to understand how we got here from there. It is far from clear that homosexuality and the vast amount of opposition to its acceptance worldwide will be swept away by the official action of a single nation.

Perhaps the key issue is whether the "condition" of homosexuality is truly a matter of choice, a genetic abnormality that may or may not be treatable, a deviant product of warped family relationships, or a sinful decision in defiance of rules and traditions, especially if those rules emanate from a sovereign deity.

In Biblical times, little if any consideration was given the prospect that some people are "born that way." The conviction that we were all created by God *de novo* in His own image seemed to mean that logically any deviation from the norm was a matter of our choice and to be judged in light of God's edicts. Homosexual cohabiting deviated from God's clear purpose for human procreation according to the laws of nature (Genesis 1:28). It may be that venereal disease was a seen as nature's punishment (Romans 1:26–27), so that the most efficient deterrent was death (Leviticus 18:22 and 20:13). Despite ancient Rome's fascination with Greek culture that they copied freely, Romans viewed homosexual practices with scorn amounting to loathing. The practice often bought a sentence of death. It was certainly the case from the beginning in Islam that adultery and homosexuality were both condemned in their holy writ (Cf. the Qur'an (4:6 and 24:2)

Down through the centuries, homosexuality has been considered a condition or a freak of nature, but it was usually only the overly action that state of affairs that was denounced. Advances in biological research raised questions as to whether the condition might be genetically based and therefore not to be treated as a crime or deviance. Sigmund Freud wrote in 1935 that "it is nothing to be ashamed of" and it "is a great injustice to persecute it."[99] Historically, close observers of human nature have insisted on the familial and cultural "shaping" of homosexuality. As early as Aristotle, it was noted that young men who had been sexually abused or otherwise tyrannized by their fathers were the most likely to gravitate toward homosexuality. Luella Cole, writing at about the same time as Freud and Kinsey, declared, "In order to pass from childhood to Adulthood the adolescent must solve a number of problems. [Among them], he must develop heterosexual interests."[100] In 1991, Clara Schuster wrote, "There is no evidence to support the hypothesis that homosexuality is biologically based so it must appear to have been conditioned."[101]

Research has been undertaken to determine the question as to whether homosexuality is born or bred.[102] Simon LeVay, a neuroscientist at the Salk Institute in La Jolla, California and a self-confessed homosexual, is lending his considerable energy and expertise to the project. Discovering that the portion of the hypothalamus in heterosexual males is twice as large as that same section in homosexuals, LeVay concluded that the difference between them indeed has a biological basis. One problem immediately presented itself: Why is it that among identical twins, who have exactly the same neural equipment, one may be homosexual but only in 11 percent of cases will both be homosexual?

Furthermore, why are so many homosexuals dissatisfied with their condition? The dissatisfaction is in most cases not simply due to the sense of isolation or being shunned by society. They simply do not want to be homosexual. Furthermore, their homosexuality appears not to be comparable to being another racial or ethnic minority. Jacquelyn Holt Park, author of a book about the complexities and sorrows of being identified as lesbian, has been confronted by those who charge that blacks cannot change their color, but homosexuals can change their sexual behavior.

To continue on that plane we need now to explore the various arguments from the perepective of religious traditions eastern and western.

Hinduism.   It would not be accurate to describe Hinduism as more "permissive" or "tolerant" of homosexuality than other religions because these terms suggest that this orientation is problematic. For the most part, Hinduism simply accepts the condition as a fact of life. According to Jawaharlal Nehru, elected prime minister of india (1947), homosexuality was neither approved nor disapproved, and is in fact "not at all common in India." Rather, it is associated with lower classes of Muslim and British immigrants. According to the Kamasutra, all forms of physical pleasure generated by lovers of either the same or opposite sexes should be encouraged, and a favorite passage in Hindu mythology (at least among homosexuals) has it that Samba, son of the great god Krishna, was both homosexual, bisexual, and a cross-dresser.[103]

Hindu literature would suggest that there are many ways a person might "make love" to someone without sexual intercourse. From recent history, we might consider Johannes Brahms, who courted through his music (recall *The Alto Rhapsody*), Elizabeth Browning through poetry (e.g., "Sonnets from the Portuguese"), and Michelangelo through his painting and sculpture. Curiously, Michelangelo courted his only true love, Vittoria Colonna more though his poetry that is less celebrated than his visual art. For years, they interwove their sentiments into a stream of letters, but he felt so inferior to her brilliance, beauty, and almost mystical nature that he lamented at the time of her sudden death: "Nothing grieves me more than the fact that, even on her deathbed, I dared to kiss only her hand and not her lips." None of these persons was homosexual.[104]

Arvind Sharma underscores that Love, according to normative Hinduism, was never simply physical desire or romantic attraction. . .for it was colored by the constraints of *dharma*, use of custom especially chastity. Because action, mind and emotion converged in the final analysis, *bhakti* devotion, synthesized a variegated emotionality with yogic concentration and acts of selfless service. *Bhjakti* was expected to be directed to a husband just as a devotee worshipped his or her chosen deity with love.[105]

Buddhism.   The two major divisions of Buddhism, Mahayuana and Hinayana (the second being the name Mahayanists gave to Theravada), present two quite different attitudes toward homosexuality. In fact, even within each of these, sharp differences can be found depending on the culture in which they are expressed. In general, Buddhists recognize only two appropriate expressions of sexuality: celibacy for priests and nuns and physical expression leading to pregnancy between husbands and wives. Theravada texts, generally forbade homosexual practices, although no punishments are prescribed. On the other hand, the Mahayana tradition (found) a more permissive attitude; in the early centuries, Buddhist monks frequently had young male lovers. However, when Buddhist missionary monks took the faith to Japan, its overall message was welcomed, but its homosexual behavior was denounced as involving bad karma. In the sober insistence of this judgment (probably rising from the prevailing cultural traditions of Japan rather than original Buddhism), those who practiced their homosexuality were thought to go straight to hell.[106]

Trying to sort this out requires the recognition that as with many religions, social and cultural practices in the countries where the original faith is introduced can have a profound effect in reshaping the way the world regards the religion. This reality should not be construed to imply that Buddhism, lacking an authoritarian structure, became weak and ineffective after it is introduced in other countries. In fact, Buddhism, today the third largest religious tradition in terms of followers among the many paths of faith in the world,[107] has vigorously advocated clear ethical precepts and reciprocal relations between priests, monks, and laypersons, seeking to bring guidance and comfort to all, including those whose sexual orientation diverges from the norm.

Confucianism.   For centuries, confucianism seemed almost fixated on the proper relations between persons and sociopolitical entities. Gender segregation kept relationships within the family focused on male interactions—son to father, brother to brother, male friend to male friend—with hardly a mention of sisters or even mothers. Indeed, Confucius scolded his eldest son for grieving publicly over the death of the boy's mother. His followers were largely unconcerned with homosexuality, rather taking it for granted until encounters with the West began through travelers such as Marco Polo, Christian missionaries, and traders. Then, acknowledging that homosexual practices might undermine the "family line" and threaten the integrity of the social fabric, Confucian scholars began to inveigh against it.

Confucian judgment on homosexuality never reached the furious level of punitive action or deadly punishment exercised among the Hebrews during the same historic period. The *Analects of Confucius* clearly portray that the focus of attention for any citizen should be on the "love of learning." Even "love of wisdom, without love of learning degenerates into utter lack of principle." As to homosexuality, "love of uprightness without love of learning degenerates into harshness."[108] Scholars had little time for what they regarded as an extraneous diversion.

Judaism.   The judgment against homosexual practices in Judaism is a polar opposite to that of the three Eastern traditions we have discussed. The condemnation is unequivocal. The word *sodomy,* as a legal term, comes to us initially from the story in Genesis (19:1–28) where "the men of Sodom, both young and old," surrounded the house where Lot, the nephew of Abraham, was staying, demanding that he send his two companions (angel visitors?) out to them for the crowd's sexual pleasure. Lot pleaded with the gathering not to commit such an abomination, offering to send his daughters out instead (which raises ethical questions quite apart from the sodomy issue!). The angel visitors intervened, striking the crowd with blindness and then urging Lot to gather together his family and flee the holocaust to follow. The context of the story makes it clear that a gang rape was being threatened, and the Lord's revenge was swift and devastating.

The legal position of the ancient Hebrew culture explicitly forbids homosexual relations: "You shall not lie with a male as with a woman; it is an abomination" (Leviticus 18:22). Furthermore, it places the practice in the same category as bestiality: "You shall not lie with any beast and defile yourself with it, neither shall any woman give herself to a beast to lie with it: it is perversion" (18:23). To reinforce the seriousness of the crime, the penalty is spelled out in unequivocal terms: "If a man lies with a male as with a woman, both of them have committed an abomination; they shall be put to death." (Leviticus 20:13). The mode of death was not made explicit but was probably by stoning.

After Rome occupied the land of Israel, the Jewish authorities were denied the right to punish by death but were able to appeal, for example to Pontius Pilate's court, to carry out certain executions including crucifixions. To be sure, some Jews on rare occasions took it on themselves to stone those whom they judged to have violated sacred tradition. A noted case was that of Stephen, being stoned (not for homosexuality but) for preaching a sermon on the apostasy while reminding them of their history of violence against their own prophets including the crucifixion of God's messiah. (Acts 7).

After the slaughter of Jews in Jerusalem by the Romans in 70 C.E. and the scattering of those that survived over Europe and North Africa, we know almost nothing of the Jews' involvement against homosexuals except the Talmud's explicit prohibition of homosexual practices.

We find a concrete linkage between Jewish ethics and judgment (but not punishment) on homosexual practice in the writings of Moses Maimonides (1135–1204). Central to his concern was what he termed the five "parts" of the human soul. In his unique anatomy of the soul, he includes the nutritive, the sensitive, the representational, the arousal, and the rational.[109] The faculty of arousal is that "by which a man desires or dislikes a thing [from which] the following sorts of actions stem: inclination and avoidance, anger and gratification . . . love and hate and many other characteristics of the soul." Such arousal, augmented by what Maimonides termed imagination, as "the evil inclination," can be judged as his reason for condemning homosexuality, which interdicts procreation. Bringing forth children, he declared, is both the natural and rational purpose of all sexual activity.

Across the eight centuries since Maimonides, Orthodox Judaism has sustained the condemnation of homosexuality. The Conservative branch of Judaism, however, has modified the stringency of such judgment on the basis of recent scientific studies that suggest the condition may not be a matter of choice after all but biologically driven.[110]

The Central Conference of American Rabbis, the world's largest group of branch, the Reform "voted overwhelmingly March 29, 2000, to allow its clergy to bless gay and lesbians unions."[111] From a purely historical perspective, this shift over many centuries from condemnation to blessing must surely be one of the more dramatic in the history of religious development.

Christianity. The Christian tradition has its share of dramatic shifts, even if not as striking as the one encountered in Judaism. The apostle Paul made it clear in his letter to the church at Corinth (I Corinthians 6:9) and to followers in Rome (Romans 1:27) that those who practice homosexual behavior have no place in the kingdom of God. Instead of sentencing such participants, however, he declared that they will doubtless suffer the natural consequences in their own flesh (a probable reference to venereal disease). Jude 7 reminds the early Christians how God punished the people of Sodom for their "un-natural lusts" using the forces of nature (Genesis 19:24). In Biblical stories, nature was often God's modus operandi including the floods of Noah's time, the plagues of Egypt, the "victory" of Elijah over the priests of Baal (I Kings 18:30–39) and his ultimate vindication (I Kings 19:9–16), and the earthquake and rending of the temple veil climaxing the crucifixion (Matthew 27:51; 28:1–5). In the growing Christian communities, homosexual practices, while denounced, appear seldom to have wrought overt punishment except for the imposition of penances or excommunication. Thomas Aquinas referred to Sodomy, which he condemns as being against nature.

Among the later reformers—Luther, Calvin, Knox, and so on—the argument is more along Biblical lines than the appeals to natural law as Aquinas had employed. The medieval Inquisition, which began around 1233, brought back increasingly harsh punishments for "sinful" sexual behavior. The death penalty was more often by hanging, but burning alive became popular, drawing huge crowds. "Fagot," referring to the bundle of sticks used to light the fire around the condemned person, became a favorite epithet for those accused of homosexual behavior. Protestant tradition in the United States seldom resorted to death by burning; even the witch trials at Salem (later proved to be a ghastly miscarriage of justice) employed hanging as more "humane." In colonial New England, homosexuals were most often punished by being put in stocks for a few hours for the public's amusement and ridicule.

Protestant churches have, at least until the early twentieth century, been reluctant to discuss their stance on homosexuality except as part of larger agendas at annual meetings such as synodicals or general assemblies. Laws on the separation of church and state have prevented church bodies from erecting legal barriers to public office, employment, places of residence, and matters of immigration or civil or human rights on the basis of sexual preference. Churches have for the most part limited their denominational position on homosexuality to issues of church membership, participation in the church's official business, and, more recently, ordination as clergy and same-sex marriages.

Public policy about removing homosexuality from its roster of crimes in Western countries has developed cautiously. In 1957, a British parliamentary committee recommended that "homosexual behavior between consenting adults in private no longer be a criminal offense." After three years of debate, the motion was voted down, but passed the House of Lords in 1965 and became effective in 1967 after being approved by both houses. Change has come even more slowly in the United States, with more than half of the states during that same time maintaining antisodomy laws. Some states (e.g., Oregon) created ballot initiatives to outlaw homosexual activity and to deny homosexuals the right to public employment as recently as 1992. South Africa was the first country to ban discrimination on the basis of sexual orientation even while laws that criminalized sex between men remained on the books. This paradox was at least partially resolved when "South Africa's highest court ruled, in 1994, that men convicted of sodomy since 1994, could demand monetary damages and have their criminal records cleared."[112]

The argument over whether homosexuality may have a basis in biology continues to resurface and to provide religious groups some incentive to engage both science and politics in debate. In 1948, the famous Kinsey Report concluded that at least 10 percent of the population in the United States was either actively or casually engaged in homosexual activities. If this were the case, is not homosexuality perhaps as natural as being born left-handed (also present in about 10 percent of the population) and therefore not a matter of choice? Some researchers found problems with Kinsey's study, including the fact that 25 percent of subjects studied were in prison on sex-offense charges, and many others interviewed had been recruited from sex-oriented lecturers or houses of prostitution (none attended church).[113] Efforts to replicate the study in a number of different countries revealed that, for example, the percentage of homosexuals in France appeared to be no more than 4.1 percent of men or 2.6 percent of women; in Britain, 1.4 percent had had homosexual encounters in the previous five years; in the United States of America, 1.2 percent of both sexes had engaged in the practice during the year before the survey; in Canada, 1 percent; in Norway, 0.9 percent of each sex had such encounters within three years of the survey. In Denmark, fewer than 1 percent were exclusively homosexual.

As noted Aristotle declared that his experience with the military convinced him that the oppressive and abusive atmosphere of the home is what led young recruits to become homosexual. This insistence on parental mismanagement of a child's life leading to sexual aberration continued through Sigmund Freud in the early twentieth century. Subsequent research into brain-cell configuration by Simon LeVay on the prospect of finding "gay genes" has, as noted sparked renewed controversy.[114] Judith Herman has proposed the hypothesis that there is a positive correlation between victimization by incest and lesbianism reported by some 38 percent of lesbians interviewed.[115]

Many churches are conflicted over the rights of members to be homosexually active; the arguments range from they're not like us, so keep them away to the Bible teaches us to "welcome the stranger that is within the gates" (Leviticus 19:18; Deuteronomy 10:19; *Cf.* Matthew 25:35; Hebrews 13:1–2). Avoiding getting lost in what some regard as the mere sophistries of such argument, the Roman Catholic church follows a 2003 Vatican ruling that same–sex marriage is "deviant and immoral"—period. The United Methodists, United Presbyterians U.S.A., Southern Baptists, and others are trying to avoid destructive attitude swings while striving to retain their stance against gay marriages (and being encouraged as they observed voters in Missouri banning same-sex marriages in 2004). On the other hand, Quakers, the United Church of Christ, the Congregationalists, and Episcopalians have opened the way for homosexuals to participate fully in all church activities, even to blessing gay marriages and ordaining known homosexuals to positions of authority. Widely noted denominations are struggling with the anxiety of congregations becoming alienated from each. A major rift in the Episcopal Church in the summer of 2004 witnessed the breaking away of several congregations from the parent body because the General Convention (the church's highest lawmaking body) had consented to the election of an openly homosexual priest as bishop of New Hampshire. The seismic worldwide reverberations have shaken to its foundations the 77 million member Episcopal Church, the third largest Christian body after Roman Catholic and Eastern Orthodox churches.[116]

Islam. The second largest of all religious bodies in the world has, at the present time, no such conflict within its ranks concerning homosexual behavior.

Muslim believers are educated from earliest age that the Qur'an is the final and irrefutable authority on all matters moral and ethical and is abundantly clear on this topic. In Sura xxvi, 165f., Lut (Lot of the Genesis story, 19:1–26) responds to the proposed homosexual activities of the men of Sodom in alarm and disgust: "Of all the creatures in the world, will ye approach males, and leave those whom God has created for you to be your mates? Nay, ye are a people transgressing all limits."[117]

In conversations initiated for a series of programs on BBC World Service in 1995 and recorded in book form in 1998, John Bowker asked pointedly about the authority of the *Qur'an*, whether new interpretations are sometimes entertained, and just how Muslims should treat homosexuals. The following were the responses. First, the Qur'an is absolute but was not envisioned to legislate for all future contingencies.

"We look on the Qur'an as the word of God. But we interpret the Qur'an, and this interpretation can be dynamic and can change with circumstances." An example would be the use of capital punishment for homosexuality (as exists in the Hebrew culture). "There is no mention in the Qur'an. There is a school of law which says that since there is no mention of this punishment in the Qur'an, therefore we reject it."[118] So how should homosexuals be treated? "The punishment for homosexuals is that you bother them until they stop. You say to them, 'You silly people, you are doing a stupid thing.' If they stop, you don't touch them, don't go near them to remind them of what they did. So it's a very merciful religion, really."[119]

Let's visit again, but very briefly, the current debate on whether homosexuality is natural because apparently it is found elsewhere nature. The idea that an act or condition is necessarily good because if found in nature is refuted in countless social situations and is the basis for many human-rights initiatives. For example, there appears to be an instinct for self-preservation prejudice involving a reaction: to people don't look like us. A preemptive strike is a great temptation in this situation. Yet God who created nature reminds us that faith supercedes instincts. "Religion has been given to us to help us transcend nature."[120] In jungles or in deserts, some male animals may appear to be mutually stimulating each other sexually when in fact that is probably all that is involved. It amounts to no more than mutual masturbation, not homosexual activity.

E. IMPLICATIONS OF HOT-BUTTON ISSUES
FOR GLOBAL ETHICS

Ours is a species perpetually on the move it seems. Migrations have apparently been our characteristic since before recorded time. In most cases, the migrants influenced changes in the social, political, and religious environments they encountered. In turn, they also experienced transformations in their own social structures, folkways, and so on. From our point of interest, the religious dynamic—whether polytheistic, monotheistic, or showing no concern with deities at all—has left its mark. Newcomers frequently awakened interest in finding a common ground for creating a workable ethical system that could unite everyone in a quest for peaceful, reliable community living. In time, the hope was for such amity to become global.

All this may seem naïve and a-historical until we review the impact of the "eastern" traditions of Hinduism, Buddhism, and Confucianism on the countries in which they settled and compare them with the impact of the "western" monotheisms of Judaism, Christianity, and Islam. Furthermore, how each of these traditions was influenced by the cultures into which they moved is a consideration. As a single example, we have noted that the female circumcision ritual has often been identified as a Muslim tradition because it has been pervasive in African nations where Islam has for centuries been the dominant religion. The fact is that female circumcision was never a Muslim ritual and is nowhere found in the Qur'an. It was Muslim immigrants simply adopted this ancient tribal practice of their new locale, probably for the same reasons that migrating Christians adopted fir trees along with wassail and mistletoe from their Germanic converts to help celebrate Christmas. Ironically, the adoptions sometimes cloud the original theological importance as when yuletime revelries overshadow God's gift of the Messiah and nightly banquets obscure the daily fasting prescribed for Ramadan.

Among the more complex traditions have included the virtual enslaving of indigenous peoples by immigrants if the latter, though numerically a minority, became a ruling "majority" as conquerors. An example would be the arrival in America of Europeans in the 16th and following centuries, often reducing the native "majority" population to subservient roles. How are the "rights" of the new minority populations to be identified, and either granted or denied in the absence of prior laws to which both populations subscribe? Historically religious bodies have played a key role identified and either granted or denied in the absence of existing laws to which both populations subscribe? Historically, most such laws have been secured through religious tradition.

Still to be deciphered and resolved are those hot-button issues with which every generation must deal in relation to its own changing and evolving sociocultural contexts. Consider only recent human population increases (from 2 billion in 1900 to 6 billion in 2000) with a shrinking amount of arable land to feed them. Contemplate the effects of pumping 5 billion tons of toxic pollutants into the air, thereby depleting earth's protective layer of ozone and increasing dangerous levels of ultraviolet rays—events that now have planetwide consequences and more and more serious implications in our quest for globally relevant ethical responses.[121] We must also revisit the challenging issues of gender roles, as well as the rights of the unborn, the rights of women facing unwanted pregnancies, and the right to express one's sexual orientation. These topics are sometimes shrugged aside as parochial and of limited importance as compared with the continued ongoing crises such as crime and capital punishment and the vastly more tragic and complex disasters occurring in "acceptable" realities of war and its inevitable carnage.

NOTES

1. The Statue of Liberty, officially titled *Liberty Enlightening the World* was sculpted in 1885 by Frederic-Auguste Bartholdi, funded by contributions of the French people, and shipped to the United States in commemoration of friendship between the two countries. It was dedicated by President Grover Cleveland in 1886. The stirring words, unique in international relations, were composed by Emma Lazarus who died in 1887.

2. Jeffrey Fleishman, "Immigration and Marriage Laws Send Culturally Mixed Couples into Exile," *Los Angeles Times,* September 6, 2004, 1.

3. Ibid., A 10.

4. Ibid.

5. Samuel P. Huntington, *The Clash of Civilizations: Remaking of World Order,* (New York: Touchstone), 202.

6. Ibid., 203.

7. Unfortunately, the written language has not yet been deciphered, but its pictographs suggest a relationship with the Brahmin culture of India and the Arabian alphabet.

8. Ninian Smart, *The World's Religions* Prentice-Hall (Englewood Cliffs, NJ: Prentice-Hall, 1989) 43.

9. Robert E., Hume *The World's Living Religions* (New York: Charles Scribner's Sons,1958), 67.

10. William A, Young, *The World's Religions,* 2nd ed. (Upper Saddle River, NJ: Pearson/Prentice-Hall, 2005), 84–87.

11. Mettanando Bhikkhu, "Buddhism and AIDS: Why Is the Religion of Compassion so Quiet?" (Thesis, Buddhism and the AIDS Epidemic in Thailand, Harvard Divinity School, 2004); available at *www.nationmultimedia.com.*

12. *Mencius 3:2.9.7–7,* quoted in Hume, *op. cit.*, 113.

13. Karl Jaspers, "Confucius, The Moral-Political Ethos," *Socrates, Buddha, Confucius, Jesus* (New York: Harcourt, 1962), 45.

14. Young, *op. cit.*, 132.

15. Charles L. Manske and Daniel N. Harmelink, *World Religions Today* (Irvine, CA: Institute for World Religions, 1996), 16.

16. Jean Duvernoy, *Le Registre d'Inquisition de Jacques Fournier* Oxford, quoted in Robert B. McLaren, *Christian Ethics, Foundations and Practice* (Englewood Cliffs, NJ: Prentice-Hall, 1994), 32–33.

17. In John 11: 47ff. we read that the chief priests and Pharisees argued about what to do. This man performs many signs. If we let him go on thus everyone will believe in him and the Romans will come and destroy both our holy place and our nation." But Caiaphus retorted, "You know nothing at all; do you not understand that it is expedient for you that one man die . . . that the whole nation should not perish?" The Gospel writer makes it clear that Caiaphus was not speaking on his own authority but as a prophet of God. It appears that he had in mind already that Jesus was to fulfill the ancient role of sacrificial lamb, and this may account for an ancient tradition that Caiaphus eventually became a convert to Christianity.

18. Rodney Stark, *The Rise of Christianity* (Princeton, NJ: Princeton University Press, 1996), 4–6.

19. Manske and Harmelink, *op. cit.,* 34.

20. John L. Esposito, ed., *The Oxford History of Islam* (New York: Oxford University Press, 1999), 305.

21. Young, *op. cit.,* 219–20.

22. R.C. Zaehner, *Hindu and Muslim Mysticism* (New York: Schocken Books, 1969) 3. A case can be made that the Eastern religions are all receptive to mystic experience, as in the profound meditative states sought in Buddhism from whence comes enlightenment and understanding of the meaning of life and of our destiny. Confucianism, however, seems to have little room for such mystical incidents inasmuch as Confucius had expressed no interest in notions of mysticism, the occult, or personal deities, and he discouraged speculation.

   Confucius' concept of Heaven, (*Tien*) from which he declared the supreme moral order of the world emanates inevitably gave rise to a quest for ways to comprehend such an order and its source, however. As noted earlier, the last section of the *Analects* identifies faith in a supreme being as the path to moral and civic rectitude, and Confucius himself was eventually deified, Book XX 3.

23. The Sunni, representing about 85 percent of the Muslim world, claim to live the faith as established by Muhammed and the four caliphs who followed him in strict compliance with the Qur'an. If the Holy Book does not address a problem of personal or community life, Muslims look to the *hadith,* verbal reports of what the Prophet said or did (or proscribed). The Shi'ites declare that the first three caliphs were usurpers and only Ali, the fourth, was an authentic spokeman. After Ali's murder, his son Husain tried to carry on but was captured and executed. The proper successors to Husain who managed to gain acceptance are called *imams* and are believed to possess supernatural authority in interpreting the Qur'an. The Shi'ites are currently the largest sect in Iraq but remain only 10 to 15 percent of Muslims worldwide.

24. Albert Hourani, *A History of the Arab Peoples* (Cambridge, MA: Harvard University Press, 1991), 72.

25. Ibid., 72–73.

26. Manske and Harmelink, *op. cit.,* (B)

27. Roderick Hindery, *Comparative Ethics in Hindu and Buddhist Traditions* (Delhi: Motilal Bamarsidass, 1978).

28. Bhikkhu, *op. cit.*

29. Peter Harvey, "War and Peace," *An Introduction to Buddhist Ethics: Foundations, Values and Issues* (New York: Cambridge University Press, 2000), 263, quoted in Young, *op. cit.,* 315.

30. Ibid.

31. Amartya Sen, *Development as Freedom* (New York: Random House, 1999), 231.

32. Ibid.

33. John L Esposito, *The Oxford History of Islam* (Oxford, England: Oxford University Press, 1999), 41.

34. A single case that has its parallels not only in the United States but in numerous European countries involves the U.S. Census Bureau's announcement that whites are no longer a majority in once all-white Orange County, California, where steady growth in Asian and Latino populations has dramatically changed the once homogenous suburban landscape. Growth in the Asian population in prosperous Irvine increased 167 percent in a decade. "All the ripple effects—such as housing, education and economic development—need to be mitigated in a way that prepares these counties to absorb newcomers in a positive way." Seema Mehta and Jennifer Mena, "O.C. Whites a Majority No Longer," *Los Angeles Times,* September 30, 2004, B1, B6.

35. Philosophers from Aristotle to Hume and Kant have argued that one cannot reason from "is" to "ought," so even if one can assert that God *is,* "the fact that there exists a God who is absolute perfection does not by itself imply that there are obligations." In the polytheistic traditions, values of the gods are really the projection of particular human values. "The monotheistic God is the integration of all values (including personhood), hence there is no ambiguity in what that God requires." We are, according to Scripture, created "in God's image"; "He is holy, so be ye holy, as He is merciful, so be ye merciful." "The principle that God's transcendence in perfection, call upon us to perfect the principles in ourselves by way of *emulatio Dei,* are those which are perfections in us, that is, the human virtues." *Cf.* Lenn Evan Goodman, *Monotheism* (Oxford: Osmun Publishers, 1981), 82, 88.

36. Ibid., 89.

37. "The possession of all things in common is said to be the natural law," Thomas Aquinas, *Summa Theologica,* Part I of Second Part Q 94, Great Books of the Western World, vol. 2 (Chicago: Encyclopedia Britannica, 1952), 225.

38. Jacques Ellul, *The Subversion of Christianity,* trans. Geoffrey Bromily (Grand Rapids, MI: 1986), 13.

39. Young, World Religions, *op. cit.,* 218.

40. Ibid., 220.

41. Harold Schilling, William A. Young, *World Religions* 1st edition, 1995, ibid 24.

42. Larry Rasmussen, *Earth Community, Earth Ethics* (Maryknoll, NY: Orbis Books, 1996).

43. James Ridgeway, *The Politics of Ecology* (New York: E.P. Dutton, l971), 29.

44. Daniel Maguire cited in Rasmussen, *op. cit.,* 10.

45. Al Gore, *Earth in the Balance* (New York: Penguin Books, l993), 242–48, 258–62.

46. Young, *op. cit.,* 435.

47. Rasmussen, *op. cit.,* 198.

48. H. H. The Dalai Lama, *Ethics for the New Millennium* (New York: Penguin Putman Books, l999), 223.

49. Ibid., 198.

50. Huston, Smith *The World's Religions* (San Francisco: Harpers 1991), 166.

51. Yi-pao Mei, *Motse, The Neglected Rival of Confucius* (Westport CT: Hyperion Press, 1973), 80f.

52. Smith, Huston, *op. cit.,* 184.

53. The words in Proverbs seem even more harsh than the modified translation, "Spare the rod and spoil the child." A more direct translation of Proverbs 13:24 reads: "He who spares the rod hates his son." The Hebrew the word for *rod* is *shebet,* which refers to the rod of the shepherd. In point of fact, the rod was never used to beat or punish the sheep but to guide and comfort them; the 23rd Psalm provides "Thy rod and thy staff, they comfort me." If a man failed to provide guidance and comfort, he must indeed hate his child, not showing the love the child needs and deserves as a child of God. This is probably the most often misquoted passage in Hebrew scripture, sometimes cited as justification for what amounts to child abuse.

54. Hans Kung, *Christianity and the World Religions* (New York: Doubleday, l986), 206.

55. Ibid.

56. Matthew Fox, *The Coming of the Cosmic Christ* (San Francisco: Harper & Row, 1988), 63.

57. John Polkinghorne, *The Faith of a Physicist* (Princeton, NJ: Princeton University Press, 1994), 87.

58. A. Yusuf Ali, *The Holy Qur'an,* 638–39.

59. Ibid., 639.

60. Iqtidar H. Zaidi, "On the Ethics of Man's Interaction with the Environment: an Islamic Approach," *Religion and Environmental Crisis* cited in Young, William A. *The World's Religions,* 2nd ed., 2005, 292.

61. Roderick Hindery, *op. cit.,* 266. It is of special interest that the Buddhist tradition took a very different stance.

62. Ibid., 243. This development evolved over a long period until it became a fixture of the cult of Amida Buddha, which had its genesis in northwest India; its substance is reported in *The Lotus Sutra,* c. 1st and 2nd centuries c.e.

63. Nancy Schuster Barnes, "Women in Early Indian Buddhism," *Women in World Religions,* ed. Arvind Sharma (New York: State University of New York Press, 1987), 108.

64. Smith, *op cit.,* 189.

65. Richard Guisso, "Thunder over the Lake: The Five Classics and the Perception of Women in Early China," cited in *Women in World Religions,* Arvind Sharma, editor *op. cit.,* 135.

66. Theresa Kelleher, "Confucianism," *Women in World Religions, op. cit.*

67. Kelleher, Ibid., 159.

68. Smith, Huston, *op. cit.,* 193.

69. Tragically, with a sweeping victory for the Communist regime in China in 1948 and a zeal for stifling all dissent, detention and execution for "subversive activities" were common. Appeals to religious sensibilities were denounced, so that Confucianism, Buddhism, and Taoism were equally ostracized. *Cf.* Ben Cowles, Thomson, *Through the Dragon's Mouth* (Santa Barbara, CA: Fithian Press, 1999), 288–91.

70. Denise L. Carmody, "Judaism," in *Women in World Religions, op. cit.,* 185.

71. Ibid., 195.

72. Ibid., 200.

73. "The other" Mary is unidentified in Matthew 28:1 where she first is mentioned but is possibly the mother of James, as suggested in Luke 24:10.

74. *Cf.* Meyer Waxman, *Judaism, Religion and Ethics* (New York, London: Thomas Yoseloff, 1967), 120.

75. Padraic O'Hare, "To Each (Her) Due," *Women and Religion,* ed. Regina Coll Mahwah (NJ: Paulist Press, 1982), 16.

76. Theo van Gogh, a descendant of the famous nineteenth century painter Vincent van Gogh, had been threatened many times for his outspoken views on women's rights and for filming of stories of incest, rapes, beating, and forced marriages in Muslim societies. The murder is under investigation as this being written. *Cf.* Sebastian Rotella and Douglas Heingarten, *Los Angeles Times,* November, 2004, A3.

77. *The Holy Qur'an, op. cit.,* xxiv 31–32

78. Smith, *The World's Religions* Harper San Francisco 1991, *op. cit.* P. 270

79. John C, Raines and Daniel C Maguire, *What Men Owe to Women* (New York: State University of New York Press, 2001), 22–23. *Cf.* Julius Lipner, "The Classical View on Abortion," *Hindu Ethics: Purity, Abortion and Euthanasia,*" ed. Harold Coward (New York: State University of New York Press, 1989), 41–70; cited in Young, William, *World Religions, op. cit.,* 346.

80. Ibid.

81. Swami Ramsukhdas, *How to Lead a Household Life* (Gorakhpur, India: Gita Press, 1994), 56. Cited in Raines and Maguire, *op. cit.*

82. Hans Kung, *Christianity and the World Religions* (Garden City, NJ: Doubleday, 1986), 30.

83. Raines and Maguire, *op. cit.,* 221.

84. H. H. The Dalai Lama, *op. cit.,* 123–24ff.

85. Arvind Sharma, ed., quoting Cheng I, in *op. cit.,* 155.

86. McLaren, *op. cit.,* 138f.

87. In *De Audacities X11,* Tertullian declared idolatry, adultery, and homicide as irremissible sins based, he declared in Acts 15:20. The writer of Acts, however, did not make them irremissible; he simply urged converts to Christianity to refrain from them. Tertullian was thus misconstruing scripture to fit his overly harsh judgment in a manner reminiscent of the Pharisees whom Jesus denounced for their harshness and rigidity.

88. The popularity of natural law as a frame of reference goes back at least to Aristotle and figures prominently in both Roman Catholicism and Protestantism. Robin Gill Edinburgh, Scotland has noted this with some misgivings pointing out that even if it could be established that procreation is the obvious primary function of sexuality, "it is far from clear that it should be the only or indispensable function. To derive an exclusive moral prescription from an empirical observation of function was to commit an extraordinary category error." As an example, one might argue that a rapist had no intention of achieving procreation, so aborting the dreaded, unwanted pregnancy might provide the only viable solution. *Cf.* Robin Gill, *A Textbook of Christian Ethics* (Edinburgh, Scotland: T & T Clark, 1985), 456.

89. Karl Barth, "The Protection of Life," quoted in *Abortion: The Moral Issues* (New York: Pilgrim Press, 1982), 94.

90. Daniel Callahan, "The Roman Catholic Position," *Abortion: The Moral Issues, op. cit.,* 63–68.

91. James W. Gustafson, "A Protestant Ethical Approach," *Abortion, The Moral Issues, op. cit.,* 191–209.

92. Brad Stetson, "A Choice That Defines Our Humanity," *Los Angeles Times,* January 22, 2001,

93. Barth, *op. cit.,* 95.

94. Mead, "Rights to Life" *ibid.,* p. 12.

95. As of this writing, the U.S.'s war on Iraq had killed 1,00,000 people while the current wars in Africa have left over a million dead. *Cf. Los Angeles Times,* October 29, 2004, and November 7, 2004, respectively.

96. John Bowker, *What Muslims Believe* (Oxford England: One World, 1998), 50.

97. Abdulaziz Abdulhussein Sachedina, *The Just Ruler* (New York: Oxford University Press, 1988), 125.

98. Ibid., 130.

99. Sigmund Freud, quoted in James W. Vander Zanden, *Human Development,* 7th ed. (New York: McGraw-Hill, 2000), 434.

100. Luella Cole, *Psychology of Adolescence* (New York: Farrar & Rinehart, 1936), 13.

101. Clara Shaw Schuster and Shirley Smith Ashburn *The Process of Human Development* (Philadelphia: J.B. Lippincott, 1992), 306.

102. David Gelman with Donna Foote, "Born or Bred?" *Newsweek,* February 24, 1992, 46–53.

103. Gilbert Herdt, "Homosexuality," *Encyclopedia of Religion,* vol. 6 (New York: Macmillan, 1987), 450.

104. In the art world recently there has been discussion that Michelangelo's bachelor status might have meant that he was homosexual. This author had the opportunity to meet and spend some time with Irving Stone shortly before his death. Author of the, *The Agony and the Ecstasy*, historical biography on Michelangelo, Stone declared there was "absolutely no evidence to substantiate such a rumor."

105. Sharma, Arvind, *Women in World Religions,* New York: State University of New York Press, 1987, *op. cit.,* 76

106. Peter Harvey, "Sexual Equality," *An Introduction to Buddhist Ethics* (Cambridge, England: Cambridge University Press 2000), 428; cited in Young, The World's Religions, *op. cit.,* 370.

107. As of 2000, the number of members placed *Christianity* first with 2,130 billion; Islam second with 1,033 billion; Hinduism third with 764 million, and Buddhism fourth with 359 million. *Cf.* Manske, Charles L., and Harmelink, Daniel N., *World Religions op. cit.*

108. Arthur Waley, trans. *The Analects of Confucius* (New York: Vintage Books/ Random House, 1938), 211f.

109. Lenn Evan Goodman, *Rambam: Readings in the Philosophy of Moses Maimonides* (New York: Viking Press, 1976), 221f.

110. Chandler Burr "Homosexuality and Biology," *The Atlantic Monthly,* 1993, 47f. *Cf.* William Byne "The Biological Evidence Challenged," *Scientific American,* May 1994, 50f.

111. "Reform Rabbis Affirm Same-Sex Unions," *Christian Century*, April 19–26, 2000, 451.

112. *Los Angeles Times*, October 10, 1998, A3.

113. J. Gordon Muir, "Homosexuals and the 10% Fallacy," *Los Angeles Times,* March 31, 1993.

114. Simon LeVay and Dean H. Hamer, "Evidence for a Biological Influence in Male Homosexuality," *Scientific American*, May 1994, 44f.

115. Judith Lewis Herman, *Father-Daughter Incest* (Cambridge: Harvard University Press, 1981), 104–5. The author of this text is indebted to a former student, Lori Keller, for an outstanding research paper on the topic Lesbianism and Incest at California State University, Fullerton, in 1986.

116. Larry B. Stammer "A New Day for Congregations," *Los Angeles Times,* August 23, 2004, B7.

117. Ali, A. Yusuf, *The Holy Qur'an,* Text, Translation and Commentary, *op. cit.,* 966f.

118. Bowker, *op. cit.,* 33–34, 50.

119. Ibid., 54.

120. Ibid., 52.

121. Gerald O. Barney with Jane Blewett and Kristen R. Barney, *Global 2000 Revisited* Arlington, VA: Millennium Institute, 36. *Cf. The Infinite Voyage*, WQED/Pittsburgh in association with The National Academy of Sciences.

CHAPTER 8

Religion, Morality and The Culture of Violence

History is little else than a picture of human crimes and misfortunes.

—Voltaire

Voltaire's observation noted above implicated not only individuals or groups but the entire human race in the depravity, atrocities, and recidivisms of our culture. Despite his confirmed agnosticism, he echoed the judgment of Hebrew scripture: "The heart is deceitful above all things, and desperately corrupt" (Jeremiah 17:9).

We have become painfully familiar with the violence, horrors, and mounting death tolls from warfare, crime, disease, and starvation during the past century. Add to this domestic violence and millions of people worldwide infected with deadly HIV and AIDS via exploitive and/or irresponsible sexual activity as well as innocent transfer. Robert McAfee Brown points out that the root of the term violence is the Latin *violare,* which includes abuse, in any form, of human rights (i.e., using, abusing, or depersonalizing other persons and thus reducing them to "things"[1]). In accepting such a definition, one must also include as violence or abuse the denial of health care and a decent standard of living to employees. Denials of resources such as food, shelter, and clean water render millions (especially in undeveloped countries) incapable of providing for their families. Students of warfare can attest to how tragedies in Africa, Asia, South America, and elsewhere have led to exasperation, revolt, and finally genocide on massive scales.

The mind-numbing litany of conditions that cripple human society as noted, has often led to hopelessness and the temptation either to give up in despair or resort to anarchy and economic exploitation. On noteworthy occasions, however, social and religious movements have succeeded in encouraging a turn to more creative efforts through benevolent giving, political reform, the arts, technical skills, and the sciences. Certainly many of the leading religions of the world have been founded in just such exigencies, and have responded impressively to minister to human need. However, before we arouse the rebuttal that we are evading an honest acknowledgement of the destructive conditions that have made ours a culture of violence, we must further examine certain underlying causes.

242

Dehumanizing people by name calling ("they're nothing but animals, cockroaches, vermin to be exterminated") is a familiar military tactic when sending soldiers into battle. It leads to the mentality that "they deserve what they get". When military incursions succeed, the victors are tempted to extend their prowess to enslavement and even to slaughter as recent developments in the Sudan and other African nations testify. Dehumanization is designed to blunt any humane consideration in confronting the enemy. International relations are rife with demeaning epithets, as the Ayatollah Khomeini's description of America as the "Great Satan" for its alleged trafficking in drugs, gambling, alcohol, and exporting of pornography via magazines, movies, and the Internet. Verbal retaliation has expressed itself in the broad-brush tactic of labeling as terrorists all who first used such epithets and then backed up their rage with armed strategies. Especially enraging to many Arabic leaders is the U.S. multibillion dollar support for Israel, even permitting Israelis to develop nuclear weapons while denying such weapons to Iran, Iraq, and so on. The United States is not innocent in this: President Ronald Reagan branded Russia the "evil empire," and President G.W. Bush charged Iran, Iraq, and North Korea with being the "axis of evil."

Without justifying such behavior on either side of the conflict, sociobiologist E.O.Wilson has long held that antisocial acts, especially the most violent ones, have been part of the evolutionary process in which sheer survival of the species made some violent action requisite.

> Human nature is a hodgepodge of special genetic adaptations to an environment largely vanished. . . . We are forced to choose among the elements of human nature by reference to value systems which these same elements created in an evolutionary age now long vanished.[2]

Half a century ago, philosopher Will Durant put this even more succinctly: "Every vice was once a virtue, necessary in the struggle for existence."[3] Durant was more explicit, too, in locating the root of violence in greed. The acquisition of both greed and violence were useful so that "not all our laws, our education, our morals and our religion can quite stamp them out."[4]

Durant's acknowledgement is by no means the end of the story. "To transmute greed into thrift, violence into argument, murder into litigation and suicide into philosophy has been part of the task of civilization."[5] The task is made more difficult by the apparent public zest for media portrayals of irresponsible sex, horror, and violence that a certain segment is happy to provide including actual murders in what Kerekkes and Slater term "snuff" films, or "the marketing of outrage."[6]

It would be absurd, to be sure, to lay all the blame for a violent culture on a modicum of media distortions. Other issues must be studied if we are to understand global attitudes toward what has been dubbed by cultural analyst George Wesigel "a spiritual malaise infecting our way of life." These issues would include public attitudes toward the death penalty, the atmosphere of international conflicts leading to the acceptance of a war mentality, and a persistent apathy to massive deforestation and other environmental disruptions that amount almost to a war against the planet. Nevertheless, we cannot be naïve, and overlook research such as a seventeen-year study of some 700 adolescents that revealed that aggressive behavior among those who watched movie and TV violence was ten times higher than for nonviewers. Such studies have rung law enforcement alarms nationwide.[7] The callous rubric often quoted by first-time killers, that the person deserved to die, is a familiar justification on the grounds that the victim was a wretched miscreant who just got what was coming to her or him. The victim might be a physician who performed abortions; a prisoner arrested as a possible spy but denied legal counsel or even a formal charge; a person of a racial, religious, or political status without whom society was better off. Meanwhile, child abuse, domestic violence, road rage, and environmental and economic exploitation all contribute to the culture of turbulence and disorder.

A. DEATH AS ENTERTAINMENT: FREEDOM AND RESPONSIBILITY

As suggested, one of the more obvious, albeit superficial, ways to measure a society's moral stature is through its people's favorite entertainment. Many people appear to relish acts of violence, especially if they believe that they serve justice. An ancient writer of Psalms, still writhing with the memory of his people being taken into slavery, exulted in the prospect of bloody revenge: "O daughter of Babylon, you devastator! Happy shall he be who takes your little ones and dashes them against the rock" (Psalm 137: 8–9).

The entertainment aspect of witnessing and then participating in such vengeful acts can be contagious, whether stimulated by historic grievances (as in family feuds, clan warfare, or international conflicts) or even by sheer fiction as in novels that identify a villain and skillfully presents the person's reasons for revenge. Theater audiences enjoy being stimulated to the point of horror and wrath. Hebrew scriptures abound in historic and legendary tales of slaughter launched from out-of-control rage against enemies that kept the fires endlessly rekindled. We may recall how the Israelites, on the assumption that God had given the land of Canaan to them, invaded and slew ten thousand men, capturing the enemy king (Adoni-bezek) and amputating his thumbs and great toes. (Judges 1:4–7) The bloody exploits of Joshua, the flourishes of Sampson ("With the jawbone an ass have I slain a thousand men," Judges 15:16), and David's exploits celebrated in songs and dances ("Saul has slain his thousands, and David his ten thousands," I Samuel 21:10–11) the boasts are passed along from one generation to the next.

Meanwhile, the Hindu Katha Upanishad reminds the faithful that for a Kshatriya warrior, nothing is better than a lawful fight, however bloody (2: 19–25). In the dramatic poem Bhagavad Gita, a Hindu knight, Arjuna, asks the Lord Krishna about the propriety of killing people, even in war (since the enemies in this case were mostly his own relatives). The answer comes via his charioteer that the souls of those slain will achieve special Kharma, so he need not worry. Besides, abandoning his duty as a warrior would make him guilty of a crime (2: 31–33). We will return to a more orderly treatment of religious traditions presently, but first note some more secular sources.

History is replete with bloody tales of punishment and revenge were popular themes for entertainment including Homer's *Iliad* and *Odyssey* (which Plato argued should be censored lest they lead the youth into irrational actions). Recall the raucous enthusiasm of crowds that filled the Coliseum in Rome who signaled the death of fallen gladiators with the infamous thumbs down. Consider also the gesture crowds that gathered to witness the unknown number of executions that Rome inflicted on malefactors (beheadings were reserved for the upper classes, and stoning and crucifixion were most frequently used for lower class criminals). At the time of Sparticus' leading a massive slave revolt (c. 72 B.C.), the combined forces of Crassus and Pompey captured thousands of his followers. Six thousands of them were crucified along the road to Rome, taunted and pelted with rocks by surging crowds. The crucifixion of Jesus was by no means an obscure event but part of a massive wave of sadism and cruelty.

We have ample evidence of the human appetite for violence in the early days of 'the common era' after the death of Christ (A.D), not least of which is found in the highly entertaining sagas of Beowulf's bloody battle with the monster Grendel and of King Arthur's noble dream of Camelot being shattered by Lancelot's reported adultery and Mordred's savagery. Tales of Kings Alfred, Charlemagne, Roland, and Robin Hood can hardly be faulted for being enjoyed; there was a theme of nobility, and even chivalry ran through these stories that minstrels and troubadours sang about. The Age of Chivalry appears to have been largely mythical, however, as the large number of executions of heretics, common criminals, or agitators for civil or religious reform attest. These executions became increasingly sadistic from stoning, hanging, burning, and strangling to ever more brutal forms of torture prior to the actual execution. Usually reserved for treason, the barbaric punishments that stretched a man on a wrack, disemboweled him, branded him with hot irons, and blinded and sometimes impaled him provide vivid justification for this section title, Death as Entertainment. One can move quickly to the howling crowds during the French Revolution's Reign of Terror to the almost carnival atmosphere of lynch mobs in some U.S. states that celebrated the deaths and as recently as the early twentieth century photographed them for use in picture postcards to send to friends and relations to "commemorate" the event.

We should not neglect the fact that voices of dissent were raised, in response to these events and religious groups such as the Quakers and Puritans published their opposition to the death penalty. Benjamin Franklin, like his French counterparts Voltaire and Montesquieu and the Italian Cesare Beccaria, sought to have them abolished with marginal success. It required two centuries for England to move from maintaining several hundred capital offences to disestablishing the death penalty in the early twentieth century. By the 1970s, it had been abolished in Austria, Brazil, Denmark, Portugal, Switzerland, Venezuela, and some U.S. states. At this writing, only the United States among major Western nations has retained the death penalty.

Even in the absence of executions, however, death continues to be a preoccupation of much of the entertainment industry around the world. Enthusiasm for tales of murders, both real and fictional, in theaters, books, radio, films and television and DVDs, is growing, having become the major means of creating powerful images of life and of death in all its forms. Among other incentives, there is money to be made. The *Los Angeles Times* published "Horror returns to make a killing" (in a January 30, 2005). Chris Lee, author of the article, underscored the popularity of low-budget but high-grossing box office triumphs such as *The Exorcist, The Chainsaw Massacre, Night of the Living Dead,* reminiscent of earlier days when *Dracula, Frankenstein, Phantom of the Opera* (in one of several remakes) appeared. A *Times* editorialist, Lee wrote, "Human nature is such that you don't turn away from horrific images. You go to the theater to be scared." The apparent reason for the availability of such films is the disproportionate cost-to-profit factor. The 2004 horror movie "The Saw" cost $1.2 million to produce but had grossed $55 million by February 2005; "The Grudge" cost $10 million but garnered $110 million.

A brief tracing of theater's evolution from stage to film may put some of this in perspective.

The origin of theater per se is not clear, but religious festivals were at its roots. In ancient Mesopotamia (c. 3,000 B.C.E.), they appear to have included recitations and enactments of folk lore and heroic exploits while preserving the most dramatic ones in ritual dance.[8] Pyramid texts found on the interior walls of Egypt's burial sites dating from the fifth dynasty (c. 2494–2345 B.C.E.) depict priests wearing animal masks and apparently performing ceremonial pageantry of historical importance. Greek drama is thought to have originated in the great Dionysia festival at Athens (c. 500 B.C.E.), which was specifically a religious event although modern critics concerned about censorship might respond negatively to its production due to fact that the nature god Dionysus was associated with sex, intoxication, and revelry. From this experience three of the greatest Greek writers of tragedy emerged: Aeschylus, Sophocles, and Euripides. A profound sense of the moral implications of a ruler's misbehavior emerged in Sophocles' *Oedipus Rex* in which the protagonist must die on behalf of his people. From this period of tragic drama arose writers of comedy; Aristophenes ridiculed the notion that the missteps of men and gods have any real importance in the cosmic scheme of things.

Out of the tug of war between comedy and tragedy came the first serious move toward censorship. As noted earlier, while he believed fervently in freedom, Plato wrote that it must be tempered by responsibility. Dramatists and producers, he insisted, must be guided by a more responsible attitude toward the moral influence of these entertainments, especially on the young. For the first time, artistic freedom and social responsibility took center stage in public forum, yet little came of it. As Thomas Gibb noted, "Great periods of achievement in theater have tended to coincide with periods of national achievement. Conversely, periods of excessive materialism such as those of the decay of ancient Greece and Rome tend to produce theater in which ostentation, spectacle, and vulgarity predominate."[9]

It is significant for subsequent generations that Plato's advocacy of censorship writers "will be forbidden to express ideas hurtful to public morals and piety"[10] observed even though not formally mandated. Graphic features such as stabbings, deadly conflict, and overly sensual displays were restricted to action "off-stage" (*obscena* from which we derive the word "obscene"). Clytemnestra's killing of Cassandra in Aeschylus' drama *Oresteia* took place off stage and was probably made more dramatic unseen than if acted out on stage (but also less conducive to imitation by impressionable youth).[11] This form of self-regulation by the producers of theatrical works became a separate entity from athletic games. It was carried as far into the future as Shakespeare, for whom the killing of Macbeth was off stage lest it be "beyond toleration and decency."

Meanwhile, as the Romans transformed gladiatorial games from athletic contests into blood sports, violence became an integral part of public entertainment. Boxing, wrestling, and bullfights were included with other sports. Spectators in the Coliseum, not unlike those who frequent boxing matches and car races today, responded with gusto when a knockout or chariot accident was sufficiently dramatic. It was common for a hapless slave to be matched in hand-to-hand combat against a seasoned gladiator. When the slave faltered and was seriously wounded, the shouting crowd would almost routinely give the thumbs-down sign to the winner to dispatch his opponent there on the sand. Within a generation, the crowds grew increasingly insistent in their demand for bloody action. In the second century B.C.E. in celebration of Trajan's military prowess, 5,000 pairs of gladiators fought in an exhibition lasting one hundred days with uncounted men slain (although on one occasion, 2000 gladiators and 230 wild animals were actually "billed to die"). This was indeed death as entertainment, and such exhibitions ceased only after Constantine embraced Christianity and in 325 outlawed all gladiatorial contests.[12]

In the new era of Rome with violence eliminated from arenas after having largely supplanted legitimate theater, houses for live drama began to spring up all over Italy, Spain, and France and in their colonies in North Africa. Their productions, however, were not noticeably ennobled by Christian restrictions against mayhem. "Their staple fare was bawdy and obscene mimes, and farces dealing mainly with drunkenness, greed, adultery and horseplay, or at best acrobatic spectacles featuring scantily clad dancers. Actors who had once been citizens of good repute were no longer esteemed."[13] For the new breed of citizen after Constantine, telling tales and legends in public gatherings reflected the practice of reciting Homer's *Iliad* and *Odyssey*. There were stories of valor and heroic sagas satisfied the never fully concealed zest for deadly conflict. These public tale recitations were of crucial importance in shaping the values of generations of youth . It is impossible to know where actual historical people and romanticized figures of fantasy meld, yet it can be argued that their stories whether told, pantomimed, or staged, lifted generations of youth (and countless elders) out of the drudgery of a harsh life.

Ironically, theater, which had been cast in a dark manner by the early church fathers, became once again a place of spiritual inspiration.

> Just as Greek drama developed from the worship of Dionysus, so medieval liturgical drama developed from the Christian liturgy, and there was a clear progression from a simple act of faith in a ritual setting, to a full scale pageant on the life of Christ.[14]

This has continued to our own time in pageants such as the centuries-old Oberammergau festival in Bavaria and in motion pictures such as *The Passion of Christ* in 2004 by Mel Gibson.

The alleged implications of the motion picture industry in stimulating and encouraging violence could engage another whole chapter. It is clear, however, that just as theater was once cast in a dark manner by the Christian church, so the modern cinema came under serious scrutiny quite early because of almost two decades of gangster films and their often bawdy, seminude sequences that even vaudeville (which was being eclipsed by silent movies) would not display. This scrutiny by social and religious groups (moral watch-dogs) came at a time when prohibition, speakeasies, and alleged gangster takeovers of whole cities' political structure were front-page news daily.

According to many historians of the movie industry, a move toward censorship was already in motion as the result of the violent reaction of audiences across the country to one particular film, D.W. Griffith's *The Birth of a Nation*. The film was first shown on February 8, 1915, in Los Angeles under the title *The Clansman*. "No other single picture has had as great an impact on the art of film making or on American society."[15] The first half of the film is a conventional documentary on the Civil War, but the second half moves to the Reconstruction period during which black people, liberated from slavery, try to assert their newfound identity by securing political authority to dominate the government of South Carolina. Despite the effort to depict this as "Civilization [being] saved, and the South redeemed from shame" in the words of Griffith's script, the film portrayed the black people as uneducated dregs, casting lustful eyes on white women. The Ku Klux Klan is portrayed as rescuing the women and restoring order. Audiences, both in the north and south, were so enraged that in some cities police had to be enlisted to quell riots. *The Birth of a Nation* was banned more often than any other film in motion picture history. In ruling to allow censorship, the Supreme Court decreed that the issue was not one of free speech. The movie industry is "a business, pure and simple . . . conducted for profit . . . capable of evil, and not entitled to constitutional guarantees of freedom of speech."[16]

Other movies began to be scrutinized, two in particular, *The James Boys* and *Night Riders*, by the Illinois Supreme Court. Acknowledging that while they depicted persons and actions connected with the history of the country, the court ruled, "It does not follow that they are not immoral, depicting exhibitions of crime, malicious mischief, arson and murder."[17]

At the height of agitation by civic, religious, and educational lobbying groups that urged government regulation of the content of films, Will Hayes, a lawyer and prominent political figure (chairman of the Republican National Committee, 1918 and a Presbyterian elder), stepped forward with an alternate plan. He became active in the newly forming Motion Picture Producers and Distributors of America in Hollywood. He was elected its president in 1922 and immediately began self-regulatory reforms in the industry by which studio executives would counsel each other on what constituted decent, uplifting fare. The plan was so successful that it warded off government censorship. Hayes went to the extent of inserting morals clauses into actors' contracts.[18] In 1930, he was one of the authors of the Production Code, which detailed what was morally acceptable and remained the standard for all Hollywood films until 1966. Out of the Hayes Office era came the "golden age" of Hollywood productions such as Cecil B. DeMille's *King of Kings* and *Ben Hur;* a spate of musical extravaganzas from the compositions of Victor Herbert, Sigmund Romberg, Rudolf Friml, and George Gershwin as well as *Fantasia, Oklahoma!* and *The Wizard of Oz* and romantic spectaculars including *Robin Hood* and *Gone with the Wind*. The list seems inexhaustible, and DeMille sought to educate the public not only to attend films to enjoy but also to embrace plots that went beyond sex and violence. This appears in what seems to have been an intended ecumenism. The *King of Kings* inaugurated a shooting schedule "participated in by representatives of the Protestant, Catholic, Jewish, Buddhist and Moslem faiths."[19] Certainly deaths occurred in the story lines of many such productions but were more often the occasion for sharing grief, insight, courage, and even nobility of character, not in themselves than for a preoccupation for entertainment's sake.

One hears a great deal of argument about whether movies and television have a direct, causal effect on the sexual and violent expressions of children and youth. Indeed, as noted, parental as well as public concern has existed since radio, movies, television, and methods to record music came on the scene. The trio of primary formative institutions, family, school, and church has been replaced by the media in a great many families. Yale University's Family Television Research Center published the following structure of the typical child's day:

> The child wakes up, immediately turns on the [TV] set, goes to school, comes home and turns on the set again. Next the family eats dinner with the set on. All watch television together until relatively late at night. There is little verbal exchange among family members until the child is put (or sent) to bed with no quiet time (for shared conversation, hopes, affection).[20]

Meanwhile, "it is now the official position of the American Psychological Association—supported by scores of studies—that viewing TV violence has a *causal* effect on aggression in both children and teens."[21] Such a seeming generalization takes on urgent meaning when we hear a news report about a five-year-old boy taken to see *Nightmare on Elm Street* who talks incessantly about the gory exploits of the key figure and the stabbing of a two-year-old girl seventeen times with a kitchen knife.[22]

Is court action leading to censorship the answer to the anxious question of whether anything can be done? Few today would urge a return to Plato's insistence on state-sponsored censorship. Would a return to having the entertainment producers (and now commercial sponsors as well) take responsibility for policing themselves as the Hayes' Office of the 1920s–60s be effective? Child developmentalist Thomas Licona's suggestions deserve considerable attention:

A. *Set a good example;* research shows that parents who watch little television and few movies tend to have children who watch little.

B. *Require children to ask permission.* Watching TV is a privilege, not a right; this is an essential element in establishing parental supervision.

C. *Regulate what children watch.* "We don't let you put trash in your stomach; we don't want you to put trash in your mind." Parents must take a stand for the values they hold.

D. *Reduce the number of hours the TV set is on.* Designate "quiet time," including one or two nights weekly when the TV set is off. Some schools have sponsored "No TV for a week" (or even a month) and found that grades improve.

E. *Make TV a special event,* rather than a pointless routine, "a mindless habit."[23]

Our ancestors east and west told stories like many in the Hebrew Bible. The Bhagavad Gita (with its graphic portrayals of war, disembowelings, and eating the enemy's vitals on the fields of Kurukseta) held listeners in rapt attention. In many cases, the dramas caused them to model their lives after violent figures. Many researchers believe that violent characters portrayed in today's books, plays, films, and video games prompt imitation. A major problem, as Licona expresses it, is a combination of parental "absence" in guidance and the fact that "network television is accountable to no one but its sponsors; cable TV to no one but its paying customers. Neither is accountable to any standards of social responsibility."[24] These factors result in a lowering of ethical expectations and an alarming increase in domestic unraveling and violence in our homes, on the streets, and even in halls of political power where preemptive wars are planned.

To a former Air Force colonel, it seems that even torture of foreign suspects in U.S. prisons, which would have shocked earlier generations, is now all but condoned.[25] These victims are not entitled to protection granted under the Geneva Convention according to the U.S. State Department despite the country's revered slogan that "all men are created equal" and merit equal treatment. Furthermore, U.S. soldiers captured and tortured in Iraq were not qualified for financial reparations, despite the Anti-Terrorism Act of 1996, which authorizes "money damages against a foreign state for personal injury or death caused by an act of torture." The reason, it was explained, is that even a modest amount of money as was requested was needed to rebuild Iraq. Our culture of violence, which is thought to be reflected in virtually all nations to a greater or lesser degree, appears sometimes to trump civility.[26]

B.   THE DEATH PENALTY: A DEAD END?

Most of the major religions base their ideas of punishment on the ground that when evil is done, usually in violation of some transcendent thou shalt not, it must be addressed, and the perpetrator brought to justice. The dominant Asian religions have no single position to which one could point as characteristic of any of the traditions in relation to capital punishment. However, the principle of *ahimsa* or nonviolence operates in Hinduism, Buddhism, and Jainism to a greater or lesser degree to eliminate or at least express general opposition to state-sponsored executions.

1.   Asian Traditions

Hinduism declares that all pain and suffering derive from evil doings and that Heaven, rather than the state, can be relied upon to punish evil (Bhagavad Gita: 7.15). The term *karma-marga* describes a position (rather than a dogma) of salvation by works. That is, redemption from death depends on what one has done, not solely by what one knows or believes. If a person does evil things, punishment belongs to heaven, not to earthly powers; *ahimsa,* "not killing" reminds us that all life—not only human life—is sacred, extending to animals and all other living things. On the basis of this tenet, even environmental preservation is a sacred duty. Because of the multiplicity of social levels (despite the fact that the caste system is legally prohibited), these positions or standards are observed with varying degrees of enforcement.

Buddhism for the most part avoids confronting evil head on by affirming that punishment of some kind awaits the evil doer. The latter, nevertheless, can redeem himself or herself with good actions (Mahavagga 6.31.7). Buddhism tends to more rigorously observe *ahimsa* than in Hinduism, which is why one finds more vigorous opposition in Buddhism to capital punishment. The law of kharma-marga is also more strictly interpreted in Buddhism, virtually dictating that rewards and punishment for actions in this life will be fulfilled in the life beyond. The state should therefore not have final jurisdiction over life and death.

While Jainism is not considered one of the "great" religious traditions in terms of sheer numbers (about 4,300,800 in the 2000), its adherents are more emphatic in interpreting *ahimsa* and *karma* in support of reverence for life than in either Hinduism or Buddhism. Through Mohandas Ghandi (1869–1948), although not a Jainister, the ideals of the Christian Sermon on the Mount and the Jain conception of *ahimsa* achieved a more specifically political influence than from either Buddhism or Hinduism. The Jain influence in India has been out of proportion to its numbers. Its rejection of anything that passes for justice involving violence or death affects its position or capital punishment.

Confucianism, with its emphasis on the essential goodness of humankind, discouraged belief in a personal god who gives laws and decrees punishment. Nevertheless, the Shu King (4.6.2) and the Meng Tzi (4.2.9) affirm that "heaven" will award punishment or happiness in response to human actions, evil or good. It is believed that the major problem with mortals, is that some deny our own essentially good nature as well as the rules that sustain it. It is a bitter irony, therefore, that on this basis, followers of Confucianism indulge in deceit, theft, and even murder without compunction. Followers believe that such persons deserve to suffer the condemnation of society and that should be swift and unhesitating.

> As expressed in Chung Tse's interpretation, When men kill others to take their property, being reckless and fearless of death, among all the people there are none but detest them. Thus such characters are to be put to death, without waiting to give them warning.[27]

2. Western Traditions

Judaism among the Western traditions offers the most succinct advice of any religion on how one achieves spiritual rectitude. Micah 6:8 says, "What does the Lord require of you but to do justice, and to love kindness, and to walk humbly with your God?" However, Amos (5: 231–23; 8:4) sharply warns God's demands for both personal and social (even national) righteousness: "Hear this, you who trample upon the needy. I take no delight in your solemn assemblies; rather let justice roll down like waters, and righteousness like an ever flowing stream." (Micah 6:8). Exodus (22:18) argues that there may be times when "justice" requires death as the only solution for criminal behavior (where heresy is regarded as criminal): "You shall not permit a sorceress to live." In Hebrew thought of the time, this may be extrapolated to enemies of the nation: "Do not spare them, but kill both man and woman, infant and suckling" (I Samuel 15:3–9). The death penalty could hardly be made more explicit (*Cf.* Exodus 15:3-10; Deuteronomy 7:2; Proverbs 6:34).

In Christianity, Jesus, like the prophet Amos, was unimpressed by the religiosity of those who made salvation a matter of obedience to rules and laws, but he insisted on what surely would today be regarded as too liberal. Matthew (25:31f.) makes it clear that our morality and indeed our salvation will be tested not by what we claim to be faith statements but by our meeting the mundane yet crucial needs of the hungry, the thirsty, the lonely, those who need clothing, the sick, and those in prison. Self-styled Christians who fail the test will be punished in the most alarming manner: "Depart from me, you cursed, into the eternal fire prepared for the devil and his angels"(Matthew 25:41).

There is no suggestion in the New Testament of God's desiring earthly punishment, certainly not state-sponsored execution. All is in God's hand: " 'Never avenge yourselves . . . vengeance is mine. I will repay,' says the Lord" (Romans 12:19). In Colonial America in the seventeenth century earlier, both the Puritans and the Quakers made a strong effort to have capital punishment eliminated. Michael Meranze reminds us in his highly original *Laboratories of Virtue* (North Carolina Press, 1996) although Pennsylvania ostensibly discontinued public executions, enforcement failed so that between 1682–1834, at least 257 individuals were executed, and public whippings and pillorying were staples for town people during Wednesday and Saturday market days, and announced as celebration of public punishment. Currently, both the National Council and World Council of Churches seek the abolition of capital punishment.

The Roman Catholic Church, despite having used capital punishment in past centuries, came to a decisive break with the past when, in 1988, the United States Catholic Conference, meeting in Washington D.C., announced that

> "abolition of Capital punishment is . . . a manifestation of our belief in the unique worth and dignity of each person from the moment of conception. The defense of life is strengthened by eliminating exercise of a judicial authorization to take human life."

While rejecting the doctrine of original sin, Islam nevertheless insists that all evil comes from a "taint" in the soul of each person (Qur'an S. xv. 13–17). Capital punishment is regarded as legitimate to address this taint; however, because Muslim societies differ from one another, great caution is urged to be sure that executions are not indiscriminately dispensed.

The Holy Qur'an teaches: "Take not life which Allah has made sacred, except by way of justice and law" (Surah vi.151), and forgiveness remains an option. When the secular law fails and God's judgment is the final court of appeals, it is important to note that while God's punishment awaits, forgiveness remains possible until the last moment. Even then, if the condemned earnestly repents and God judges the penitent's motives to be genuine, the punishment will be withdrawn (lxxix 35–41). God's forgiveness is inexhaustible.[28] It is significant for those seeking a religious foundation for ethics, whether local or global, that the Qur'an offers little or no justification for state-sponsored executions.

In some parts of the world, it appears that if respected leaders identified as Muslims, Christians, or "believers" of some other tradition favor beheadings, hangings, burnings, or preemptive military strikes, it may be argued that all such punishments are acceptable because they are done "in the name of" religion. Where a clear separation of church and state prevails, however, the support for capital punishment on religious grounds risks losing its credibility. Perhaps ironically, a rejection of capital punishment on the basis of religious faith takes on new significance. A basic religious argument for opposing the death penalty is its denial of human redemption. Instead of allowing an individual to live and make amends for his or her crime, the lethal injection becomes the state's easy way out. This was crystallized in the case of Karla Faye Tucker, the woman executed by Texas authorities in 1998. She had spent fifteen years on death row during which she experienced a religious conversion that, according to people who knew her, redirected her life toward service to God and helping other inmates. "What" it was asked, "was the greater value to Society—Tucker's removal to the death chamber, or her presence as a reminder that even the most damaged lives can be redeemed and turned to usefulness?"[29]

Capital punishment also involves the consideration of also more secular matters. In the United States, keeping a prisoner in jail costs about $30,000 per year. Imposition of the death penalty raises the annual cost to $120,000 for added security and legal fees and so on related to judicial appeals. Given a life expectancy of thirty years in jail, a sentence of life without possibility of parole costs the state about $900,000 dollars while the death sentence (assuming the fifteen years for appeals) costs $1,800,000! The parsimonious citizen might demand that we cut the time between arrest and execution. In a nation of laws, however, this would violate the prisoner's Constitutional rights by which his innocence might be established.

Even for the nonreligious, there are other ethical issues to be raised. These include there being no verifiable deterrent effect in executing supposed criminals; inequitable distribution of sentencing along racial, ethnic, and gender lines; execution or innocent for crimes they did not commit; the degrading of a society's values; and so on.

The question of whether the death penalty is a deterrent to crime and advances the moral order of society has been argued since Henry VIII of England set a record of 72,000 executions during his thirty-eight-year reign. As recently as the early nineteenth century, England listed 250 capital crimes including stealing a lady's handkerchief, damaging a fishpond, and associating socially with gypsies. When it was discovered that pickpockets were at their most efficient circulating in crowds gathered to watch the execution of pickpockets, serious study of the efficacy of the death penalty began. By 1982, England had joined ninety-six other nations in abolishing the penalty. As noted, the United States stands almost alone (with Nigeria, Saudi Arabia, Taiwan and Yemen). China and Iran in executions, and carried out more than 80 percent of all of the world's executions between 1992 and the date of this writing. Interestingly, Venezuela was the first major Western nation to abolish the practice, as early as 1863.[30]

Research suggests that execution not only does not deter crime but actually stimulates it. The United States is not only the single major country in the Western world that advocates the death penalty but also the one with the highest murder rate.[31] States in the United States that held capital punishment to be legal averaged *9.1* murders for every 100,000 people in 1992 (the last date for published statistics); states without the death penalty averaged only *4.9* murders per 100,000.[32] Lewis E. Lawes, former warden of Sing Sing prison, stated that of 150 men he led to the electric chair, not one would say he had given any thought to the possible penalty when he committed murder.[33]

Another concern is that the death penalty is often meted out to one criminal or group of them disproportionately to other distinctive groups. It has been discovered, for example, that the execution of black killers of white people far exceeds that of whites who kill blacks. "A 1990 study of 2,500 Georgia murder cases revealed that 22 percent of black defendants who murdered whites were sentenced to death, while only 3 percent of whites who killed blacks received death sentences.[34] Carroll Picket, often called Death House Chaplain at the Huntsville, Texas, prison (and who initially favored the death penalty) noted, "It is still true that the overwhelming majority of criminals put to death in this country are people of color, and people who are poor. In 1982 100 prisoners in Texas were under sentence of death. He adds that as of 2003, "281 more have been executed and there are 500 on death row. What kind of deterrence is that?" Pickett has changed positions.[35]

As to gender, a 1995 record revealed that only 2 percent of 5,434 women on death row since 1973 were actually expected to be executed; only one woman was.[36] Those who oppose capital punishment may have a sense of relief that only one execution took place, but the question of why the unbalanced clemency on the basis of gender remains.

Little attention seems to be given to the fact that a large number of convicted young criminals (teens and younger) are demonstrably mentally retarded and incapable of making the moral judgments to contain their rage when they feel they have been assaulted or driven to desperate acts by hunger or homelessness. The Southern Poverty Law Center reminds us that once convicted, a prisoner has no Constitutional right to a lawyer, and historically even if he is fortunate to acquire one by appointment of the judge, many such appointees have been known to sleep through the proceedings or come totally unprepared. In a 1989 case in Alabama, a juror declared she would not have voted for capital punishment if the defense attorney (twice dismissed from the courtroom for drunkenness) had revealed evidence of the condemned man's mental retardation. The convict was nevertheless executed.[37]

In another case, the judge deemed the fact that a notoriously heavy drinking lawyer was to defend a man facing a death sentence as being inconsequential. Gerald Uelmen, a law professor at the University of Santa Clara, reported that the alcoholic lawyer had actually been arrested for drunk driving on his way to court.[38]

Another aspect of how ineffective the death sentence is in deterring crime is in the landmark case of a man who spent fifteen years awaiting execution when a group of journalism students at Northwestern University proved his innocence via evidence both the prosecuting and defense attorneys should have exhibited.[39] This was the case that prompted Illinois Governor George Ryan, earlier a strong advocate of the death penalty, to declare a moratorium on all executions and released a group of wrongly convicted inmates from death row while a two year fact-finding study was conducted.[40]

Again, evidence of the failure of executions to deter crime is in the fact that the death penalty sometimes interferes with the conviction process itself before sentence is even imposed. Jurors have often admitted finding the sentence so repugnant that, rather than err on the wrong side of humane concern, their deliberations actually resulted in freeing the perpetrator of a crime.[41]

Still another concern is that the availability of death penalty puts arresting officers at greater risk. For example, after several killings of police officers in Austria, an

Austrian police officer claimed that the death penalty was such a dire threat that armed criminals went to extremes to avoid capture. The police argued that if the death penalty were removed, lives could be saved. Capital punishment was abolished, and indeed the death rate of police officers dropped.[42]

Discrimination on the basis of age poses a separate but increasingly strident challenge to our judicial system. The United States is one of few countries in the world that executes juvenile offenders. Should a youth of sixteen be considered eligible for the death sentence? Seventeen states of thirty-eight with capital punishment argue that sixteen-year-olds may be considered adults if they use "adult" weapons such as guns and knives in killing their victims. Why not age fourteen? Note below the following report of Supreme Court action in 2005. Or what about age five? An obvious negative? What then should we conclude about the five-year-old boy referred to earlier in Thomas Licona's case study who used a knife to stab (seventeen times) a two-year-old playmate? Did her death make him an adult murderer? Child development specialists attest that even a very young child, if suffering painful abuse, might grab a gun (if one is within reach) and is capable of killing the abuser whether an adult or a neighborhood bully. Members of Amnesty International in Norway, wrote to President Bill Clinton in 1999 urging him to halt states from executing juvenile offenders who may well have been pushed to the edge of emotional instability as well as those who are the mentally impaired. In Spain, demonstrators chanted against the United States for an impending execution of a Spanish citizen without respecting his right to meet with his nation's consul. Leaders of Germany, Canada, Thailand, and other nations have routinely complained about their citizens being executed by the United States without being granted their treaty-guaranteed rights. Mike Farrel has cautioned that the U.S. use of capital punishment, at almost any age, is turning the country into "an international human rights pariah."[43]

On March 1, 2005, the U.S, Supreme Court abolished the death penalty for juveniles, ruling that it was excessive and cruel to execute a person who was under eighteen when the crime was committed.[44] This has been good news indeed for those opposed to such a penalty, but some caution is in order. The vote was close (5 to 4), and might yet suffer a reversal as in the 1972 case of *Furman vs. Georgia*, essentially ending executions in that state. Four years later, however, a Georgia death penalty statute was held to be Constitutional, setting the stage for the resumption of executions.

Geography and the "states' rights" theory pose another problem for achieving equity for all Americans. For example, while citizens living in Maine, Michigan, Iowa, or Wisconsin will not face execution in those states, but a person who lives in Texas between 1976 and 2003 could have been executed. Executions, said Sheldon Olson, provost of the University of Texas, "is the lasting legacy of slavery. We are more likely to use it in the South because we have a legacy of dehumanizing people through slavery." Writing in December 1998, Robert Bryce reported his efforts to update his research: "There is no question that execution is far more common in the South than in other parts of the country. Of the 495 executions in the U.S. since 1976, 81 percent occurred in Southern states.[45] By 2003, the total nationwide had risen to 821.[46]

The execution of innocent people is perhaps a civilized society's worst nightmare. Nobel Laureate Bishop Tutu of South Africa rejoiced in the abolition of the penalty in 1995, saying "it's making us more civilized." In the United States, however, a veritable litany of cases can be recited in which, after fifteen or more years on death row and within days of execution, prisoners have been exonerated by last-minute discovery of (sometimes actually suppressed) evidence and set free. By April 12, 2002, it had been announced that the one hundredth death-row inmate had been released because of false evidence and/or DNA evidence had proved that the accused could not possibly have committed the crime.[47]

Questions and problems attend a theme for this section involving reasons for and methods of committing the crimes. Complications become urgent matters when the criminal acts are in obedience to those in authority and to defy such authority (as in military settings) is to expose oneself to charges of insubordination and treason. Consider the order of the Nazi army occupying Czechoslovakia during World War II to execute all the adult males in the town of Lidice for allegedly killing Gestapo leader Reinhard Heydrich. Were the soldiers who obeyed guilty of murder? Were those who refused guilty of treason? How will a judgment be reached on the fatal injuries to captives in prison compounds when the interrogators believed they were complying with rules that appear to deny prisoners certain rights just as those held in Abu Graeb and Guantanamo Bay have been denied? Are the interrogators guilty of murder, deserving capital punishment?

These issues cannot be avoided in a world where we must perennially debate whether the rules of war trump those of civil law. In the final analysis, as Michael E. Endres, professor of criminal justice at of Xavier University noted:

> Even apart from religious and moral arguments, the issue of the death penalty is linked to the fundamental matter of the kind of society in which we wish to live. It is all too easy to kill trees for another concrete roadway; the animal for its pelt, the enemy, the fetus, the aged, the defective—and the killer himself. We ought to guard against the growth of a mentality which sees the destruction of life as the solution to any problem including that of violence. It is too simplistic.[48]

Admirable that his sentiment is, it does not deal in a direct way with the fact that great numbers of people—in some societies, a large majority—are quite satisfied with and indeed insist upon the death penalty as part and parcel of the kind of society in which we wish to live. This is usually defended for security's sake and, we should admit, is an avenue for revenge as a means for "closure" to a traumatic loss and the violation of some innocent persons. Furthermore, there is no consensus as to how an end to capital punishment is to be implemented, or how to educate coming generations other than from religious and moral arguments. The task is both urgent and extraordinarily complex and without the underpinning of religion as a vital and constantly renewed resource may be beyond purely human instigation and resolution. Asserting what we "ought" to do is seldom persuasive.

C. THE "JUST" WAR

It can be argued that in one sense, war is an extrapolation of the death penalty: Those who have afflicted us must be brought to justice. Depending on the extent of the affliction, warfare might appear to be the reasonable and—in the judgment of the ancient Roman jurists, Aquinas, Hegel, and Lorimer—examples of "just" warfare.

The analogy breaks down when we considers the fact that tens of thousands of innocent people may be killed in warfare in addition "enemies."

Historically organized religions have been very much invoked in military conflicts. Egyptian tomb depictions and Greek and Roman paintings, poetry, and sculpture reveal a preoccupation with warfare and giving national conflicts a strong religious component. We need here to remember the distinction between religion per se and "the religions." *Religion,* as noted, is rooted in the Latin *re-ligio,* "bound back" to some divine source, which is sometimes called upon to bless or justify the community and/or state and its subsequent furtherance and defense.

Patriotism has almost always been emphasized in the name of that Source when national security has been threatened. Even Adolf Hitler, scornful of traditional German religious life (and not infrequently silencing pastors such as Martin Niemoeller with imprisonment for speaking against Nazi activities), found it useful to make occasional pietistic reference to the Almighty in public addresses. At the close of World War II, theologian Emil Brunner wrote with impassioned reason that, while he identified himself tentatively as a pacifist, he had to acknowledge that

> "war is the readiness of the state to support the recognized aims of its policy [and] belongs to the very nature of the state. So long as the law of the jungle prevails between states the right of self-defense is an elementary condition of its existence. Pacifism of the "absolutist" variety is practically anarchy."[49]

Just before that war's end, Albert Einstein, whose pacifism and anti-nationalistic warnings were a theme in many of his writings, declared in a reflection on the Holocaust,

> Behind the Nazi party stands the German people, who elected Hitler after he had in his book and in his speeches made his shameful intentions clear. The Germans as an entire people are responsible for these mass murders and must be punished as a people if there is justice in the world.[50]

Before proceeding with further commentary, it will be useful to gain insights from several of the major religious traditions including some to which we have given scant attention before.

Hinduism is sometimes referred to as the "glue" of life among India's vast and ethnically diverse population, the diversity being the product of successive invasions from times immemorial, bringing Caucasoid, Mongolian, Australoid, and Negroid races into the mix.

Conflicts among them were almost inevitable, but the emergence of Hinduism (c. 1500–2000 B.C.E.) mediated among the competing groups with its message that we are all part of each other as we are all part of the World Soul. An often quoted passage from the Upanishads is "That Soul! That art Thou! Whoever thus knows 'I am Brahma' becomes this All"— repeated nine times in the Chandogya Upanishads.[51] The ideal for life here on earth is peace, not war (Bhagavad Gita, 1.31-38; 1.45; 2.65).[52]

It is nevertheless true that of the four major castes in the Hindu structure for society, the Kshatriya, believed to have been designated by Krishna since the dawn of creation, reflects the fact that the history of India was one of almost constant warfare. Furthermore, in the Bhagavad Gita, the Lord Krishna, disguised as a charioteer for the noble knight Arjuna, declared that while both life and death are illusions, he should not hesitate to kill in battle; immortality for the victims is assured (1:28-45; 2:4–8, *Cf.* Katha Upanishad 2:18–19). Until the days of Ghandi when the caste system was proscribed, strict obedience to the laws of Manu (established c. 250 C.E.) that required obedience to the caste regulations, especially the retention of the warrior caste to counter all-too-frequent invasions, was the condition for salvation. The extraordinary influx of Muslims begun around the twelfth century has continued to the recent conflicts in Kashmir, and the open hostility between India and Pakistan is particularly troubling since India has achieved nuclear power. Hinduism has no specific or enforceable plan for outlawing war.

Buddhism, in contrast with Hinduism, makes explicit its objection to violence in any form. The Mahavagga (6.31.13) as well as the Dhammapada (194) condemns all intentional killing, emphasizing peace as the only true path to happiness. Rod Hindery makes the point sharply by contrasting this with the Bhagavad Gita's recrimination of Arjuna's "defective pity" and "appeal to Arjuna's honor and fame as a warrior."[53] The task of a warrior is to enforce rules which may, at times, call for acts of war. The Buddhist response is that the aim of all should be to learn to live peacefully with all others. The effectiveness of this simple message was revealed in the near conversion of the third emperor of India (304–236 B.C.E.). "This warrior king turned partly against war and caste, and toward a layman's moral interpretation of Buddhist dharma."[54]

Initially, Buddhism held great appeal for thousands in India, which had suffered centuries of invasions and internal conflicts. One reason for its gradual decline was the difficulty in sustaining the denouncement of military service. In a border conflict with Magadha, King Mimbisara, a patron of the Lord Buddha, learned that a large number of his finest warriors had been won over to the Buddhist nonviolent stance and wanted to be ordained as monks. Threatened with furious reaction by fellow soldiers, the king sought out the Lord Buddha and assured him of royal protection for his order but with the request that no more persons in royal service be ordained. The Buddha agreed, and a rule that continues to the present day was enacted, the first such formal agreement between secular and religious orders on the need for a military presence even in times of peace.[55] But "with the ordinary world such as it is, a strong state and even an army are necessary evils; therefore it is permissible for a lay Buddhist to serve as a ruler or a soldier."[56]

His Holiness the Dalai Lama, a Buddhist priest and winner of the Nobel Peace Prize, reflecting on the violent career of our species, has charged:

> It is a sad fact of human history that religion has often been a major force of conflict. Even today individuals are killed, communities destroyed, and societies destabilized as a result of religious bigotry and hatred. It is no wonder that many question the place of religion in human society.[57]

Hans Kung would underscore the Dalai Lama's lament, putting it even more sharply: "The most fanatical, the cruelest political struggles are those that have been colored, inspired, and legitimized by religion."[58] Kung, a staunch supporter of ecumenical interaction among all the religions, also affirms, "There is a significant connection between ecumenism and world peace. Anyone who feels a sense of obligation toward the world community, who takes seriously the fragility of all human arrangements . . . must know what is at stake here." An active participant in the Parliament of the World's Religions, and seeking both a rationale and strategy, Kung asks,

> What should a declaration on a global ethic contain? Such a declaration must penetrate to a deeper ethical level, the level of binding values, irrevocable criteria . . . and not get stuck at the legal level of laws. It should be capable of securing a consensus; must be self-critical . . . not just addressed to "the world" but also and primarily to the religions themselves.[59]

In full accord with Kung's assessment, His Holiness the Dalai Lama is equally insistent that what is *not* to be sought is an amalgam of all religions as if "one size fits all." He states, "I believe the best way to overcome ignorance and bring about understanding is through dialogue with members of other faith traditions" and illustrates this with reference to his own meetings with the late Thomas Merton, a Catholic monk, which were deeply inspiring. "Once we have experienced the benefit of love and compassion, and of ethical discipline we will easily recognize the value of others' teachings." Meanwhile, he continues,

> It is essential to have a single-pointed commitment to one's own faith. This involves individual practitioners finding a way at least to accept the validity of the teachings of other religions while maintaining a whole-hearted commitment to their own. What is required is that we develop a genuine sense of religious pluralism in spite of different claims of different faith traditions. In this regard I find the concept of a world parliament very appealing.[60]

If there is to be peace on earth, it cannot be limited to renouncing military action. At the individual level, he says, "Relinquish your envy, let go your desire to triumph over them. Instead try to benefit them. If you cannot, for whatever reason, be of help to others, at least don't harm them. This, then, is my true [Buddhist] religion, my simple faith."[61]

Jainism, the oldest personally founded religious tradition in India, was begun by one Mahavira (c. 599-527 B.C.E.) some thirty years before the advent of Buddhism with a clear intent to reform Hinduism. It never succeeded in displacing either and today has only about 4,303, 000 members worldwide. Its asceticism, suppression of the ego and all aspects of self-aggrandizement, and absolute condemnation of war, however, have made an unmistakable impact on other traditions around the world where lust for power seems to be the hallmark of the human race. The recurring theme of "never kill anything for any reason" and similar injunctions (Sutrakritanga 1.3.4.19-20; 1.11.9-11) was in effect the gauntlet thrown down before warmongers but seldom picked up.

Perhaps the major reasons for lack of numerical growth of Jainism lie in their very reticence of self-promotion and the fact that they emerged at a time of unprecedented religious creativity throughout the East, which in itself was a major reason for the rise of antiwar, peace-promoting religions. This was a period when Lao Tse and Confucius were active in China, Zoroaster in Persia (later to be named Iran), Shinto in Japan,[62] and the great prophets of Israel—Amos, Jeremiah, Ezekiel, and Isaiah—Jain influence on both business and architecture has left a lasting impression in the affairs of the east, yet its doctrine of ending warfare appears to have had success only within their own ranks and results in increasingly rare conversions into Jainism.

Meanwhile,we find the third oldest of the major religions, Shinto ("the divine Way") in Japan. It has no attributable founder but is believed to have emerged around 660 B.C.E. Some historians find in it a synthesis of Buddhism and Confucianism,[63] and others would include Taoism, because it's name, Shin Tao, is derived from the Chinese translation of the Japanese *Kami-no michi*, "way of the gods." The gods are myriad in number, the chief among them being the sun goddess Amaterasu from whom the line of emperors derive. The mikado, the reigning emperor, is thus sacred and infallible. Japan's emblem of the rising sun on its national flag reminds every Japanese citizen of his or her duty to enforce the laws of the goddess upon the rest of the world. If this means war as the requisite method, so be it. Bushido "the way of the warrior," is the closest approximation to a code of ethics that Shinto provides.[64] The most earnest prayer is addressed to the sun goddess: "Let the land under heaven enjoy peace and be free from war."[65]

For centuries, Japan was a relatively peaceful nation, reflecting its declared isolationist policy, which was broken by the invasion of Commodore Perry (1853–1854) who, with nine heavily armed ships, forced upon the country diplomatic and trade agreements.[66] In 1882, the government authorities divided Shintoism into secular and sectarian aspects. Sectarian Shinto was accorded status as a religion in company with Buddhism and other traditions. The secular branch became more like a patriotic cult that displayed formidable attack strategies including the *kamikaze* pilots ("God's mighty wind") of World War II who crashed their planes onto the decks of U.S. ships.

Taoism, a relatively small religious tradition today, representing only about 2.6 percent of the world's population, appeared on the stage of history roughly 600 B.C.E., half a century later than Shintoism but had a significant influence on it. Most notably, it provided the concept of *Yin* and *Yang*, the ruling principle of a balanced nature. A declaration in the *Tao-Teh-King* had particular appeal: "The wise esteem peace and quiet above all else. The good ruler seeks peace and not war . . . Arms are not blessed, but full of sorrow."

Unfortunately, such platitudes have little lasting effect in the face of mounting corruption, crime, the ravages of disease and wars often fought to alleviate the effects of privation, as recent tragedies in Africa have revealed. Taoism fell into disrepute early in its formative years, owing to some degree to its almost utopian vision of possibilities while advocating "extreme disinterestedness and utmost calm." Confucius ridiculed such unrealistic detachment from the world even in the presence of war. Opposition to Confucianism, which was on the rise, alienated many while Taoism's lack of missionary efforts made countering Confucianism (or any other rival for attention) ineffective. Taoism's retreat into animism, polytheism, demonolatry, and a closeted practice of magic virtually sealed its fate as a minority religious tradition.

Zoroastrianism represents another tradition that at one time commanded great respect but, due at least in part to its growing advocacy of violent warfare to secure its dominance over other traditions, has almost faded from history. Depending on one's sources, Zoroaster (also called Ahuramazda) was born as early as 6000 B.C.E., 1400 B.C.E, 1000 B.C.E. or (most likely) 660 B.C.E.[67] Most Biblical scholars today choose the 660 date for Zoroaster's birth and praise his influence on both Hebrew and Christian scriptures and events that they reveal. The concept of Satan, for example, comes from Zoroastrianism as do an elaborate demonology and visions of angels as "the heavenly host" employed in the New Testament episode of the annunciation of Jesus' birth (Luke 2:13–14). King Cyrus, who liberated the Jews from bondage in Babylonia (Persia), was a Zoroastrian to whom God referred as a messiah, "the Lord's anointed" (Isaiah 45:1), and (perhaps) "the anointed one" (Daniel 9:25) who will oversee the rebuilding of Jerusalem.

As a youth, Zoroaster was known for his kindness to the poor and animals. At thirty, he experienced the presence of the one true god, Ahura Mazda, which launched his career as a religious leader. Along the way it also seemed to encourage a militancy against opposition and eventuated in an attitude that made him feel he must convert the world. Included in the sacred writings of the faith, the Yasna, (43, 8f), we find the seeds of violence to come: "To the wicked, would that I could be in very truth a strong tormentor." A supporter of war where it seemed indicated, Zoroaster declared "good treatment is prescribed toward good people, but ill treatment toward the wicked." An ambivalence toward the use of force against adversaries emerged: "Resist them then, with weapon" (Yasna 31:18) and rationalized "with enemies fight with equity. With a friend proceed with the approval of friends." Probably first among the living monotheistic religions to proclaim that God is the guarantor of moral order throughout the universe, it is not unlikely that the Maji in Luke's gospel concerning Jesus' nativity were Zoroastrians trained in the astronomy of the time. Referred to in tradition as kings, it seems also probable that they carried swords. The pessimism that germinated among the Isrealites after the captivity, and the largely failed restoration of Jerusalem under Antiochus was greatly relieved by the Jewish contacts with Zoroastrian visions of heaven and hell, the struggle between good and evil, light and darkness, and the final triumph of good.

Judaism had its roots not in battles or invasions but in the peaceful migration of Abraham and his extended family (as well as flocks and herds) from the land of his fathers to "the land that I [God] will show you . . . and I will make of you a great nation" (Genesis 12:1–2). Traveling from southern Mesopotamia up the ancient Tigris-Euphrates valley to Canaan through Syria to Palestine—making contact with the Hivites and Perrizites and negotiating peacefully with the Hittites—they traveled down to Egypt, and finally back to Palestine where Abraham lived out his days without any record of having drawn a sword. It would not be for another five centuries after bondage in Egypt and a return to the Promised Land that warfare would become a recurrent reality. Now, it seemed, the God of Israel would become "a man of war" (Exodus 15:3). From Moses' time through the occupation of the land they believed had been promised by God, the battles of such romantic heroes as Samson and heroic women like Deborah, warfare was a part of their national vocabulary.

After numerous victories and defeats, botched kingdom politics under Saul, David, and Solomon, and a divided Israel, some profoundly prophetic voices were raised to warn the Hebrew people of impending doom for their violent and corrupt ways. They had been a chosen nation not for privilege but to "walk in the light of the Lord" (Isaiah 2:5). They were not to depend on weapons of war, horses, and chariots (Isaiah 31:1; Hosea 1:7) to gain political and military dominance. Instead, they were to fulfill God's purposes by beating their "swords into plowshares and spears into pruning hooks" and to "study war no more" (Isaiah 2:4) because they had become "impudent and stubborn" (Ezekiel 2:4) and a "stiff necked people" (Exodus 32:9; Deuteronomy 9:6), God's punishment would be severe: "You only have I known of all the families of then earth, therefore I will punish you" (Amos 3:2). An unexpected rejoinder to Israel's pleas for divine aid!

What was to happen next was a series of disasters: the siege and fall of Jerusalem (c. 587), mass deportation into Babylonian captivity until release by Cyrus of Persia (c. 538). After their deliverance, many Hebrews returned to rebuild Jerusalem but countless others simply scattered across Europe while some established an "elephantine colony" in Egypt.[68] Persia remained the dominant power throughout the Middle East for several generations until the growing Greek culture over whelmed it (c. 459–404) to be overwhelmed in its own time by the Romans. Judaism, much influenced by Hellenic thought, served an important role both culturally and geographically because Israel's land formed a bridge between Western Asia and Africa. Under Roman rule, the Jews were not permitted a standing army or use of the death penalty, but as long as the leaders (i.e., the high priests, scribes, and Pharisees) maintained at least relative peace over their people, they could stay in power.

Failing that in the judgment of the Romans, the Jews were all but exterminated in 70 C.E., and the remnant engaged in the great diaspora. From that time to our own, after being marginalized citizens in countless countries for two millennia, Judaism has not found it possible to use military force nor the appeal of a holy war to advance its cause. Today, in the wake of the Nazi-driven holocaust of World War II, the "never again" motto of the survivors of that horrendous tragedy, and the creation of the state of Israel, that situation has altered dramatically. The stage of history is now the scene of the most debated confrontations in modern times. Weapons of war including highly sophisticated guns, rockets, helicopter gunboats, and the threatened use of atomic ordinance, place not only Israel but also many other nations in the cross-hairs of catastrophe

Christianity was born into a world of raging conflicts, international wars, and domestic violence. Its essential message has been not of returning violence with violence but of responding with good instead of evil, of encouraging efforts at reconciliation, and of striving to set up the conditions for enabling and sustaining peace in the name of God's love revealed in the life, death, and resurrection of Christ. It was a deceptively easy message to articulate but so difficult to make persuasively that martyrdom seemed for at least three centuries the most likely destiny for those who proclaimed the gospel. As the church grew, it declared war to be so contrary to Christian love that not only must members not participate in killing (whether as soldiers or executioners for the state) but also soldiers were to be restricted from joining the church.[69] Origen, one of the greatest minds of the early church, declared pacifism a central feature of the faith, and that their love, labor, and prayers were doing more than Roman arms to preserve the realm. Will Durant describes in terse prose what followed in the life of Rome:

> They turned from Caesar preaching war, to Christ preaching peace; from incredible brutality to unprecedented charity; from a life without hope or dignity to a faith that honored their humanity.[70]

After the emperor Constantine embraced Christianity (c. 315), succeeding rulers found it imperative to debate a rationale for a "just" war given the constant threat of attack from pagan tribes beyond the borders of Rome. Augustine, bishop of Hippo in Africa, elaborated such a position in declaring that wickedness must be restrained by force in necessary: "The sword of the magistrate is divinely commissioned." To be just, a war must be waged under the authority of the prince; its object was to punish injustice and restore peace; it must be fought without hatred or vindictiveness and indeed in full obedience to Jesus' command to love the neighbor and pray for the enemy in a spirit of love. As Christianity gathered in numbers and began migrating across Europe, eastward into Constantinople, and eventually north to Russia, it became evident that well-trained and ordered troops were needed. The rise of feudalism, battles with Scandinavian invaders, the looming prospect of the Crusades, and the romanticizing of chivalry under legendary King Arthur are too complex to detain us here. We encounter at this point perhaps the most scholarly publication on the "just war" by Thomas Aquinas, who wrote:

> In order for a war to be just, three things are necessary. First, the authority of the sovereign by whose command the war is to be waged. According to the words of the Apostle (Romans 13:4) 'He beareth not the sword in vain: for he is God's minister, an avenger to execute wrath upon him that doth evil.' Secondly, a just cause is required. Augustine says, 'A just war is one that avenges wrongs, when a nation or state has to be punished, or to restore that which was seized unjustly.' Thirdly, it is necessary that the belligerents should have a right intention . . . not for motives of aggrandizement or cruelty, but with the object of securing peace, of punishing evil doers, and of uplifting the good.[71]

Since Aquinas' day, countless debates have been held on his rationale for a just war, or whether all wars should be denounced and Christian churches should take a wholly pacifist stance. It is one of the ironic "about face" reversals in the church's history that from the virtual denouncing of military action in the third century, the church embraced a virtual enforcement of militarism by the time of the first Crusade in 1096. Pope Urban's stirring "Deus Vult" ("God wills it") in a sermon at Clermont, France, was said to be echoed by the entire congregation, and the arrival of the invading army with the Cross painted on soldiers' shields, in Constantinople, Antioch, and finally Jerusalem in 1098, was the scene of massive slaughters.[72] After a succession of crusades, culminating in the utter tragedy of the Children's Crusade of 1212, the Muslim forces turned the tide, and by 1244 had regained Jerusalem. "Henceforth for more than six centuries it was held by by succession of Moslem rulers . . . and was not again to be in Christian hands until the twentieth century."[73]

Differences in attitudes toward war, as well as antagonism toward the church's official stance on who may be saved and by what means, led to the truce of God in the twelfth century. It forbad battles on Saturday through Sunday and sought to curb jousts and tournaments as popularizing the shedding of blood. Objections also were raised to building vast, costly cathedrals in the presence of grinding poverty and exposed the enrichment of bishops to levels of wealth even beyond that of kings. Wars based on clashes of conscience and religious doctrine led to centuries of religious wars and reformations, which inevitably led to cries for separation of church and state to avoid either using the other to gain political power. This was by no means a universal quest, and space does not afford opportunity to examine the quasimilitary exploits of explorers and their accompanying armies and conquistadors in the New World during the sixteenth and succeeding centuries. Perhaps the Thirty Years War (1618–1648) fought mainly in Germany provides the best illustration of how religious wars were actually less a matter of religion as of politics and territorial and dynastic disputes following the Reformation. "Rivalries between ambitious monarchs, generals and adventurers, reinforced by national loyalties may have been more important. Had the religious element not been present, they alone might have produced the war."[74]

The period 1648–1815 and the defeat and exile of Napoleon witnessed numerous intranational skirmishes and revolutions that largely ignored religious issues except for using quasireligious slogans to justify armed conflicts. From then until 1914, there has never been a period so nearly free from war. In popular discussion, what was to become World War I was dismissed: with comments such as it won't last, give them six months and they'll solve their problems. Soldiers on battlefields in France actually celebrated their first Christmas by leaving their trenches to visit the enemy and sing Stille Nacht together. Candle-lit Christmas trees, where a few pine and fir permitted, appeared along trench lines. "Perhaps two thirds of the whole front observed the truce, which some places lasted a week [before] the commanders ordered their men back to the trenches.[75] After a century of relative peace, the end of that crucial Christmas truce witnessed the change to a century whose wars have cost as many as 187,000,000 human lives.[76]

Is religion powerless to halt this growing trend toward homicidal violence? Alan Geyer calls militarism "the world's number one mental health problem" in noting the observation of Harold and Margaret Sprout of Princeton University that "militarism has a dehumanizing effect" and is "ultimately anti-humanist not (alone) because people get killed in war but because *it is a theology* which sanctifies the war system" (italics mine).[77] Nearly every Christian denomination has denounced militarism, but the World Council of Churches has been reluctant to make such denunciation a condition for membership, noting that Christians must be sensitive to the variety of cultures' economic and political systems in which armed forces serve. The issue then seems to be not whether Christianity is a religion of peace but whether individual Christians and their churches can exemplify the command of the gospel to "love your enemies, and do good, and lend expecting nothing in return . . . Be merciful even as your Father is merciful" (Luke 6:36–36).

Islam is second only to Christianity among all the world's religions in numbers of adherents, having grown from 400 million in 1959 to over 1.4 billion in 2000.

Muhammed was essentially a man of peace, denouncing the constant bloody skirmishes among the tribal groups of his homeland, which has been involved in military encounters almost since its inception. Its astonishingly rapid expansion across Europe within a century of Muhammed's death inevitably involved meeting military opposition with military retaliation. This has led scholars like Samuel Huntington to conclude that Islam "has always had bloody borders," which raises the crucial question as to whether Islam as a religion is inherently militaristic.[78] David Hawkin stoutly refutes such an insinuation,[79] noting that even the current struggles between modern Israel and Palestine beg the question: "Does this reflect an inherent philosophy of militarism or more a philosophy of *Realpolitik?*"[80]

Doubtless the most frequently used word among non-Muslims to characterize Islam is *jihad,* thought to imply violent "holy" wars. This perpetuates a serious misunderstanding. "It has a more complex meaning arising from the Arabic *jahada,* "he made an effort. The underlying sense is one of striving: 'to strive in the cause of God: There are many ways you can strive: using your mouth, explaining what Islam means; with your wealth by giving to orphans; giving your life to God."[81] *Jihad* is by no means restricted to physical battle in the military sense. Indeed the warfare most important to wage is "the warfare within oneself . . . against evil impulses, against the tendencies toward idolatries—that is the elevation of nonspiritual and nondivine things to the chief status in one's soul or one's heart. The greater *jihad* is the fight within yourself, the lesser *jihad* is the warfare outside."[82]

This is not to infer that there is no support of outward and very physical military expressions of *jihad.* The Qu'ran states quite clearly: "Those who believe and strive with might and main in God's cause with their goods and persons, they are the people who will achieve [salvation]" (S. ix. 20).

This may not only involve fighting but also killing (S. ii. 190–192), especially when it is "in the cause of God and oppressed men and women" (S. iv. 74–76), and in self-defense or being grievously wronged (S. xxii. 39–41). If the oppressor ceases, however, one must forgive as "God is oft forgiving" (S. Ii. 192–193).

It has often been noted that while the Qur'an is the final authority on Islamic beliefs and actions, there is a rich resource in the Hadith, the body of traditions from the time of Muhammed and his associates, touching on matters of faith, morals, ethics, governance, and so on. Among the most engaging speculations arise from their encounter with other (and earlier) monotheistic religions, notably Judaism, Zoroastrianism, and Christianity. In his travels, Muhammed encountered all of these and, presumably, was influenced to some degree by their beliefs, for example, in "the trans-human world of spiritual forces; the sacred quality of all beings; a supreme divine being; the ethical responsibility of all human beings. These religions also taught the brotherhood of all mankind."[83] As noted earlier, Islam shares with virtually every other major and many minor religions some variation on the Golden Rule.

Given this, how does it happen that Islam has been considered by many historians to be the most militant of the major religious traditions, actually requiring on some occasions to take the sword against any opposition to the Muslim faith (Qur'an iv. 77; ix, 29;)[84], and how did it develop that Muhammed's armies became so well trained and disciplined in such a short time as to be able to conquer so much of the world of his day?

The answer to the first part of the question is perceived in simply tracing the development from the time of Muhammed's overpowering experience of God's summons in the flight from Mecca in 622 (which became the start of the Islamic calendar, dated A.H. (an abbreviation from the Latin anno hegire). From winning the hearts of the people of Medina to establishing military and political rule over Mecca (630–632), Muhammed sent emirates to Greece, Persia, Egypt, and Abyssinia, demanding of their kings accept his faith. "The Abyssinians are reported to have to the listened to the preaching Prophet with great respect and awe."[85]

For 28 years after Muhammed's death, four of his closest comrades, Abu Bekhr, Omar, Othman, and Ali, carried on his leadership. A serious, almost catastrophic division arose upon Ali's death when the question arose as to how the successors to Muhammed should be identified. One faction, the *Sunnites,* self-declared definers of the true faith as "traditionalists," had embraced the first four caliphs, as they were called (from the Arabic khalifa, or rightful successor). *Sunnites* today represent the larger of the two groups (some 85 percent of all Muslims).[86] The second faction, called *Shiites,* adhere to the belief that Ali, the son of Muhammed's wife Fatima, was the true inheritor of authority and proclaimed a more liberal faith that eventually ranged from mysticism to pantheism.

The two factions have perpetually struggled for religious eminence and the authority to become a caliph at the individual level. Thus, the caliphate emerged, often established amid violent military rivalry.

At least six caliphates who prevailed from early seventh to the twentieth centuries (1924) can be readily identified: (1) Omayyad (660–750) ruled from Damascus to Spain and North Africa; (2) Abbaside (750–1258) held its capital in Baghdad until the Mongols invaded and executed the last Abbaside caliph; (3) Fatimite (910–1171), ruled Egypt and North Africa; (4) Spanish (755–1236) was centralized in Cordova; (5) Moorish (1238–1492) was primarily at Granada, and marked the conspicuous termination of the Islamic caliphate in Spain because of the purge of both Jews and Muslims in 1492; and (6) Ottoman–Turkish ascended to power in 1299. It continued until the sultan, residing at Constantinople, was deposed in 1922. That date also coincided with the complete secularization of Turkey under the direction of Mustafa Kemal, "father of the Turks," commonly called Ataturk.

The fate of the caliphate provides almost an index to the rise and decline (but not "fall"!) of Islam's presence in the world. From its seventh century emergence through its dynamic expansion and spawning of vast empires and sultanates and to its being marginalized as a world power by European colonialism, Islam was subjugated by Europe's imperial powers in the nineteenth century.

Muslim responses ranged from dismay, defeatism, and a desire simply to accommodate and be absorbed to reform, emigration to new lands or to fight back in a *jihad* against all forces that threatened the group's identity.[87] The latter proved fruitless in the face of European military supremacy, and violence often led to retaliatory violence and vendettas. The former found a modicum of hope in the fact that democratic ideals such as the equality and brotherhood of all, while not fully realized in institutional Islam, are nevertheless a basic commitment of those who believe, as the Qur'an expresses: "Surely those who say, 'Our Lord is God,' and remain steadfast, they shall not fear, nor shall they grieve"[88], the phrase quoted by Iraqi Prime Minister Ibrahim Jafari in his swearing-in ceremony in May 2005.

Armed conflicts between Sunni and Shiites, bloody exchanges between insurgents and domestic leadership, the ongoing murderous confrontation between Israel and Palestine, and the invasion of Iraq by U.S. forces resulting in tens of thousands of casualties have cast a dark cloud over prospects for peace in our world. Prime Minster Jafari invited to insurgents to "participate in our rebuilding and development. The dialogue of words will lead to what you couldn't achieve with the dialogue of bullets and the culture of betrayal."[89]

Are wars then justifiable in the tradition of Islam? If we take the Qur'an literally, the answer is yes, and indeed may be required (Qur'an iv. 74–76). Bowker confirms: "If Muslims are in a state of war, then it is compulsory. If there is defensive *jihad* going on in his locality, he is not allowed to hold back"[90] but only under extreme circumstances, and never for greed (e.g., exploiting a neighbor's goods or property, and never for the sake of revenge, which is a form of idolatry).

The greatest fulfillment of *jihad* is in the war within one's self, a war to purge and cleanse the self. This requires that we stop romanticizing about just wars and collaborate through our faith traditions to achieve a just peace.

D. WAR AGAINST THE PLANET

A certain romanticism clings to the concept of globalization (*cf.* the effort of ancient rulers to unite the known world around a given ideology or simply to control it for political reasons or economic advantage). Usually, as in the case of Hammurabi (c. 1792–1750 B.C.), globalization was backed up with military might and some well-codified laws. It appears, however, that the main thrust of Hammurabi's reign was to control only Mesopotamia, particularly the Euphrates waters that fed critical agricultural irrigation projects.

However, Hebrew scriptures present Abraham's response to a summons from a god who represents a global aspiration as unique as one can find: "The Lord said, 'Go from your country, and your kindred and your father's house to the land that I sill show you. And I will make of you a great nation . . . and by you all the families of the earth sill bless themselves.'"(Genesis 12: 1–3).

A missionary zeal to enrich and ennoble life, not for conquest or exploitation, also emerged in Buddhism, when the son of King Osaka (c. 250 B.C.) carried to Ceylon the message of how the Buddha had renounced his own blessedness and taught his followers to toil for the world's welfare: "For when the world's welfare is concerned, who would be slothful or indifferent?" (Mahavamsa 12:55).[91,92]

Neither Hinduism nor Confucianism launched any kind of global program in the early centuries. Not until 1917 was a Hindu missionary society begun in Bombay. Despite its slogan "to make the whole world Hindu," its missionary effort remained very limited and declined further after the death of its founder, G.B. Vaidya. It was largely through the Parliament of the World's Religions meeting in Chicago in 1897 that the work of the Vedanta Society was presented through Vivekananda, as having a global message (but not a global program). The society was able to give Hinduism a fully international appeal and seal its success at the Parliament's meeting in 1993.

Recall, however, that Judaism began at its beginning with a clearly global outlook and rationale. "Declare [God's] glory among the nations, His marvelous works among all the peoples" (Psalm 96:3). However, Israel's firm embrace of religious freedom, devoid of any attempt to enact laws to guide the actual practice of religion, has been its hallmark across the centuries. Even contemporary Israel makes no posture as a theocratic state and supports no "missionary" activity in the Buddhist or Christian sense.

Christianity, on the other hand, has from its inception held to a global focus. The gospels portray Jesus' birth as being accompanied by an announcement from God's angels of "good news of great joy to all people" (Luke 2: 8-10), not just to the local Jewish or Roman world. The first visitors to the birth place after the shepherd's departure were "wise men from the East" (Matthew 2:1–2), whom many scholars conclude were from Persia. If so, they may well have been Zoroastrian scholars, representatives of a foreign culture. At the close of his earthly ministry, and after his resurrection, Jesus instructed his disciples to "go and make disciples of all nations . . . teaching them to observe all that I have commanded you" (Matthew 28:19–20). This is echoed in Mark's gospel: "Go into all the world and preach the gospel to the whole creation" (Mark 16:15).

The crucial element to note here is that what was commanded was not for the disciples to attract converts to a new institutional religion but to feed the hungry, tend people's thirst, welcome strangers, clothe the naked, heal the sick, and visit those in prison (Matthew 25:36–36). Such mundane caring eventually expanded to creating schools, hospitals, training centers for medical and legal education, and even university-level training in the arts. In time, globalization of the faith included agricultural training and international economics. The motive was not personal or institutional gain but love (Matthew 5:44; John 13:35).

Islam, the second largest of the world's religions, has from its beginning nurtured a zeal for expanding the influence of the faith and, like Christianity, not confining itself to drawing people to its rituals and prayers but also building hospitals, schools, and some of the first and finest universities in Europe and Egypt after the Dark Ages. The missionary zeal to reach out to other nations while planting a firm home state led to the demand of the some 90 million Muslims in India for a separate, autonomous state, which in 1947 became a reality in Pakistan.

Given the centuries-old global strategies employed by religious leaders and sometimes secular enterprises practiced by people who were only nominally religious, one must ask how the term *globalization* has become so identified with business and economics as to have a veritable "lock" on its meaning. An easy, albeit superficial, explanation might be that, after the collapse of the feudal system and the growth of mercantilism, it was quite natural for enterprising business owners to look farther afield for customers. But explanation overlooks the reason relating to the vast new opportunities for foreign travel and trade beginning in the age of exploration. European businesses were already involved in trade with India and China, for example, when Christopher Columbus (and others, e.g., Ferdinand and Isabella with their appetite for wealth and power) realized establishing new travel routes would greatly facilate trade. Technological advances in manufacturing and mining were, of course, also part of the new realities as well as improvements in banking, insurance, transportation, and communication. Adam Smith's book *The Wealth of Nations* (1776) helped popularize opposition to governmental interference with business practices (*laissez-faire*) that had undermined mercantilism and gave businesses an opportunity to globalize their activities in a transnational climate. That this might encourage the exploitation of cheap labor, which in turn would put employment on the home front of participating nations at risk had not been considered.

While ecology had its barest beginning in the work of Theophrastus and Aristotle, it crept into our religious vocabulary only via zoologist Ernst Haekel's adoption of the Greek *oekologie,* "place of living relationships," as recently as 1918. So when did the word *crisis* appear to reference the interaction between globalization and ecology? Perhaps the first formal word of alarm came when Charles Dickens urged Parliament to revoke the death penalty for anyone who broke a loom in a factory. Mill owners enjoyed growing economic power through exports and foreign trade enhanced by the invention of the loom so essential a tool that they valued even at the price of human life. Naturalist George Grinnell raised notice of another approaching danger in the United States in 1886 over the slaughter of barn swallows and the extinction of the passenger pigeon by the millinery trade's demand for feathers for women's apparel. Grinnell's published article led to the creation of the Audubon Society, which in turn sought legal limits on disruptions of the environment by industry.

On a far more dramatic level, the potato famine in Ireland in 1845, which claimed the lives of a million people from sheer starvation, is a lesson in the horrific total dependence of a nation on a single crop. Some South American countries have been similarly enticed to confine their produce to a single commodity (coffee, bananas, etc.) without reckoning with the vagaries of weather, blight, or insect infestation. These unpredictables can make a whole nation of people vulnerable. In fact, the blight that destroyed the Irish crop began during a severe climatic change that originated as far away as Peru. The blight then spread via exports to the United States and to the Netherlands (which had not become dependent on a single crop) before settling on Ireland with devastating consequences.[93]

The massive migrations of people from Ireland and other impoverished European countries to North America, especially the United States brought even more demands on the natural and industrial environments for housing, clothing, and food while the number of inventions and agricultural and manufacturing innovations attempted to meet the needs of the greatly increased population. Meanwhile other developments like deforestation, air and water pollution, and overfishing rivers and streams, and contamination from transport enterprises (diesel engines fouling the air) were changing the whole environment. This was reflected in *Our Plundered Planet,* a 1948 book that shook a generation, detailed the consequences of deforestation, strip mining, and faulty waste and sewage disposal.[94] This was followed in 1962 by Rachel Carson's *Silent Spring,* which brought a new awareness that our ecological balance has been seriously compromised by needless overuse of insecticides, fungicides, and pesticides, creating an imbalance between predators and natural prey that may make even human habitation unsustainable.[95]

Globalization must be understood not simply in terms of what some nations did to each other and the environment in the interests of making more goods and profits. Nobel Laureate Joseph Stiglitz notes that while governments once sponsored international trade to encourage good relations as well as profits (and the more nations involved, the better), today the concept of globalization arouses fierce debate and even riots. "Why," he asks,

> has globalization that has brought so much good, helped many countries grow population-wise; helped economic development, enriched much of Asia and left millions of people far better off. . . . Why has it become so controversial? Many people in the world live longer than before, and their standard of living is far better.[96]

Stiglitz is quick to acknowledge, however, that

> proponents of globalization associate it with triumphant capitalism, American style [which] has not brought promised economic benefits. A growing divide between the haves and have-nots has left increasing numbers in the Third World in dire poverty. Despite repeated promises of poverty reduction made over the last decade of the twentieth century, the actual number of people living in poverty actually increased by almost 100 million. This occurred at the same time that total world income increased by an average of 2.5 percent annually.[97]

Dwight Hopkins insists that globalization has become little more than

> the vehicle of cultural invasion. The tendency is to create a monoculture . . . the undermining of economic, cultural and ecological diversity; the acceptance of a technological culture as developed in the West. The indigenous culture and its potential for human development are vastly ignored.[98]

Rehearsing the downside of a movement as powerful as globalization is helpful, however, only if we can view its potentials for good and make conscious and conscience-driven decisions about how to utilize its positive contributions. As Stiglitz insists: "Globalization is here to stay. The issue is how we can make it work. And if it is to work, there have to be global public institutions to help set the rules."[99] A relatively small-scale application of this might be two old rivals, China and Taiwan, developing mutual support. The latter has moved energetically into the electronic industry, having become "number one" as provider of 70 percent of the world's chip foundry services, 72 percent of notebook PCs, and 79 percent of the world market for PDAs. Most are actually made in China, however; more than 1 million Taiwanese live on the mainland. "All the manufacturing capacity in China is overlaid with the management and marketing expertise of the Taiwanese, along with all their contacts in the world."[100] One must be cautious in optimism, but it appears that a long-running cross-straight drama is in a tense new phase.

Vice President Al Gore proposed a more truly global effort in his *Earth in the Balance.* He refers us to the Marshal Plan created by General George Marshall and President Harry Truman after the close of World War II. "In a brilliant collaboration that was unprecedented, several relatively wealthy nations, and several relatively poor nations— empowered by a common purpose—joined to reorganize an entire region of the world and change its way of life."[101] The Plan addressed a host of problems including disruptions in lifestyle due to massive bombings and obliteration of cities (e.g., much of London, Paris, Berlin, Nürnberg, Moscow) that cost millions of lives during the war and severe displacement afterward, resulting in migrations, unemployment, hunger, and lack of medical care, and adequate housing exacerbated by environmental destruction as a result of wholesale deforestation, loss of agricultural resources, and massive air and water pollution. In many instances drawing on the ethical commitment of leaders in U.S. business, the Marshal Plan was able to offer practical solutions instead of only ideological platitudes. The Plan provided vast new opportunities for employment and rebuilding as well as the sense of being part of a truly global embracing community. Three emphases were proffered in keeping with the urgency of resolving these crises: (1) democracy should be the preferred form of political organization planetwide; (2) modified free markets would be the preferred form of economic organization, and (3) each individual should feel that he or she is part of a truly humane civilization. This third is the most difficult to achieve, requiring dependence in many cases on people who give mere lip service to the ideas without wholehearted effort.[102]

The financial cost of the Marshall Plan from 1948–1951 to the United States was enormous: nearly 2 percent of its GNP, or $100 billion annually in 2002 terms. It enjoyed strong bipartisan support in Congress. Far from harming the free enterprise system, it was deemed the most effective way to foster its healthy operation.[103]

Vice President Gore proffered strategic goals to facilitate achieving the preceding objectives. Although directed initially to environmental concerns, these goals have a much broader application.

1. *Stabilize the world's population* to protect the environment from depletion of sustainable food supplies and preventing the earth from becoming a vast desert. This objective does not involve re-igniting the smoldering birth control arguments or inviting governmental eradication of unplanned births. Stabilizing the ratio of births to deaths by natural causes will reveal the natural corollary in industrial nations with low rates of infant mortality and high rates of literacy and education. This provides reasonable conditions to strive for.

2. *Create and develop environmentally appropriate technologies* that can be transferred to all nations, especially those in the third world. The latter would pay for them by discharging the various agreed upon obligations incurred as participants in this global Marshall Plan.

3. *Establish global agreement on a system of economic accountability* that assigns appropriate values to the moral and ecological consequences of routine choices made by individuals (e.g., the entertainment media), the marketplace (identifying products produced and marketed that may foul the air and water

and cause cancers or other health hazards), and the major businesses and nations (larger macroeconomic choices in making including excessive competition or war).

4. *Negotiate a new international agreement* embodying regulatory frameworks, prohibitions and enforcement mechanisms including cooperative planning incentives and mutual obligations necessary to make the overall plan a success. This clearly is the most complex of tasks and necessitated the fifth strategic goal.

5. *Establish a cooperative plan for educating the world's citizens about our global involvement.* Implementing this goal will necessitate a massive effort to disseminate information about local, regional, national, and global threats not only to the natural environment but also to the total human environment (such events as precipitated the long-held secret slave trade in Africa during much of the seventeenth through nineteenth centuries). Doing this will entail making international agreements about freedom of the press so that governments will not dictate what news items to publish or omit. Implementation will also necessitate a far greater self-discipline on the part of the news media (as well as the entertainment industries) because they will not exploit subject matter that could cause great harm to the public under the pretense of freedom of speech for the sake of profit.[104]

Much of the preceding may seem more like naive utopianism than objective realism or even a responsible rejoinder to humanity's apparent proclivity for self-aggrandizement and lust for power. It may be that in our wistful yearning for embracing a pluralism that will bring forth a transformed humane endeavor, we have simply fallen into what Robin Gill calls being "trapped by globalization."[105] One way to identify our culture today, he suggests, is to see it as "a confusing mixture of postmodernity and globalization." If postmodernity tends to fragment knowledge, morality and truth, and globalization reinforced by international travel, trade, entertainment, and communication, it also tends to relativize local communities and marginalize once cherished forms of morality. Under the illusion that globalization makes us more generous and open to the world, a new generation is being lured into atomistic individualism and increasingly self-centered consumerism.[106]

E. IMPLICATIONS FOR GLOBAL ETHICS

How much active influence the many organized religions have exercised to reduce warfare and promote peace is something historians and religious scholars will continue to debate for generations to come as they have in the past. As weapons of war become more sophisticated, destructive, and above all available, however, it becomes increasingly urgent that we revisit these religious traditions to identify what we have in common.

Few examples of the callous transformation of tragedy into amusement have been so disturbingly displayed as that of published photos revealing the torture of detainees at Abu Graeb prison in Iraq. That episode pales, however, in the light of musical videos being brought back from the war by U.S. soldiers, who in 2004 photographed the carnage of battle replete with "charred, decapitated and bloody corpses" then added soundtracks of heavy metal music, the lyrics of which included: "Don't need your forgiveness. Die, don't need your prayers," so the films could be displayed "as entertainment" back home.[107] "It's like a trophy," said Pfc. Chase McCollough, "something to keep." "I have a lot of pictures of dead Iraqis," echoed Spc. Jack Benson. "Everybody does." What happens in this situation the culture is endorsing.[108]

As we have asked before, what are the implications of such a case for global ethics? Is there anything in the annals of the major religious traditions to address this painful revelation and to suggest a remedy acceptable to all religious bodies?

Likewise, we must raise the question about capital punishment. Although outlawed in nearly 100 countries, it is still permitted in Nigeria, Saudi Arabia, Taiwan, China, Iran (the latter two have executed nearly 80 percent of all such sentences since the l980s), and the United States where it is permitted in thirty-eight states for convicted criminals aged 16 years and up.[109] The topic is on the table for many organizations like the World Council of Churches.

The question of whether war is justifiable remains largely unanswered. There is no single religious body that can speak for all others, so the question is made more complex by the effort to fashion a "global ethic" when it remains unclear whether we are actually to seek an ethical position that is free from being labeled either a global ideology transcending all religions or a syncretistic cocktail of "the best" (undefined) of all religions. As Hans Kung pointed out in his preface to *A Global Ethic,* doing this requires that what we must follow is not a generalized study of religious ethics (plural) but a given ethic (singular).[110] "The fundamental ethical demand on all human societies or institutions should be a basic principle, the beginnings of which one finds in every great religious or ethical tradition: "every human being must be treated humanely." The Golden Rule can be similarly demonstrated in all of the great traditions: "Do not do to another what you would not want to be done to you."[111] It may be questioned whether this phrasing is actually equivalent with the more positive expression: *Do* unto others as *you would have them do* unto you (not merely avoid doing what you would not want them to do), (Matthew 7:12). If in either case this advice seems too simplistic, another question is raised: If people in every great religious or ethical tradition really believe this, why do we not have peace on earth?

Many great religious teachers have grounded the seeming proclivity to violate what we know to be right and humane in a host of social, political, psychological, and even biological forces. The almost universal term is *sin*. It ostensibly arises from an impulse that cries out to be free from all restraints and to violate even the will of the lord of creation if there be such, whose standards for the good life impose limitations on our freedom. While the Eastern religious traditions tend not to dwell on sin, Judaism, Christianity, and Islam focus on our willfull separation from the deity, which sin implies as a condition of rebelliousness that alienates us from the lord of life. We haven't adequate space here to deal with so controversial a subject as it deserves except to note that the consequence of sin is the death of the self unless God forgives and restores the broken relationship.

Ethics is sometimes put forward as the application of the more basic virtue of morality to the common experiences of daily life and from which arise in ascending order social customs, laws, manners, and etiquette as discussed in an earlier chapter. A person may consider himself or herself to be decent and civilized simply because he or she has learned the rules of social life, but without any consideration of their immoral underpinnings. In the United States in the nineteenth century America, many people displayed a refined manner in social gatherings but saw no inconsistency on later attending a public lynching or rejoicing in news from the cavalry that a whole Native American village had been massacred. Much more could be said about large, well enculturated crowds attending sixteenth century witch burnings, or in ancient Rome screaming approval at gladiatorial games and public crucifixions.

Happily, we are not left without hope about the human condition or its capacity for ethics, whether on the merely local or global levels. "We all have a responsibility for better global order (and) it is clear there will be no new global order without a new global ethic."[112] The first line of action must be in the home where all of our earliest evaluations and actions are guided by the wisdom and caring of parents. Obviously this is a tall order in societies where single-parent families are becoming more than more common. Mealtime and bedtime prayers and stories can reinforce in the child's mind the significance of the moral and ethical commitments of the family.

Beyond the family is the neighborhood, especially the school where disciplined learning (rooted in the concept of *discipleship,* far removed from its popular connotation as punishment and coercion) includes sharing experiences and socializing processes with peers as well as teachers, some of whom come from diverse cultural and racial backgrounds. Beyond the schools is a host of agencies (churches, police and fire departments, businesses, hospitals, concert halls, each with its own specialized rules and regulations, many of which were inspired by what Urie Bronfenbrenner called the "macrosystem" of overarching economic and political controls.[113]

Obviously, not all children will grow into the same kind of adults as their parents or siblings, certainly not simply because they share so much of the same "ecological" heritage. Some features will be more instrumental in character development than others. Not all parents have experienced them in the same way. Great enthusiasm, resentment, or indifference toward political parties, as one example, help shape the attitudes of the children. In fairly recent history, a significant number of organizations have provided forums for discussion of such issues that we have addressed in the preceding chapters. They also encourage more experimentation with novel ideas, such as in the training of parents, teachers, religious leaders, politicians, economists, environmentalists, scientists, artists, and so on in ways to facilitate moral development from all parts of the social spectrum, from individual to global. A few of these organizations that might help visualize the broader participation include The World Council of Churches, Society for Buddhist-Christian Studies, European Societas Ethica, Inter-religious Federation for World Peace, Islamic Research Foundation, Federation of Jain Associations, Council for the Parliament of the World's Religions, World Conference on Religion and Peace, Federation of Zoroastrian Associations, World Fellowship of Buddhists, Islamic Research Foundation, and the World Council of Synagogues.

This list is very brief and does not include the almost countless number of churches, temples, mosques, and so on, many of which have well-educated leaders competent in family counseling as well as in ethics applicable at almost every social and cultural level. Those who are not so trained are encouraged to become involved and share what skills and insights they do possess. Many of the latter individuals are active in such agencies as the YMCA and YWCA, Boy Scouts and Girl Scouts, Jewish Chautauqua Society, the Newman Club, Red Cross, Salvation Army, and Goodwill Industries, all of which have indispensable gifts that enrich nations around the world.

What is here urged is active participation, not in quest of a single global ethic, although that may indeed be a final goal. Instead, let there be a shared search through diversified religious and ethical configurations for practical methods applicable to forgiveness, healing, and rebuilding in a war-ravaged world with its plethora of both personal and ecological abuses, crime, deceit, disease, and poverty. This is a tall order indeed but nonetheless urgent.

EPILOGUE: MORAL DEVELOPMENT IN AN INTERDEPENDENT WORLD

> *Let no one be deceived: There is no global justice without truthfulness and humaneness.*
> *Council for a Parliament of the World's Religions*

An atmosphere of pessimism pervades many academic and professional conferences, where a "post" syndrome prevails: We live in a *post*modern, *post*industrial, or *post*-Christian world. It appears to many that there is little hope that we can either discover or create moral guidelines to direct us through the new millennium. This book has been designed to affirm new possibilities and to encourage interdisciplinary, intercultural dialogue that respects each tradition for its potential gifts without developing a merely syncretistic agenda.

The much advertised global village may be conceptually overdrawn given the great diversity of our cultures, languages, religions, and political systems. In light of the human penchant for confrontation and the availability of unprecedented powers of destruction, however, it becomes increasingly clear that developing a global commitment to the moral quest rather than to sheer economic and military hegemony is imperative. This may well be our greatest single challenge if the current century is not to be our last.

NOTES

1. Robert McAfee Brown, *Religion and Violence* (Philadelphia: Westminster Press, 1973), 7.
2. E.O. Wilson, *On Human Nature* (Cambridge, MA: Harvard University Press, 1978), 196.
3. Will Durant, *The Story of Civilization* (New York: Simon and Schuster, 1942), 50.

4. Ibid., 52.

5. Ibid., 53.

6. David Kereke and David Slater, *Killing for Culture* (Creation Books, 1998); vii, 237.

7. Rosie Mestel, "Adolescent TV Watching Linked to Violent Behavior," *Los Angeles Times,* March 29, 2002. *Cf.* Robert Moss, "Making Movies Mean and Ugly," *Saturday Review of Literature,* October 1980, 14f; Michael Medved, "A Sickness of the Soul," *Los Angeles Times,* February 6, 1992, B11; Newton Minow and Craig LaMay, "From Wasteland to Land of the Wasted," *Los Angeles Times,* July 10, 1993.

8. E.C. May, *The Circus from Rome to Ringling, Encyclopedia Britannica,* vol. 4 (Chicago: Encyclopedia Britannica, 1974), 635 ff.

9. Thomas Gibb, "Art of Theater," Encyclopedia Britannica, 213.

10. Plato, Laws. Great Books of the Western World, vol. 7 (Chicago: Encyclopedia Britannica), cited in Will Durant, *The Life of Greece* (New York; Simon and Schuster. 1939), 523.

11. Phyllis Hartnoll, *The Theater: A Concise History* (New York: Thames and Hudson, 1998), 13.

12. "Gladiators," *The New Encyclopedia Britannica,* vol. 4 (Chicago: William Benton Publisher, 1973), 564.

13. Hartnoll, *op. cit.,* 29.

14. Ibid., 35.

15. Edwards de Grazia and Roger K. Newman, *Banned Films: Movies, Censors, and the First Amendment* (New York: R.R. Bowker, 1982), 3.

16. Ibid., 5.

17. Ibid., 9.

18. Matthew Bernstein, ed., *Controlling Hollywood* (New Brunswick, NJ: Rutgers University Press, 1999), 74–79.

19. Richard Maltby, *The King of Kings and the Czar of All the Rushes,* cited in Bernstein, *op. cit.,* 74.

20. Dorothy G. Singer, "How Much Television Is Too Much?" *Families,* January 1982, cited in Thomas, Licona, *Educating for Character* (New York: Bantam Books, 1992), 395, 454.

21. Ibid., 407.

22. Ibid.

23. Ibid., 408.

24. Ibid., 409.

25. David Savage, "Whitehouse Turns Tables on American POWs," *Los Angeles Times,* February 15, 2005, A-1, A-5.

26. Ibid,. A-5.

27. Cited in William A.Young, *The World's Religions,* 322.

28. A.Yusuf Ali, *The Holy Qur'an,* S. xxxix 53 and n.4324.

29. "On Execution," *The Christian Science Monitor,* February 5, 1998, 20f.

30. *Los Angeles Times,* April 21, 1992, H5.

31. Sigmund Roos, "Death Penalty's Lessons," *The Christian Science Monitor,* November 13, 1997, 19.

32. Ibid.

33. Robert B. McLaren, *Christian Ethics, Foundations and Practice* (Englewood Cliffs, NJ: Prentice Hall, 1994), 228.

34. "Death Penalty's Lessons," *The Christian Science Monitor,* December 13, 1997, 19.

35. Jerry L. Van Marter, "Capital Punishment on Trial," *Presbyterians Today,* March 2003, 17.

36. "Women on Death Row," *USA Today,* July 25, 1995, 2A.

37. McLaren *op, cit.,* 229.

38. Stuart Banner, "The Death Penalty's Strange Career," *The Wilson Quarterly,* Spring 2002, 74.

39. Maura Dolan, "State Court Strongly Enforces Death Penalty," *Los Angeles Times,* April 9, 1995.

40. Marc Haefele, "Support for the Death Penalty Slowly Draining Away," *Los Angeles Times,* October 22, 2000, M6.

41. Ibid.

42. Rugene Block, *And May God Have Mercy* (San Francisco: Fearon), 25.

43. Mike Farrell, "Executions Put State and Nation on the Killing Stage," *Los Angeles Times,* December 22, 1999, B17.

44. David Savage, "Supreme Court Bans Executions of Juveniles," *Los Angeles Times,* March 2, 2002, 1.

45. Robert Bryce, "Why Texas Is Execution Capital," *Christian Science Monitor,* December 14, 1998, 1.

46. Jerry Van Marter, *Presbyterians Today,* March 2003, 17.

47. Kris Axtman, "U.S. Milestone: 100th Death Row Inmate Exonerated," *The Christian Science Monitor,* April 12, 2002, 1.

48. Michael Endress, *The Morality of Capital Punishment* (Mystic, CT: Twenty-Third Publications, 1985), 131.

49. Emil Brunner, *The Divine Imperative* (Philadelphia: Westminster Press, 1947), 469.

50. Albert Einstein, *Out of My Later Years* (New York: The Philosophical Library, 1950), 265. First written in 1944.

51. Robert Hume, *The World's Living Religions* 26. Injury to any living creature is thus a violation of one's self and an assault on Brahma. Cf. Svetasvatara, Upanishad, 4.11; *S.E. Frost, The Sacred Writings of the World's Great Religions,* 407.

52. In contrast with Hinduism, note Young, *op. cit.,* 314.

53. Roderick Hindery, *Comparative Ethics in Hindu and Buddhist Traditions,* 145.

54. Ibid., 235.

55. David Hawkin, ed., *The Twenty First Century Confronts its Gods* (New York: State University of New York Press, 2004), 174.

56. Ibid., 175.

57. H.H. the Dalai Lama, *Ethics for the New Millennium* (New York: Penguin Books, 1999), 219.

58. Hans Kung, *Christianity and the World's Religions* (New York: Doubleday, 1986), 442.

59. Hans Kung and Karl-Josef Kuschel, *A Global Ethic* (New York: Continuum, 1993), 58–59.

60. H. H. the Dalai Lama, *op. cit.,* 224–25.

61. Ibid., 224–35.

62. Charles L. Manske and Daniel L. Harmelink, *World Religions Today,* 17; Robert N. Bellah, *Tokugawa Religion: The Cultural Roots of Modern Japan* (New York: Free Press, 1985); H. Byron Earhart, *Japanese Religion* (Belmont, CA: Publisher), 1982.

63. Manske and Harmelink, *op. cit.,* 17.

64. The Kamikaze pilots of World War II who were willing to commit suicide by crashing their planes onto the decks of American ships, in the fulfilling of that pledge, are a stark reminder. *Kamikaze* means literally "God's mighty wind."

65. Frost, *op. cit.,* 408.

66. "Matthew Perry," *Encyclopedia Britannica,* vol. 11, (Chicago: 887–88).

67. Hume, *op. cit.,* 201. (*Cf. Encyclopedia Britannica,* vol. 19, *op.cit.,* p. 1169f).

68. "Chronology of the Old Testament," *The Interpreter's Dictionary of the Bible* (New York: Abingdon Press, 1962), 580–99.

69. Kenneth Scott Latourette, *A History of Christianity* (New York: Harper, 1953), 243.

70. Will Durant, *Caesar and Christ* (New York: Simon and Schuster, 1944), 667.

71. Aquinas, Thomas, *Summa Theologica,* Part II (Great Books of the Western World, Chicago: Encyclopedia Britannica, 1971), 578.

72. Latourette, *op. cit.,* 410.

73. Ibid., 412.

74. Ibid., 884.

75. John Man, *The War to End Wars, 1914–1918* (Pleasantville, NY: Reader's Digest Association, 2000), 23.

76. Larry L. Rasmussen, *Earth Community, Earth Ethics* (MaryKnoll, New York: Orbis Books, 1997), 2.

77. Alan Geyer, *The Idea of Disarmament: Rethinking the Unthinkable* (Elgin, IL: The Brethren Press; and Washington, DC: The Churches' Center for Theology and Public Policy, 1982), 206.

78. Samuel S. Huntington, *The Clash of Civilizations? The Debate* (New York: Foreign Affairs, 1996), 254–59.

79. David J. Hawkin, *The Twenty First Century Confronts Its Gods, Globalization, Technology and War* (New York: State University of New York Press, 2004), 19.

80. Ibid., 20.

81. John Bowker, *What Muslims Believe* (Oxford: One World Press, 1998), 78.

82. Bowker, Ibid., 79–80.

83. Irta M. Lapidus, "Sultanates and Gunpowder Empires," *The Oxford History of Islam,* ed. John L. Esposito (Oxford, UK: Oxford University Press, 1999), 348.

84. John Bowker, *God: A Brief History* (London, England: DK Publishing, 2002), 360f.

85. Jane I. Smith, "Islam and Christendom," *The Oxford History of Islam, op. cit.,* 306. The respect came "especially [with] the description of Mary, mother of Jesus, leading them to affirm that this was indeed God's revelation."

86. Manske and Harmelink, *op. cit.,* 81.

87. Esposito, *op. cit.,* 644f.

88. Ashraf Khalil and Patrick J McDonnell, "Iraqi Leaders Take Office," *Los Angeles Times,* May 4, 2005, A1, A5.

89. Ibid.

90. Bowker, *What Muslims Believe, op. cit.* 79.

91. Quoted in Hume *The World's Living Religions, op. cit.,* 81.

92. David Lukas, "Field Guide," *Los Angeles Times,* May 10, 2006, F3.

93. Al Gore, *Earth in the Balance* (New York: Penguin Books, 1992), 69f f.

94. Fairfield Osborn, *Our Plundered Planet* (Boston: Little, Brown, 1948).

95. Rachel Carson, *Silent Spring* (Boston: Houghton-Mifflin, 1962).

96. Joseph E. Stiglitz, *Globalization and Its Discontents* (New York: W.W. Norton, 2002), 4.

97. Ibid., 5.

98. Dwight N Hopkins, *Religions/Globalizations* (Durham, NC: Duke University Press, 2001), 27.

99. Stiglitz, *op. cit.,* 222.

100. Bruce Einhorn, "Why Taiwan Matters," *Business Week,* May 16, 2005, 76f.

101. Gore, *op. cit.,* 296.

102. Ibid., 298.

103. Ibid., 304.

104. Ibid., 305–307

105. Robin Gill, *Moral Leadership in a Postmodern Age* (Edinburgh: TT & T Clark, 1997), 56–57.

106. Ibid.

107. Louise Roug, "Extreme Cinema Verity," *Los Angeles Times,* March 14, 2005, A-1–A-14.

108. Ibid.

109. Warren Richey, *The Christian Science Monitor,* October 31, 2002, 1,2.

110. Kung, *op. cit.,* 7.

111. Ibid., 54.

112. Ibid., 18.

113. Urie Bronfenbrenner and A.C. Crouter, *Families in Society,* cited in James W. Van der Zanden, *Human Development,* 7th ed. (Boston: McGraw-Hill, 2000), 8–10.

Credits

CHAPTER 3

Page 69: adapted from *The Ecology of Human Development,* Urie Bronfenbrenner (Cambridge, MA: Harvard University Press), 1979.

CHAPTER 6

Page 161: (left) Dave King © Dorling Kindersley, courtesy of the Natural History Museum, London; (right) Embassy of Pakistan.

Page 162: "Shiva as Lord of the Dance (Shiva Nataraja)," India, Tamil Nadu, Chola period, c. 970. Copper alloy, H. 26 3/4 in (67.9 cm). Asia Society, New York: Mr. and Mrs. John D. Rockefeller 3rd Collection. 1979. 20 photograph by Lynton Gardiner

Page 164: (top) Government of India; (bottom) Amit Pashricha © Dorling Kindersley, courtesy of the Indian Museum, Kolkata (Calcutta), India.

Page 166: Index Stock Imagery, Inc.

Page 168: Italian Government Tourist Board.

Page 169: *Les Archives Photographiques d'Art et d'Histoire.*

Page 170: (top) SuperStock, Inc.; (bottom) Church of San Vitale, Ravenna, Italy/Canali PhotoBank, Milan/SuperStock.

Page 171: A.F. Kersting.

Page 172: Corbis.

Page 175: (top) Art Resource, N.Y.; (bottom) AKG-Images.

Page 176: © British Library, London, UK/ © British Library Board. All Rights Reserved/ The Bridgeman Art Library.

Page 177: Art Resource, N.Y.

Page 182: Neg. No. 329853. Photo, Logan. Courtesy Dept. of Library Services, American Museum of Natural History.

Index

DATE DUE